Trade Union Law

EMPLOYMENT LAW LIBRARY

Trade Union Law

Nick Humphreys

Series editor: Simon Auerbach, Partner
Pattinson & Brewer

First published in Great Britain 1999 by Blackstone Press Limited,
Aldine Place, London W12 8AA. Telephone: 0181-740 2277

© Nick Humphreys 1999

ISBN: 1 85431 832 2

British Library Cataloguing in Publication Data.
A CIP catalogue record for this book is available from the British Library

Typeset by Montage Studios Limited, Horsmonden, Kent
Printed by Livesey Ltd, Shrewsbury, Shropshire

Contents

Preface

Trade union law has come a very long way in a very short time. In the space of 30 years it has been essentially 're-invented' three times to the point where it is now unrecognisable as the old-style 'collective *laissez faire*' of self-regulation. It now consists of a common law core overlaid with a complex statutory code of regulation. This book attempts to cover both areas.

As the emphasis of trade union law has changed from time to time, it is important to consider case law in the context of the time when various cases were decided. Where possible and relevant, I have drawn readers' attention to this fact.

Neither, it would seem, are the changes over yet. The incoming Government in its election manifesto promised to allow union recognition where a union has the support of a majority of the workers at an undertaking. These promises have led to the White Paper 'Fairness at Work', the main proposals of which are incorporated in the text of this book (and which, true to Sod's Law, was published several weeks after the original submission of the manuscript thus delaying publication while the text was revised!).

Some reform has already occurred, albeit in a minor way. The first change is contained in the Employment Rights (Dispute Resolution) Act which was passed on 8 April 1998. The main effects of the Act, for the purposes of this book, will be that industrial tribunals are to be re-styled as employment tribunals and union officials will now be amongst the categories of person allowed to advise in relation to agreements contracting out of statutory rights.

The second reform is contained in the Employment Rights (Increase of Limits) Order 1998 (SI 1998 No. 924) which was passed on 1 April 1998. The increased awards payable under the Order have been incorporated within the text.

Lastly, the Government has now implemented the White Paper proposal to reform the law relating to 'check-off' arrangements under s. 1 of the Deregulation and Contracting Out Act 1994, by passing the Deregulation (Deduction from Pay of Union Subscriptions) Order 1998. This provision removes the need for workers who are union members to have to confirm every three years that union-related deductions can still be made from their salaries. It also removes the need for employers to notify such workers one month in advance that an increase in deductions is to be made.

Further reform is also proposed in relation to consultation in collective redundancy and transfer of undertaking situations. While at the time of writing only a consultation paper has been issued, amendments to this area are expected to come onto the statute book in the near future and are likely to deal with the following:

(a)   mandatory consultation with union representatives in the case of a collective redundancy/transfer situation where a union is already recognised (in place of the current situation where an employer can choose between a union and an employee representative);

(b)   elections for employee representatives to ensure the independence of such representatives, and, in the event that no representative is elected, an obligation to provide information to individual employees within the workforce who would be affected;

(c)   an extension of the workforce to whom the duty to consult is owed. It appears that the current position, where only those who may be dismissed are consulted, will be extended to one where those who may be 'affected' by a transfer or redundancy are consulted;

(d)   an extension of the duty to consult so as to provide for consultation in all cases of redundancy (as opposed to the current position where consultation occurs only where 20 or more employees are to be dismissed as redundant);

(e)   a duty on employers to provide training to employee representatives on how to handle the information that they are provided with; and

(f)   an extension of the maximum award to 90 days' pay (as opposed to the current four weeks' pay) in the event of a failure to consult.

Finally, under reg. 23 of the Working Time Regulations 1998 (SI 1998 No. 1833), trade unions or groups of workers (acting under a workforce agreement as defined in sch. 1 of the Regulations) may collectively modify or exclude the rights existing under the 1988 regs. 6(1)–(3) and (7) (length of nightwork), 10(1) (daily rest breaks), 11(1) and (2) (weekly rest periods), 12(1) (rest breaks) and also the reference periods used in the computing of the rights.

In the usual way, I have incurred a number of debts of gratitude in the course of writing and I would particularly like to thank the following people: Craig Oliver and Sharon and Paul Edelstyn, who reviewed and proof read draft copy and provided a wealth of helpful comments (I would add that any errors that remain are mine and not theirs); Simon Auerbach, the Series Editor, for setting me on the right path in relation to the initial draft chapter submitted to Blackstone Press; Blackstone Press for their patience and perseverance when I failed to submit the final proof by the initial submission deadline; Michael Parker, a partner at Bower Cotton, for allowing me to use various of Bower Cotton's IT applications; and last, but by no means least, Julia Gaisford, who managed to dig me out of an substantial hole during editing of the text and for putting up with me generally.

Nick Humphreys
January 1999

Abbreviations

ACAS	Advisory, Conciliation and Arbitration Service
CAC	Central Arbitration Committee
CBI	Confederation of British Industry
CPAUIA	Commissioner for Protection Against Unlawful Industrial Action
CROTUM	Commissioner for the Rights of Trade Union Members
DTI	Department of Trade and Industry
EAT	Employment Appeal Tribunal
ERA 1996	Employment Rights Act 1996
ILO	International Labour Organisation
JIC	Joint Industrial Council
NIRC	National Industrial Relations Court
TUC	Trades Union Congress
TULRA 1974	Trade Union and Labour Relations Act 1974
TULRCA 1992	Trade Union and Labour Relations (Consolidation) Act 1992
TUPE 1981	Transfer of Undertakings (Protection of Employment) Regulations 1981
TURERA 1993	Trade Union Reform and Employment Rights Act 1993

Copyright Acknowledgements

Eclipse Group Limited, 18–20 Highbury Place, London N5 1QP (use of Industrial Relations Law Reports)

Incorporated Council of Law Reporting for England and Wales, 3 Stone Buildings, Lincoln's Inn, London WC2A 3XN (use of official reports and the Weekly Law Reports)

Table of Cases

Table of Statutes

1 Institutions and Sources of Trade Union Law

1.1 THE HISTORY AND SOURCES OF TRADE UNION LAW

1.1.1 Introduction

Trade unions have been subject to legal regulation for much of their history. Indeed, it is only in this century that unions have been allowed a relatively free hand in the way that they are able to conduct affairs between their members and employers or employers associations. Understanding the history of trade unions is important in order to understand fully the current legislation relating to trade unions and the perceived need for intervention in every facet of union activity. The following is a brief account of trade union history which can essentially be broken down into five phases, these being:

(a)   the position pre-1824;
(b)   the reform of trade unionism up to 1906;
(c)   the Industrial Relations Act 1971;
(d)   the social contract era; and
(e)   the reforms of trade union law post-1979.

1.1.2 The history of trade unions

1.1.2.1 The position prior to 1824
Before 1824 trade unions were regulated by a total ban on the recognition of workers collectives. Regulation was provided variously by the Statute of Labourers 1351, the Statute of Artificers 1563, the Poor Law 1601, the Master and Servant Acts and the Combination Acts. These pieces of legislation collectively empowered justices of the peace (usually employers) to fix rates of pay for servants, to prevent withdrawals of labour by employees and to make combinations of workers unlawful.

The early wage fixing legislation was initially introduced to ensure that skilled workers could not take advantage of the consequences of the plague which had substantially reduced the workforce available to employers. The legislation provided that all able bodied workers could be compelled to work at rates of pay in line with those prior to the Black Death.

The main feature of the Master and Servant Acts was the absence of a contract of employment upon which to hang the working relationship. A person could be compelled to work by the local justices, and failure to work could be enforced by criminal penalties. However, to the extent that a master refused to provide work, he could be punished only by civil sanctions.

The Combination Acts of 1799 and 1800 had a different aim. Socially and politically Britain was aware of the then recent French Revolution and took the view that any combination of the working classes should outlawed. To this end, the Combination Act 1800 outlawed all agreements put forward by workers to bring about changes in working conditions, rates of pay, and the like. Again, prosecutions were heard by magistrates and were plentiful.

Another feature of the times was the attitude of the judiciary to organisations of workers. Judges took the line that, even with the welter of legislation hemming workers in, any organisation of workers attempting to bring about changes in working conditions was of itself an illegal conspiracy to be dealt with by the criminal law. An example was *R* v *Mawbey* (1796) 6 TR 619, where Grose J said of workers (at p. 636) that: '. . . each may insist on raising his wages if he can, but if several meet for the same purpose it is illegal and the parties may be indicted for a conspiracy.'

The main engine of change for this line of legislation and judicial thought was the industrial revolution. One of the consequences of the revolution in manufacturing processes was an increase in the hardship associated with working conditions. Social thinking was forced to adapt. Ultimately, the liberal views of the likes of Jeremy Bentham came to the fore prompting the second era of trade unionism, the period up to 1906.

1.1.2.2   The law up to 1906

1.1.2.2.1   The Benthamites   The period between 1800 and 1906 was a time of great change for trade unions. The first notable change caused by the Benthamites was the acceptance that trade unions should have legality. The recognition came in the form of the Combination of Workmen Act 1824 and the Combination Laws Repeal Amendment Act 1825. These Acts recognised that workers' combinations were of themselves lawful, but still contained various criminal offences that could be committed by such combinations. In particular, s. 3 of the 1825 Act created a loosely worded selection of offences that could be committed by combinations, in the form of threats, molestation, intimidation or obstruction. The offences were regularly used. It should be added, the law allowed combinations the right to bring about changes in the conditions of employment only at individual establishments, and any attempt to influence the working conditions at other places of employment could be dealt with under s. 3 of the 1825 Act .

Despite s. 3 unions continued to prosper. This was largely due to increasing professionalism in their organisation, which in turn led to their social acceptability. Instead of being seen as 'secret societies' they started to build funds for their members, to appoint professionals to look after members' interests and to lobby more effectively for change in the law. The overriding aim of unions of this era was to change working conditions and not to change society by means of class action.

1.1.2.2.2   Reform of the Combination Acts   Further reforms followed. In 1859, the Molestation of Workmen Act introduced restrictions on the meaning of 'molestation' under s. 3 of the Combination Laws Repeal Amendment Act 1825. It provided that molestation did not occur where a combination of workers attempted peacefully to persuade workers to leave work in strikes aimed at changing hours or conditions of employment where the workers being persuaded would not be in breach of their contracts of employment.

More was to follow. Under the Master and Servant Act 1867, imprisonment of workers for individually breaching their contracts of employment became an exceptional punishment rather than the norm that it had been under the Master and Servant Act 1823. Despite the new Act, prosecutions still continued to follow in large numbers. Judicial attitudes to unions were also largely conservative. In *Hornby* v *Close* (1867) 10 Cox CC 393, it was decided that unions were unlawful if they had as their objects the raising of wages and the organisation of labour, due to such aims being in restraint of trade.

In the same year as *Hornby* v *Close* was decided, a Royal Commission was set up to investigate the disturbances arising out of an industrial dispute that escalated into what became known as the 'Sheffield outrages'. The Commission was chaired by Sir William Erle. Two schools of thought emerged from the Commission. A majority expressed the view that legality should be granted to unions, in return for which they would be forced to abandon rules that were perceived to be in restraint of trade. However, a minority view recommended the granting of complete legality to unions together with immunity from the law relating to restraint of trade and the criminal consequences of conspiracy.

1.1.2.2.3   Developments after the Royal Commission   Following the Royal Commission the minority view expressed above started to filter through. Still more reforms followed between 1871 and 1875. The changes were the Criminal Law Amendment Act 1871, the Trade Union Act 1871, and the Conspiracy and Protection of Property Act 1875.

The 1871 Amendment Act removed the last vestiges of the Combination Acts by repealing the 1824 and 1825 Acts and also the Molestation of Workmen Act. The 1871 Act confined molestation to cases of violent threats. This said, it introduced new offences in the form of criminal harassment. These offences still exist today in s. 241 of the Trade Union and Labour Relations (Consolidation) Act (TULRCA) 1992 (see 10.3.2.3). However, liability for criminal conspiracy was also removed by the 1871 Act where the conspiracy consisted of doing an act which was not of itself illegal.

Whereas the Criminal Law Amendment Act made changes to the criminal law, the Trade Union Act of 1871 was a milestone as regards the constitution and civil status of unions. Under s. 3 of the Act, 'the purposes of a trade union'were not to be viewed as unlawful simply because the union acted in restraint of trade. The downside to this recognition was that s. 4 did not allow the courts 'to enforce directly large parts of the unions agreements with members ... or ... with other unions'. Thus, union affairs were effectively removed from the jurisdiction of the courts.

Another major impact of the Trade Union Act 1871 was to provide for the Administrative Register under s. 6 of the Act. The register provided for registration with the Registrar of Friendly Societies. Although (ultimately) minor tax benefits did accrue, it was thought that the Act did nothing as to the status of unions as unincorporated associations. The courts were eventually to take a different view on this (see 2.1.5 *et seq.*).

The Conspiracy and Protection of Property Act 1875 was the third of the changes. By s. 17, it repealed the Master and Servant Acts, thereby making it no longer a criminal offence to withdraw labour from one's employer. It did retain some criminal liability where the strikes would endanger life or property (s. 5 — see 10.3.2.2) and also where the strike was in one of the public utilities (s. 4 — repealed by the Industrial Relations Act 1971). Lastly, it provided the basis of the right to strike by removing criminal liability from the acts of a conspiracy of workers acting in furtherance or contemplation of a trade dispute unless the acts would of themselves be criminal in nature.

By the time the Victorian era had finished, unions were on a sound legal footing and were generally regarded as lawful. However, the courts had other ideas and these came to a head in *Quinn* v *Leathem* [1901] AC 495. Here, the plaintiff was an employer of non-union labour. The defendant was a union activist and was keen to establish a closed shop. He informed the plaintiff and one of his biggest customers that unless the non-union labour was dismissed, industrial action would be visited upon them. The plaintiff lost his customer as a result and sued for conspiracy under the common law. The matter reached the House of Lords who found in favour of the plaintiff. Lord Lindley stated (at p. 538):

A combination not to work is one thing, and is lawful. A combination to prevent others from working by annoying them if they do is another, and is *prima facie* unlawful.... A threat to call men out given by a trade union official to an employer of men belonging to the union and willing to work with him is a form of coercion, intimidation, molestation or annoyance to them and to him very difficult to resist, and, to say the least, requiring justification. None was offered in this case.

Ultimately, in 1906, the unions were able to obtain exemptions from liability in tort by means of the Trade Disputes Act of that year. This Act provided immunity in tort as regarded breaches of contracts and conspiracy. It was supplemented on a number of occasions (as will be seen in Chapter 6), but apart from this Act and the Trade Union Act 1913 (providing for trade union financing of political objects) the

Government actively refrained from legislating to affect the workplace save for provisions for bare minimum standards for employers and employees as regards safety, compensation and the like. Regulation of the workplace was instead left to trade unions and employers, who bargained for employees at a works or national level for the purposes of workforces as a whole rather than for individuals. This so-called 'collective *laissez faire*' was to last until 1971 with the introduction of the Industrial Relations Act of that year.

1.1.2.3   The Industrial Relations Act 1971

The Industrial Relations Act 1971 was introduced in response to a perceived need for widespread trade unions reforms. Between 1906 and 1971 much had changed in both the workplace and the economy in Britain. Factors such as inflation and unemployment, which had been marginal in the economy for years, both started to increase. More people were looking for jobs in the economy due to the baby boom and increasing numbers of women moving full-time into the workplace. The ability of the economy to absorb the influx decreased due to increasing mechanisation. Against this background, governments of both the left and right tried to maintain full employment policies.

One of the key problems facing employers towards the end of the 1960s occurred at a local level in the form of the power that trade unions had in being able to wring changes from an employer who, either by himself or acting through an employers' association, had negotiated a national level collective bargain. Local level shop stewards, for reasons of their good productivity, their desire to obtain better terms and conditions, the establishment of a closed shop or simply to keep pace with inflation, would use what came to be known as 'wild cat'strikes. These strikes would take place at short notice upon the breakdown of negotiations between a union representative and an employer. The unionised staff would immediately stop work and economic pressure would be brought to bear upon the employer. The problem with this form of industrial action attracted the attention of a Royal Commission chaired by Lord Donovan (Donovan, *Report of the Committee on Trade Unions and Employers Associations*, Cmnd 3623, London: HMSO, 1968). The Report examined private sector manufacturing based industries and came to the conclusion that reform of factory level bargaining was necessary, but that this should be achieved ultimately through education of union activists. The Report, with one member dissenting, rejected calls for full legal intervention in the area of industrial relations. However, in 1971 the Conservative administration came to power and implemented the Industrial Relations Act as part of a prices and incomes policy.

The Act worked at two distinct levels, these being the granting of individual rights and the attempted control of collective activity (commonly referred to as 'corporatism'). The Act made a number of changes to the law as it had evolved up to this point. The central feature was registration of trade unions. Registration provided corporate status to unions and made unions liable to have their rule books subject to court supervision. It was a voluntary process, but in return for registration unions received exclusive bargaining rights, bargaining information, tax benefits and immunity from action in tort. Unregistered unions were fully liable for the torts that they committed and received none of the other benefits. Another feature of the Act was that collective agreements were conclusively presumed to be binding unless written with a clause expressing them not to be so (see 3.7.3 with regard to the current position). Further still, employers could enforce the provisions of the Act in the National Industrial Relations Court ('NIRC' — established by the Act), as could the Government in an emergency situation by gaining a 'cooling off' order.

In spite of all the carrots that were offered to unions to register, most refused to do so; and in order to undermine the Act and the Government that had introduced it, the TUC instructed its members sitting on industrial tribunals to resign, which the vast majority of them duly did. Notwithstanding the unions' decision not to comply with the Act, employers refused to use the powers that they were given to seek redress in the NIRC. Ultimately, the Government used its new emergency powers in only one case — *Secretary of State for Employment* v *ASLEF (No. 2)* [1972] ICR 19. Here, railworkers had withdrawn their goodwill from the working relationship by introducing an overtime ban and a work-to-rule as a result of a dispute over pay. The effect of the action was to cause massive train timetabling problems, whereupon the Government made an application to the NIRC. The argument put forward by ASLEF was that in withdrawing their goodwill they were not actually in breach of their contracts of employment. This view was ultimately rejected by the Court of Appeal who duly granted the cooling off order. A ballot was subsequently held which provided massive support for the union. Ultimately, a pay settlement was granted on very favourable terms to the union. Despite substantial union provocation to use the emergency powers again (most notably in the case of the miners strike of 1974), they were not resorted to.

The Conservative Government ultimately gave way to another Labour Government in 1974 and the Industrial Relations Act was repealed shortly afterwards.

1.1.2.4   The social contract

The Labour administration of 1974 was elected on the promise to provide a social contract for the people of Britain. The gist of the agreement was that Government would provide a policy of full employment coupled with the provision of certain social and employment benefits, in return for which a prices and incomes policy would be instituted with the TUC helping to keep the incomes end of the bargain.

The first piece of employment-related legislation was the Trade Union and Labour Relations Act (TULRA) 1974. The Act repealed the Industrial Relations Act 1971 and attempted to re-state much of the pre-1971 law while adding a few modifications culled from the 1971 Act. Blanket exemption in relation to union liability in tort was re-established under s. 14 of TULRA 1974. Registration of unions was abolished (s. 8) and collective agreements were once more treated as being non-binding save to the extent that an agreement contained a clause stating that the agreement was to be binding upon the parties to it (s. 18).

Further legislation was also forthcoming. The Employment Protection Act 1975 introduced a number of new employment institutions: ACAS (ss. 1–6, see 1.2.1); the Central Arbitration Committee (s. 10, see 1.2.2); the Employment Appeal Tribunal (s. 87) and the Certification Officer (s. 7).

Additionally, the 1974 Act granted extensive new rights to trade unions and their members. Of particular importance were: the introduction of compulsory arbitration for the recognition of trade unions (ss. 11–16); the duty to disclose bargaining information to unions (ss. 17–21, see below at 3.2); the introduction of procedural limits on an employer's right to make compulsory redundancies (Pt IV, see 3.3); the right to participate in the actions of an independent trade union (ss. 53–56, see 5.5); the right to time off for union duties (ss. 57–58, see 5.4); and the removal of trade disputes disqualification from unemployment benefit (s. 111).

Further rights were granted to unions under the Trade Unions and Labour Relations (Amendment) Act 1976, most notably by making the dismissal of a non-closed shop employee automatically fair.

The response of union executive committees to the measures introduced by the Government was to protest that they could not keep their members from asking for pay rises. The Government, it was felt, had not gone far enough in relation to the social contract. Not enough legislation had been introduced to protect the disadvantaged in society and the very low paid. The problem was partly the fault of the International Monetary Fund (IMF), who helped Britain out of the economic problems of the 1970s which were caused by excessive public spending, and partly the fault of full employment policy, bad management of resources in the workplace and poor industrial relations policies generally (the last two of which led to wage induced cost push inflation and, ultimately, increased redundancies due to increasing uncompetitivness of British industry). The IMF provided financial help at a cost — cutting back on public spending.

As a result of this perceived betrayal, workers took matters into their hands at a local level. This took the form of nation-wide strikes by the very low paid in public sector employment. The social contract ultimately suffered a meltdown in the infamous 'Winter of Discontent', with unionised labour out on strike and hitting as its main victims those who most needed help themselves — the old, who were denied light and heat, and the public generally, who were denied basic social facilities such as rubbish collection.

The problem as far as the public were concerned was that the unions simply could not be called to account. They were immune from liability in tort and had no restrictions on their taking of industrial action save for those contained within the union rulebook. The final outrage was that unemployment continued to rise as more and more of the old manufacturing based businesses either closed down or rationalised their operations by investing in new technology with the result that jobs were lost. Unemployment rose above 1 million, and by the time of the election accounted for around 5 per cent of the workforce.

The Conservative party campaigned for the election on a promise to revamp the economy by abandoning central planning on prices, incomes and employment and using market forces to set the levels for each in the economy. Part of this reform necessarily involved changes to the way in which trade unions went about their business. They were perceived to be a corrupting influence on markets, setting wage levels higher than they would be if left to negotiations between employers and individual employees. The Conservatives also promised that the knock-on effect would be full employment by the setting of realistic wage levels for each employee, thereby allowing employers to employ more people at the market rate for labour. The Conservatives were ultimately elected, partly on the back of the famous 'Labour isn't working' campaign.

1.1.2.5   The Conservative reforms

The changes made by the incoming Conservative Government were introduced, significantly, in a series of piecemeal amendments over the course of a decade rather than *en bloc* as the Industrial Relations Act had been. The first change came in the form of the Employment Act 1980. The main applications to trade unions of this Act were: provision of State funds for secret ballots and workplace ballots (ss. 1–2); the power for the Secretary of State to issue Codes of Practice on industrial relations (s. 3); the right not be unreasonably excluded or expelled from a trade union (ss. 4–5); the repeal of immunity for secondary picketing and limiting immunity for picketing to picketing at place of work only (ss. 16–17, see 7.4.5); and the repeal of the union recognition machinery (s. 19).

More legislation was to follow in the form of the Employment Act 1982. This Act made further in-roads into the rights that unions had enjoyed in the 1970s by: narrowing the closed shop exceptions relating to unfair dismissal and increasing the compensation available to employees dismissed as a result of the closed shop (see 5.5.4.2); introducing legislation preventing the use of union membership or recognition requirements in supply contracts and, to the extent that they existed, removing exemptions from liability in tort for inducing a contractor to introduce these requirements; removing the immunities that existed in tort actions against unions (while at the same time protecting union assets held in provident funds and political funds and also capping the amount of damages that could be awarded against a trade union found to have committed a tort); and, lastly, narrowing the meaning of 'trade dispute'.

Mrs Thatcher's Conservatives were not finished with the unions yet though. More legislation followed in the form of the Trade Union Act 1984. The Act had as its cornerstone the notion that unions should be democratic and exist for the benefit of their members. The main thrust of the Act was the introduction of new balloting requirements for unions in respect of elections for union leadership offices (see 4.2.8), confirming industrial action and for the retention of the political fund together with regulation as to the meaning of political objects, and check-off arrangements.

The 1984 Act was promulgated and ultimately introduced with a large industrial conflict in full swing, the miners' strike of 1984–85. The strike provided the catalyst for further legislation, this time taking the shape of the Employment Act 1988. It seized upon the dissatisfaction of individual mineworkers and the litigation that had taken place between them and their unions. The 1988 Act sought to make changes in the rights that individuals had as against the collective rights of the union. It introduced rights: to ballots before industrial action (see 4.2.4); not to be unjustifiably disciplined by a union (see 4.2.3); to control the expenditure of trade union funds by trustees of a union (see 4.2.7); and, lastly, extending the Government's stand on the closed shop, removed the right to be fairly dismissed as a consequence of the closed shop or to have other discriminatory action taken against a unionised employee.

Despite the fact that as a result of the Government's changes between 1979 and 1980 unions were now radically reformed and had been effectively handed over to individuals rather than acting in the collective interests of their members with the closed shop having been overhauled so as to promote the Government's ideology, it was decided that more changes were needed. These came in the form of the Employment Act 1990. The 1990 Act had a number of objects as its purpose, although it is difficult to establish a coherent theme to the statute. The most important of the reforms were, first, the extension of Government policy on trade union membership to its logical conclusion. This resulted in discrimination by employers for reason of membership or non-membership of a trade union being outlawed in the case of job applicants (see 5.3). Secondly, further reform was made to the law relating to balloting, and an extension was made to the liability of trade unions so as to make them liable for the unlawful action of union officials where a union failed to condemn action taken by union officials without a union's authority (see 7.5.2.2). Other reforms also included an extension of the power of the Home Secretary to issue Codes of Practice and an extension of the powers of the Commissioner for the Rights of Trade Union Members.

By now, the law relating to trade unions had become a complex bundle of rights existing in a number of different statutes. It needed consolidation, and this was ultimately to follow in the form of TULRCA 1992. Unfortunately, the Government implemented further reforms under the Trade Union Reform and Employment Rights Act (TURERA) 1993 (most notably by introducing the right not be denied membership of a union), but thankfully chose to amend TULRCA 1992 rather than to have it as free-standing legislation. TULRCA 1992 as amended is therefore the central piece of legislation for this book.

This said, a package of reforms proposed in the White Paper 'Fairness at Work' is to be implemented in the near future. The text of this book deals with the reforms as and when they appear.

1.2 INSTITUTIONS OF TRADE UNION LAW

A number of different institutions exist in relation to trade unions and exercise varying functions under either statute or agreement or convention. The following are the most important of the bodies.

1.2.1   The Advisory, Conciliation and Arbitration Service

The Advisory, Conciliation and Arbitration Service (ACAS) was set up under the Employment Protection Act 1975 and derives its continued existence from ss. 247–253 TULRCA 1992. It is a body corporate (s. 247(2)) and is separate from the Government having the power to appoint its own staff, being such number as it thinks fit, subject to the consent of the Secretary of State (s. 250(2)). The primary management body of ACAS is the Council, consisting of nine ordinary members (with three coming from employers organisations and three from organisations representing workers) and a chairman, all of whom are appointed by the Secretary of State (s. 248). The Council is empowered to determine its own procedure including the quorum necessary for meetings (s. 248(5)). The terms of appointment of members of the Council are set out in ss. 249–250 but members cannot be appointed for a term exceeding five years.

ACAS is additionally required to produce a report and financial statement each year (s. 253).

The purpose for the creation of ACAS was to facilitate the use and, where necessary, reform of collective bargaining between employers and unions, or as ACAS has said of itself, 'to improve industrial relations and employment practice, to minimise conflict and to encourage all people at work to be involved in and committed to the success of their organisations'.

The statutory duty of ACAS generally is now contained in s. 209 TULRCA 1992, which states that: 'It is the general duty of ACAS to promote the improvement of industrial relations in particular by exercising its functions in relation to the settlement of trade disputes under sections 210 and 212.' The full remit of ACAS is now set out in Pt IV, Ch. IV of TULRCA 1992, and in the context of trade unions extends to four matters, these being:

(a)   the giving of advice;
(b)   the issuing of Codes of Practice;
(c)   inquiry, collective conciliation and mediation;
(d)   arbitration.

ACAS is subject to judicial review where, in exercising the above functions, it acts in a way that no reasonable body charged with its function would (see *ACAS* v *UKAPE* [1980] IRLR 124 on this point).

The power of ACAS to intervene will be exercised only where it is the case that the protagonists are 'parties' to a 'trade dispute'. These two concepts are defined in s. 218 of TULRCA 1992 and are provided in the wider definition of 'trade dispute' that exists for the purposes of that Part of the Act. The distinction between the definitions of 'trade dispute' in s. 218 and under s. 244 (discussed at 7.2.2) is that the s. 218 definition is necessarily wider so as to head off potential industrial disputes before they happen. Section 244, however, exists to help define who will be able to claim immunity when industrial action is taken.

Section 218 defines 'a trade dispute' as being one between employers and workers, or workers and workers for a particular list of reasons, these being identical to those in s. 244 (see at 7.2.2). Under s. 218(4), a dispute to which a trade union or employers' association is a party is treated as if it were a dispute to which workers or employers are parties. Thus where a trade union consisting of workers for one or more different employers is in dispute with a particular employer, workers of the other employers would be treated as being in dispute with the particular employer subject to the dispute. Section 218 does no more than require that the dispute be connected with one of the list of reasons and therefore any connection, provided that it is not contrived, will be enough for ACAS to become involved.

ACAS has been given a power to levy charges for the work that it provides by virtue of s. 251A of TULRCA 1992, and does levy these in relation to some of its minor activities such as the giving of conferences. It does not charge for its industrial trouble-shooting roles though. The specific functions of ACAS are considered in more depth immediately below.

1.2.1.1 Provision of advice
The power to provide advice is derived from s. 213(1) of TULRCA 1992. The power exists to provide advice on request or otherwise to employers, employers' associations, workers or trade unions. ACAS also has a power under s. 213(2) to issue such publications as it thinks are likely to affect industrial relations.

1.2.1.2 The issuing of Codes of Practice
ACAS is given power to formalise advice that it gives as Codes of Practice under s. 199(1) of TULRCA 1992. It has a statutory duty to issue Codes where it is the case that they affect:

(a)   time off for trade union officials as dealt with under s. 168;

(b)   time off for trade union members to carry out trade union activities under s. 170; and

(c)   disclosing information to trade unions for the purposes of collective bargaining.

The duty to issue these Codes is contained in s. 199(2) of TULRCA 1992.

The procedure for issuing Codes or draft Codes is set out in s. 200. A draft Code must first be prepared for general public comment, and ACAS may make any modifications it thinks fit in the light of comments that it receives from the public (s. 200(1)). Thereafter, the Code is sent in draft form to the Secretary of State who either approves the same and lays it before the two Houses of Parliament, or who rejects it and gives his reasons for doing so (s. 200(2)). If within 40 days of the Secretary of State issuing the draft either of the two Houses of Parliament resolves against the draft being issued, the Code cannot be issued, but failing that it is issued in the form of the draft laid before Parliament (s. 200(3) and (4)).

Once issued a Code can be revised by ACAS, but all revision must take place with the approval of Parliament, again in the form of laying the revised Code and waiting for 40 days to see if an objection of either House is raised (s. 201). ACAS can also request the Secretary of State to revoke a Code once it is issued, although if the Secretary refuses to do so he is bound to provide his reasons (s. 201(2)).

The effect of ACAS Codes of Practice is that they are not law themselves but can be used as evidence in any proceedings before a tribunal or the Central Arbitration Committee (CAC) (s. 207(1), (2)).

It should be noted that the Secretary of State also has powers to issue Codes of Practice under s. 203. The procedure for issue requires the Secretary to consult with ACAS in formulating his Codes (s. 204(1)), and again requires the approval of both Houses of Parliament in issuing, revising and revoking a Code (ss. 204–206).

Codes of Practice issued by the Secretary of State are likely to arise where ACAS feels unable to issue a Code. A good example is the Code on Picketing. Again, the effect of such a Code of Practice is that it can be used in evidence. However, the scope of a Code issued by the Secretary of State is wider in that it can be used as evidence in court proceedings as well as before a tribunal and the CAC (s. 207(3)).

The Codes of Practice can be highly persuasive. An example is the case of *Thomas* v *NUM (South Wales Area)* [1985] IRLR 136. The problem arising was that groups of picketing miners attended picket lines at colliery gates on a daily basis. Six members of the group were selected to stand at the gates and another larger group was placed back from those at the colliery gates, from where they hurled abuse at those miners who had decided to return to work. An injunction was sought to prevent harassment of the returning workers. Scott J, in granting the injunction so as to limit the number of pickets at the colliery gates, relied on the Code of Practice on Picketing and stated that para. 31 of the 1980 Code of Practice (now para. 51 of the 1992 Code):

> ... does not make it a criminal offence or tortious to have more than six persons on a picket line. Nor is less than six any guarantee of lawfulness. The paragraph simply provides a guide as to a sensible number for a picket line in order that the weight of numbers should not intimidate those who wish to go to work. I am directed by [what is now s. 207(3) TULRCA 1992] to take this guidance into account.
>
> I do so and propose, therefore, to restrain the South Wales Union ... from organising picketing or demonstrations at colliery gates by more than six persons.

1.2.1.3   *Inquiries, collective conciliation and mediation*
The functions of inquiry, collective conciliation and mediation are all aimed at resolving the causes of the disputes or industrial disputes likely to take place or in progress. The power of ACAS to engage in these functions is found in ss. 214 and 210 respectively. As to inquiries, ACAS is empowered to enter into an inquiry if it thinks fit for the purposes of looking at industrial relations generally, in a specific

industry or even in a particular undertaking or part thereof (s. 214(1)). The findings of the inquiry and any recommendations that ACAS feels appropriate may be published, but only after sending a copy of the inquiry document to the parties interested and, if ACAS thinks fit, taking account of their views.

The power of ACAS to arrange collective conciliation is exercised either at the request of one or more of the parties to a trade dispute, or by ACAS of its own initiative (s. 210(1)). In carrying out this function, ACAS may refer the parties to a third party for conciliation (s. 210(2) and must also encourage the parties to use any trade disputes machinery that already exists as between them (s. 210(3)).

In many collective agreements there exists an automatic reference to ACAS in the event of a trade dispute. Of the references to ACAS in 1995 for collective conciliation, 35 per cent of the references came from unions, 10 per cent came from employers, 43 per cent were joint references (explained partially by the use of automatic reference clauses) and the remainder were instituted by ACAS of its own volition.

1.2.1.4 Arbitration

The power for ACAS to refer a matter to arbitration is set out in s. 212 of the 1992 Act. Arbitration can be provided where a trade dispute exists or is apprehended. However, in order for a reference to arbitration to take place, there must have been a request for arbitration by one or more of the parties to the dispute and all of the parties to the dispute must consent to the referral (s. 212(1)). ACAS is then empowered to refer the matter either to an ACAS appointed arbitrator or to the CAC. ACAS is not allowed to make a reference to arbitration where there are agreed procedures in place between the parties for negotiation or resolution of trade disputes unless it is satisfied that either the procedures have broken down, or that there are special reasons justifying the reference (s. 212(3)). In any event, prior to referring to arbitration, ACAS should consider whether the dispute could be adequately resolved by conciliation. Conciliation is a valuable stage in the proceedings. If it is successful, there is no need for the parties to go to arbitration (and unnecessary time and cost can thereby be saved). Further, the conciliation officer can also help the parties in deciding what terms of reference will be provided to the arbitrator in the event that the concilation is ultimately unsuccessful.

ACAS has a panel of some 80 arbitrators to choose from, and in most cases the arbitration will be carried out by one arbitrator acting alone. In certain more complex cases a panel of arbitrators can be appointed. Under s. 212(4)(a) of TULRCA 1992, one of the panel must act as the chairman of the panel.

The procedure at an arbitration is left to the arbitrator. It is unusual to have legal representation (it is discouraged) and the manner of arbitration is usually designed so as to avoid legal formality.

Lastly, it should be noted that under s. 212(5) the result of the arbitration is not binding upon the parties in dispute unless they consent to its being so.

1.2.2   The Central Arbitration Committee

The Central Arbitration Committee (CAC) was created in 1975 and took over the functions of the former Industrial Arbitration Board. The CAC is now governed by Pt VI of TULRCA 1992. Under s. 259, it is the duty of ACAS to provide staff (from the officers and employees of ACAS), accommodation, equipment and other facilities for the CAC.

The CAC has a permanent seat in London and is chaired by a person appointed by the Secretary of State after consulting with ACAS (s. 260(2)). The Committee also has one or more deputy chairmen (appointed again by the Secretary of State after his consultations with ACAS (s. 260(3))) and is also made up of members from both sides of industry. The terms of appointment and remuneration are dealt with under ss. 261–262.

The CAC can hear cases referred to it by ACAS only where both sides have consented to a referral. It will hear cases involving industrial disputes or the enforcement of disclosing bargaining information (under s. 183, see 3.2.5).

The proceedings of the CAC are dealt with under s. 263 of the 1992 Act. The CAC ordinarily sits with the chairman and such other members as the chairman directs. It can sit in two or more divisions if the chairman thinks it expedient, and to the extent that a division is sitting without the chairman the functions of the chairman are carried out by a deputy chairman (s. 263(1)).

The CAC generally takes a pro-active approach to the cases that come before it. It is usual for a chairman or deputy chairman, together with an ACAS conciliation officer, to approach the parties at the start of a case to attempt to reach a joint result in the case rather than having the CAC sitting as would a judge in normal adversarial proceedings.

In hearing a case, the CAC can determine its own procedure (s. 263(5)) and can sit in private where it considers it expedient to do so (s. 263(3)). The CAC has no power to administer oaths or to compel the attendance of witnesses. To the extent that the CAC is not unanimous in its decision, the chairman is entitled to act in the case with the full powers of an umpire (s. 263(4)). Upon the CAC making a decision, it has a duty to publish that decision (s. 264(3)). It should again be noted that any result of arbitration decided upon by the CAC is not binding upon the parties except to the extent that they agree that it will be so.

The CAC rarely sits on voluntary references made to it. The last such reference to it was in 1989.

The White Paper 'Fairness at Work' has made recommendations to increase the role and the powers of the CAC in relation to recognition and de-recognition disputes. When the White Paper recommendations are implemented, the CAC will be able to decide any of the following matters:

(a)   whether a trade union has reasonable support amongst the employees for whom it is seeking recognition;

(b)   the appropriate 'bargaining unit' in a workplace;
(c)   whether a sufficient majority of employees in a workplace support recognition; and
(d)   the procedure to be followed for negotiations between an employer and a trade union.

The issue of recognition is dealt with more fully at 3.2.1.

The CAC also has a duty to publish an annual report and prepare financial accounts for submission to ACAS in order that ACAS can report to the Secretary of State (s. 265).

1.2.3   The Trades Union Congress

The Trades Union Congress (TUC) is the collective body for trade unions. It was established in 1868. It has no overall power to bind member unions with regard to TUC policy.

The TUC has under its constitution the power to become involved in disputes between member unions. The principles were agreed at the 1939 TUC Conference at Bridlington (commonly referred to as the 'Bridlington Principles'). The Principles cover such matters as union influence, membership recognition of other bodies and transfers of members from union to union. The introduction to the Principles states that they are not contractual in effect but that all affiliated unions accept the Principles as 'a binding commitment for their continued affiliation to the TUC'.

The TUC has a specialist division constituted to hear claims between unions under the Bridlington Principles, this being the TUC Disputes Committee. Prior to 1993, the Bridlington Principles prevented a union from recruiting a new member where it was the case that that member was a clearly ascertainable member of another affiliated union, was under discipline from such a union or where there was good reason not to have the member otherwise accepted by the union. A good example of the rule and the power of the Disputes Committee was the case of *Cheall v APEX* [1983] IRLR 215. Here, the applicant sought a right to be heard by the Disputes Committee after he joined APEX from the TGWU. The TGWU objected to the Disputes Committee which ordered the termination of Mr Cheall's membership. Cheall was denied the opportunity of putting forward representations to the Committee. In an appeal to the House of Lords, their Lordships upheld the right of the Disputes Committee to order expulsion, notwithstanding the lack of an appearance by Cheall. They were of the view that union decisions over membership were entirely within the bounds of union discretion. The position has now changed following the amendments made by TURERA 1993 to TULRCA 1992, dealing with the right to membership of a union (see 3.2.9.2). Accordingly, the Bridlington Principles have had to be modified so as to take account of the changes, and now members of the TUC acknowledge:

... that they will not knowingly and actively seek to take into membership the present or recent members of another union by making recruitment approaches, either directly or indirectly, without the agreement of that organisation.

Members are now required to attempt to resolve disputes amicably before referring the matter to the Disputes Committee making, where necessary, any appropriate payment for loss of income to the complainant union suffering from the poaching of its members. If the parties cannot agree, the matter is then referred to the Disputes Committee who can make such order for compensation as it thinks fit if the case is proven. Ultimately, if a union that has actively engaged in poaching fails to adhere to a decision of the Disputes Committee, it can be excluded from the TUC under the TUC Rules.

1.2.4   The Certification Officer

As noted at 1.1.2.4 above, the Certification Officer was created by s. 7 of the Employment Protection Act 1975. The regulation surrounding the Certification Officer is now carried over into Pt VI of TULRCA 1992.

The Certification Officer is appointed by the Secretary of State after consulting with ACAS (s. 254(2)). Assistant Certification Officers can be appointed by the Certification Officer and he can delegate to the appointed assistants such powers within his remit as he thinks fit (s. 254(3), (4)). Facilities for the Certification Officer have to be provided by ACAS, including staff and accommodation (s. 254(5)). ACAS is also required to pay to the Certification Officer any sums needed for the performance of his duties (s. 254(5A)). It is also obliged to pay him and any assistant appointed such sums as are necessary for remuneration, pension, travelling and retirement gratuity as are approved by the Secretary of State and the Treasury (s. 255).

The powers of the Certification Officer are the following:

(a)   to maintain lists of trade unions and employers associations;
(b)   to determine the independence of trade unions;
(c)   to keep annual returns and accounts from trade unions;
(d)   to secure observance of the statutory procedures on engagements, amalgamations and changes of name by unions;
(e)   to supervise the statutory requirements relating to political funds;
(f)   to act as a decision-making body in matters relating to the alleged non-compliance with rules relating to elections to trade union office;
(g)   to ensure that there is independent scrutiny of elections to trade union executive positions; and
(h)   to retain custody of documents submitted under earlier enactments in respect of annual returns, accounts, copies of rules and other documents that were required under the Trade Unions Acts 1871–1964, the Industrial Relations Act 1971 or TULRA 1974 (s. 257).

The Certification Officer is allowed to adopt such procedure as he thinks fit (s. 256(1)) in matters conducted in front of him, but is required to have regard to whether he will make known the identity of any individual lodging a complaint (s. 256(2)). This latter provision is designed to provide some measure of secrecy for 'whistle-blowers'. To the extent that expenses are incurred in the course of hearings held by the Certification Officer, the Secretary of State can make provision for the payment of them although consent from the Treasury is again required (s. 256(3)).

1.2.5   The Commissioner for the Rights of Trade Union Members

The Office of Commissioner for the Rights of Trade Union Members (CROTUM) was introduced under the provisions of the Employment Act 1988. The current legislation relating to the constitution of the CROTUM is found in ss. 266–271 of TULRCA 1992. The office was established to provide help to union members contemplating bringing action against their union for a number of defined reasons.

The Commissioner is required to be appointed by the Secretary of State and is provided with an official seal upon taking office for authenticating any documents issued in the carrying out of functions (s. 266(2), (3)). The Commissioner is entitled to delegate any of the functions of his office to a person authorised by him on his staff, and it should be noted that the Commissioner and any member of staff authorised by him do not enjoy Crown status or immunity in any proceedings brought against them (s. 266(4), (5)).

The terms of appointment and remuneration of the Commissioner are dealt with under ss. 267–268. It is not possible for a Commissioner to be appointed for a single term exceeding five years (s. 267(2)) and remuneration, pension and retirement gratuities of a Commissioner must be approved by the Secretary of State and the Treasury (s. 268(2)–(5)). Expenses incurred in the performance of the Commissioner's duties are treated in a similar fashion (s. 270).

The Commissioner is allowed to appoint such staff as he thinks fit in the performance of his duties subject to the approval of the Secretary of State and the Treasury (s. 269(1)), and is required to file an annual report and accounts with the Secretary of State (s. 270). The Secretary of State is required to lay the report before both Houses of Parliament (s. 270(1)).

The powers of the Commissioner in relation to an individual making an application to him for assistance are dealt with in ss. 109–114 of TULRCA 1992. A guide ('Guide for Trade Union Members') has been issued by the Commissioner and is available free to trade union members. It sets out in basic terms the areas in which the CROTUM is able to provide representation. Section 109 makes provision for three categories of assistance, these being, first, assistance in respect of proceedings or prospective proceedings for a trade union's breach of a statutory duty as listed in s. 109(1), i.e.:

(a)   an application to the court under s. 15(3), i.e. an application for an order authorising a member to take or continue proceedings on behalf of a trade union, or for other proceedings under that section;

(b)   an application to the court under s. 16, being one for a remedy to prevent union trustees from unlawfully using union property;

(c)   an application under s. 26 for failure to maintain a register of union members or to secure the confidentiality of such a register;

(d)   an application to the court under s. 31 to receive a remedy for a union's refusal to allow a member access to its accounting records;

(e)   an application under s. 45C for a remedy in a case where a union appoints a person to a position on its executive and the appointee has been convicted under s. 45A for a breach of one of the disclosure duties set down in s. 45 (these being the duty to supply a copy of union rules, accounting records, annual returns, statements for members, accounts and audit and members' superannuation details);

(f)   an application to the court under s. 56 for a union's failure to comply with requirements as to election for office;

(g)   an application to the court under s. 62 to prevent industrial action not having the support of a ballot;

(h)   an application to the court under s. 71 to prevent a union unlawfully using funds for political objects;
or

(i)   an application to the court under s. 81 for failure to comply with the requirements as to political ballots.

The second category of assistance is provided under s. 109(2), this being for proceedings or prospective proceedings for breach of union rules relating to the following matters:

(a)   the appointment or election to or removal of a person from a union office;
(b)   disciplinary proceedings against a person, including expulsion from a union;
(c)   the authorising or endorsing of industrial action;
(d)   the balloting of members;
(e)   the application of union property;
(f)   the imposition, collection or distribution of any union levy; or
(g)   the constitution or proceedings of any committee, conference or other union body.

The final category is set down in s. 109(3), this being proceedings or prospective proceedings for breach of any order issued by the Secretary of State and relating to the conduct of any trade union, official of a union or any trustee of union property.

In deciding whether or not a case is fit to receive aid, the Commissioner is specifically bound to take account of the factors in s. 110(2) of the 1992 Act, which requires him to consider whether the case raise a question of principle, whether it is unreasonable to expect the complainant member to undertake the case without help and whether there is substantial public interest in the case to be brought. The Commissioner can look at cases outside this list though.

Further, under s. 110(3), if the Commissioner, in dealing with cases involving political ballots where the Certification Officer has ruled in favour of a union member, considers the case would have a reasonable prospect of having an enforcement notice granted, he is bound to grant an application by a union member to the extent necessary for the securing of the order to remedy the defects committed by the union and in ensuring that they do not happen again.

The Commissioner is, however, limited in respect of the cases that he can grant aid to. Under s. 110(4) members of the union other than the complainant member must be affected by the breach of union duty, or similar breaches must have been or might be committed in respect of other union members.

As regards the time frame for making a determination on an application put to the Commissioner, he is required to consider the application 'as soon as is reasonably practicable' after receiving the application and decide whether to grant the application and, if so, the extent to which to grant it (s. 110(1)). To the extent that the Commissioner decides not to grant an application put to him, he is required to notify the applicant of the decision. The Commissioner has a discretion as to whether or not to give his reasons for not granting an application (s. 110(5)).

The method by which assistance is granted is dealt with in s. 111. The Commissioner is bound to notify an applicant of a decision to grant aid under s. 111(1)(a) and can also give an applicant a choice of ways in which financial assistance will be granted (including the placing of restrictions on a grant, such as a requirement for an applicant to contribute towards his own costs: s. 111(1)(b)). Practically, the types of assistance are very wide. They can include the giving of advice by a solicitor or counsel (s. 111(2)(a)). Also, it is possible for an applicant to be provided with representation in proceedings, or to receive such help as would normally be provided by a solicitor or barrister (s. 111(2)(b)).

If the assistance relates to the conduct of proceedings, the Commissioner is bound to agree to indemnify an applicant in respect of any liability to pay costs or expenses arising by virtue of a judgment or court order in the proceedings (subject to any duty upon an applicant to contribute to his costs as specified under s. 111(1)(b): s. 111(3)(a)). The Commissioner may also agree to indemnify an applicant in respect of any liability for costs arising out of a compromise or settlement designed to avoid or end the proceedings (s. 111(3)(b)), and can also indemnify an applicant in respect of an undertaking that such an applicant may be required to give in order to obtain an interlocutory injunction (s. 111(3)(c)).

Other procedural issues in a grant of aid by the CROTUM are, first, a requirement to notify a person against whom proceedings have been or are to be commenced of the fact that an applicant is receiving aid (s. 111(4)). Secondly, any expenses or sums payable to an applicant in order to compromise a claim that are recovered in the proceedings are subject to a first charge in favour of the Commissioner (s. 111(5)). This obviously needs to be borne in mind when negotiating a settlement. Thirdly, the title of court proceedings may include an endorsement to the effect that an applicant is 'assisted by the Commissioner for the Rights of Trade Union Members'. The effect of such an endorsement is not to make the Commissioner a party to the proceedings and the omission of the wording is simply treated as an irregularity that does not nullify the proceedings or any steps taken in them (s. 112)). Lastly, to the extent that an applicant to the CROTUM procures the provision of aid in a case by fraud, the Commissioner is entitled to recover all sums paid to that applicant or to any other person as a result of the fraud (s. 113).

The Commissioner has been used nine times a year on average since the introduction of the office. As a consequence, it has been proposed in the White Paper 'Fairness at Work' that the office should be abolished and additional powers granted to the Certification Officer to cover the current range of functions of the Commissioner.

1.2.6   The Commissioner for Protection Against Unlawful Industrial Action

The office of Commissioner for Protection Against Unlawful Industrial Action (CPAUIA) was established by TURERA 1993 and was introduced to provide aid for individuals who might suffer as a result of breaches of the right created under s. 22 of that Act. The right was inserted as s. 235A of TULRCA 1992 (this being the right for an individual to complain that industrial action would or would be likely to affect the supply of goods or services or reduce the quality of goods or services supplied (see 9.3.1)). The Commissioner was established by s. 22 of TURERA 1993 and was consolidated into TULRCA 1992 as s. 235B. The powers and duties of the Commissioner are similar to those of the CROTUM and regard should be had to 1.2.5 above.

1.2.7   The International Labour Organisation

The International Labour Organisation (ILO) was founded in 1919 by the Treaty of Versailles, Arts 387–427. The Organisation works by having representatives from three different fields within a member State, these being workers, employers and government. The Constitution of the ILO was revised in 1944 by the Declaration of Philadelphia and makes a number of important policy statements about employment law generally, most notably, that 'labour is not a commodity', that 'freedom of expression and of association are essential to sustained progress' and that 'poverty anywhere constitutes a danger to prosperity everywhere'. Above all, the yardstick for government in making labour policy is that 'all human beings irrespective of race, creed or sex, have the right to pursue both their material well-being and their spiritual development in conditions of freedom and dignity, of economic security and equal opportunity'. Britain was one of the countries that played a founding role in the creation of the ILO, and a substantial amount of early 20th-century employment law in the UK was created as a result of ILO Conventions or ILO Recommendations (e.g., the Employment of Women, Young Persons and Children Act 1920, the Hours of Employment (Conventions) Act 1936 and the Merchant Shipping (International Conventions) Act 1936).

The ILO has three main bodies, these being the International Labour Conference, the Governing Body and the International Labour Office. As to the International Labour Conference, this normally meets once a year and is attended by four representatives of each member State, i.e., two government members, one member representing employers and one representing employees (ILO Constitution, Art. 3(1)).

The Governing Body consists of 56 governmental members and 28 each of workers and employers representatives, with the distribution of the seatholders being on a geographical basis. Members of the Governing Body are elected every three years at Conference, although 10 seats are reserved for States of industrial importance, one of which is the United Kingdom. The Governing Body arranges such matters as the activities of the ILO, the agenda of the Conference and appoints various committees and the Director-General of the International Labour Office.

The International Labour Office is the secretariat of the ILO and has its base in Geneva.

There are two sources of law that come from the ILO — Conventions and Recommendations. Recommendations are used most commonly as a device for fleshing out Conventions. Under Art. 19(5) and (6) of the ILO Convention, each member State must submit Conventions and Recommendations within 18 months of Conference to the national authority competent to enact legislation. The national body cannot 'bur[y] or set aside without due consideration' an instrument put forward in this fashion (per ILO Official Bulletin 1944). The British Government complies with its obligations by the laying of White Papers before Parliament setting out the views of the Government. To the extent that the views are not adopted by Parliament, no further obligation falls upon the member State, save for certain reporting requirements as may be required by the Governing Body from time to time. Similar requirements exist in relation to Recommendations.

A State that ratifies a Convention is required to 'take such action as may be necessary to make effective' the content of the Convention. Ratification must be unconditional. In order for a Convention or Recommendation to be ratified a two-thirds majority of delegates at the Conference is required, and this is normally only after the matter has been heard by Conference at two successive sessions. Conventions of the ILO also contain a power for member States to denounce previously adopted Conventions. The power is normally contained in the final articles of a Convention. Denunciation is not usually possible in the first 10 years following adoption; and thereafter, if a State has not exercised the right, the State will be bound for further periods of five years. In order to denounce a Convention it is necessary to inform the International Labour Office, and the denunciation becomes effective one year after receipt by that body.

Enforcement of ILO law takes place by referring either the Constitution or a Convention to the International Court of Justice. The International Labour Office tends to be the main interpreting body. Interpretations are placed in the Official Bulletin. There also exists a Committee on Freedom of Association composed of nine members appointed by the Governing Body whose remit is to examine failure to comply with the principle of freedom of association. Complaints can be made either by a member State against another member, by the Governing Body or by employers or workers organisations to the Committee.

The position of the British Government in relation to ILO Conventions has changed in the years following the election of Mrs Thatcher in 1979. Prior to 1979, the UK had ratified over 80 Conventions, although a number have since been denounced (to make way for changes to the law on wages policy in public sector contracts, wages councils and places and hours of working). Perhaps the greatest difficulty in recent years as regards Britain has been the problems caused by the incompatibility of the free market approach to employment with unionised labour. Examples of the tensions are the complaint put forward by the TUC in 1981 following the unilateral revocation of the Civil Service Pay Agreement and the subsequent refusal by the Government to refer the matter to the Civil Service Arbitration Tribunal. It was alleged that this violated Conventions 87 of 1948 (Freedom of Association), 98 of 1949 (Right to Organise and Collective Bargaining) and 151 of 1978 (Right to Organise in the Public Sector). This complaint was upheld in part by the Committee on Freedom of Association ('the committee', one of the committees appointed by the Governing Body), as were complaints in 1984 on the Government's decision to remove union membership rights at GCHQ (alleged breach of Convention 87 of 1948, complaint again made by the TUC) and, additionally, in 1987, that the Teachers Pay and Conditions Act contained provisions that would be in breach of Conventions 98 of 1949 and 151 of 1978 (the complaint here being made by the National Union of Teachers and the World Confederation of Organisations of the Teaching Profession).

While it is the case that a decision that a complaint is justified carries substantial moral weight against a non-complying member, no sanctions ultimately attach for failing to comply. Therefore, to the extent that a Convention is not contained in a piece of domestic legislation, failure to comply with it causes no problems for the Government. This said, there is an increasing move on the part of the European Court of Justice to follow generally accepted principles of international law in determining the outcome of European cases, and there is the possibility that the United Kingdom may ultimately be influenced by the ILO in this way (see, in particular, Grief, N., 'The Domestic Impact of the European Community on Human Rights as Mediated Through Community Law' [1991] PL 555–67). It remains to be seen if the policy of the new Labour Government will change in this regard.

1.2.8   The Confederation of British Industry

The Confederation of British Industry (CBI) is the central business organisation in Britain. It represents employers both to the public in the United Kingdom and also at an international level in the European Union. Article 3 of the charter of the CBI lists its objectives as being:

To provide British business with the means of formulating, making known and influencing general policy on industrial, economic, fiscal, commercial, labour, social, legal and technical questions and to act as a national reference point for those seeking industry's views; to develop the contribution of British industry to the national economy; to encourage the efficiency and competitive powers of British industry and to provide advice, information and services to British industry to that end.

The CBI is chaired by a part-time elected President who serves for two years. The President is elected by members who are companies or business associations. Ultimately, the Director General of the CBI and the permanent staff of the CBI deal with day-to-day policy issues, meetings with ministers and the like.

The CBI maintains contact with the TUC (see 1.2.3) through a variety of different channels, these being the National Economic Development Council, the Manpower Services Commission, the Health and Safety Commission and ACAS (see 1.2.1). Informal links also exist between the CBI and the TUC, but it should be noted that the CBI does not ultimately engage in collective bargaining on its own account.

1.2.9 The Department of Trade and Industry

The Department of Trade and Industry (DTI) is responsible for implementing employment policy insofar as it concerns ACAS, tribunals, industrial relations policy, and pay and redundancy issues. These functions came to the DTI following the closing down of the Employment Department in 1995. The Department used to carry out its duties directly in relation to conciliation and arbitration until these functions were transferred to ACAS in 1974. Apart from providing for general employment policy in the areas described, another function of the DTI is to institute courts of inquiry under s. 215 of TULRCA 1992.

Courts of inquiry can be created where it is the case that a trade dispute exists or is apprehended and the Secretary of State feels the need to inquire into the causes of and circumstances of the dispute (s. 215(1)). A court created in this fashion is required to inquire into the matters within its remit, to make a report (and any minority reports if necessary) and lay the report(s) before both Houses of Parliament (s. 215(2) and (3)). The reports when laid cannot take account of any evidence from a trade union or individual business unless it is the case that the information was given to the court as evidence, or has been provided with the consent of the secretary of the union or permission of the business in question. This restriction against disclosure also applies to members of the court (s. 215(5)).

The constitution of a court of inquiry is dealt with under s. 216 of the 1992 Act. It consists of either a chairman and such other persons as the Secretary of State thinks fit to appoint, or it can simply be one person sitting alone. If needs be, the Secretary of State can give powers to the court to call witnesses and documents and to administer oaths (s. 216(5)).

Courts of inquiry are rarely used as a means of establishing the cause of an industrial dispute. The most notable exception to this in recent years was the court chaired by Lord Scarman in the dispute at the Grunwick photographic company (ultimately being reported as *Grunwick Processing Labs Ltd v ACAS* [1978] ICR 231 in the subsequent litigation that followed ACAS's recommendation to allow recognition of the union at the centre of the dispute).

1.2.10   The European Community

European law has a part to play in the regulation of trade unions. The position of European law in the United Kingdom has been weaker than in other member States due to the British Government's initial failure to adopt what would have been the 'Social Chapter' of the Treaty on European Union (OJ 1992, C/224) at the inter-governmental summit at Maastricht in November 1991. However, one of the first employment-related measures of the new Labour administration has been to adopt the Social Chapter.

The Maastrict Treaty is binding on the signatories to the Treaty and Protocol. It has three key themes. These are (i) to clarify the right of the European Community to engage in matters relating to social policy, (ii) to extend the concept of qualified majority voting and (iii) to stimulate the development and growth of dialogue between workers and managers. Article 1 of the Treaty sets down its main aim, this being:

> ... the promotion of employment, improved living and working conditions, proper social protection, dialogue between management and labour, the development of human resources with a view to lasting high employment and the combatting of exclusion.

To the extent that measures are introduced under the Treaty, some can be dealt with on the basis of qualified majority voting (these being health and safety, working conditions, information and consultation of workers, equality between the sexes and integration of excluded groups: Arts 2(1) and 2(2)), while other matters require unanimity of member States to invoke change (these being social security, protection of workers faced with termination of employment, representation and collective defence of the interests of workers, rights of third-country nationals legally resident in the Community and financial provision for promoting employment and job creation: Art. 2(3)).

It should be noted that the Treaty does not apply to pay, the right to associate or the right to strike or impose lock-outs (Art. 2(6)). To this end, the Treaty patently excludes the notion of developing collective bargaining throughout the Community.

Articles 3 and 4 are aimed at promoting consultation between workers and managers in the public and private sector on issues that affect social policy, and ultimately, if headway cannot be reached by signatories to the Treaty allows the European Commission to put forward proposals to achieve this aim.

2 The Nature and Status of Collective Organisations

2.1 TRADE UNIONS

2.1.1 Trade unions defined

The definition of a trade union is found in s. 1 of TULRCA 1992, which states that a union is:

> ... an organisation (whether temporary or permanent)—
>
> (a) which consists wholly or mainly of workers of one or more descriptions and whose principal purposes include the regulation of relations between workers of that description or those descriptions and employers or employers' associations; or
>
> (b) which consists wholly or mainly of—
>
> (i)   constituent or affiliated organisations which fulfil the conditions in paragraph (a) (or themselves consist wholly or mainly of constituent or affiliated organisations which fulfil those conditions), or
>
> (ii)   representatives of such constituent or affiliated organisations,
> and whose principal purposes include the regulation of relations between workers and employers or between workers and employers' associations, or the regulation of relations between its constituent or affiliated organisations.

The definition needs to be examined as regards a number of different points.

2.1.1.1 'Organisation'

The concept of an organisation confers some notion of a body with a structure. In considering what this was, the NIRC decided in *Frost* v *Clarke & Smith Manufacturing Co. Ltd* [1973] IRLR 216 that a mere body of workers claiming to be

a union for the purposes of claiming sole bargaining rights under the Industrial
Relations Act 1971 was not an organisation since (at p. 218): 'They had no name,
they had no constitution, they had no rules, they held no meetings, they kept no
minutes, they had no offices, they had no property, they had no funds; indeed they
had none of the attributes of an organisation.'

2.1.1.2 'Regulation of workers'

The definition also requires that the body has as one of its principal purposes the
regulation of relations between workers and employers or employers' associations.
The meaning of 'principal purposes' has been considered judicially. In *Midland Cold
Storage Ltd* v *Steer* [1972] ICR 435, the issue was whether a body of shop stewards
of two unions at the Port of London could amount to a trade union. The matter arose
when the plaintiff sued the shop steward defendants for refusing to handle goods
destined for the plaintiff and which had caused it substantial disruption. The
activities of the defendants, apart from organising industrial action, were not clear.
The plaintiff sought an injunction, a declaration and damages against the defendants
on the ground that the defendants, as a union, had acted unlawfully. The court had to
determine whether the defendants (as members of a 'Joint Shop Stewards
Committee') constituted a union capable of having proceedings served against it.
Megarry J (as he then was) decided that they were not. He said (at p. 443):

> I am far from satisfied by the evidence ... that the 'principal objects' of the
> committee 'include the regulation of relations between workers of that description
> or those descriptions and employers or organisations of employer'. There is little
> satisfactory evidence about the composition or activities of the committee, apart
> from some evidence relating to 'blacking'; and although the committee appears to
> intend to secure the employment of registered dockworkers by the plaintiffs,
> I cannot infer that, once this achieved, the committee has any ambition to 'regulate
> relations' thereafter ...

This said, provided that there is satisfactory evidence of organisation and the desire
to regulate, that appears to be adequate for the purposes of establishing a union. A
good example in this regard is *British Association of Advisers and Lecturers in
Physical Education* v *National Union of Teachers* [1986] IRLR 497. The case
concerned the plaintiff's exclusion from a national pay negotiating body for four
categories of local authority education employees (the 'Soulbury Committee'). The
background to the exclusion was that the plaintiff had entered into an agreement with
the defendant in 1961 for its members to become members of the defendant union at
a reduced subscription. It was also agreed that the plaintiff association would at all
times retain its autonomy. In 1982, the plaintiff wrote to the defendant withdrawing
its collective membership. In 1985, the defendant put forward a motion to the
Soulbury Committee that the plaintiff should be removed from the Committee. The
motion was carried and it was then that the plaintiff sued for breach of contract

relating to its exclusion and asked for an injunction and damages. In the High Court, the claim was struck out on the grounds that the plaintiff was not a union and therefore had no *locus standi* to bring the claim. The main issue in the case was essentially whether or not the plaintiff had as one of its principal objects the 'regulation of relations between workers ... and employers or employers' associations'. The plaintiff appealed and in the Court of Appeal the claim was reinstated. The Court of Appeal made two important points. First, Neill LJ dealt with the constitution of the plaintiff association. This stated that: 'The Association shall be concerned with the professional interests of its members'. Neill LJ said of this (at p. 500):

In my judgment, when one is dealing with persons who are of professional standing and one speaks of the professional interests of the members, one is not confining one's attention simply to the status of the profession to which they belong, but is dealing in a wider context with the interests of the individual members in their profession. It seems to me that in the context of this constitution the phrase 'professional interests' is apt to cover the interests of individual members in their profession including their interests *vis-à-vis* their employers.

Secondly, Ralph Gibson LJ added (at p. 501):

We are concerned with an association that has a total membership of 402. The Act does not require, for an association to qualify as a trade union, that it be of any particular size or that it demonstrate any particular capacity or effectiveness or frequency of intervention in its role of regulation of the relations between its members and their employers. It qualifies if it demonstrates that it has a principal purpose to regulate those relations and is an association wholly or mainly of workers.

2.1.1.3   *Representative unions and divisions of unions as unions*
The definition in s. 1 also makes provision for bodies representative of a collection of unions to be categorised as unions themselves (s. 1(b)). Examples of this are the TUC and the International Transport Workers Federation. The converse is equally true: where a union is a collective of different trades or exists in a number of different regions, it is possible to have separate unions within a main union, e.g., the National Union of Mineworkers (see, *Thomas* v *NUM (South Wales Area)* [1985] IRLR 136). The consequences of being found to be a smaller union are important with regard to the issue of remedies and the quantum of damages that can be awarded against a union by reference to its size (see 8.3.2.4).

2.1.2   Listing

Once a union has fulfilled the basic definition of a trade union, it can apply to be listed. Listing is a mechanical process dealt with under ss. 2–5 of TULRCA 1992.

The duty to keep a list of trade unions is imposed upon the Certification Officer by s. 2(1). The bodies to be listed are those who existed on the list under s. 8 of TULRA 1974 and other organisations satisfying the criteria of Pt I of the 1992 Act (s. 2(1)). The list is a public document and can be inspected by members of the public at all reasonable hours without payment of charge (s. 2(2)). The Certification Officer is also bound to include a copy of the list in his annual report (s. 2(3)).

2.1.2.1 Procedure for listing
The statutory listing procedure is set down in s. 3 of TULRCA 1992. Application by an unlisted organisation is initially made to the Certification Officer (s. 3(1)). The Certification Officer can specify a model form to be used in the listing process, and an organisation requesting to be listed must also supply a copy of its rules, a list of officers, the address of the main or head office and the name that it is to be known by, together with a fee for registration (s. 3(2)). The Certification Officer is then bound to list the body if he is satisfied that the body is a trade union (as defined in s. 1), that the matters in s. 3(2) have been complied with and that registration of the name is not prohibited due to its similarity with that of another listed organisation, a body that was registered as a trade union under the Trade Union Acts 1871–1964 or registered under the Industrial Relations Act 1971 as a trade union (s. 3(3)–(4)).

2.1.2.2 Removal from the list
The Certification Officer also has a power to remove the name of an organisation from the list where:

(a) although a body is listed, it appears in fact that it is not a trade union (s. 4(1));
(b) he is requested to remove the body from the list by the organisation (s. 4(3)(a)); or
(c) he is satisfied that the body no longer exists (s. 4(3)(b)).

In a case where the Certification Officer decides to remove a listed body, he is required to give the body notice of the fact and must consider any representations made to him by the body received by him during the notice period. The notice period cannot be less than 28 days (s. 4(2)).

2.1.2.3 Appeals against refusal to list or removal from the list
To the extent that an organisation is either refused entry on the list or has its entry terminated, an appeal lies to the Employment Appeal Tribunal (EAT) on either a point of fact or (unusually) of law (s. 9).

The Certification Officer should not be called as a witness to any appeal. In *The Certification Officer* v *Squibb UK Staff Association* [1979] IRLR 75 (a case involving a refusal to grant a certificate of independence, dealt with below at 2.1.3), Lord Denning MR said of the function of the Certification Officer (at p. 77):

[The Certification Officer] appeared so as to oppose the appeal and justify his own decision. He gave evidence as if he were a party and was cross-examined at length as if he was a party. I must say I think that was undesirable. The Certification Officer is a judicial position. He has to be impartial and independent. He has to give his determination and support it with written reasons. I cannot believe it is right that he should be cross-examined on those reasons. He should not be cross-examined any more than a justice of the peace or a planning inspector or arbitrator or any of the many people who have to make decisions from which there is an appeal. Such a person can be asked to supplement his reasons and to give further reasons: or the matter can be remitted to him for reconsideration. . . . No doubt on any appeal there is public interest involved. So there should be someone present to support the decision of the Certification Officer. . . . In one of these cases I think that the public interest should be safeguarded by the Treasury Solicitor.

2.1.2.4 Advantages of listing
Listing is important to a trade union in a number of ways. First, it provides evidence that the union is a union (s. 2(4)) and a certificate can be issued to a body claiming to be a union that its name has been included on the register (s. 2(5)).

Secondly, to the extent that a union provides provident benefits (as defined in s. 467(2) of the Income and Corporation Taxes Act 1988), those benefits are exempt from income tax, corporation tax and capital gains tax provided that the union is listed.

The third advantage to a union is that where a union is listed, property of the union (which is required under s. 12 of TULRCA 1992 to be held by union trustees) can be vested in new trustees or transferred by the process in ss. 13–14 of the 1992 Act, which relies simply on the resolution of appointment of a trustee as being sufficient to vest the property in a union trustee (no vesting deed is required).

The final and most significant advantage is that once a union has been listed, it can apply for a certificate of independence.

2.1.3 The certificate of independence

2.1.3.1 Introduction
The grant of a certificate of independence is of fundamental importance to a trade union from the point of claiming trade union rights. The formulation of the main union statutory rights requires that the union must be both independent and, in some cases, recognised as well (see Chapter 3 generally with regard to recognition).

The requirement of independence for the grant of rights is to ensure that collective rights are exercised by truly independent bodies as opposed to staff associations which may simply provide a means for a personnel department to impose informal control over the workforce. Further, since the rights include, *inter alia*, the power to bargain away the right to strike, the use of the Certification Officer as an outside check to ensure independence guarantees that union members are protected from management infiltration that could deprive them of their ability to take industrial action. As Kilner-Brown J put it in *Association of HSD (Hatfield) Employees* v *Certification Officer* [1978] ICR 21, at p. 24:

> Parliament will not tolerate the recognised and certificated existence of a band of people claiming to be an independent trade union when in reality they are unable to offer a vigorous challenge to the employers on behalf of their members whether collectively or individually.

2.1.3.2 Independence

As with listing, the 1992 Act provides a statutory formulation for the grant of a certificate of independence. The first requirement for a union applying for a certificate is that the union is independent. Section 5 provides a definition of independence and states that a union will be independent where it:

> (a)   is not under the domination or control of an employer or group of employers or of one or more employers' associations, and
> (b)   is not liable to interference by an employer or any such group or association (arising out of the provision of financial or material support or by any other means whatsoever) tending towards such control . . .

The test works at two levels asking, first, whether the union is actually just an emanation of an employer and, if not, secondly, whether the union could be forced to defer to the wishes of an employer.

2.1.3.2.1 Limb 1 — Independence from an employer

As to the first limb of the test, the Certification Officer publishes a booklet, *Guidance for trade unions wishing to apply for a certificate of independence*, which deals essentially with two issues, these being the procedure for obtaining a certificate of independence and also the criteria used for determining independence. The criteria are broadly similar to those put forward in the case of *Blue Circle Staff Association* v *The Certification Officer* [1977] IRLR 20. In this case, the appellant was appealing against the refusal of the Certification Officer to grant a certificate of independence. The appellant association had been formed in 1971 to cover salaried staff of the Blue Circle Group of Companies. In 1975, it had made constitutional changes to attempt to make it independent of management, but under its rules the body was heavily infiltrated by management at all levels. The Certification Officer rejected the application for a certificate of independence and relied upon eight criteria (approved by the EAT) (these now being reduced to the following in the above booklet):

(a)   History of the organisation. The body should not have a recent history of having been created by management. If it was created by management but has since evolved into being the author of its own destiny, history can be ignored.

(b)   Membership base. The Certification Officer tends to frown upon bodies that derive their membership solely from one employer. A limited base such as this makes the body more vulnerable to pressure from an employer and ultimately independence requires an ability to withstand pressure. This said, the Certification Officer has approved a number of single employer unions and a good example (until privatisation) was the National Union of Mineworkers.

(c)   Organisation and structure. The main issue here is that the body should not be infiltrated by management and should be truly independent and able to make its own decisions. Of particular importance is whether senior employees are able to be members, since this potentially allows a degree of management interference.

(d)   Finance. In the case of a union receiving a direct subsidy from an employer, this is probably enough to be fatal to a claim of independence. However, independence also requires a sound asset base which allows a body to ward off the withdrawal of any financial facilities (such as check-off).

(e)   Employer provided facilities. This will include any administrative support that is provided to the body, while also dealing with such matters as time off for members. In the case of single employer organisations, the process that the Certification Officer adopts is to cost the provision of the facilities to see if the body could cope financially with the withdrawal of them. The provision of facilities should not necessarily be determinative of the grant of a certificate. Regard must also be had to the ACAS Code of Practice on Time Off for Trade Union Duties and Activities 1991. This Code recommends, at para. 28, that employers should provide such facilities as noticeboards, accommodation for meetings, a telephone and office space. Other factors may therefore have to be taken into account.

(f)   Negotiating record. This is of importance to a claim for independence. A weak success rate in negotiations is not necessarily probative of lack of independence, but a strong success rate can help to outweigh defects in any of the above factors. According to the Certification Officer, negotiation is the point at which independence and success overlap. An effective union is likely to be an independent one.

Other good examples of cases involving applications for independence on these criteria are *A. Monk & Co. Staff Association* v *Certification Officer* [1980] IRLR 431 and *Association of HSD (Hatfield) Employees* v *Certification Officer* [1978] ICR 21. In the *Monk* case, the association in question was a one employer association and had evolved from an association initially formed to combat interest in recruitment at the firm by an established union (the Association of Clerical and Transport Staff). It had already made two previous unsuccessful applications to the Certification Officer when it made the application that led to the appeal. The Certification Officer again turned down the application holding that the association was not independent and was also likely to suffer from interference from the employer of its members (discussed below at 2.1.3.2.2). The association appealed and the EAT found against the Certification Officer. It took the view that although the union was not as strong as some (having a membership of 481 and assets at the bank of around £13,000), it had the determination to carry on in the event that the employer withdrew facilities that it provided. Further, it had an established record of negotiations with the firm. To the extent that it was prepared and able to carry on in the event of the employer withdrawing facilities, it was independent.

Likewise, in the *HSD* case, the association was formed out of the workers at Hawker Siddeley Dynamics at Hatfield. It boasted a membership of some 800 employees. Following nationalisation of the aerospace industry, the association became fiercely independent of the management of HSD. HSD was visited by the new head of British Aerospace, and he refused to have dealings with the association on the grounds that it was not a union. The association was incensed and applied for a certificate of independence. This was refused by the Certification Officer. On hearing the appeal, the EAT took the view that following the nationalisation of HSD and the fierce opposition of the association to the management initially, it was clear that the association was independent and could therefore be provided with a certificate.

2.1.3.2.2   Limb 2 — The likelihood of interference   The second limb of the test (s. 5(b)) focuses upon a body's ability to resist external pressure from an employer. Two possibilities of formulation exist in relation to the Act's test of being 'liable to interference by an employer'. The first is that 'liable to interference' refers solely to the time that a union applies for certification (this view being favourable to an applicant union). The second is that a union could be liable to interference at some point in the future, if, for example, the union tried to take industrial action (this view is obviously unfavourable to applicants).

As to the correct view, the leading case is *The Certification Officer* v *Squibb UK Staff Association* [1979] IRLR 75. Here, the association had again evolved from a single employer association and had sought independence from the management of the employer. The employer recognised the body as having sole negotiating rights for members of staff. It had a membership of 231 and had funds of around £1,100. Against these facts, the employer provided a number of facilities for the association such as check-off, office facilities and time off for union officials. The Certification Officer refused the grant of a certificate to the union. The union appealed to the EAT and was successful, but on appeal to the Court of Appeal, the Certification Officer's decision was reinstated. Shaw LJ stated (at p. 79):

The phrase 'liable to' when used otherwise than in relation to legal obligations has an ordinary and well-understood meaning, namely, 'subject to the possibility of'. Counsel for the union has in fact contended that it means 'subject to the likelihood of' ... I see no warrant in the context of the legislation or in practical common-sense for so limited a construction of the words 'liable to'. If adopted, it would impose upon the Certification Officer the need for an exercise in clairvoyance with much uncertainty developing in the outcome.

Another good example of the question of interference was the case involving workers at the Government Communication Headquarters (GCHQ), *Government Communications Staff Federation* v *Certification Officer* [1993] IRLR 260. The case arose initially out of the decision of Margaret Thatcher to ban outside trade unions at GCHQ, claiming that the interest of the nation was at stake if unions went on strike there. The staff at GCHQ were allowed to form their own departmental staff association approved by the Director of GCHQ. The appellant body was the result. The body was accorded sole negotiation rights for its members and ultimately applied for a certificate of independence which was refused. On appeal, the EAT agreed with the Certification Officer. The association's continued existence was always contingent on the permission of the Director of GCHQ and therefore it could never be independent.

2.1.3.3   Granting and revoking the certificate
The grant of a certificate of independence is dealt with in ss. 6–9 of TULRCA 1992. Applications must be to the Certification Officer on such form as the Certification Officer approves, together with the fee for registration from time to time in force (s. 6(1)). To the extent that an application is received from a body that is not listed (see 2.1.2 *et seq.* above), the Certification Officer is bound to refuse an application for a certificate of independence (s. 6(3)).

The Certification Officer is bound to come to a decision on the granting of a certificate within a period of one month from the date of receiving an application from a union, and during that time he must make such enquiries as he thinks are necessary to establish independence before making his determination (s. 6(4)–(5)). The Certification Officer is bound to give reasons for any refusal to grant a certificate (s. 6(6)) and he must keep a record of all certificates of independence that are granted and allow free public access to the record at all reasonable hours (s. 6(2)).

Once the Certification Officer has granted a certificate of independence, he can review the decision and withdraw the certificate if he is of the opinion that the body is no longer independent (s. 7(1)). If he is minded to review a certificate, he must inform the union and enter a notice of the proposal in the record kept by him (s. 7(2)). Again, since the function being undertaken is essentially judicial in nature, the Certification Officer is required to make such enquiries as he thinks fit and take into account any representations that are submitted to him before making his decision and either confirm the certificate or withdraw it and provide his reasons for doing so (s. 7(3)–(6)).

2.1.3.4   Evidential effect of the certificate
The certificate of independence or the absence of it (including where it has been revoked) is conclusive evidence as to whether or not the union is independent, and any document purporting to be a certificate of independence and signed by either the Certification Officer or a person appointed by him to sign such certificates is presumed to be a certificate of independence until the contrary is proved (s. 8(1)–(2)).

The 1992 Act also allows for certified copies of a certificate of independence to be presumed to be valid as evidence (s. 8(3)).

Lastly, to the extent that proceedings are commenced in front of a court, the EAT, the CAC, ACAS or an industrial tribunal and an issue arises as to whether or not a union is independent, then to the extent that no certificate can be provided and no entries exist on the record kept by the Certification Officer, the case must be stayed pending a determination by the Certification Officer under the procedure for an initial grant of a certificate (s. 8(4), (5): see above at 2.1.3.3).

2.1.3.5 Appeals

As with a refusal to list or removal from the list, an appeals procedure lies in the event that a union is dissatisfied as to a refusal to grant or revocation of a certificate of independence. The appeal lies on grounds either of fact or of law and is to the EAT. Regard should be had to 2.1.2.3 above for a full discussion of this area.

2.1.4 Recognition of trade unions

2.1.4.1 Introduction

After a trade union has gained a certificate of independence from the Certification Officer, the next important hurdle for the union to cross is that of recognition by an employer (or two or more associated employers). The importance of recognition lies in the increased rights that a trade union derives as a result of recognition (see Chapter 3).

Recognition is not currently a compulsory process save for one situation. This is where an employer is proposing to transfer an undertaking. Where it is the case that the transferring employer recognised a union or unions, the transferee employer is also bound to afford recognition to the union or unions and any collective agreements that have been entered into are deemed to be modified to that effect (Transfer of Undertakings (Protection of Employment) Regulations 1981, SI 1981 No. 1794, reg. 9).

Proposals were put forward by the Labour Party in the 1997 election campaign that recognition could become compulsory once Labour were in power where it was the case that a majority of a relevant workforce voted in favour of union recognition. Detailed proposals have yet to emerge in this area with regard to the time frame for the proposed changes. The current position is therefore left to the common law which places a voluntary emphasis upon the concept.

Recognition does have a statutory definition at s. 178(3) of TULRCA 1992, and means: 'the recognition of the union by an employer, or two or more associated employers, to any extent, for the purposes of collective bargaining; and 'recognised' and other related expressions shall be construed accordingly.' A full definition of what amounts to collective bargaining is found at s. 178(2) and essentially covers the same areas as trade disputes. The net result is that recognition occurs where an employer or associated employers recognise a union for one or more of the purposes laid down by TULRCA 1992. Furthermore, since s. 244(1)(g) provides that a trade dispute can also arise out of a union's claim to be recognised by an employer, the effect is to allow lawful industrial action in relation to recognition-related disputes.

Recognition can be broken down to address three general propositions that have emerged from the case law concerning the issue.

2.1.4.2   Recognition — the three propositions

2.1.4.2.1   Proposition one   Case law relating to recognition shows clearly that recognition can be expressly or impliedly agreed by the parties. In *National Union of Tailors* v *Charles Ingram & Co. Ltd* [1977] IRLR 147, an employer in a poor financial position had laid off a large number of staff without consulting the applicant union, which the employer would have been obliged to do in the event that the union was recognised (see 3.3). One of the issues facing the EAT on appeal was whether or not the union was recognised as it claimed. Phillips J dealt with the law relating to recognition at p. 148, stating:

> 'Recognition' plainly, we think, implies agreement — which, of course, involves consent. That is to say it is a mutual process by which the employers recognise the union, which obviously agrees to be recognised and it may come about in a number of different ways. There may a written agreement that the union should be recognised. There may be an express agreement not in writing. Or, as we think, it is sufficient if neither of those exist but the established facts are such that it can be said of them that they are clear and unequivocal and give rise to the clear inference that the employers have recognised the union. This will normally involve conduct over a period of time.
>
> Of course, the longer that state of facts has existed the easier it is in any given case to reach a conclusion that a proper interpretation of them inevitably leads to the conclusion that the employers have recognised the union.

Cases since *National Union of Tailors* v *Charles Ingram* followed the approach taken in that case and have found that the question of recognition is one of mixed fact and law to be determined from the particular case being dealt with. Another example is *National Union of Gold, Silver and Allied Trades* v *Albury Bros Ltd* [1977] IRLR 173; aff'd [1978] IRLR 504, CA. Here, the issue again arose out of a collective redundancy and the question was whether or not the appellant union should have been consulted after tentative steps had been initially taken between the company and the union. The facts were slightly more unusual in that one of the legal arguments put forward turned on the issue of the words 'recognition … to any extent' in s. 178(3). The matter was dealt with again by Phillips J in the EAT (his judgment being upheld by the Court of Appeal), who took the view that the use of the words 'to any extent' were used to denote recognition for a particular purpose or purposes rather than recognition arising out of limited contact. Eveleigh LJ, in the Court of

Appeal, added of recognition (at p. 506) that 'it entails not merely a willingness to discuss but also to negotiate in relation to one or more [of the matters set down in s. 178(2) of TULRCA 1992]. That is to say, to negotiate with a view to striking a bargain upon an issue. . .'.

Other examples of a failure to recognise include *Amalgamated Union of Engineering Workers* v *Sefton Engineering Co. Ltd* [1976] IRLR 318, where meetings between the employer and two union representatives as workers representatives were held not to constitute recognition; *Transport and General Workers Union* v *Dyer* [1977] IRLR 93, where one previous negotiated ending to a strike did not amount to recognition; and *Cleveland County Council* v *Springett* [1985] IRLR 131, where courteous replies to questions put by a union did not amount to recognition.

Examples of cases in favour of recognition are *National Union of Tailors* v *Charles Ingram*, above; *Union of Shop, Distributive and Allied Workers* v *Sketchley Ltd* [1981] IRLR 291 (for facts, see 2.1.4.2.2); and, more doubtfully, *Joshua Wilson & Bros Ltd* v *Union of Shop, Distributive and Allied Workers* [1978] IRLR 120, where the employer was found to have recognised a union through observing JIC conditions, allowing a trade union representative to post notice of wage changes on a noticeboard and allowing a union representative to collect union subscriptions while on the employer's premises.

2.1.4.2.2 Proposition two   The second issue that arises from the cases is that once an employer is taken to have recognised a union, he cannot, in the absence of formal withdrawal of recognition, argue that he did not intend to recognise. This point was established in *Union of Shop, Distributive and Allied Workers* v *Sketchley Ltd* [1981] IRLR 291. Here, a collective agreement had been entered into between the union and employer granting the union rights of recognition in relation to representation of workers, check-off, etc. The union was stated not to have rights in relation to the negotiation of terms and conditions of employment, and this point was expressly made to the union in various correspondence. In January 1980, the employer decided that it would be necessary to implement a programme of redundancies and again informed the union that it would not be able to take part in any negotiations. On 28 February 1980, the union held a meeting of its members and informed the employer that the outcome of the meeting was that its members would be taking strike action unless the union granted rights to represent the workers' interests. The result was that on 29 February a written agreement was entered into allowing the union rights of audience in relation to proposed redundancies. The union was subsequently to ask for protective awards (dealt with below at 3.3) when the employer failed to consult the union and imposed redundancies. The EAT held that the union had been recognised and was therefore able to claim the protective awards. Browne-Wilkinson P (as he then was) stated (at p. 295):

In our view, an employer who enters into an agreement with a union relating to the terms and conditions of employment of members of their union runs a severe risk that the inference will be drawn that such an employer has recognised the union as having negotiating rights in that field.

It is obviously open to the parties to restrict the context of such an agreement by a clause expressly stating that a union is not being recognised for the purposes of negotiating terms and conditions.

2.1.4.2.3 *Proposition three*

Recognition also raises the question as to whether or not an employers' association can enter into an agreement that binds all of its members to deal with a trade union. The matter arose in the case of *National Union of Gold, Silver and Allied Trades* v *Albury Bros Ltd* [1977] IRLR 173; aff'd [1978] IRLR 504, CA, where one of the issues facing the court was whether or not the respondent employer was bound by a collective agreement that had been entered into by the North Area Goldsmiths' and Jewellers' trade section of the British Jewellers' Association and the union. Phillips J, in the EAT, said of this point:

> We do not think that the mere fact that a trade association has negotiated with a union an agreement relating to terms and conditions of employment, etc. is by itself sufficient to establish that an employer who is a member of the association has, for that reason alone, recognised the union within the meaning of [s. 178(3) of TULRCA 1992]. Such a conclusion would seem to us to be contrary to the generally accepted meaning of recognition in industrial circles, where it is understood to postulate some kind of direct contact between the unions and the employers for the purpose of negotiating terms and conditions of employment, etc.

Accordingly, without more, mere membership of a trade association that has signed a collective agreement with a union will not impose a duty to recognise.

2.1.4.2.4 *Withdrawal of recognition*

There is currently no legal duty to carry on recognising a union once recognition has been initially granted by an employer (*Associated Newspaper Ltd* v *Wilson* [1995] IRLR 258). In its pre-election manifesto, the current Labour Government promised to impose recognition where a union had the support of the majority of workers in a workplace. The proposal has yet to be implemented, though, and much debate exists as to what the 'majority of workers in a workplace' means.

Furthermore, an employer is free to withdraw recognition at any point in time after recognition has been granted, and the only liability that will occur is an obligation to honour recognition rights during any period of notice that may have been given to a union, or, possibly, to the extent that a collective agreement has been revoked, to honour rights granted to individual employees (see *Robertson* v *British Gas Corporation* [1983] IRLR 302 but, to contrary effect, see *Cadoux* v *Central Regional Council* [1986] IRLR 131).

2.1.5   Status and legality of trade unions

2.1.5.1   Introduction
Trade union status is dealt with under s. 10 of TULRCA 1992. The Act grants to trade unions a special status as a collection of individuals who are able to do or have done to them a specific category of things under a collective name, that being the name of the union. Trade unions are therefore effectively distinguished from both incorporated and unincorporated associations. In arriving at this peculiar state of affairs, it is necessary to bear in mind the history surrounding trade unions.

2.1.5.2   The history of trade union status
Prior to the Trade Union Act 1871, trade unions were treated as just another form of unincorporated association. It followed that if a union was to be sued or was itself to sue, it had to do so by way of a collective action. It was thought that the 1871 Act, which had introduced the concept of registration for trade unions (see above at Chapter 1), made no difference to this position. However, in the case of *Taff Vale Railway Co.* v *Amalgamated Society of Railway Servants* [1901] AC 426, the House of Lords took the view that trade unions enjoyed a somewhat different status. The case arose out of the alleged victimisation of one member of the union who had presented a claim for a pay rise to the company's managers. The union took a stand over the matter and a strike was called. The company, determined not to be beaten into submission, imported strike-breakers to carry on the business of the railway. Further, it took steps to ensure that the union did not harass members of staff still working. An injunction was granted against the union at first instance, but on appeal the Court of Appeal overruled the judgment of Farwell J holding that, since the union did not have any legal capacity, it could not be sued. The company appealed to the House of Lords which unanimously reinstated the trial judge's decision, albeit for different reasons. Two reasons emerged for the decision. First, it was held that to sue a union was simply an extension of a representative action, and therefore it was perfectly possible to sue the union in its own name. Secondly, and alternatively, two of the Law Lords took the view that upon its registration the union was transformed into a quasi-corporate entity whose status could be lost upon deregistration (although see the case of *Lawlor* v *Union of Post Office Workers* [1965] Ch 712, where an unregistered union was sued in its own name).

Whatever the position, it was at last possible to sue not only the individual members of a union but also the union itself, with the consequence that, between 1901 and 1906, when the Trade Disputes Act was passed, union funds were open to attack when enforcing judgments against unions.

In 1971, things changed. The Industrial Relations Act of that year was passed, and one of the central themes of the Act was registration of unions. This had the effect of conferring corporate status on such bodies. Unions that chose not register were treated as unincorporated associations (although having some benefits of corporate status). As discussed in Chapter 1, the 1971 Act was a disaster. It was replaced in

1974 by the Trade Union and Labour Relations Act which created the current position (consolidated under s. 10 of the 1992 Act), i.e., that trade unions are not to be treated as bodies corporate save that they can do the following things:

  (a) make contracts;
  (b) sue or be sued in proceedings relating to property, founded on tort or contract or any other cause of action;
  (c) bring or have brought against them proceedings for a criminal offence alleged to have been committed by them or in their name.

The current position, it is submitted, is a move away from the position postulated by the House of Lords in the *Taff Vale* case. It ties in with neither of the two theories put forward in that case, because the 1992 Act now expressly states that a union is not a body corporate. Further, it is not correct to talk in terms of action brought or taken being representative since it is the union that benefits or suffers from the proceedings (see below).

2.1.5.3   Analysis of the actions that can be taken by or brought against a union in the name of the union

2.1.5.3.1   Matters arising in contract   To the extent that a union is involved in a contract, it cannot make the contract itself and must therefore act through the means of an agent. It follows that the ordinary rules of the law of agency and warranty of authority will apply in any potential disputes arising where a union tries to disown a contract alleged to have been made by it.

2.1.5.3.2   Issues of civil litigation   Problems arise in relation to civil litigation at two levels. First, there is a question as to whether or not a union must sue or be sued in its own name, or whether it is still possible to use the device of representative action (RSC Ord. 15, r. 12). The better view appears to be that it is still possible to use a representative action but that all persons represented (i.e. the entire union membership) must have similar interests in the outcome of the litigation.

  In *News Group Newspapers* v *SOGAT 82* [1986] IRLR 337, injunctions were sought against branches of the first defendant union and also the second defendant, the National Graphical Association, for torts committed in the context of the Wapping dispute. It was alleged that the action ought to be taken in the form of a representative action since a dispute existed as to whether the local branches of the unions were in fact unions in their own right under the definition in s. 1 of TULRCA 1992. Stuart-Smith J, while accepting that a representative action could be maintained in an appropriate case, took the view that on the facts he was concerned with, a representative action was inappropriate since the members clearly had divergent views. He showed the problems that can arise with a representative action when dealing with a large class of members (at p. 354):

Only a small proportion of any one branch are directly involved in the dispute. Some of those who are will have taken an active part in the commission of torts, others may have disapproved and condemned such conduct in their colleagues. Of those who are not directly involved some may approve or authorise such tortious action on the part of the branch committee, which pending a delegate meeting of the branch is empowered to act for the branch, others may not; even on the committee itself opinion and action may be divided.

The representative action was duly struck out in this case, and in most cases the appropriate procedural device will be for the union to sue or be sued in its own name.

The second problem that arises in the context of civil litigation is the question of whether or not a union can sue for defamation. The most recent case on point is *Electrical, Electronic, Telecommunications and Plumbing Union* v *Times Newspapers Ltd* [1980] QB 585. The case concerned an allegedly libellous article published by the defendant in November 1977. A preliminary issue was raised in the proceedings concerning the personality of trade unions, namely whether, following TULRA 1974, a union could have a personality capable of being defamed. The matter was dealt with by O'Conner J, who took the view that since the 1974 Act stated that unions were not to be treated as bodies corporate, it took unions away from the previous law contained in *National Union of General and Municipal Workers* v *Gillian* [1946] KB 81 which relied on the Trade Union Act 1871 concept of status derived from *Taff Vale* (above at 2.1.5.2). This, it will be remembered, worked partly on the view that unions were quasi-corporate bodies and therefore could have personalities. Accordingly, since unions were unincorporated associations with certain rights to sue or be sued, they did not have personalities (in the view of O'Connor J) and they could not sue for defamation. He went on to add that it would not be possible to use a representative action to further the claims of union members either, since each member would have different interests in the outcome of the case if damages were recovered.

It is submitted that this view as to the lack of personality is not correct on a number of grounds. First, the issue of legal personality distinct from membership was not addressed by the House of Lords in the *Taff Vale* case in either of its two possible formulations of status. The House treated unions as juridical persons at best. If this is so, the law has not changed following the 1974 Act (and the consolidation in 1992). Secondly, although O'Connor J dealt with the issue of representative actions by refusing on the grounds that individually each member of a union would have a different interest, and therefore the use of a collective action was not appropriate, he did not go on to consider whether or not a collective reputation could be damaged. It has long been held that it is possible to damage a collective reputation and regard should be had to, e.g., *Cook* v *Batchelor* (1802) 3 Bos & Pul 150. Thirdly, the House of Lords appears to have accepted, albeit *obiter*, that a union can be defamed. In dealing with a libel action brought against a local authority in the case of *Derbyshire CC* v *Times Newspapers Ltd* [1993] 1 All ER 1011 their Lordships were referred to the *Gillian* case in the course of proceedings, although, regrettably, not the *EETPU* case. Lord Keith, in approving the trade union cases, said of them (at p. 101): 'The trade union cases are understandable upon the view that defamatory matter may adversely affect the union's ability to keep its members or attract new ones or maintain a convincing attitude towards employers.'

Given that the *EETPU* case is directly decided on the basis of defamation, it seems that there may yet be some mileage left in defamation cases brought by trade unions.

2.1.5.3.3   Property-based disputes   The property of a union is vested in its trustees under s. 12 of TULRCA 1992. The property is stated to be held 'for it' under s. 12(1). This gives rise to the question whether, since a union is an unincorporated association with no personality beyond that of the members of the association, the formulation modifies the rules relating to private purpose trusts.

The general rule in relation to private purpose trusts is that they are void (*Morice* v *Bishop of Durham* (1804) 9 Ves 399). Further, while it has been held that it is possible to construe that an unincorporated association holds property for the benefit of its members rather than for pure purposes (*Re Denley* [1969] 1 Ch 373), it has also been held that, to the extent that a gift is for a class of members both existing and future without further qualification, the trust will necessarily fail since future members might be able to obtain an interest in property outside the perpetuity period (*Re Grant* [1979] 3 All ER 359).

The way in which the problem has been resolved is to find that property is held by a union for the benefit of the union itself. In *Hughes* v *TGWU* [1985] IRLR 382, it was held that members of a union have no proprietary interest in the assests of the union either individually or in common with other members. This means that during a period of union membership, a member has a right to use the property of the association to which he belongs according to the union rules. His relationship is contractual rather than proprietary in nature.

If a union decides to wind itself up, it would appear that the members at the time of the dissolution are those entitled to claim the property pursuant to their contracts of membership and, to the extent that the contract of membership provides no means of distribution, each takes in equal shares (see *Re Bucks Constabulary Fund (No. 2)* [1979] 1 All ER 623).

2.1.5.3.4   Criminal proceedings   Section 10(1)(c) of TULRCA 1992 is vital to the issuing of criminal proceedings by or against a union:

10.—(1)   A trade union is not a body corporate but—

. . .

(c)   proceedings for an offence alleged to have been committed by it or on its behalf may be brought against it in its own name.

Since a union is stated to have no legal personality, it needs the qualification to make it answerable because unincorporated associations are simply treated as being a collection of their members.

2.1.6   Special register bodies

Special register bodies are a hangover from the Industrial Relations Act 1971, ss. 84–86. The special register was created to allow professional bodies, who, as a minor part of their functions, entered into collective agreements for their members with employers or employers' associations, powers to register under the Act so as to gain the benefits of registration without raising the question of whether such bodies were unions. The register was closed when registration was abolished under TULRA 1974. However, provisions were made for bodies that had registered to stay on the register. Very few bodies now remain, and those that do must be either registered under the Companies Act 1985 or have been granted letters patent or a charter (TULRCA 1992, s. 117). Special register bodies are bodies corporate.

2.1.7   Legality of trade unions

The issue of union legality again owes much to history. From their inception, unions were treated as being illegal due to their purposes being contrary to public policy by way of restraint of trade. The restraint arose as a result of a member divesting himself of his ability individually to negotiate his own terms and conditions of employment (*Hornby* v *Close* (1867) 2 LR QB 153). The consequences of the restraint of trade doctrine were removed by the Trade Union Act 1871, ss. 2–3. However, the doctrine was still to play an important part in the running of unions. This was due to s. 4 of the 1871 Act, which made union rules unenforceable before the courts. The reasoning behind s. 4 was that while Parliament was happy for unions to exist for the benefit of their members, it would be unfortunate if a union could rely on the rulebook to create a binding contract between itself and a member which it could then enforce through the courts by means of an injunction so as to force a strike. As a result, the courts initially took the view that they would not enforce rulebook provisions (see *Russell* v *Amalgamated Society of Carpenters and Joiners* [1912] AC 421, where a union member's widow tried to enforce a requirement in the defendant's rules in order to receive a provident benefit and the House of Lords held that where some of the rules of the union were in restraint of trade, the rules that were not could not be severed).

However, other areas of the law had shown that not all restraint of trade was unlawful. In *Nordenfelt* v *Maxim Nordenfelt Guns and Ammunition Co. Ltd* [1894] AC 535, the House of Lords had held that while restraint of trade was *prima facie* unlawful, reasonable restraint of trade could be justified under the common law. This view ultimately filtered through into trade union cases and the courts, through somewhat convoluted means, took the view that s. 4 of the Trade Disputes Act could be avoided in an appropriate case. Section 4 worked by declaring that 'Nothing in this Act shall enable any Court to entertain any legal proceedings' in relation to the union rulebook. What the courts did was to ask whether a union was in restraint of trade at common law. If it was not, the Act was not necessary to legalise it and it was therefore possible to enforce the union rules. The matter appeared to be beyond dispute after *Osbourne v Amalgamated Society of Railway Servants* [1911] 1 Ch 540 and *Amalgamated Society of Carpenters and Joiners v Braithwaite* [1921] 2 AC 440.

Ultimately, s. 4 of the Trade Disputes Act 1871 was repealed by the Industrial Relations Act 1971.

The modern view as to the legality of unions is set down in s. 11(1) and (2) of TULRCA 1992. This provides that the purposes and rules of a union are not to be treated as unenforceable or unlawful merely because they are in restraint of trade.

It is worth noting, though, that the courts are still prepared to use the doctrine of restraint of trade in an appropriate case. An example is *Boddington v Lawton* [1994] ICR 478. Here, members of the Prison Officers Association sought a declaration that they were allowed to use funds of the association to pay towards the defence of members being sued for trespass, false imprisonment and breach of duty. The claims arose as a result of industrial action taken by the association which had resulted in patients at a mental hospital being locked in their rooms for longer than would normally be the case. In an earlier case involving the association, it had been decided that the Prison Officers Association could not engage in a trade disputes. This arose due to the fact that prison officers are not 'workers' for the purposes of the Act, rather they are office holders (*Home Office v Evans* (unreported) 18 November 1993). Lord Nicholls V-C took the view that the rules of the association were in restraint of trade and therefore constituted an unlawful contract. When faced with the contention that due to evolution over a period of years the rules of a trade union were in the public interest, his Lordship rejected this notion and stated (at p. 487) that cases going back to *Hornby v Close* (1867) 2 LR QB 153 and as recent as *Goring v British Actors Equity Association* [1987] IRLR 122 had held union rules to be in restraint of trade and that: 'It would be most undesirable for judges now to hold that, to reflect changes in social conditions, the common law in this field has developed and is now to the contrary effect of what has been established and acted on for so many years.' His Lordship went on to add that since the rules were unenforceable in any event, it did not matter if the trustees carried on funding the defences of the members who were being sued.

Ultimately, it would appear that at common law a trade union must be taken to act in restraint of trade, but the problems created by the common law can be avoided by s. 11 of TULRCA 1992.

2.2 EMPLOYERS' ASSOCIATIONS

2.2.1 Introduction

Employers' associations were formed in this country to perform a fundamentally different role to that of unions. Whereas unions were created to provide collective power for workers, employers have always been holders of collective power in the form of capital. Employers' associations evolved after the First World War into bodies that took part in national level collective bargaining, but as has been explained in Chapter 1, when national level bargaining broke down in the 1960s, their role changed to providing assistance to small businesses who lacked knowledge and expertise in dealing with unions. The role of employers' associations has continued to decline (especially during the 1980s) and in the 1990s it is to provide advice and consultancy services to their members, lobbying of the EU and to represent members' interests at a national and international level. The main employers' body in Britain is the CBI (see above at 1.2.8).

In the same way that unions are regulated under TULRCA 1992, employers' associations also come under scrutiny. They are now dealt with in Pt II of the Act.

2.2.2   Definition and status

An employers' association is defined in s. 122(1) of TULRCA 1992 as:

... an organisation (whether temporary or permanent)—

(a)   which consists wholly or mainly of employers or individual owners of undertakings of one or more descriptions and whose principal purposes include the regulation of relations between employers of that description or those descriptions and workers or trade unions; or
(b)   which consists wholly or mainly of—
(i)   constituent or affiliated organisations which fulfil the conditions in paragraph (a) (or themselves consist wholly or mainly of constituent or affiliated organisations which fulfil those conditions), or
(ii)   representatives of such constituent or affiliated organisations,
and whose principal purposes include the regulation of relations between employers and workers or between employers and trade unions, or the regulation of relations between its constituent or affiliated organisations.

The definition shows that an employers' association must fulfil two criteria, these being membership and purpose.

As to membership, one of three types of membership is available to an employers' association: employers or individual proprietors; constituent or affiliated organisations which are themselves employers' associations; or representatives of constituent or affiliated organisations which are themselves employers' associations. Further, in order to rank as an employers' association, the body has to carry out as one of its principal purposes the regulation of relations between either employers and workers or trade unions, or, in the case of organisations consisting of constituent or affiliated organisations, regulation between the constituent or affiliated members.

When looking at the regulation of employer and workers, it has to be considered whether the association is responsible to the members for these purposes. In *Greig* v *Insole* [1978] 1 WLR 302, the plaintiff claimed damages against the respondent in tort for denying him his ability to earn his living as a professional cricketer. The defendant was a member of the committee of the Test and County Cricket Board (TCCB), the body that regulates cricket in Britain. The TCCB claimed that it was immune from action in tort as it was an employers' association (this was a possible defence at the time under TULRA 1974). The High Court decided that this was the case. While it was accepted that the TCCB was an association made up of employers, the body was not accountable to its members in relation to the way it carried out regulation of working conditions, instead it accounted to the International Cricket Council. Further, since it had power to prevent employment arising in the first place, Slade J doubted whether such rules could fall within the definition of regulating relations between workers and employers. The TCCB was therefore not able to take advantage of the definition.

It should be noted that unlike a trade union, an employers' association can be either an incorporated or unincorporated body under s. 127(1); and where it is unincorporated, it has the same rights and obligations as a trade union (see above at 2.1.5 *et seq.*).

2.2.3 Listing

2.2.3.1 Introduction
As with trade unions, it is possible for an employers' association to be listed with the Certification Officer. Listing is dealt with under ss. 123–126 of TULRCA 1992. The bodies entitled to be listed are those satisfying the definition of an employers' association in s. 122 and bodies who were listed under the provisions of TULRA 1974 (s. 123(1)). The list, as with the list of trade unions, is a public document and can be inspected at all reasonable hours free of charge (s. 123(2)). The evidential effect of being listed is that it provides proof that a body is an employers' association, and a certificate can be issued to the body which can be admitted in evidence (s. 123(4)–(5)). The Certification Officer is bound to attach a copy of the list to his annual report (s. 123(3)).

2.2.3.2 The listing process
The mechanics of listing are dealt with by s. 124 of TULRCA 1992. Any association, whenever formed, that is not included on the list is entitled to apply for listing (s. 124(1)). Applications should be in the form specified by the Certification Officer from time to time but must include, as a bare minimum, a copy of the rules of the association, a list of the association's officers, the address of the main or head office, the name by which the association is known and the prescribed fee set by statutory instrument (s. 124(2)).

When an employers' association provides the above information to the Certification Officer then, provided that he is satisfied that the organisation is an employers' association and entry on the list is not prohibited by reason of the association having the same or a similar name as a body registered under either the Trade Union Acts 1871–1964 or the Industrial Relations Act 1971, or currently listed under TULRCA 1992, he must list the body.

2.2.3.3   Removal from the list
Again as with trade unions, it is possible for the Certification Officer to remove an organisation from the list. This can occur where either the Certification Officer is satisfied that the organisation does not qualify as an employers' association, or where he is either requested to remove the organisation by the organisation or is satisfied that the organisation no longer exists (s. 125(1) and (3)). If the reason for removal is that Certification Officer believes that the body is not an employers' association, he must give the body at least 28 days' notice of his decision to remove it from the list and consider any representations made to him by the organisation within that period (s. 125(2)).

2.2.3.4   Appeals against decisions of the Certification Officer
If an organisation is unhappy about the Certification Officer's refusal to list it or removal of it from the list, it is entitled to appeal to the EAT (s. 126(1)). The right of appeal, as with trade unions, is on the grounds of both fact and law (s. 126(3)). If the EAT is satisfied that an organisation either is an employer's association or remain on the list, the EAT must declare accordingly and order the Certification Officer to takes such steps as are necessary to ensure that the organisation is placed on the list or remains listed (s. 126(2)).

As to calling the Certification Officer as a witness in proceedings, regard should be had to 2.1.2.3 above.

2.2.3.5   The advantages of listing
Unlike trade unions who derive a number of advantages upon being listed (see above at 2.1.2.4), only one advantage accrues to an employers' association upon listing, i.e., the simple procedure for vesting of property in the trustees of an employers' association. The procedure is the same as for trade unions and regard should be had to 2.1.2.4 above.

2.2.3.6   Other advantages of employers' associations
Employers' associations gain two other advantages under TULRCA 1992 as a result of their status as employers' associations. First, benefits accrue under the Friendly Societies Acts in relation to insurance on the lives of children under 10 (arising from s. 99 of the Friendly Societies Act 1992) and also in relation to charitable subscriptions and contributions to other registered societies (arising under s. 52 of the Friendly Societies Act 1974). The extension is provided by s. 129(3) of the 1992 Act.

Secondly, under s. 130 of TULRCA 1992, to the extent that judgment is awarded against an employers' association, the members, trustees and officials of the association are not liable to satisfy the judgment out of their own assets, even if the association is unincorporated. It should be noted that, unlike trade unions, employers' associations have had no immunity in tort whatsoever since 1982 (immunity did exist prior to this but was removed by the Employment Act 1982). Furthermore, unlike trade unions, the 1992 Act does not specify the circumstances in which an employers' association can be responsible for the wrongs of its officials (see 7.5.2 with regard to the position of trade unions).

2.2.3.7 Administrative obligations of employers' associations
Employers' associations are subject to a number of administrative obligations. These are the same as would apply to a trade union and the 1992 Act simply makes reference to the provisions applying in like manner. The provisions imposed under s. 131 are the following:

(a)   the duty to supply copies of rules (s. 27);

(b)   the duty to keep accounting records (s. 28);

(c)   the duties in respect of annual accounts, returns and audits (s. 32(1), (2), (3)(a), (b) and (c) and (4)–(6) and ss. 33–37);

(d)   the investigation of financial affairs (ss. 37A–37E);

(e)   matters relating to members' superannuation schemes (ss. 38–42);

(f)   the exemption for newly formed organisations (s. 43(1));

(g)   the discharge of duties in the case of an organisation having branches or sections (s. 44(1), (2) and (4)); and

(h)   the offences in relation to non-compliance (ss. 45 and 45A)).

Employers' associations incorporated under the Companies Act do not have to comply with ss. 33–35 of TULRCA 1992 in relation to the appointment of auditors (since they have to be appointed under the Companies Act), but ss. 36 and 37 will apply as to the rights and duties of the auditors.

Where it is the case that an employers' association is made up wholly or mainly of constituent or affiliated organisations or representatives thereof (a federated employers' association (s. 135(1)), the matters in (a)–(e) above do not apply (s. 135(1)–(3)).

Lastly, in relation to the administration of an employers' association, it should be noted that, unlike trade unions, they do not have to disclose in their annual return details of the salaries and benefits paid to their officers (defined in s. 136 of TULRCA 1992) and neither are they caught by increased disclosure provisions relating to accounts introduced under the Employment Act 1988.

2.2.3.8 Political objects of employers' associations
Employers' associations are entitled to have political objects, and to the extent that they do they are caught by the same rules as trade unions in relation to balloting, etc.

(TULRCA 1992, s. 132: see Chapter 4). If the association is a federated association and has voted not to operate a political fund, there is nothing to prevent a component association from collecting contributions towards a political fund from such of its members as are not exempt from contributing to the fund (s. 135(4)).

2.2.3.9 Amalgamations and changes of name

An unincorporated employers' association is able to merge with another association in the same way that unions are capable of merging, and the rules on mergers are again borrowed from the corresponding provisions in relation to unions (see Chapter 9). The provisions are contained in s. 133 of TULRCA 1992 (although some minor changes are introduced to the balloting rules under s. 133(2)).

In relation to changing an organisation's name, the provisions are contained in s. 134. In the first instance, the organisation must either have a name changing provision in its rules, or must use the organisation's rules to procure a power to change the name of it (s. 134(1)). The change of name cannot take effect in the case of either an incorporated or unincorporated association until such time as the Certification Officer is notified of the change (s. 134(2)). The Certification Officer also has a power to refuse a name change where it is the case that the association has adopted a name that is the same as or similar to that of either an existing employers' association or union (s. 134(3)). A change of name does not affect any existing legal liability of an unincorporated association (s. 134(4)).

3   Rights of Recognised Trade Unions

3.1   INTRODUCTION

The rights accruing to an independent and recognised trade union are:

(a)   to have relevant information disclosed to facilitate collective bargaining;
(b)   to be consulted in respect of large scale redundancies;
(c)   to be consulted in relation to a transfer of an undertaking;
(d)   to be consulted in respect of health and safety matters; and
(e)   to be consulted in the case of a union representing workers of a public authority where a previous practice of consultation exists.

Rights and obligations can also accrue by way of collective agreements between an employer or employers and one or more trade unions.

3.2   THE RIGHT TO INFORMATION FOR COLLECTIVE BARGAINING PURPOSES

3.2.1   Introduction

The duty to provide information to a recognised trade union for the purpose of collective bargaining was introduced by s. 17 of the Employment Protection Act 1975. The legislation is now consolidated as TULRCA 1992, Pt IV, Ch. 1. The aim of the legislation is to provide a level playing field in collective bargaining. When originally enacted, it was possible for all independent unions to enforce the right by means of the statutory mechanism established by ss. 11–16 of the 1975 Act which enacted a duty to recognise. Once recognition was achieved, an employer was bound to provide information. However, a union cannot claim unlimited information from an employer under the duty. In 1977, ACAS issued a Code of Practice on the

Disclosure of Bargaining Information which deals with the type of information that ought to be disclosed (see 3.2.2.2 with regard to the Code generally).

The duty to recognise was removed by the Employment Act 1980. The issue of compulsory recognition has now been reviewed and revised and is one of the most controversial of the current reforms proposed under the White Paper 'Fairness at Work'. In the White Paper, the Government has stressed that collective bargaining, when properly carried out, is good for industrial relations. It has therefore proposed to introduce compulsory recognition for bargaining in connection with pay, hours and holidays (with training also possibly to be covered) in two situations. These are, first, where a 'bargaining unit' within a workforce has the support of a defined majority of the relevant workforce under a properly conducted ballot. It is proposed that a bargaining unit will be one or more unions representing either the whole or a defined class of a workforce. It is proposed that, where possible, recognition should be voluntary between unions and employers. If it is not possible to achieve voluntary recognition, the CAC will be required to determine whether a union has the requisite support of the workforce (the idea being to prevent frivolous applications). The proposed majority of the relevant workforce in a ballot is at least 40 per cent of those eligible to vote (a threshold chosen so as to avoid votes being carried by way of apathy).

If more than one union is involved in a request for recognition, the unions must act jointly as a bargaining unit. This is to prevent disputes between unions within a workplace. Under the proposed procedure, the CAC will be barred from hearing competing claims as to the correct union to be recognised.

It is also proposed that employers will be able to apply for derecognition in the event that support for a recognised union falls below the threshold. It has been suggested that employers will not be able to apply for derecognition until three years after the date upon which a previous CAC reference is determined so as to allow for the procedure to bed in.

Lastly, under the first head of recognition, it is not proposed that the recognition machinery will apply to employers having fewer than 20 employees.

A simpler form of recognition is proposed in cases where over half of the workers in a workforce are already union members. Where this is the case, recognition will be automatic.

While the duty to provide information to an independent recognised union still exists, it can be circumvented by an employer failing initially to recognise or subsequently derecognising a union (although as regards a union that is currently recognised, an employer cannot escape an existing duty to provide information simply by saying that it no longer recognises the claimant union). An act of derecognition will apply only to future duties to disclose (see, for example, *Selfridges Ltd and the Manufacturing Science Finance Union* (CAC Award 91/1) and *Ackrill Newspapers Ltd and the National Union of Journalists* (CAC Award 92/1)).

The duty to disclose bargaining information is available to both Crown employees (TULRCA 1992, s. 273) and Parliamentary staff (ss. 278–279), although the right to enforce the duty is not available (ss. 184–185).

3.2.2   The general duty of disclosure

The duty to disclose is contained in s. 181 of TULRCA 1992, which provides that an employer shall disclose on the request of representatives of an independent trade union recognised by the employer the information required by the remainder of that section. The duty arises at all stages of the collective bargaining process. Requests to an employer for information must be in writing to an employer by representatives of a union (s. 181(3)). An employer is only bound to disclose information within its possession or within the possession of an associated employer (s. 181(2), and, for the definition of 'associated employer', see s. 297). Regard should also be had to *Ayrshire Bus Owners (A1 Service) Ltd and the Transport and General Workers Union* (CAC Award 91/2).

While the Act states that information should be provided to a union upon request, it does not provide a time limit for an employer to comply with the request, and theoretically there is nothing to stop an unscrupulous employer from withholding information until such time as it suits the employer to disclose. Obviously, such action would be contrary to good industrial relations practice if carried out on a frequent basis, and it would probably be better for an employer to derecognise rather than provoke a union by constantly dragging its feet.

The information to be provided is dealt with in s. 181(2), which creates a conjunctive two-limb test in deciding whether the information needs to be disclosed.

3.2.2.1   Limb 1 — material disadvantage
The first limb focuses on the 'level playing field' ideal and requires consideration of whether a union would be impeded to a material extent if requested information was not supplied to it (s. 181(2)(a)). In addressing this limb of the test, the CAC has taken the view that what must be looked at is whether a union would be hampered generally without provision of a particular type of information rather than whether a failure to provide specific information will be harmful in a particular bargain (*Daily Telegraph Ltd and the Institute of Journalists* (CAC Award 78/353), *Beecham Group Ltd and the Association of Scientific, Managerial and Technical Staffs* (CAC Award 79/337) and *BP Chemicals and the Transport and General Workers Union* (CAC Award 86/1)). Thus, s. 181(2) looks to the general nature of the information sought and addresses the question of whether the union will be able to prepare to bargain adequately.

It has been argued that if an employer refuses to take part in collective bargaining with an independent trade union which it has recognised then the union cannot be materially disadvantaged as a result of the employer failing to provide information to the union since there are no negotiations in which to use that information (*BL Cars*

Ltd, MG Abingdon Plant and the General and Municipal Workers Union and the Transport and General Workers Union (CAC Award 80/65)). In the *BL* case, the CAC agreed that the failure of the employer to consult deprived the union of the statutory right and the union was not entitled to the information claimed. However, the position was revisited in *BP Chemicals and the Transport and General Workers Union* (CAC Award 86/1). Here, the company and union were in disagreement over the provision of information relating to the company's pension scheme. The company took the line that it was not bound to disclose the requested information since even if it did disclose, it would not negotiate. On the evidence before it, the CAC ordered disclosure. It took the view that the company had recognised the union for the purposes of negotiation over pensions, and since the information related to pensions the union was entitled to it. In short, it did not relate to a discretion of management (which the CAC stressed was the point of the *BL* case, which related to a factory closure, a matter entirely within management discretion).

3.2.2.2   Limb 2 — good industrial relations practice
The second limb of the test requires a consideration of whether it would be in the context of good industrial relations generally to release the requested information (s. 181(2)(b)). In considering this issue, regard can be had to the ACAS Code of Practice on Disclosure of Information to Trade Unions for Collective Bargaining Purposes ('the Code') which can be used as evidence of what is good practice but is expressly stated not to be conclusive evidence (s. 181(4)).

At para. 11, the Code provides some examples of the types of information that should be disclosed. The paragraph starts with a general caveat, stating:

> Collective bargaining within an undertaking can range from negotiations on specific matters arising daily at the workplace affecting particular sections of the workforce, to extensive periodic negotiations on terms and conditions of employment affecting the whole workforce in multiplant companies. . . . Consequently, it is not possible to compile a list of items that should be disclosed in all circumstances.

Paragraph 11 then goes on to list certain types of information that it is generally considered good practice to disclose, this being information in relation to pay and benefits; conditions of service; manpower resources; performance and finance of an undertaking. Paragraph 12 of the Code adds that the requirements are not exhaustive.

Although TULRCA 1992 does itself talk in objective terms by referring to good industrial relations practice, if a dispute arises as to what amounts to good practice in a particular case, it is desirable that evidence be provided to support a contention. Provided that evidence is relevant, it is possible to adduce proof as to what is considered to be good practice at other firms or in other industries. For examples of the duty to disclose being upheld, see *Tyne and Wear Passenger Transport Executive and the General Municipal Workers Union* (CAC Award 82/10) and *BP Chemicals and the Transport and General Workers Union* (CAC Award 86/1). For cases where it has been decided that no duty to disclose exists, see *Daily Telegraph Ltd and the Institute of Journalists* (CAC Award 78/353) and *Standard Telephone and Cables Ltd and the Association of Scientific, Technical and Managerial Staffs* (CAC Award 79/484).

3.2.3 Exceptions to the duty to disclose

While s. 181 of TULRCA 1992 creates a general duty to disclose collective bargaining information to independent recognised unions, the duty can be avoided in the circumstances set down in s. 182(1). This creates six categories of cases in which disclosure will not be ordered against an employer. They are:

(a)   Where it would be in the interests of national security not to disclose. It is possible for a Minister of the Crown or a person acting on his behalf to certify that the disclosure of information would be prejudicial to national security. Further, if such a certificate is provided, it is conclusive proof of its contents (s. 183(6)).

(b)   Where disclosure would contravene an enactment.

(c)   Where the information requested was originally disclosed to an employer in confidence and therefore to disclose the same would amount to a breach of confidence by the employer. It should be noted that an employer cannot simply claim that information is confidential and therefore immune from disclosure. However, if information is requested from a third party source, there seems to be nothing to stop an employer from requesting from that the information be passed on to the employer on the basis that the employer has a duty to keep the information confidential. Regard may be paid to a number of cases on the issue of confidentiality, notably, *Joint Credit Card Co. Ltd and the National Union of Bank Employees* (CAC Award 78/212), *Ministry of Defence and the Civil Service Union* (CAC Award 80/73) and *Seifert Sedley & Co. and the Association of Scientific, Technical and Managerial Staffs* (CAC Award 80/152).

(d)   Where the information specifically relates to an individual. While it is the case that a union is prevented from making enquiries about named individuals, it is entitled to information relating to particular posts. It follows, therefore, that if only one person occupies such a post, the union is entitled to the information notwithstanding that it relates clearly to that person occupying the post. Examples of this point occurred in *University of Lancaster and the Association of University Teachers* (CAC Award 79/300), *British Aerospace, Dynamics Group, Space and Communications Division, Site B, and the Association of Professional, Executive, Clerical and Computer Staff* (CAC Award 80/69) and *Cloride Legg Ltd and the Association of Clerical, Technical and Supervisory Staffs* (CAC Award 84/15).

(e)   Where disclosure of the requested information would cause substantial harm to a business undertaking other than any effect which might arise through collective bargaining. In this defence it seems that the CAC is willing to take a very pragmatic view as to what will cause substantial harm. This is reflected in that disclosure orders have been granted which show that the CAC will often allow some, but not all, of the information requested by a union to be disclosed in an appropriate case. Sensitive information is information that is objectively sensitive, not information that is claimed to be sensitive by the employer. An example of a CAC decision ordering partial disclosure of information is *Hoover Ltd and the General and Municipal Workers' Union* (CAC Award 79/507), a claim that unit cost and unit price information was sensitive if it fell into the hands of a competitor. The CAC took the view that certain categories of information relating to manufacturing cost, budgeted expenditure and the basis for budget forecasts should not be disclosed.

(f) Where the information has been obtained by the employer for bringing, prosecuting or defending any legal action.

3.2.4 Complaints of failure to disclose

To the extent that an employer fails to comply with the duty to disclose, a union can bring a complaint under the procedure set out in s. 183 of TULRCA 1992. A complaint lies to the CAC and can be brought where an employer either fails to disclose the information requested under s. 181 (s. 183(1)(a)) or fails to confirm such information in writing (s. 183(1)(b)). A complaint to the CAC must be in writing and should be in such form as the CAC may require.

Upon receipt of a claim, the CAC is required to consider whether it thinks that the complaint could be disposed of by way of a conciliated settlement. If it is of the view that this is likely, it is bound to refer the matter to ACAS and to notify the union and employer of the referral (s. 183(2)). It is then the duty of ACAS to resolve the dispute. If, after a referral to ACAS, the complaint cannot be resolved ACAS is required to inform the CAC of this fact.

In the event that a complaint is either not referred to ACAS or ACAS decides that a case that has been referred cannot be dealt with by conciliation, the CAC proceeds to hear and determine the complaint and makes a declaration after the case stating whether or not the complaint is well-founded. A decision can be wholly or partially favourable to a complainant union (see, for example, *Hoover Ltd and the General and Municipal Workers' Union* (CAC Award 79/507) (s. 183(3)). In the course of proceedings before it, the CAC is entitled to hear from anyone other than a union or an employer who has an interest in the outcome of the proceedings. Section 183(4) adds that, to the extent that an interested third party is not heard in the proceedings, the validity of the proceedings is not affected.

Upon making a finding for a union, s. 183(5) requires that the CAC's declaration must specify the following matters:

(a) what information it has been found necessary to disclose;
(b) the date on which the employer either refused to supply the requested information or refused to confirm the information in writing; and

(c)   a period of time within which the employer is bound to make good his failure to supply or to confirm. In specifying a time limit, the CAC must allow a period of at least one week from the date of the declaration.

The CAC cannot specify what matters it thinks ought to be disclosed in the future as between the parties and, to the extent that it tries to do so, it can be judicially reviewed. In *R* v *Central Arbitration Committee ex parte BTP Trioxide Ltd* [1981] ICR 843, Forbes J stated (at p. 859):

> I feel confident that these provisions only entitle the committee to deal with a complaint relating to a past failure and information already refused and do not permit a declaration of what the committee prospectively considers the employer in future cases should disclose.

3.2.5   Enforcing a declaration

Where an employer fails to comply with the terms of a declaration within the time specified for compliance, a union is able to present a further complaint to the CAC under s. 184(1) of TULRCA 1992. Again, as with the initial complaint, the further complaint must be in writing in such form as the CAC determines. Upon receiving the subsequent complaint, the CAC is bound to hear the claim and determine whether it finds the complaint well-founded, whether wholly or in part (s. 184(2)). The CAC is again entitled to hear anyone it thinks has a legitimate right to be heard in a dispute. As with an initial complaint, a failure to allow a non-party to be heard does not affect the validity of the proceedings (s. 184(3)). To the extent that the CAC finds wholly or partly for a complainant union, a declaration is required to this effect.

As the purpose of the information to be disclosed is usually to negotiate terms and conditions for employees, after a declaration has been granted it is possible for a union to request in writing that an order be granted that one or more employees (but not workers) have the terms and conditions of their contracts of employment modified in the form of the request made by the union (s. 185(1)). If the employer discloses or confirms in writing the information requested by the union, the right to modified terms and conditions is lost. Any claim that has been presented by a union is treated as being withdrawn where the information is supplied at any time prior to the CAC deciding on the claim (s. 185(2)).

If the CAC does not consider the terms and conditions claimed appropriate, it may substitute its own terms. An order for terms and conditions can be expressed to take effect at any point in time back to the date of an original complaint (s. 185(3)). Terms so modified take effect as implied terms and continue in effect until such time as they are either varied by a new CAC order or a collective agreement between a union and employer incorporated into the contract of an employee, or are replaced by terms agreed between an employee and an employer (s. 185(5)).

Two qualifications need to be borne in mind when requesting modified terms. First, the CAC can award amended terms to a union only to the extent of its recognition (s. 185(4)). Therefore, if a union is only partially recognised by an employer, e.g., for the purposes of dealing with an employer's pension scheme, the union cannot seek an order modifying terms and conditions in respect of matters such as pay, hours of work, etc. Secondly, the CAC cannot impose an order in respect of terms fixed by statute (s. 185(7)), although in the case of terms where minimum standards are fixed by statute, it is possible for the CAC to increase the statutory minima.

It should be noted that the remedial provisions of ss. 184 and 185 do not apply to Crown employees (s. 273(2)).

3.3 CONSULTATION RELATING TO LARGE SCALE REDUNDANCIES

3.3.1 Introduction

The duty to consult with trade unions in respect of large scale redundancies was introduced by s. 99 of the Employment Protection Act 1975 (now s. 188 of TULRCA 1992) which was the method used to adopt the Collective Redundancies Directive 75/129. The Collective Redundancies Directive was modified by the amending Directive 92/56. In the meantime, it was alleged by the European Commission that the UK had failed to implement the original form of the Collective Redundancies Directive and proceedings were instituted in the European Court of Justice (*EC Commission* v *United Kingdom* [1994] IRLR 412, which duly confirmed this to be the case). In order to comply with the spirit of the Directives, the Government took remedial steps by enacting TURERA 1993 and the Collective Redundancies and Transfer of Undertakings (Protection of Employment) Regulations 1995, SI 1995 No. 2587. At the same time, the extent of national law was cut back. The Employment Protection Act 1975 had envisaged consultation in *all* cases of redundancy and laid down minimum periods of consultation in respect of larger scale redundancy. The changes enacted by TURERA 1993 and SI 1995 No. 2587 moved the duty away from consultation in relation to single redundancies and towards collective redundancies only. Since part of the changes were enacted by statutory instrument under s. 2(2)(b) of the European Communities Act 1972 (which empowers the Government to implement matters arising out of or related to EC rights or obligations), it was not surprising that a challenge was launched. The grounds of attack were that the removal of the right to consultation in respect of single redundancies arose only under national law and therefore using regulations under the provisions of the European Communities Act was *ultra vires*. The case mounting the challenge was *R* v *Secretary of State for Trade and Industry ex parte UNISON* [1996] IRLR 438. The Divisional Court found against the claim, with Otton LJ holding (at p. 443), that a literal interpretation of the phrase 'related to' could be adopted. Since the national law on consultation was related to EC law (albeit that it had been wider in scope), it was possible to amend it using the European Communities Act.

The main thrust of the amended legislation now is that an employer must consult either a recognised trade union or an elected employee representative (see 3.3.3.2 with regard to electing employee representatives). If there is more than one independent trade union recognised by an employer, the employer can discharge his duty to consult only by consulting all of those unions (*Governing Body of the Northern Ireland Hotel and Catering College* v *National Association of Teachers in Further and Higher Education* [1995] IRLR 83).

The consultation must take place 'in good time' where it is the case that the employer is proposing to make 20 or more people redundant over a period of 90 days at the same establishment (TULRCA 1992, s. 188(1)). The employer has an unfettered choice as to whether he consults with either union representatives or employee representatives (s. 188(1B)).

What amounts to 'good time' depends upon the degree of redundancy measures being implemented (see 3.3.2). Further, the DTI must be informed of such redundancies when they take place.

3.3.2 Scope of the duty

The duty to consult arises in a case where an employer is proposing to dismiss as redundant 20 or more employees at the same establishment within a 90-day period. An employer in this position is required to consult all persons who are appropriate representatives of the employees who may be dismissed (s. 188(1)). Problems have arisen in relation to the formulation of s. 188(1) in that it does not appear properly to implement Art. 2 of Directive 75/129. The Directive states that an employer is bound to consult where he is 'contemplating collective redundancies'. Under s. 188(1), the duty arises where an employer is 'proposing to dismiss'. An argument exists that the duty under the Directive arises *before* an employer has made a definite decision to dismiss (a broad formulation of the duty) whereas the obligation at national law arises *after* the decision has been taken (a narrower formulation). No EC decision has been pronounced directly on the point, although in *Dansk Metalbejderforbund* v *H. Nielsen* [1986] CMLR 91, Advocate General Lenz took the view (at p. 96) that the broader formulation was to be favoured.

The argument has been adopted in the English courts and put forward in a number of cases. The first of these was *Hough and APEX* v *Leyland DAF Ltd* [1991] IRLR 194, followed by *Re Hartlebury Printers* [1992] IRLR 516, *R* v *British Coal Corporation ex parte Vardy* [1993] IRLR 104 and *Griffin* v *South West Water Services Ltd* [1995] IRLR 15.

In *Hough*, the case concerned the unamended formulation of s. 99 of the Employment Protection Act 1975 and the unamended Collective Redundancies Directive. The facts involved the dismissal of the respondent's security staff and the consultation of APEX some four months after an initial decision to implement the redundancy programme. In the EAT, Knox J took the view that there was a difference between the formulation of the Directive and s. 99. He thought that 'contemplating' under the Directive was an elastic concept covering a multiplicity of circumstances (i.e., at one end of a spectrum an idea that change might be necessary, moving to having a firm idea as to how to implement change at the other end). His Lordship considered that the term 'proposing' as used in the Act was certain in nature. This said, since contemplating was elastic, it was possible to read the Directive in line with national law by consulting at the stage of having made a decision (the narrow formulation).

The next case was *Re Hartlesbury*. This involved an application to bring a claim against administrators for a failure to consult unions when a decision to wind up a company in administration was taken. Morritt J also took a narrow view on the formulation, holding, ultimately, that national law did comply with the Directive due to the flexible interpretation of the word 'contemplating'.

In the *Vardy* case, a judicial review of the decision of British Coal to close 31 collieries without consulting trade unions was undertaken. The decision to close was ultimately quashed with Glidewell LJ in the Divisional Court holding, *obiter*, that the duty to consult under the Directive was not a duty to consider how to implement the redundancies proposed by an employer (the narrow formulation) but rather a duty to consider whether there should be redundancies in the first place (the broad formulation). He was willing to construe national legislation in the light of the Directive.

Lastly, in *Griffin*, the plaintiff commenced an action against the defendant for failing to consult. The defendant had received a report in November 1993 recommending that a re-organisation should take place that would lead to large scale redundancies. The company decided that proposals would be discussed with representatives in May 1994. A claim was launched under the Directive contending that since the company was a successor to the former South West Water Authority, it was an emanation of the State, and that therefore the Directive could be relied upon directly against the employer. Further, since the Directive was wider in scope than national law, it had not been complied with because, it was claimed, consultation had not taken place at an appropriate point in time. An injunction was therefore sought by the plaintiff to prevent breaches of the duty to consult. Blackburne J held that the duty to consult arises only at the time that the employer has identified the employees to be made redundant (the narrow formulation) and is able to give them the information in Art. 2(3) of the Directive (covering such matters as the reasons for the redundancies, the number and categories of workers to be dismissed, the time frame over which the redundancies are to take place, the criteria for selection, etc.), and therefore failed to follow the judgment in *Vardy*. He also took the view that it was not possible to rely on the Directive due to its being insufficiently precise and unconditional and therefore not capable of direct effect. Accordingly, while he was prepared to accept that the defendant was an emanation of the State, he felt that the employer had complied with the Directive.

Problems do arise from the decision in *Griffin*, most notably that the information in Art. 2(3) of the Directive does not envisage that individual employees have been identified. It also does not appear that the learned judge was directed to the opinion of the Advocate General in *Dansk Metalbejderforbund*.

It is submitted that the weight of authority in England clearly acknowledges that there is a distinction between the formulation of the EC Directive and s. 188 of TULRCA 1992. Further, since the primary reason for consultation is to see whether it is possible to achieve the employer's objectives in another way without the need for job losses (see s. 188(2)(a)), it is further submitted that in order to provide a purposive interpretation, and thereby comply with the spirit of the Directive, it is necessary to consult at a point in time prior to having decided that redundancies are necessary.

3.3.3   Time limits for consultation

3.3.3.1   General
The provisions of s. 188(1) of TULRCA 1992 require that an employer shall consult the appropriate representatives of those employees who may be dismissed in 'good time' (s. 188(1)). The phrase is taken directly from Art. 2(1) of the Directive and replaces the original requirement in the Employment Protection Act 1975 that the consultation should begin 'at the earliest opportunity'.

The meaning of 'good time' must be considered in the light of the purpose of the duty to consult, i.e. to see whether job losses are actually needed. In *Transport and General Workers Union* v *Ledbury Preserves* (1928) Ltd [1985] IRLR 412, Peter Gibson J in the EAT said of the duty (at p. 413):

> It seems to us ... that there must be sufficient meaningful consultation before notices of dismissal are sent out. The consultation must not be a sham exercise; there must be time for the [appropriate] representatives who are consulted to consider properly the proposals that are put to them.

Similar views were expressed in *National Union of Teachers* v *Avon County Council* [1978] IRLR 55, *Spillers French (Holdings) Ltd* v *USDAW* [1979] IRLR 339 and *E. Green & Son (Castings) Ltd* v *Association of Scientific, Technical and Managerial Staffs* [1984] IRLR 135.

Section 188(1A) sets down the minimum periods of consultation required, stating that, in any event, the requirements of consultation are:

(a)   where the employer is proposing to dismiss 100 or more employees as mentioned in subsection (1), at least 90 days, and
(b)   otherwise, at least 30 days,

before the first of the dismissals takes effect.

As to when the dismissals take effect, this has been considered by the EAT on a number of occasions. In *E. Green & Son (Castings)* v *Association of Scientific, Technical and Managerial Staffs* [1984] IRLR 135, the EAT considered that the phrase 'takes effect' should mean the point in time at which the first of the dismissals is proposed actually to happen. As Nolan J stated (at p. 140):

> It is implicit ... that the reference in [s. 188(1A)] to a period 'before the first of those dismissals takes effect' is a reference to the first of the proposed dismissals. The whole section is concerned with looking forward to projected dismissals at a future date and with imposing upon the employer the requirement to disclose information about his plans for those dismissals. In the event, not all of those dismissals may occur; or they may occur at different dates from that originally proposed. Clearly, however, the employer cannot reasonably be required to provide information and to consult [appropriate representatives] other than what he anticipates at the outset of the 90 day period.

Therefore, if employees were to attempt to take advantage of the notice requirements, e.g., by alleging that an employer had agreed to allow workers to leave for redundancy at a date within the protected period, they ought not to be able to claim the remedies provided for by TULRCA 1992. In *Association of Scientific, Technical and Managerial Staffs* v *Hawker Siddeley Aviation Ltd* [1977] IRLR 418, the employer had proposed to make redundant 320 employees on 18 August 1976, with the first of the proposed redundancies taking effect not before 15 November 1976 so as to comply with the 90-day consultation period. An employee asked to be able to leave on 27 August 1976 on the grounds that he was not actually doing any work for the employer. He was duly allowed to go, whereupon the union claimed for protective awards (see 3.3.6.4). The industrial tribunal held on the facts that the employers had breached the requirements of the Act by not consulting 90 days prior to the first dismissal, but ultimately did not award a protective award. It is submitted that the decision is wrong in law in the light of the decision in *E. Green & Son* in that the Act does not require an employer to consult for 90 days, it simply requires the employer to take steps to ensure that consultation is implemented 90 days prior to the first proposed (as opposed to actual) dismissal.

In attempting to calculate the period of consultation an employer is not bound to take into account employees in respect of whose proposed dismissal consultation has already begun (s. 188(3)). The subsection applies only where it is the case that an employer discovers a genuine need to implement further redundancies after an initial batch has been decided upon.

Further, if an employer were to attempt to take advantage of s. 188(3) by seeking to impose redundancies in two or more batches so as to comply only with the lesser of the two minimum consultations periods (e.g., as where 100 employees are to be dismissed and the employer attempts to introduce the dismissal in two separate batches of 50), the employer's actions would be examined closely by an industrial tribunal if a complaint were made (see 3.3.6 with regard to enforcement of the right).

3.3.3.2   Failure to comply with time limits in cases of no employee representatives

It needs to be borne in mind that the right to consultation is available either to independent recognised trade unions or to elected employee representatives. Since there is currently no obligation for an employer to recognise a union, the issue of electing employee representatives and the consequences of a failure to do so on the part of the employees need to be addressed.

An employer is required in the absence of recognising a union to invite any of the employees who may be dismissed to elect employee representatives. No machinery is laid down in the 1992 Act for the holding of elections and it would appear that such an election is entirely a matter for the employees whose jobs are affected. The Act does provide a definition of what amounts to a representative in s. 196, but this merely states that the representatives can be either *ad hoc* for the purposes of the redundancy, or can be recognised generally by the employer.

To the extent that the employees facing dismissal by redundancy fail to make a choice of representative, the employer is able to comply with the obligations imposed in relation to consultation under s. 188(7A). Under this subsection, provided an employer has issued an invitation to elect representatives and the invitation was issued 'long enough' before the consultation is required under ss. (1A), i.e. either 30 or 90 days as the case may be, the employer is deemed to have complied with the requirements of notice if, after the employees subsequently select representatives, the employer provides the representatives with the information required in a reasonable time. Taking the subsection to its logical conclusion it would seem that, if the employees faced with redundancy fail to elect representatives upon being invited to do so by their employer, they have no right to be consulted. Indeed, this was the outcome reached by the Divisional Court in *R v Secretary of State for Trade and Industry ex parte UNISON* [1996] IRLR 438, subject to one caveat — that being that an employer must issue an invitation in good time.

3.3.3.3   Failure to comply with time limits in special circumstances

Another category of case exists in which it is possible for an employer to fail to comply with the time limits, and that is where special circumstances exist which render it not reasonably practicable to comply with the consultation requirements (s. 188(7)). The 1992 Act does not go on to provide a definition of what amounts to 'special circumstances', but case law has attempted to provide some guidance to this end. In *The Bakers Union v Clarkes of Hove Ltd* [1978] IRLR 366, the appellant company had dismissed nearly its entire workforce of 368 on the same day for redundancy without consultation. The respondent union had lodged proceedings in the industrial tribunal and the employer had defended on the grounds that special circumstances existed, namely, that the company was insolvent. The industrial tribunal held that this did not amount to special circumstances. The matter was ultimately appealed to the Court of Appeal which held that special circumstances were things out of the ordinary run of events. Insolvency *per se* was neutral and the cause of the insolvency would have to be looked at to determine whether the case was special or not. In *Association of Patternmakers & Allied Craftsmen* v *Kirvin Ltd* [1978] IRLR 318, the Scottish EAT held that an employer cannot claim special circumstances where it is the case that 'he has shut his eyes to the obvious'. They went on to add:

> Insolvency by itself is not a special circumstance and it may well be foreseeable. What can be a special circumstance, however, may be the fact, if proved, that the employer has continued trading in the face of adverse economic pointers in the genuine but nonetheless reasonable expectation that redundancies will be avoided.

Other examples of special circumstances have occurred in cases such as *Hamish Armour* v *Association of Scientific, Technical and Managerial Staffs* [1979] IRLR 24 (the refusal of a Government loan), *USDAW* v *Leancut Bacon Ltd* [1981] IRLR 281 (the unexpected withdrawal of banking facilities and appointment of a receiver), *GMB* v *Rankin and Harrison* [1992] IRLR 514 (the appointment of receivers and sudden redundancy of part of the workforce in order to achieve a sale of the business of the employer as a going concern) and *AEEU and GMB* v *Clydesdale Group plc* [1995] IRLR 527 (dismissal of employees for redundancy following a court order to wind up the employer).

Having established what can amount to special circumstances, it is necessary to go on to consider whether the circumstances render it not reasonably practicable to comply with the duty to consult. The issue of reasonable practicability is again left to the discretion of tribunals hearing cases of failure to consult. Guidance on this was given in the case of *Union of Construction, Allied Trades and Technicians* v *H. Rooke & Son (Cambridge) Ltd* [1978] IRLR 204. Here, Phillips J in the EAT stated (at p. 205):

> What is in issue here is the compliance with a binding obligation of the law imposing substantive legal obligations in favour of third parties. In such cases, for example under the Factories Acts, the words 'reasonably practicable' are often used as a formula for justification, if the circumstances warrant it, of non-compliance with some such obligation. But it would be extraordinary if it could be held that it was not reasonably practicable to comply with such a statutory provision merely because the person upon whom the obligation lay was, even if for good reason, ignorant of the existence of the provision.

It should be noted that an employer cannot claim special circumstances as a defence to a failure to consult where it is the case that the employer is controlled by another person who fails to provide the employer with necessary information. This point is expressly excluded from the ambit of special circumstances by the caveat to s. 188(7) which was added by s. 34 of TURERA 1993.

Lastly, if an employer seeks to assert that there were special circumstances, it is for the employer to show that they did exist and that he took all reasonable steps to comply with the consultation requirements (s. 189(6)).

3.3.3.4   Varying the time limits
Under s. 197 of TULRCA 1992, the Secretary of State retains a power to vary the minimum notice periods. If the power is exercised, the notice period cannot be varied below the 30-day minimum set down in Art. 4(1) of the Directive (s. 197(1)).

3.3.4   The place of employment at which the right can be claimed

The 1992 Act imposes the duty to consult only where an employer proposes to dismiss the requisite number of employees and the employees are employed at one establishment. No definition of what amounts to an establishment is contained in either the Act or the Directive. This said, extensive case law exists at both national and European level on this point. The national courts have held in *Secretary of State for Employment* v *Vic Hallam Ltd* (1969) 5 ITR 108 that an establishment can be defined in the following way:

> For my part, I find it quite impossible to give any exclusive definition or test as to what constitutes an establishment. The tribunal said that they approached the matter as one of broad common sense. For my part I think that is the correct approach in deciding whether as a matter of fact and degree any particular premises do constitute an establishment. But it seems to me there are certain indications which help in the matter. The first is one to which I have already referred, exclusive occupation of premises; secondly some degree of permanence ... and thirdly, as it seems to me, some organisation on the premises, an organisation of the men who are working there. Finally, the question whether a particular premises is an establishment is bound up with the question of where the men who are working there are being employed in or from ... When one finds, as here, a place in which there is no organisation of staff whatsoever, no administration is carried out, there is a strong pointer, as it seems to me, to it not being an establishment. (*per* Lord Parker CJ at p. 110)

This *dictum* was approved by the House of Lords in *Lord Advocate* v *Babcock and Wilcox Ltd* [1972] 1 All ER 1130.

The position in Europe has been looked at in the case of *Rockfon A/S* v *Specialarbejderforbundet i Danmark* [1996] IRLR 168. Here, the European Court of Justice took the view that:

... the term 'establishment' appearing in art. 1(1)(a) of Directive 75/129/EEC must be understood as meaning, depending on the circumstances, the unit to which the workers made redundant are assigned to carry out their duties. It is not essential, in order for there to be an 'establishment', for the unit in question to be endowed with a management which can independently effect collective redundancies.

An establishment, it seems, is a local employment centre bearing the hallmarks of organisation yet not necessarily having its own independent management.

One of the problems with the requirement of having the redundancies from a single establishment is that it is possible for an employer with a number of different establishments to implement a redundancy programme involving more than 20 employees in a 90-day period that does not require consultation, by simply choosing staff to be selected as redundant from the different sites. Since the chances are that each will be treated as being a different establishment for the purposes of the Act, the duty to consult will not arise.

3.3.5   The content of consultation

The general nature of the consultation is set down in s. 188(2) of TULRCA 1992. This requires the two sides to discuss ways of avoiding the proposed dismissals, reducing the numbers of employees to be dismissed and mitigating the consequences of the dismissals. The employer is bound to undertake the consultation with a view to reaching agreement with the appropriate representatives. The Act goes on to provide details of specific information that an employer is required to provide to appropriate representatives. These are is set down in s. 188(4) and consist of the following:

(a)   reasons for the employer's proposals;

(b)   the numbers and descriptions of employees whom the employer is proposing to dismiss as redundant;

(c)   the total number of employees of any such description employed by the employer at the establishment in question;

(d)   the proposed method of selecting employees who are to be dismissed as redundant;

(e)   the proposed method of carrying out the dismissals, with due regard being given to any existing procedure, including the period of time over which the dismissals are to be implemented;

(f)   the proposed method of calculating the amount of any redundancy payments to be made (if the same deviates in any way from an existing enactment) to the employees who are to be dismissed.

The information is required to be in writing (s. 188(4)) and must be given to each of the appropriate representatives by being delivered to them, or sent by post to an address notified by them to the employer or, in the case of trade union representatives, sent to the union at the address of the union's main or head office (s. 188(5)).

In order that the representatives are able adequately to consult with the employees who are affected by the employer's decision, the employer is required to give access to the appropriate representatives to the employees. Further, the employer is under a duty to provide to the representatives accommodation and such other facilities as it may be appropriate to provide (s. 188(5A)).

3.3.6 Remedies for failure to consult

3.3.6.1 General

Where it is the case that an employer fails to consult with appropriate representatives of his workforce in good time, the remedy that is provided is initially in the form of a complaint to an industrial tribunal (s. 189(1)). The persons who can complain to the tribunal are:

(a) where it is the case that employee representatives have not been consulted, any of the representatives who have not been consulted;

(b) where it is the case that a trade union has not been consulted, the union in question; or

(c) in any other case any or all of the employees who have been made redundant.

If the tribunal finds that the complaint is well grounded, it is obliged to make a declaration to that effect and may also make a protective award (s. 189(2)).

The concept of a protective award is defined in s. 189(3). It amounts to an order requiring an employer to pay remuneration to employees who have been dismissed as redundant without consultation and within the protected period. That remuneration must be paid for the duration of the protected period. The protected period is defined in s. 189(4) as beginning on the the earlier of the date on which the first of the dismissals to which the complaint relates takes effect, or the date of the award, and it lasts for such period as the tribunal decides is just and equitable in all the circumstances having regard to the seriousness of the employer's default, but in the case of 100 or more employees being dismissed has a limit of 90 days and in the case of 20–99 employees being so dismissed has a limit of 30 days.

Any complaint under s. 189 has to be presented to a tribunal either before the date on which the last of the dismissals to which the complaint relates takes effect, within three months beginning with that date, or within such period as the industrial tribunal shall consider reasonable if it is not reasonably practicable to comply with that requirement (s. 189(5)). As to which of these dates should be used, it appears that if dismissals have actually taken place, the actual date of dismissal is the one to be used for considering the protected pay period. If it is the case that an employer is proposing to ignore the consultation obligation and is to make employees collectively redundant, the end of the protected period is the date of the tribunal award (*GKN Sankey Ltd v National Society of Metal Mechanics* [1980] IRLR 8).

It has been suggested that the correct dates to use should in fact be the same dates as those for the period of consultation referred to in s. 188 (see 3.3.3). This view was proposed in *General and Municipal Workers Union v British Uralite Ltd* [1979] IRLR 413 and *E. Green & Son (Castings) Ltd v Association of Scientific, Technical and Managerial Staffs* [1984] IRLR 135. It is submitted that the better view is the one proposal in the *GKN Sankey* case in that it has the advantages of imposing a clear, literal construction on the Act rather than twisting the wording of the Act to find one protected period when on the face of it the Act clearly envisages two separate periods and provides different definitions for each.

The amount of the award is dealt with under s. 190(2). An employer is obliged to pay a week's pay (calculated in accordance with the Employment Rights Act 1996, Pt XIV, Ch. II) to each employee for each week of the period. To the extent that fractions of a week are brought in to the calculation, a week's pay is reduced proportionately.

3.3.6.2   Reducing or avoiding protective awards
Some provisos to the payment of and amount of an award do exist. They are set out below.

3.3.6.2.1   Exercise of the just and equitable discretion   First, there is the issue of the 'just and equitable' discretion open to the tribunal. What the tribunal is bound to take into account when focusing on the length of the award is the loss of the chance of consultation, and therefore the possibility of avoiding redundancies through consultation, rather than any immediate financial loss that employees suffer as a result of the employer's failure to consult. In other words, the protective award is compensation for an employer's failure to consult.

It follows that an employer should still be ordered to pay a protective award even though his employees may have been dismissed one day and employed by a new employer the next day at a higher rate of pay (thereby suffering no loss). The EAT so held in *Spillers-French (Holdings) Ltd v Union of Shop, Distributive and Allied Workers* [1979] IRLR 339. This logic was extended in *Sovereign Distribution Services Ltd v Transport and General Workers Union* [1989] IRLR 334, where the EAT stated that, even though an employer might be able to show that consulting with appropriate representatives would not have made a difference, a protective award could still be ordered. This is because the purpose of the legislation is to ensure that consultation takes place.

Employers can also ask to have taken into consideration, when assessing the seriousness of their breach, the fact that they have tried to find alternative employment for the employees who are to be made redundant (see *Spillers-French*). Again, this seems logical. An employer taking these steps is attempting to reduce the seriousness of his breach of duty and is thereby behaving equitably towards the complainants. It follows that he should receive credit from a tribunal when it exercises its discretion.

Another point that has arisen in relation to the exercise of a tribunal's discretion is whether the appropriate representatives must prove that a loss has arisen as a result of a failure to consult. It was held by the Scottish EAT in *MSF v GEC Ferranti (Defence Systems) Ltd (No. 2)* [1994] IRLR 113 that it is up to those claiming a protective award to show that they have suffered a loss. This, it is submitted, incorrectly places the burden of proof. It may well be impossible for the appropriate representatives to show that employees have suffered any loss. Indeed, this seems to fly in the face of the decision in *Spillers-French (Holdings) Ltd v Union of Shop, Distributive and Allied Workers* [1979] IRLR 339. What the employees have lost is a chance to be consulted. It is submitted that the tribunals should follow the practice in other areas of the law in exercising their discretion to award a protective award, notably the law of contract, which recognises that although it may be impossible to calculate the loss of a chance, it still can be recovered (see *Chaplin v Hicks* [1911] 2 KB 786). Accordingly, it is submitted that it should be for the employer to put forward convincing reasons as to why he should be excused from paying a protective award.

3.3.6.2.2 Termination of employment during the protected period A number of possibilities exist in relation to the way in which employment terminates. These are dealt with under the 1992 Act and, depending upon the way termination of the contract of employment occurs, it may have the effect of either terminating the right to a protective award or merely reducing it.

The first way in which termination of employment can affect the right to a payment is where an employee dies during the protected period. In such a case, s. 190(6) of TULRCA 1992 provides that the award is reduced and has effect as if the protected period had ended on the employee's death.

The second possibility is that an employee is either fairly dismissed for a reason other than redundancy during the protected period, or that the employee unreasonably terminates the contract of employment during the notice period. Redundancy for these purposes is defined in s. 195 of TULRCA 1992 (as opposed to the definition set down in s. 139 of the Employment Rights Act 1996). Where either of these cases occurs, the right to the protective award is lost in any period where, but for the dismissal or termination, the employee would have been employed (s. 191(1)).

The third possibility is that an employer may make an offer either to renew an employee's contract or to re-engage the employee. The offer does not have to be in writing (s. 191(2)). Where termination of the previous contract occurs in this fashion, and the renewal or re-engagement would take effect before the end of the protected period with the contract being either the same, substantially the same or where the renewal or re-engagement would amount to a suitable offer of employment to a particular employee, then if the employee unreasonably refuses that offer of employment, he is not entitled to a protective award in any period during which, but for his refusal, he would have been employed (s. 191(2)–(3)).

If the contract is renewed and the employee is re-engaged in suitable alternative employment, the employee is entitled to a trial period of four weeks beginning on the date on which he starts work under the contract as renewed or substituted, or for such longer periods as the parties may agree in writing (s. 191(4)–(6)). Any agreement entered into providing for a longer trial period is required to be entered into before the employee starts work under the new contract and is required to specify the end of the trial period and the terms and conditions that apply after the end of that period. Where an employee terminates a renewed contract or one under which he has been re-engaged during the trial period, or the employer gives notice to the employee for a reason arising out of the new terms of the contract, the employee will remain entitled to the protective award unless the employee has acted unreasonably in terminating the contract. Since it is the case that these provisions are similar to those relating to trial periods in cases of redundancy, regard should be had to the redundancy cases on the meaning of the unreasonable rejection of a contract, in particular *Carron Co.* v *Robertson* (1967) 2 ITR 484 and *Hindes* v *Supersine Ltd* [1979] ICR 517.

3.3.6.2.3 Excluded employees The next group of cases in which an employee cannot claim a protective award is where the employee falls into a class of persons who are not eligible due to being excluded either by statute or voluntarily.

The categories of statutory exclusion are short-term employees (s. 282), share fishermen (s. 284), overseas employees (s. 285) and persons in the police service (s. 280). Police officers do not qualify as they are not employees for the purposes of the 1992 Act.

In relation to those who are voluntarily excluded from the right to a protective award, it is possible by means of a collective agreement to contract out of the statutory scheme where a collective agreement provides for a scheme that is at least as favourable as the statutory scheme and has been approved by the Secretary of State (s. 198(1)–(2)). The Secretary of State provides an exemption from the Act by means of a statutory instrument under s. 198(2). However, he is not allowed to issue an Order unless a collective agreement provides:

(a)   a grievance procedure in cases where employees allege that an employer has not followed a collective agreement; and

(b)   machinery for referring a dispute to arbitration, or allows a claim to be made to an industrial tribunal (s. 198(3)).

3.3.6.3 Enforcing protective awards
Where an employer has been ordered to make a protective award and has failed to do so, it is possible for an employee to apply to an industrial tribunal for an order for the remuneration due under the protective award (s. 192(1) and (3)). An employee must

present a claim within a three-month time limit beginning with the date of the failure, although the tribunal does retain a power to extend the time limit if it is satisfied that it was not reasonably practicable for an applicant to present the claim in that time (s. 192(2)). The remedy of complaint is available only under s. 192 and not under Pt II of the Employment Rights Act 1996 (s. 192(4)).

3.3.6.4 Protective awards and recoupment
For the purposes of social security legislation, a protective award is treated as earnings and is therefore subject to the provisions relating to recoupment. A discussion of the law relating to recoupment is beyond the scope of this book and regard should be had to more general employment law or social security law texts.

3.3.7 Protection for appropriate representatives

Protection is provided to employee representatives and trade union officials from being either victimised or unfairly dismissed as a result of being an appropriate representative. In the case of victimisation, the remedies provided to trade union members are by means of s. 146 of TULRCA 1992 (see 5.4 et seq.), whereas for employee representatives the protection comes under s. 47 of the Employment Rights Act 1996.

If the employer resorts to unfair dismissal, the protection is provided by s. 152 of TULRCA 1992 (see 5.5 et seq.), and employee representatives gain protection by means of s. 103 of the Employment Rights Act 1996.

Lastly, appropriate representatives have the right to paid time off work to carry out their functions, and this arises under ss. 168–169 of TULRCA 1992 for union representatives and s. 61 of the Employment Rights Act 1996 in the case of ordinary employee representatives.

3.3.8 Notification to the Department for Education and Employment

Where an employer is proposing to dismiss a group of employees as redundant in circumstances to which the duty to consult would apply, an obligation to inform the Department for Education and Employment also arises. If an employer is proposing to dismiss as redundant 100 or more employees at the same establishment, the duty on the employer is to inform the Secretary of State at least 90 days before the first of the dismissals. Where an employer is proposing to dismiss 20 or more but fewer than 100 employees, the employer is bound to notify at least 30 days before the first dismissal (TULRCA 1992, s. 193(1)–(2)).

The notice is required to be in writing and must be delivered to the Secretary of State at such address as the Secretary of State directs. It is required to state who the appropriate representatives are for the purposes of consultation and also when consultation started. It can also contain such other particulars as the Secretary of State declares relevant (s. 193(4)). The Secretary of State may request such further information as he thinks fit upon receiving the employer's notice (s. 193(5)). The Secretary is required to send a copy of the employer's notice to each of the appropriate representatives named in the employer's notice (s. 193(6)).

The employer can deviate from the procedure to notify the Secretary of State where special circumstances exist. These amount to the same type of circumstances for failing to consult with appropriate representatives as have already been discussed above at 3.3.3.3. Again, even if an employer fails to notify the Secretary of State due to not being provided with necessary information by a person controlling the employer either directly or indirectly, that will not constitute special circumstances (s. 193(7)).

Failure to notify the Secretary of State is a criminal offence and can be punished on summary conviction by a fine not exceeding level 5 on the standard scale (s. 194(1)). Where an employer is found guilty and the employer is a company, if the company has committed the offence with the consent or connivance of an officer of the company, the officer can also be prosecuted (s. 194(3)). Only the Secretary of State or an officer appointed by him may issue criminal proceedings for this offence.

3.4 THE DUTY TO CONSULT ARISING ON THE TRANSFER OF AN UNDERTAKING

3.4.1 Introduction

The duty to consult in respect of a transfer of an undertaking arises, as with the duty to consult in the event of large scale redundancies, as a product of European law. In this case, the duty arises under the Acquired Rights Directive 77/187/EEC. It is implemented in national law in the form of the Transfer of Undertakings (Protection of Employment) Regulations (TUPE) 1981, SI 1981 No. 1794. As with many other pieces of national legislation which owe their origins to European law, TUPE 1981 did not meet the standards of the Directive introducing them. It was widely anticipated that the European Commission would launch infringement proceedings against Britain alleging, *inter alia*, that the UK had failed to implement a duty to consult with appropriate representatives of an employer's workforce in the event of a transfer of an undertaking. The proceedings duly appeared in the form of *EC Commission* v *United Kingdom* Case C-382/92 [1994] IRLR 392. The result of the proceedings was a shock to no one. The Government was so confident of losing that it had already taken remedial steps in the form of TURERA 1993. The outcome of the case (coming after the enactment of the 1993 Act) went further than the Government had anticipated though. It required that appropriate representatives of workers should have the right to be consulted in the absence of a recognised, independent trade union. To this end, it was necessary to remedy the omission in TUPE 1981 by introducing the Collective Employment and Transfer of Undertakings (Protection of Employment) (Amendment) Regulations 1995, SI 1995 No. 2587.

3.4.2 The scope of the duty to consult

The duty to inform and consult arises under TUPE 1981, reg. 10 when a relevant transfer takes place. A relevant transfer is one under which the whole or part of an undertaking is transferred from one employer to another and retains its own identity after the transfer. Regard should be had to the recent case of *Betts* v *Brintel Helicopters Ltd* [1997] IRLR 361, implementing the European case of *Suzen* v *Zehnacker Gebaudereinigung GmbH* [1997] IRLR 255 as to when an undertaking will be transferred.

The duty to consult falls on both the transferor employer and the transferee employer. It imposes a duty on them to consult appropriate representatives of the employees of their workforces where the employees may be affected by the transfer or the measures taken in connection with it, whether or not they are employed in the undertaking or the part of it to be transferred (reg. 10(1)).

Appropriate representatives will be either employee representatives elected by the employees, whether on an *ad hoc* basis or generally, or they may be representatives from an independent recognised trade union (reg. 10(2A)). Again, as with the right to consult in the event of collective redundancies, the employer has a free hand in deciding whether to consult with representatives of the workforce or with a recognised trade union. It would presumably be possible to injunct an employer seeking to consult with employee representatives, as opposed to a recognised trade union, where a binding collective agreement existed.

A further point to note is that, as with collective redundancies, there are no regulations clarifying how employee representatives are to be elected. This again leaves the matter up to the employees concerned and leaves open the problems of possible vote rigging, etc. that could occur with an unregulated election.

3.4.3 The content of consultation

The information to be discussed is dealt with by TUPE 1981, reg. 10(2). This provides that an employer shall inform the appropriate representatives of the following:

(a)   the fact that a transfer is to take place, the approximate time of the transfer, and the reasons for the transfer;

(b)   the legal, social and economic implications of the transfer on the employees who are likely to be affected by the transfer;

(c)   the measures that an employer envisages will be taken in connection with the transfer in relation to the affected employees, or if he does not envisage any measures being taken, this fact; and

(d)   if the employer is the transferor, the measures which the transferee envisages he will take in relation to employees transferred under the provisions of the Regulations, or if no measures are to be taken, that fact.

In order for an employer to carry out the consultation required by (d) above, the Regulations also provide that a transferee employer must inform the transferor at such time as will enable the transferor employer to comply with the duty of consultation (reg. 10(3)).

The method by which the information is to be delivered is dealt with by reg. 10(4). This requires, in the first instance, that the information shall be given to the appropriate representatives. In the alternative, it can be sent to them by post at an address notified by them to the employer. Further still, if the representative is a union representative, the employer can discharge the duty to provide information by delivering the information by post to the union at the address of the union's main or head office.

It should be noted that appropriate representatives have no say over the way in which information is provided to them. Provided that the employer meets with the requirements of reg. 10(2), representatives are not entitled to ask for originals of documents or to request that information should be delivered to them in a particular format. Regard should be had to *Institution of Professional Civil Servants* v *Secretary of State for Defence* [1987] IRLR 373.

3.4.4   Time scale for consultation

The time scale for the provision of the information is rather vague. The Acquired Rights Directive requires that consultation shall be 'in good time'. Regulation 10(2) of TUPE 1981 translates this, somewhat Delphically, into a requirement that the necessary information shall be provided 'long enough before a relevant transfer' to enable consultation with appropriate representatives of the affected employees to take place. In the *Institution of Professional Civil Servants* case (above), the High Court held (at p. 375), that the duty to consult can take place only after the employer has decided to transfer but long enough before the transfer for the consultations to be meaningful. What amounts to 'long enough before' is, therefore, a question of fact in each particular case.

3.4.5   Purpose of consultation

If measures are to be taken by an employer in relation to a transfer, the duty of the employer is to consult the representatives of workers affected by the proposed measures with a view to securing agreement to those measures (TUPE 1981, reg. 10(5)). In the course of the consultation, the employer is bound to listen to and to reply to any proposals that are put forward by representatives of the affected workers (reg. 10(6)).

3.4.6 Defences for an employer who has failed to consult

3.4.6.1 Special circumstances

Again, as with the duty to consult in the case of redundancy, a special circumstances defence may exist for an employer who has failed to consult 'long enough before' a relevant transfer. Such an employer is required to carry out all reasonable steps to ensure that consultation takes place in the event that special circumstances exist (TUPE 1981, reg. 10(7)).

As to what can amount to special circumstances, regard should be had to 3.3.3.3 above.

If an employer does allege that special circumstances existed, it will be up to the employer to prove this in any claim that arises for failure to consult. The employer will also have to show that he took reasonable steps in any event (reg. 11(2)).

3.4.6.2 Failure to elect appropriate representatives

An employer is bound to consult only with appropriate representatives. If none exists, the duty does not arise. To this end, if an employer has issued an invitation to elect appropriate representatives 'long enough before' the time that the employer was bound to consult, and the invitation has not been acted upon, the employer is treated as having complied with the provisions of the Regulations insofar as they relate to the duty to consult (reg. 10(8)).

3.4.7 Facilities

Appropriate representatives are entitled to be provided with accommodation and other facilities necessary for their needs, and are entitled to access to the affected employees (TUPE 1981, reg. 10(6A)).

3.4.8 Remedy for failure to consult

Under TUPE 1981, reg. 11(1), where an employer is alleged to have failed to consult, an application can be made to an industrial tribunal by any of the following categories of persons:

(a) any employee representative not consulted;
(b) any trade union representative not consulted; or
(c) any of the employees who are affected by the transfer.

Where an issue arises that a transferring employer has failed to consult about the measures that are to be taken by a transferee employer, the transferor employer will be in breach of the consultation duty unless the employer can show that he gave notice of the fact that he was going to disclose to the transferee employer and that the transferee employer did not comply with the duty to disclose under TUPE, 1981, reg. 10(3) (reg. 11(3)).

If a tribunal finds that a complaint is well-founded, it must make a declaration to that effect and may then go on to award 'appropriate compensation' (reg. 11(4)). Appropriate compensation is such sum as the tribunal finds just and equitable, but the Regulations provide a cap on the maximum amount awarded, this being fixed at four weeks' pay (reg. 11(11)). It is uncertain whether this amounts to an appropriate sanction for the purposes of the Acquired Rights Directive.

The person ordered to pay the compensation will be either the transferor or, in the case of a transferee who has failed to comply with the obligation to disclose the measures that he will take and who has been given notice by the transferor of a need to do so, the transferee (reg. 11(4)).

If either the transferor or transferee fails to comply with a compensation order, a fresh complaint can be made to an industrial tribunal alleging failure to comply (reg. 11(5)). If the tribunal finds that the complaint is well-founded it can order that the compensation is paid (reg. 11(6)).

In the case of a claim under either reg. 11(1) or reg. 11(5), the claim must be brought within a three-month period beginning with the date on which the transfer is completed (in a claim under reg. 11(1)), or the date of a tribunal's reg. 11(4) Order (in a claim brought under reg. 11(5)). It is possible in a reg. 11(1) claim to present a claim prior to the transfer taking place. In *South Durham Health Authority* v *UNISON* [1995] IRLR 407, the EAT stated that the Regulations should be given their normal everyday meaning. This did not include a start date, and to that end it was possible to present a claim prior to the transfer taking place.

As with most limitation periods, it is possible for the tribunal to extend the three-month period if it considers it just and reasonable to do so.

3.4.9 Protection of appropriate representatives

Protection is provided to employee representatives and trade union officials from being either victimised or unfairly dismissed as a result of being an appropriate representative. In the case of victimisation, the remedies provided to trade union members are by means of s. 146 of TULRCA 1992 (see 5.4 *et seq.*), whereas for employee representatives the protection comes under s. 47 of the Employment Rights Act 1996.

If the employer resorts to unfair dismissal, the protection is provided by s. 152 of TULRCA 1992 (see 5.5 *et seq.*), and employee representatives gain protection by means of s. 103 of the Employment Rights Act 1996.

Appropriate representatives also have the right to paid time off work to carry out their functions, and this arises under ss. 168–169 of TULRCA 1992 for union representatives and s. 61 of the Employment Rights Act 1996 in the case of ordinary employee representatives.

3.4.10 Excluded employees

The right to be consulted does not accrue to an employee who ordinarily works outside the United Kingdom under the terms of his contract of employment (TUPE 1981, reg. 13(1)).

3.4.11 Appeals

Under s. 13(1) of the Tribunals and Inquiries Act 1971, it is possible to appeal a decision of an industrial tribunal to the EAT only and not to the High Court. The appeal lies only on a point of law (TUPE 1981, reg. 11(10)).

3.5 CONSULTATION IN RESPECT OF HEALTH AND SAFETY MATTERS

3.5.1 Introduction

A full-scale review of the law relating to health and safety in employment is beyond the scope of this book and regard should be had to more specialist texts generally. A brief review of the law relating to consultation on health and safety matters is therefore all that will be undertaken here.

3.5.2 The duty to consult

From 1 October 1996 a duty has existed for all employers to consult with their employees 'fully and effectively' in all matters relating to health and safety at work. The duty arises under the Health and Safety (Consultation with Employees) Regulations 1996 SI 1996, No. 1513, reg. 3. Prior to this, it was possible for recognised unions to appoint union safety representatives under the provisions of the Safety Representatives and Safety Committees Regulations 1977, SI 1977 No. 500, under which a duty to consult has existed since 1 January 1993 (reg. 4A, 1977 Regulations). The 1977 Regulations have continued in force but apply solely to recognised trade unions (reg. 3(1)). An employer must be notified in writing before a union safety representative can start to exercise his statutory functions (reg. 3(2), 1977 Regulations). The statutory functions are set out in reg. 4 of the 1977 Regulations. Various other statutory rights and duties accrue, these being:

    (a)   upon the giving of written notice by a safety representative to an employer, a right to inspect the workplace (reg. 5);

    (b)   a right to inspect the workplace where a notifiable accident or dangerous occurrence has taken place, or where a notifiable disease has broken out upon the giving of notice (reg. 6);

(c)   a right to inspect and take copies of documents which an employer is bound
to keep in order to comply with the Health and Safety at Work, etc. Act 1974 ('the
1974 Act') save to the extent that the document relates to an identifiable individual
and provided that the representative has given reasonable notice.

If recognition of a union does not exist, the employer is bound to consult either
directly through the workforce or with a representative of the workers (known as a
'representative of employee safety' (reg. 4(1)(b) of the 1996 Regulations).

Employers caught by the 1996 Regulations are bound to provide such information
on health and safety matters, within their knowledge, as is necessary to enable the
representative to participate fully and effectively in consultation (reg. 5(1) and
5(2)(a), 1996 Regulations). Representatives of employee safety have slightly wider
rights to be provided with information under the 1996 Regulations due to reg. 5(2)(b)
allowing them access to information under the Reporting of Injuries, Diseases and
Dangerous Occurrences Regulations 1995, SI 1995 No. 3163.

The information that is provided to both groups under the 1996 Regulations should
be such as to allow the representatives to carry out their functions under reg. 6, these
being:

(a)   to make representations on behalf of employees to the employer relating to
potential hazards and dangerous occurrences;
(b)   to make representations to the employer on general matters relating to the
health and safety of workers whom the representative represents;
(c)   to represent the interests of employees in consultations with inspectors under
the provisions of the 1974 Act.

Representatives of employee safety are entitled to time off for training and
employers are bound to provide facilities to such representatives (reg. 7, 1996
Regulations). Trade union safety representatives do not have similar statutory rights
under the 1977 Regulations but are able to use their bargaining position to gain
facilities (and union safety representatives will usually be trained by their union in
any event).

3.5.3   Right to pay for time off

Both union safety representatives and representatives of employee safety are entitled
to paid time off to carry out their functions. In the case of union safety
representatives, the right accrues under reg. 4(2) and the Schedule to the 1977
Regulations; and in the case of representatives of employee safety, the right arises
under reg. 7(3) and sch. 1 of the 1996 Regulations.

3.5.4 Protection for health and safety representatives

Protection against dismissal and victimisation accrues to health and safety representatives of both classes under the Employment Rights Act 1996. As regards victimisation, an employee is allowed to present a claim to an industrial tribunal where an employer subjects the employee to a detriment short of dismissal on account of his activity as a safety representative, under s. 44 of the 1996 Act. The right not to be unfairly dismissed for health and safety reasons arises under s. 100 of the 1996 Act. The two-year qualifying period and upper age limit are both removed in cases arising under this section (ss. 108(2) and 109(2) respectively).

3.6 THE COMMON LAW RIGHT TO CONSULTATION IN PUBLIC AUTHORITY UNIONS

3.6.1 Introduction

The right under this head is a common law right and occurs where a previous practice of consultation has existed between a public body and a union representing workers of that body. The right arises on the basis of a legitimate expectation of consultation and can be traced to the decision in *Council of Civil Service Unions* v *Minister for the Civil Service* [1985] ICR 14. In this case, for reasons of national security, the Minister for the Civil Service issued an Order in Council preventing workers at Government Communications Headquarters (GCHQ) from belonging to a union. The House of Lords held that, but for the justifying factor of national security, the union might have succeeded in its claim. Lord Fraser of Tullybelton stated (at p. 28): '... even where a person claiming some benefit or privilege has no legal right to it, as a matter of private law, he may have a legitimate expectation of receiving the benefit or privilege, and, if so, the courts will protect his expectation by judicial review as a matter of public law.'

3.6.2 Legitimate expectation

An attempt to define what amounts to a legitimate expectation was first promulgated in the *Council of Civil Service Unions* case. Lord Diplock stated (at p. 35) that, for a legitimate expectation to arise, a state of affairs must exist as between a decision-maker and another person depriving the other person of that:

> ... which either (i) he had in the past been permitted by the decision-maker to enjoy and which he can legitimately expect to be permitted to continue to do until there has been communicated to him some rational grounds for withdrawing it on which he has been given an opportunity to comment; or (ii) he has received assurance from the decision-maker will not be withdrawn without giving him the

opportunity of advancing reasons for contending that they should not be withdrawn.

It follows from what Lord Diplock says that although it is possible to withdraw rights based upon legitimate expectations, a public body can do so prospectively only after it has given the person or body having the legitimate expectation notice of its intention to do so and has given that person or body a right to comment upon the withdrawal of the expectation.

3.6.3   Examples of legitimate expectation

Other examples of where the right to be consulted based on legitimate expectation has been used are *R* v *British Coal Corporation and Secretary of State for Trade ex parte Vardy* [1993] IRLR 104, which concerned a review of the decision of the Secretary of State to close down a number of British Coal collieries without consulting the mineworkers' unions. A judicial review found that the unions did indeed have a legitimate expectation of consultation based upon previous consultations. The consultation procedure could therefore not simply be withdrawn on the whim of the Secretary of State and the unions had a right to make representations prior to the procedure being abandoned.

Re NUPE and COHSE's Application [1993] IRLR 202 was a further instance where it was held that a public body's failure to consult over redundancies could be judicially reviewed on the ground of denial of a legitimate expectation if the unions concerned could show that they had the expectation that they were claiming, and that as a result of the public authority's failure to consult they would suffer substantial hardship.

3.7   COLLECTIVE AGREEMENTS

3.7.1   Introduction

Collective agreements are agreements that exist between unions and employers (or collectives of either or both groups) for the purposes of regulating the procedures that will be adopted by the union and employer, or terms and/or terms and conditions for workers.

Collective agreements may be either those falling within the statutory definition of a collective agreement, or those falling outside the definition. They can be either contractual or non-contractual in effect depending upon the point in time that the agreement was reached, the intention of the parties and the content of the agreement. They can also bind individual employees in their effect. All of these points and the impact of TUPE 1981 will be examined further below.

3.7.2   Collective agreements defined

A statutory definition exists of what a collective agreement is. It should be noted that the definition is the basis for all the rights accruing to both unions and individuals under TULRCA 1992 insofar as they relate to a collective agreement.

The definition is found in s. 178 of TULRCA 1992 and provides:

(1)   In this Act 'collective agreement' means any agreement or arrangement made by or on behalf of one or more trade unions and one or more employers or employers' associations and relating to one or more of the matters specified below; and 'collective bargaining' means negotiations relating to or connected with one or more of those matters.

(2) The matters referred to above are—

(a)   terms and conditions of employment, or the physical conditions in which any workers are required to work;

(b)   engagement or non-engagement, or termination or suspension of employment or the duties of employment, of one or more workers;

(c)   allocation of work or the duties of employment between workers or groups of workers;

(d)   matters of discipline;

(e)   a worker's membership or non-membership of a trade union;

(f)   facilities for officials of trade unions; and

(g)   machinery for negotiation or consultation, and other procedures, relating to any of the above matters, including the recognition by employers or employers' associations of the right of a trade union to represent workers in such negotiation or consultation or in the carrying out of such procedures.

(3)   In this Act 'recognition', in relation to a trade union, means the recognition of the union by an employer, or two or more associated employers, to any extent, for the purposes of collective bargaining; and 'recognised' and other related expressions shall be construed accordingly.

While this definition is wide, it is possible for agreements to fall outside its parameters, and in such cases the agreements are not covered by the TULRCA 1992 (see, for example, *Universe Tankships Inc. of Monrovia* v *ITWF* [1982] IRLR 200 — a payment of money by an employer as a goodwill gesture was held not to fall within the list in s. 178(2)).

It should be noted that when one is looking at the content of an agreement, terms cannot be implied into such agreements in the same way as with normal contracts. A presumption exists, it seems, that where an agreement is silent as to a particular point, the point was left out of the agreement on purpose on the grounds that it was either too controversial or too complicated to justify any variation of the agreement. Therefore, rather than having judicial correction of such agreements (as might occur with other contracts), they are left as they are found (*Ali* v *Christian Salvesen Food Services Limited* [1997] IRLR 17.

3.7.3 Status of collective agreements

Collective agreements can fall into one of three categories. The first category deals with agreements concluded before 1 December 1971 or outside the statutory definition of a collective agreement (see 3.7.2 above). The last two categories deal with agreements concluded under either the Industrial Relations Act 1971 or the regime that replaced it. Each will be looked at in turn.

3.7.3.1   Agreements prior to 1 December 1971 or outside the statutory definition
The legal status of the first category of agreements is governed by the common law rules relating to the construction of contracts which focus on, amongst other things, whether the parties to an agreement intended that it should be legally binding as between them. The leading case on the point is *Ford Motor Co. Ltd* v *AEF* [1969] 2 QB 303. The case concerned agreements entered into between Ford and the defendant union which governed various matters relating to dealings with unions at Ford and terms and conditions for employees. The defendant union was in a minority of unions representing workers and, after agreement for new terms had been reached with the majority of the other unions, it took strike action to hold out for better terms. Ford sued for breach of contract (the collective agreements) and sought an injunction. In order to determine whether the union had breached the terms of an enforceable agreement, it was necessary that the agreements were intended to be legally binding. Lane J held that when one was trying to determine whether the parties had intended an agreement to be binding, one had to look at the full facts of the case. After reviewing numerous cases, articles and Donovan Commission evidence, his Lordship held (at p. 329) that: 'the general climate of opinion on both sides of industry has overwhelmingly been in favour of no legal obligation from collective agreements.' He added further (at p. 330):

> The conclusion which I have reached is this; ... If one applies the subjective test and asks what the intentions of the various parties were, the answer is that so far as they had any express intentions they were certainly not to make the agreement enforceable at law. If one applies an objective test and asks what intention must be imputed from all the circumstances of the case, the answer is the same. The fact that the agreements *prima facie* deal with commercial relationships is outweighed by the other considerations, by the wording of the agreements, by the nature of the agreements, and by the climate of opinion voiced and evidenced by the extra-judicial authorities. Agreements such as these, composed largely of optimistic aspirations, presenting grave practical problems of enforcement and reached against a background of opinion adverse to enforceability, are, in my judgment, not contracts in the legal sense and are not enforceable at law. Without

clear and express provisions making them amenable to law, they remain in the realm of undertakings binding in honour.

Therefore, as between the parties, ordinarily such collective agreements will be binding in honour only unless a clause is included making a document justiciable by the courts. This is not necessarily true where the terms are incorporated into individual contracts of employment though, and regard should be had to 3.7.7 below on this point.

3.7.3.2   Agreements after 30 November 1971 and prior to 16 September 1974
Agreements covered by this period would fall into the regime set up by the Industrial Relations Act 1971. By s. 34(2) of that Act, if a collective agreement (as defined by s. 166 of the Act) was entered into, it was conclusively presumed to be binding as between the parties.

This said, it was possible to contract out of the provision by having a clause inserted into a written agreement which conclusively presumed that the agreement was to be non-binding (s. 34(1)).

It needs to be borne in mind that the 1971 Act was introduced against a spirit of non-cooperation by unions and, as a result, the vast majority of agreements from that era included a s. 34(1) clause.

3.7.3.3   Agreements made after 16 September 1974
Any collective agreements (as now defined by s. 178 of TULRCA 1992) entered into after this date fall to be governed by the provisions of TULRA 1974 and, latterly, by TULRCA 1992. The modern provisions with regard to enforceability are set down in s. 179 of the 1992 Act and there is now a presumption that, unless an agreement is in writing and contains a clause stating that it is intended to be binding as between the parties to it, it is conclusively presumed to be non-binding (s. 179(1)). To the extent that an agreement does comply with these requirements, it is conclusively presumed to be binding (s. 179(2)).

3.7.4   Non-binding clauses in binding agreements

While as was discussed at 3.7.3 *et seq.* above, some agreements are presumed to be binding as between the parties, not all clauses contained in them are capable of being enforced by a court. Such clauses fall into two categories, discriminatory clauses and no industrial action clauses.

3.7.4.1   Discriminatory clauses
To the extent that a clause in a collective agreement seeks to discriminate against a person on grounds of either sex or race it is void under the provisions of s. 77 of the Sex Discrimination Act 1975 and s. 72 of the Race Relations Act 1976 respectively. It should be noted that these provisions relate to agreements which are presumed to

be legally binding. It should be further noted that there is a similar provision in relation to disability under s. 9 of the Disability Discrimination Act 1995.

In relation to non-binding agreements, a provision also exists under s. 6 of the Sex Discrimination Act 1986 which declares that any provision in a non-binding collective agreement that purports to discriminate against women is void. The amendment was made following the ruling of the European Court of Justice in *EC Commission* v *United Kingdom* [1984] IRLR 29, which concluded that, such agreements, while not being enforceable, were capable of setting benchmarks in industrial relations and therefore could fall foul of the Equal Treatment Directive (76/207). No similar provision exists in relation to either race or disability discrimination.

3.7.4.2   No industrial action clauses
Clauses entered into between an employer and a union which contain a no industrial action clause are presumed to be non-binding as between the employer and individual employees unless they conform with the requirements of s. 180 of TULRCA 1992. This requires that the following conditions are observed:

(a)   that the agreement which contains the clause is in writing;

(b)   that the agreement contains a clause expressly stating that the clause or clauses are to be incorporated into individual contracts;

(c)   that the agreement itself is reasonably accessible to employees at their place of work and that employees are able to inspect the document during working hours; and

(d)   that a union entering into such an agreement is an independent union.

Any such clause must also be actually incorporated into individual contracts (s. 180(2) — see 3.7.6   below as to incorporation).

The provisions exist as a safeguard for workers who would otherwise lose their right to take action in the event that it is necessary to bring about a change in working practices. Such agreements should be entered into only after a union has thought long and hard about the implications of such a clause. The requirement of independence on the part of a union also stops staff associations (over which an employer might exert considerable pressure) from negotiating away the right to take action. It should be noted that it is not possible to contract out of the provisions of s. 180(2) (s. 180(3)).

3.7.5   Collective agreements and transfers of undertakings

Where a collective agreement has been entered into between an employer and a union, and the employer then transfers the undertaking or part thereof containing members of the union with which the agreement has been made, the question arises whether the transferee employer is bound by the agreement. The answer to this question is found in reg. 6 of TUPE 1981, which enacts Art. 3(2) of the Transfer of Undertakings Directive (77/187) and provides that:

Where at the time of a relevant transfer there exists a collective agreement made by or on behalf of the transferor with a trade union recognised by the transferor in respect of any employee whose contract of employment is preserved by Regulation 5(1) above, then,—

(a)   without prejudice to section 18 of the 1974 Act or Article 63 of the 1976 Order (collective agreements presumed to be unenforceable in specified circumstances) that agreement, in its application in relation to the employee, shall, after the transfer, have effect as if made by or on behalf of the transferee with that trade union, and accordingly anything done under or in connection with it, in its application as aforesaid, by or in relation to the transferor before the transfer, shall, after the transfer, be deemed to have been done by or in relation to the transferee; and

(b)   any order made in respect of that agreement, in its application in relation to the employee, shall, after the transfer, have effect as if the transferee were a party to the agreement.

The effect of the provision is that where a collective agreement exists, its obligations are transferred upon the undertaking being transferred. There is a certain amount of 'window dressing' in this provision. Most collective agreements are non-binding as between a union and an employer. The effect of the transfer is that a transferee is bound by an agreement to the same extent as a transferor. It follows that if a transferor was not legally bound, a transferee is not bound either and is therefore free to ignore any such agreement if he thinks fit.

One caveat needs to be added to the foregoing, and this is that a transferee can only ignore the agreement as regards a union. To the extent that an agreement has incorporated terms into an individual contract, the transferee is bound to comply with such terms. In *Whent v T. Cartledge Ltd* [1997] IRLR 153, the respondent company had taken over the running of the street lighting functions of the London Borough of Brent. The council had in a place a collective agreement governing terms and conditions of employment for employees. Upon the undertaking being transferred, the transferee wrote to the union representing the transferred workers and told it that recognition was being withdrawn. They also wrote to individual employees and informed them that the collective agreements would no longer have any effect. The applicants lodged claims under the Wages Act 1986, claiming that since their individual contracts contained terms set from time to time by the collective agreements, they were entitled to rely on the terms. The employer argued that, to the extent that an obligation did transfer, it was only to honour the last collective agreement and not any new national agreements that were subsequently reached. The EAT agreed with the employees and held that the obligation to honour the agreements as updated from time to time passed to the transferee. To the extent that the employer wanted to vary the terms, it would have to be done by individual agreement with each employee (although the impact of reg. 12 needs to be borne in mind in this regard).

3.7.6   Incorporation of collective agreements into individual contracts

As to when a collective agreement becomes incorporated into an individual contract, this is very much a question of fact in a particular case (see, for example, *Robertson* v *British Gas Corporation* [1983] IRLR 302, *Cadoux* v *Central Regional Council* [1986] IRLR 131, *Marley* v *Forward Trust Group Limited* [1986] IRLR 369, *Whent* v *T. Cartledge Limited* [1997] IRLR 153 and *Burke* v *Royal Liverpool University Trust Hospital* [1997] ICR 730). The fact that a clause in an agreement is non-binding as between a union and an employer does not stop the clause becoming incorporated by reference as a term in an individual's contract.

   This said, not every term that is referred to is capable of becoming incorporated. Terms which seek to act collectively are generally not thought appropriate to be incorporated into individual contracts (see, for example, *R* v *Industrial Disputes Tribunal ex parte Portland UDC* [1955] 3 All ER 18 — where a disputes procedure was held not to have become incorporated; *Gallagher* v *Post Office* [1970] 3 All ER 712 — a requirement for union recognition was held not to have been incorporated; and *Lee* v *GEC Plessey Telecommunications* [1993] IRLR 383 — an agreement for enhanced redundancy packages was held not to have been incorporated). Nevertheless, each case in this area very much depends on the particular facts. In three other cases on redundancy packages, different courts have come to three different results. In *Young* v *Canadian Northern Railway Co.* [1931] AC 83, the Privy Council held that an agreement relating to redundancy procedure was not incorporated into the plaintiff's contract. In *Alexander* v *Standard Telephones & Cables Limited* [1990] IRLR 55, the High Court dismissed an application for an injunction preventing a breach of redundancy procedure agreements (on the grounds that it would compel the employer to employ those he did not wish to employ). However, Aldous J recognised that there was a serious issue to be tried in the case. Most recently though, the Court of Session held in *Anderson* v *Pringle of Scotland Limited* [1998] IRLR 65 that an interdict could be granted where a LIFO redundancy agreement between an employer and a union was breached, on the ground that the same was capable of being incorporated into individual contracts. Commenting upon the authorities generally, Lord Prosser stated that he could not see a difference between the position under English law and that under Scots law. He added (at p. 67): '... I am satisfied that in principle it is a matter of circumstances rather than law that interdict will usually be refused.'

   The importance of the facts of a case cannot be over-stressed in this area.

4 Trade Union Obligations

4.1 TRADE UNION MEMBERS AND ACTION AGAINST THE UNION

4.1.1 Introduction

Trade union members now have a wide degree of control over their union through both contract and statute. This has not always been the case though. While the policy of the Conservative Government from 1979 was to curb the power of trade unions members, this has, perversely, also partially resulted in the growth of their statutory rights.

At common law, the rule book of a union is treated as a contract between the members and the union. As such it is, and always has been, subject to interpretation by the courts in the same way as other contracts. Of particular use to union members in this regard is the implication of terms by courts into the membership contract and the use of public policy to challenge terms in rule books that may be unfair to members.

These areas will be examined in turn, starting with the common law rules concerning the union rule book.

4.1.2 Common law rights of union members

4.1.2.1 Introduction

As stated above at 4.1.1, union rule books create a contract of membership between unions as quasi-corporate entities and their members (see 2.1.5 *et seq.* as to the capacity of unions to enter into contracts). Most of the litigation in the area has arisen either with regard to the disciplinary function exercised by a union, or as a result of the closed shop. The courts have promoted rules concerning the construction and interpretation of rule books in the light of these issues.

4.1.2.2   Nature of the rule book

How the rule book should be construed has been the subject of a number of competing theories. In *Bonsor* v *Musicians Union* [1954] 1 All ER 822, the plaintiff was expelled from the defendant union for failing to pay a weekly union subscription. He sued for an injunction preventing expulsion. Although the matter eventually reached the House of Lords, in the Court of Appeal, Denning LJ suggested that union rules were 'not so much a contract, ... but ... more a legislative code laid down by some members of the union to be imposed on all members of the union. They are more like bye-laws than a contract'. He then added that, as such, the rules were judicially reviewable in the same way as a public body acting outside its authority.

The 'bye-law' theory appears to have been rejected though by the House of Lords in the case of *Faramus* v *Film Artistes Association* [1964] 1 All ER 25. Here, the facts concerned the exclusion from membership of a purported member of a trade union on the ground that he was ineligible for membership prior to having joined the union. Lord Evershed stated (at p. 30):

> ... I agree entirely with the view ... that there is here no true analogy between the rules of this union and the bye-laws of some corporation which would entitle the court to treat the rule (as they could treat a bye-law) as ineffective and invalid if outside the law-making power conferred on the makers of the rules.

To the extent that the case ultimately dealt with the issue of joining a union rather than actual membership itself, it is uncertain how far it goes in the destruction of the bye-law theory. In any event, as is noted below at 4.2.2, unions are now subject to statutory controls upon admission to membership.

The final and prevailing theory relating to rule books is the 'contract theory'. This theory treats the rule book as a contract of membership which should be construed in the same way as any other contract. It was initially disputed but seems now to be the accepted doctrine.

One of the first modern cases to examine the contract theory was *Lee* v *Showman's Guild* [1952] 2 QB 329. Here, the plaintiff had been fined for breaking union rules on competition, having not surrendered a fairground pitch to a rival upon being ordered to do so by his union. He did not pay that fine and was expelled from the union pursuant to an automatic expulsion clause within the rules. The plaintiff sued for breach of contract and the case reached the Court of Appeal, which was then required to construe the union rule book in this light. Denning LJ stated that:

> [trade unions] wield power as great, if not greater, than any exercised by courts of law. They can deprive a man of his livelihood ... They are usually empowered to do this for any breach of rules which ... they impose and which he has no real opportunity of accepting or rejecting. In theory their powers are based on contract. The man is supposed to have contracted to give them these great powers; but in practice he has no choice in the matter.

Despite the judgment of Denning LJ, the House of Lords has confirmed that it is proper to construe union rule books as contracts. In *British Actors Equity Association v Goring* [1978] ICR 791, the House of Lords was faced with the construction of a set of rule-changing provisions within a union rule book. Viscount Dilhorne held (at pp. 794–95):

> While it cannot be said that the rules are a fine example of legal drafting, I do not think that, because they are the rules of a union, different cannons of construction should be applied to them than are applied to any written documents. Our task is to construe them so as to give them a reasonable interpretation which accords with what in our opinion must have been intended.

In order to reach an understanding of what the parties were taken to have intended, regard must be had to the particular circumstances of a case, including the nature and size of the union, formal reliance on rules and resources open to a union generally. Likewise, the court should not give an overly sophisticated construction to the rules. As was stated by Lord Wilberforce in the case of *Heaton's Transport (St Helens) Ltd v TGWU* [1972] ICR 308, at p. 393:

> ... trade union rule books are not drafted by parliamentary draftsmen. Courts of law must resist the temptation to construe them as if they were; for that is not how they would be understood by the members who are the parties to the agreement of which the terms, or some of them, are set out in the rule book ... Furthermore, it is not to be assumed, as in the case of a commercial contract which has been reduced into writing, that all the terms of the agreement are to be found in the rule book alone; particularly as respects the discretion conferred by the members upon committees or officials of the union as to the way in which they may act upon the union's behalf. What the members understand as to the characteristics of the agreement into which they enter by joining a union is well stated in the section of the TUC handbook on the Industrial Relations Act which gives advice about the content and operation of unions' rules. Paragraph 99 reads as follow: '... Custom and practice may operate either by modifying a union's rules as they operate in practice, or by compensating for the absence of union rules. Furthermore, the procedure which custom and practice lays down very often vary from workplace to workplace within the same industry, and even within different branches of the same union.'

Therefore, in examining the rule book the following need to be addressed:

(a)   Union rule books are to be construed as contracts made between unions and their members.

(b)   In arriving at the correct construction, the court is to have regard to all the circumstances surrounding the particular case, including external evidence of terms which are unwritten and may arise from custom and practice of the union and its members.

(c)   Courts should arrive at a construction that members would have understood and not be over-reliant upon strict legal construction of the wording.

4.1.2.3   Access to the courts — ouster clauses

Rule books may contain clauses making a union the final arbiter of any disputes that occur as between a member and a union. The problem that arises in relation to these clauses is one of public policy. The courts are the proper forum for the resolution of a legal matter and, as such, have often intervened in disputes in all areas of the law when a challenge to their jurisdiction arises. The law in relation to trade unions is no different. What needs to be examined, however, is what is being excluded from the court. Ouster clauses essentially fall into one of three categories:

(a)   clauses that attempt totally to remove the court's jurisdiction on matters of fact;

(b)   clauses which seek to remove the court's jurisdiction to hear disputes on points of law; and

(c)   clauses which attempt to delay access to the courts until internal remedies have been exhausted by the union members.

As to the first of these categories, there is, *prima facie*, nothing wrong with clauses that make unions the sole arbiters of questions of fact. In *Lee v The Showman's Guild of Great Britain* [1952] 2 QB 329, Denning LJ stated (at p. 342): '[Unions and their members] can, of course, agree to leave questions of law as well as questions of fact, to the decision of the domestic tribunal. They can, indeed, make the tribunal the final arbiter on questions of fact ...'

As to the second category, ouster clauses purporting to restrain the court from examining a question of law, Denning LJ added to his judgment in *Lee* (at p. 342):

... they [unions and the members] cannot make the [domestic tribunal] final arbiter on questions of law. They cannot prevent its decisions being examined by the courts. If parties should seek, by agreement, to take the law out of the hands of the courts and put it into the hands of a private tribunal, without recourse at all to the courts in case of any error of law, then the agreement is to that extent contrary to public policy and void.

The third category of clause, those which seek to influence the time at which the member can have recourse to the court, is slightly more problematic. The approach at common law is dealt with in the cases of *White v Kuzych* [1951] 2 All ER 435 and *Leigh v NUR* [1970] Ch 326. In the former case, the Privy Council was of the opinion that internal remedies should be exhausted if there existed a requirement in the rule book to that end. However, in the latter case, Goff J took a more pragmatic approach. His view was:

> ... [W]here there is an express provision in the rules that the plaintiff must exhaust his domestic remedies, the court is not absolutely bound by that because its jurisdiction cannot be ousted, but the plaintiff will have to show cause why it should interfere with the contractual position ... [In] the absence of such a provision the court can readily, or at all events, more readily, grant relief without prior recourse to the domestic remedies, but may require the plaintiff to resort first to those remedies.

This sentiment was echoed by the Court of Appeal in the case of *Longley* v *NUJ* [1987] IRLR 109. The Court stressed in this case that a plaintiff would have to show cause in order to invoke the aid of a court. Cause might amount, for example, to the domestic tribunal refusing to allow the member a right of appearance (see 4.1.2.4.2).

To the extent that a plaintiff cannot show cause then, ordinarily, the proper course for a court is to stay the proceedings until resolution of the matter by the domestic tribunal concerned.

The common law is subject to statutory intervention. Section 63 of TULRCA 1992 contains a provision dealing with clauses delaying access to the courts. The section is primarily aimed at domestic proceedings taking an unnecessarily long time to be resolved. Under s. 63(2), where proceedings take more than six months to resolve then, notwithstanding that they are almost complete, a member has a right to have the dispute heard by a court. The right of court access is not absolute though. To the extent that the court finds that the member has contributed to the delay in the proceedings as a result of unreasonable conduct, it can extend the six-month period of investigation for such length of time as it thinks fit in all the circumstances (s. 63(4)).

It should be noted that it is possible to apply to the court in a rule book dispute prior to a domestic tribunal commencing, although in the light of the foregoing such cases will be rare.

4.1.2.4 *Construction of rule books*

Once it is accepted that rule books are contracts in the same way as other contracts, courts are then faced with the task of construing them. While there is a substantial body of case law in this area, it is now of much reduced significance due to the statutory rights that were granted to union members during the reforms of the 1980s, and also as a result of the closed shop reforms which substantially reduced the number of challenges that were brought. This said, the common law principles are still of importance due to the remedies that are available (most notably injunctions).

In considering how to construe a particular rule book, the courts will pay attention to the impact of any express terms, terms which are implied and the impact of public policy.

4.1.2.4.1   Express terms of the rule book   As stated above at 4.1.2.2, courts are required to construe rule books as they would appear to a reasonable trade union member. Of particular use to union members will be the help that can be derived from the construction of rules for election of candidates to minor offices of a union. As can be seen at 4.2.8 below, union members are entitled to stand as candidates in elections for major union offices unless they are reasonably excluded from doing so (TULRCA 1992, s. 47). However, the statutory right extends only to the major union offices; there is no similar provision in relation to minor posts that a member may wish to stand for, such as that of shop steward. To this end, the common law rules are still of importance. To the extent that the rules provide that any class of members can stand as a candidate for elections, the exclusion of a member who satisfies the class requirements under the union rules will be unlawful. In these circumstances, the court will be able to provide a remedy. In the case of *Leigh* v *NUR* [1970] Ch 326, the applicant successfully obtained an injunction preventing his union from refusing to allow him to stand as a candidate in elections for the post of union president after he had shown that he met the candidacy requirements. Another example is the case of *Annamunthodo* v *Oilfield Workers' Trade Union* [1961] 3 All ER 621. Here, the appellant had been expelled from the respondent union on the grounds that he had publicly alleged embezzlement of union funds by the president of the union. He had been charged as a result with four breaches of a union rule, each of which provided for a maximum penalty of a fine. He was later expelled under a provision which he had not been charged with. The Privy Council ordered the expulsion to be set aside. It was not open to the respondent to impose a harsher penalty than that expressly provided for under the rules.

Other examples of terms that have come under the scrutiny of the court are a rule requiring compulsory attendance at union branch meetings (*MacLelland* v *NUJ* [1975] ICR 116), a purported alteration of rules in defiance of a court order (*Clarke* v *Chadburn* [1984] IRLR 350) and strike balloting rules (*Taylor* v *NUM (Derbyshire)* [1984] IRLR 440). As to the last of these provisions, regard should also be had to the statutory provisions under s. 62 of TULRCA 1992 allowing a member to have a right to hold a strike ballot, noted at 4.2.4 below.

Once a breach of rules has been established, regard should be had generally to the issue of remedies under the common law set out below at 4.1.3 *et seq.*

4.1.2.4.2   Implication of terms into the union rule book   To the extent that the rule book is a contract, it can have terms implied into in the same way as any other contract (see, for example, the judgments in *Southern Foundries Ltd* v *Shirlaw* [1939] 2 KB 206 and *The Moorcock* (1889) 14 PD 64 with regard to the officious bystander and business efficacy tests). Terms can be implied on an *ad hoc* basis or as a result of the particular nature of the membership contract. Not every claimed term will necessarily be implied though. An implied term can be alleged by both union and member alike. However, when looking at the contract, the tendency is to give the contract a meaning that is favourable to the member and not to extend the powers of the union over the member. Therefore, generally, the court will not imply a power of discipline over the members of a union (see *Spring* v *NASDS* [1956] 1 WLR 585, *Laby* v *Warwickshire Miners Federation* [1912] 2 Ch 371 and also *Leigh* v *NUR* [1970] Ch 326. To contrary effect, see *McVitae* v *Unison* [1996] IRLR 33, where it was held that a union had an implied power to discipline members in respect of matters arising prior to the creation of the union from three separate unions).

Likewise, not every term alleged in a contract by a member can be supported. The court is required to remember that the union exists, primarily, to promote the greater good of its collective membership. In the case of *Iwanuszezak* v *GMBATU* [1988] IRLR 219, a union had negotiated revised work patterns with an employer that were to the benefit of a majority of the union's members working for the employer. One member claimed breach of an implied term in the rule book, this being that the union was required to act for his benefit. Since he had been adversely affected by the changes, he claimed that he should be provided with a remedy. The claim was struck out. Lloyd LJ in the Court of Appeal held (at p. 220), that while the union should look after the interests of its members, the order of interests was collective first and individual second. Accordingly, there had been no breach.

This said, it has been held that express terms within the union rule book empowering a committee of the union to act in a particular fashion can be tempered by the requirement of reasonableness. For example, in the case of *Esterman* v *NALGO* [1974] ICR 625, a union had voted on the taking of industrial action. When the result was published, only 49 per cent of those voting had resolved in favour of action. Notwithstanding this, the union resolved to take action and instructed members not to take part in the administration of local elections. The plaintiff refused to cooperate with the order and was disciplined and found guilty of breaching a rule which read: 'Any member who disregards any regulation issued by the branch or is guilty of conduct which, in the opinion of the executive committee, renders him unfit for union membership, shall be liable to expulsion.' The plaintiff sued claiming that the union was in breach of contract. The High Court granted an injunction, Templeman J holding:

An Act of Parliament carries penalties for its breach, but it is a fallacy to assume that every democratically elected body is entitled to obedience to every order on pain of being found guilty of being unfit to be a member of an association. It must depend on the order and it must depend on the circumstances and, in my judgment, if implicit obedience is to be exacted, those who issue the order must make quite sure that they have the power, that no reasonable man could be in doubt that they have the power and that they are making a proper exercise of the power, and that no reasonable man could say to himself that 'this is an order which I have no duty to obey'.

As to when this requirement will operate, each case will turn on its own particular facts. However, it is worth noting that the position in relation to contracts of employment is somewhat different and the EAT has held that express terms are not controlled by a requirement to act reasonably (see *White* v *Reflecting Roadstuds Limited* [1991] ICR 733).

4.1.2.4.3 Public policy and the union rule book   Union rule books can also be overridden by the requirement of public policy. Not every provision contained in a membership contract will be binding, even if a union member has signified his consent in writing. A union will be required to observe basic principles of natural justice in the treatment of its members. Natural justice requires that members of a union have a right to a hearing, that such hearing is free from bias and that a union cannot act as judge and jury in its own cause. While the concept of natural justice is derived from the area of public law, State control of the workings of a domestic tribunal has always been frowned upon by the courts, and to this end the public law remedies of certiorari, mandamus and prohibition are not available to union members.

As rule books operate as contracts, public policy can either be incorporated into the rule book as an implied term, or it can operate as a device to remove express terms within rule books where such terms seek to deny natural justice.

The concept of natural justice in relation to the rule book is of particular importance when considering the disciplining of union members. Further, it was important in relation to the closed shop through which unions used to be able to deny to individuals the right to earn a living. As can be seen in Chapter 7, this is now no longer possible due to the reforms of the 1980s. However, union membership can still be beneficial and the courts are prepared to intervene in order to ensure that unions behave fairly towards their members. In *Breen* v *AEU* [1971] 2 QB 175, Lord Denning MR stated that (at p. 190) unions are:

> ... domestic bodies which control the destinies of thousands ... They can make or mar a man by their decisions. Not only by expelling him from membership, but also by refusing to admit him as a member ... Often their rules are framed so as to give them a discretion. They claim that it is an unfettered discretion. They go too far ... They are not above the law, but subject to it. Their rules are said to be a contract between the members and the union. So be it. If they are a contract, then it is an implied term that the discretion should be exercised fairly. But the rules are in reality more than a contract. They are a legislative code laid down by the council of the union for the benefit of the members ... Even though its functions are not judicial or quasi-judicial, but administrative, still it must act fairly.

While this proposition is derived from the period prior to the changes of the 1980s, the principle is still good law today. It shows that union rule books are open to challenge either on the basis of an implied term requiring unions to act fairly, or by means of public policy to strike out express terms.

4.1.2.4.3.1 Public policy as an implied term   The implied term theory works on the basis that a reasonable man would conclude that the principles of natural justice would not be excluded.

Natural justice requires a right to a hearing. The case of *Annamunthodo* v *Oilfield Workers' Trade Union* [1961] 3 All ER 621 can be used as an example of this presumption. The facts are as stated above at 4.1.2.4.1. In the judgment of the Privy Council, Lord Denning stated:

> Counsel for the respondent union sought to treat the specific formulation of charges as immaterial. The substance of the matter lay, he said, in the facts alleged in the letter as to the meetings which the appellant had attended and the allegations he had made. Their Lordships cannot accede to this view. If a domestic tribunal formulates specific charges, which lead only to a fine, it cannot without notice resort to other charges, which lead to far more severe penalties.

Regard should also be had to *Lee* v *Showman's Guild* [1952] 2 QB 329.

4.1.2.4.3.2 Deletion of terms by operation of public policy   The courts are also prepared to strike out express terms due to their failure to comply with public policy. To the extent that union rules expressly seek to exclude some aspect of natural justice, they have consistently been held to be void. In *Edwards* v *SOGAT* [1971] 1 Ch 354, a trade union rule book had a term providing that, to the extent that a temporary member of the union was more than six weeks in arrears with union dues, that member was to be automatically expelled from the union with no right of appeal. The plaintiff, through an oversight by a union official, did not have his subscriptions collected and was accordingly expelled. He sued claiming damages for breach of contract. The Court of Appeal found for the plaintiff, Sachs LJ holding that once a member had been admitted to a trade union, there was no right for the union to expel the member in an arbitrary fashion not in accordance with the principles of natural justice.

Further, in the case of *Roebuck* v *NUM* [1978] ICR 676, the plaintiffs had appeared as witnesses against the union in a libel action brought by the union's president against a local newspaper. The union rules contained a rule providing that members of the union could be disciplined by the area executive committee for action which, in the opinion of the committee, was likely to be detrimental to the union. The president of the union brought charges against the plaintiffs and acted as the prosecutor of the charges before the committee. The committee, which was also chaired by the president, found the charges to have been proved and imposed sanctions accordingly. The members sued for a declaration that the finding was in breach of the principles of natural justice, notwithstanding the proper constitution of the meeting. The High Court found for the plaintiffs. Templeman J held that disciplinary proceedings had to be constituted so as to avoid the appearance of bias to a reasonable man. This requirement had evidently not been complied with.

It should be noted that not every claim of a failure to comply with the rules of natural justice will succeed. Natural justice can be invoked to help a member only where some principle of public policy requires it. In the case of *Cheall* v *APEX* [1983] ICR 398, the plaintiff had been a member of a union with which he had become disenchanted. He then joined the defendant union and did not reply to a question raised upon joining which asked whether he had belonged to any other unions. Both his previous union and the defendant union were governed by the Bridlington Principles which regulate, *inter alia*, the recruitment of members between unions. It subsequently came to the attention of the defendant union that the plaintiff had not declared his membership of his former union. The matter was referred to the TUC Disputes Committee which found the defendant union to have improperly recruited the plaintiff contrary to the Bridlington Principles and recommended that the plaintiff be expelled. This duly occurred, whereupon the plaintiff sued claiming that his inability to appear before the Disputes Committee amounted to a denial of natural justice. The House of Lords disagreed. There was no principle of public policy to which the Bridlington Principles were contrary and, to the extent that the plaintiff was not faced with the loss of his job as a result of his expulsion, he had no cause of action. Regard should be had now to 4.2.2 dealing with the right not to be expelled from a trade union.

4.1.2.4.4   Shortcomings of the contract of membership   The principal shortcoming of the contract model of union membership is that the contract requires there to have been a valid agreement in place between member and union. To the extent that this is lacking, no common law rights can be claimed under the rule book. The case of *Faramus* v *Film Artistes Association* [1964] 1 All ER 25 graphically illustrates this point. The defendant union had a rule requiring that, in order to be eligible for membership, applicants must have had no criminal convictions. The plaintiff, had, in his youth, been sentenced to a custodial prison sentence. He did not enter this conviction on his application for membership and was admitted to the union. After eight years of membership the plaintiff's conviction came to light, whereupon the defendant purported to revoke his membership. The plaintiff sued claiming an injunction to prevent his expulsion, which he argued was in breach of the rules of natural justice. Ultimately, the House of Lords refused to grant the application. Lord Evershed, giving the judgment of the House, stated that the union rules were clearly drawn up. No right of natural justice could be implied as the plaintiff had never been a member of the union under its membership requirements. It followed that he was not being expelled and there was therefore no term of a contract that had been breached. This still remains the position under the common law, although regard should be had to the provisions under s. 174 of TULRCA 1992 in relation to the right not to be excluded from membership of a trade union (see 4.2.2 below). This said, it is worth noting that the shortcomings of the common law position are, in practice, less obvious as a result of the reform of the closed shop due to the decreased significance of union membership in relation to the ability of an individual to obtain employment.

4.1.3   Remedies for breach of the membership contract

4.1.3.1   Introduction
The usual common law rules in relation to remedies for breach of contract will be applied to the case of a breach of the rule book. Therefore, depending on the consequences of a breach of the rules, a member of a union will be able to recover damages or gain an injunction and, in either case, has the possibility of obtaining a declaration as to the rights and duties under the contract.

4.1.3.2   Damages
In relation to a breach of the rule book by the union the general rules relating to damages will attach to a successful claim by a union member. This will mean that the member will be able to recover damages to the extent that he has suffered a loss and to the extent that the loss is reasonably foreseeable. This has been the position since *Bonsor* v *Musicians' Union* [1955] 3 All ER 518, when the House of Lords reversed the previous authority on the point, *Kelly* v *National Society of Operative Printers' Assistants* (1915) 84 LJKB 2236, which had held that due to a union being an unincorporated association made up of all the members of the union, a member would be suing himself if he sued for breach of contract. This point is now beyond doubt given the quasi-corporate status of a union under s. 10(1) of TULRCA 1992.

In awarding damages, the court will not be required to take into account any injury to feelings that the member may have suffered, this being in line with the general rule in relation to commercial contracts as set down in *Addis* v *The Gramophone Co. Ltd* [1909] AC 488. Further, the member will be required to take reasonable steps to mitigate potential loss and, to the extent that this does not happen, no damages can be awarded for the loss representing a failure to mitigate (*Edwards* v *SOGAT* [1971] Ch 354).

It should also be noted that unlike damages awarded against a union for tort, there is no limit to the potential liability of the union for breach of contract (TULRCA 1992, s. 20(1)).

4.1.3.3   Injunctions
An injunction is an important remedy for a union member, particularly one facing expulsion from his union. The injunction can be gained at an interlocutory stage with the rules set down by the case of *American Cyanamid Co.* v *Ethicon Ltd* [1975] AC 295 applying (see 8.2.2 *et seq.* generally with regard to injunctions). This will mean that from the point of view of a member trying to enforce the rule book, no more than a serious question need be shown coupled with a consideration of where the balance of convenience lies. The courts are readily prepared to grant an injunction in favour of a union member to uphold the contract of membership. For example, in the case of *Porter* v *NUJ* [1980] IRLR 404, the House of Lords, when considering an application brought by the plaintiff for an injunction to prevent his expulsion from the defendant union for failing to strike, granted the injunction. Notwithstanding a

legally and factually complex background to the case, the House was prepared to accept that the balance of convenience lay with maintaining the status quo prior to the expulsion.

To the extent that an injunction is granted at an interlocutory stage, two practical benefits will accrue to the member. First, many of the cases brought against unions for breach of the membership contract do not proceed to trial with the result that the member will retain membership. Secondly, the injunction can force the union to take back a member or risk contempt proceedings with the possible fines, imprisonment and sequestrations that this form of enforcement can bring with it (regard should be had to RSC Ord. 45, r. 5). Reinstatement in the union is not available under the provisions for expulsion from a union contained within TULRCA 1992 (see 4.2.4 below).

4.1.3.4 Declarations
A declaration as to the rights of the parties can be readily obtained as a final remedy in a case for breach of contract. At an interlocutory stage, however, it is rarely if ever available. In *International General Electric Co. of New York Ltd* v *Commissioners of Customs and Excise* [1962] Ch 784, the Court of Appeal held that an interlocutory remedy declaring the rights of the parties could not possibly exist except perhaps in an exceptional case. *Clarke* v *Chadburn (No. 2)* [1984] IRLR 350 appears to have been such a case. Here, Megarry V-C granted an interlocutory declaration coupled with an injunction to prevent an unlawful change of rules purportedly taken by the NUM, on the grounds that a substantial number of members would have been affected which thereby justified the sparing use of his available discretion. Such a remedy is rarely called for and the grant of an interlocutory injunction will be adequate in most cases.

4.1.3.5 Fast track procedure in construction disputes
While a full discussion of the law of civil procedure is beyond the scope of this work, it is worth noting that, as with other contracts where a point of construction arises, it may be possible to use the summary procedure contained in RSC Ord. 14A to resolve a rule book dispute. If all that is involved in a dispute is simple determination of a provision within a rule book, the procedure will save the time and inconvenience of a full trial. However, if a dispute goes beyond these simple parameters then a full trial may well be the inevitable result.

4.1.3.6 Public law remedies
In challenging the validity of the rule book or a union's action, it is not possible to obtain the public law remedies of certiorari, mandamus or prohibition when alleging *ultra vires* action on the part of the union (see, in particular, the judgment of Lord Parker CJ in *R* v *Criminal Injuries Compensation Board ex parte Lain* [1967] 2 QB 864, at p. 882).

4.1.4 Aid in proceedings against trade unions

To the extent that a union member is forced to take action at common law to enforce the contract of membership, assistance to the member is now available from the Commissioner for the Rights of Trade Union Members. When the office of the Commissioner was initially introduced by the Employment Act 1988, no assistance was available for breach of union rules. This position was changed by the Employment Act 1990, and the right to assistance for a complainant member is now contained in s. 109(2) of TULRCA 1992. A complainant can be assisted where there has been an actual or threatened breach of union rules in relation to one of the matters listed in s. 109(2). Regard should be had to 1.2.5 above for the powers of the Commissioner generally.

4.2 STATUTORY RIGHTS

4.2.1 Introduction

The rights given to modern trade union members were expanded progressively during the 1980s (as has been discussed in Chapter 1) and commonly provide for redress to an individual member where that member personally suffers as a result of a union's unlawful action. The following individual rights are now available under statute:

(a) not to be unjustifiably expelled from the union;
(b) not to be unjustifiably disciplined;
(c) to a ballot prior to the taking of industrial action;
(d) to vote on the existence of a union political fund;
(e) to abstain from contributions to the union political fund;
(f) to inspect union accounts;
(g) to have regular elections for union officials;
(h) to stand as a candidate for union office; and
(i) to prevent unlawful use of union property.

4.2.2 The right not to be unjustifiably excluded or expelled from a trade union

4.2.2.1 Introduction
The right of a member not to be expelled or excluded from a trade union greatly cuts back the concept of freedom of association. It is, however, a long-standing in-road into the freedom of trade unions to manage their own affairs. A right not to be unreasonably excluded from membership has been available to trade union members in one form or another since the Industrial Relations Act 1971, apart from a short period between 1976 and 1980 when the Trade Union and Labour Relations

(Amendment) Act 1976 removed the right. It was reintroduced by the reforms of the Employment Act 1980. The right, while doubtless still important to aggrieved individual members, is of less utility today than in the days when the closed shop operated and denial of membership could amount to unemployment.

The old-style right focused upon the reasonableness of the action on the part of a trade union in excluding a member. This was replaced by s. 14 of TURERA 1993, which introduced new substantive provisions in the form of ss. 174–177, TULRCA 1992. The right in its modified form cuts back the effect of the old Bridlington Principles, which allowed the TUC's Disputes Committee to recommend that a union member be expelled from a union in a case where rival unions were in dispute over the membership of the member (see *Cheall* v *APEX* [1983] IRLR 215 for an example of the operation of the old-style Bridlington Principles). Following the introduction of s. 14 of TURERA 1993, the Bridlington Principles were revised and it is now no longer possible for the Disputes Committee to recommend expulsion of a member.

The net effect of the new provisions is that a trade union now has no automatic right to deny membership or expel members, notwithstanding contrary provisions in a union rule book (for a fuller discussion of the common law impact upon the union rule book, see above at 4.1.2 *et seq*.). There are, however, a number of cases in which it is still possible to deny membership by exclusion or expulsion.

4.2.2.2   The right not to be excluded or expelled

Section 174(1) of TULRCA 1992 sets up the right not to be excluded or expelled from a trade union unless the exclusion or expulsion is permitted by s. 174(2), which provides a closed category of permitted circumstances. These are where:

(a)   a member does not satisfy, or no longer satisfies an enforceable membership requirement under a union's rules. An enforceable membership requirement is further defined in s. 174(3) (again by means of a closed class of cases), these being restrictions on membership by virtue of any or all of employment in a particular trade, industry or profession; an occupational description (including grade, level or category of appointment); and/or possession of specialist skills or qualifications;

(b)   a member no longer qualifies for membership as a result of having moved out of a particular geographical boundary relevant for trade union membership;

(c)   a union regulates the affairs of members with one particular employer or group of employers and a member ceases to work for that employer or group of employers; and

(d)   the exclusion or expulsion is entirely due to a member's conduct. Again, as with unjustifiable disciplining of trade union members (see below at 4.2.3), it was thought necessary to restrict the concept of what amounts to conduct. Conduct is therefore defined by s. 174(4) of TULRCA 1992. To the extent that a union can show that a member's conduct falls foul of union rules and outwith the excluded categories under TULRCA 1992, the common law construction of the rule book will be the only available help to a member (see above at 4.1.2.2).

Conduct is inadmissible if it is conduct relating to a member being or ceasing to be, or having been or having ceased to be either a member of a trade union, or an employee of a particular employer or at a particular place, or a member of a political party (s. 174(4)(a)). Conduct to which s. 65 of TULRCA 1992 applies cannot be used by a union to justify exclusion or expulsion (this being essentially the individual acting in his own interest rather than in the collective interest of the union (s. 174(4)(b))).

Conduct is further defined in s. 177(1)(b) as including any statements, acts or omissions on the part of an employee.

Exclusion and expulsion are also partly defined in s. 177(2)(a) and (b) of TULRCA 1992. The former subsection deals with exclusions and covers the situation where the member is not informed one way or the other as to whether he is to be granted membership, but there has been such an inordinate delay that this would reasonably appear to amount to an exclusion. This is deemed to be an exclusion.

While the Act has provided this partial definition of exclusion, the EAT has recently interpreted the definition in *NACODS* v *Gluchowshi* [1996] IRLR 252. Here, the respondent had been suspended from the privileges of membership of the appellant union following his appointment to the post of director of a company run by a branch of the union as an employment agency. The suspension was to last until such time as the company met various union requirements. In the meantime, the respondent had continued to pay subscriptions to the appellant union and issued proceedings in the industrial tribunal claiming that his suspension amounted to an exclusion from the benefits of the union. The industrial tribunal agreed that the definition of exclusion was wide enough to cover a suspension from membership benefits. However, on appeal, the EAT held that this was not so. The member had only to comply with the requirements of the union and he would be restored to his full rights.

As to the provision in s. 177(2)(b), an expulsion includes an automatic termination of membership upon the occurrence of some condition subsequent in a union's rules which a member has triggered.

To the extent that a union has unlawfully excluded or expelled an individual, the individual has an initial right of complaint to an industrial tribunal under s. 174(5).

4.2.2.3 *Procedure and remedies*

An applicant must lodge a complaint within six months of exclusion or expulsion, or within such other extended period as a tribunal considers reasonable in all the circumstances (s. 175)). If a tribunal finds a complaint proved, it must make a declaration to that effect (s. 176(1)). Thereafter, much will turn upon a union's reaction to the finding by the tribunal.

A complainant cannot take further steps in pursuing his remedy for a period of four weeks after the initial declaration has been made by the tribunal. This period is to allow a union to review its action and, ideally, to revoke it.

If a union is not minded to revoke an exclusion or expulsion, the applicant can press forward to a compensation hearing to be heard by the EAT (s. 176(2)). The EAT can make such award of compensation as it thinks just and equitable in all the circumstances of the case up to the maximum of the basic and compensatory awards for unfair dismissal provided under the Employment Rights Act 1996 (ss. 176(4) and (6)), currently £18,600. Further, the EAT is required to provide a minimum award to an applicant of £5,000 (s. 176(6)).

In the case of a union revoking exclusion or expulsion, a compensation hearing is referred to an industrial tribunal (s. 176(2)). Industrial tribunals can make an award of such compensation as they think just and equitable up to the same maximum amount (s. 176(4) and (6)). An industrial tribunal cannot make a minimum basic award though. It should be noted that both the EAT and an industrial tribunal can make such deduction as they fit on the basis of an applicant's contributory fault (s. 176(5)).

As to whether it is possible to be compensated for injury to feelings as a result of expulsion, regard should be had to *Bradley* v *NALGO* [1991] IRLR 159, where the EAT held that such an award could be made but would be modest and only possible in cases where the sole cause of the injury to feelings was the expulsion itself and not some other cause.

Lastly, two points should be noted. First, the statutory right is expressly declared to be in addition to any pre-existing rights that an applicant may have to challenge a union's action under the common law (s. 177(5)) (see 4.1.2 *et seq.* above). Secondly, neither industrial tribunals nor the EAT have power to order a union's unlawful action to be rescinded. This is unlike the common law position which can achieve rescission of action through an injunction preventing breach or purported breach of the contract of membership (see 4.1.3.3 above).

4.2.3   The right not to be unjustifiably disciplined

4.2.3.1   Introduction
The right for a member not to be unjustifiably disciplined was one of the more controversial rights introduced by the 1980s reforms. It was originally introduced under s. 3 of the Employment Act 1988 and has been condemned for undermining the collective position of organised labour by giving individual members a right not to strike if they so choose, notwithstanding a properly conducted strike ballot. To this end, it has been labeled a 'scabs' charter' (see McKendrick, E., 'The Rights of Trade Union Members — Part I of the Employment Act 1988' (1988) 17 ILJ 141 at pp. 149–150).

The name of the right is somewhat misleading, in that there is no need for an objective decision as to whether disciplinary action taken by a union is reasonable. Instead, regard is simply had as to whether action falls within an exhaustive list of automatically unjustifiable reasons for disciplining a member. The right is now contained within s. 64 of TULRCA 1992.

4.2.3.2 *Discipline*

Discipline for the purposes of the 1992 Act will amount to any of the following matters done or purportedly done, and which are set out in s. 64(2):

(a) expulsion from a union, or a branch or section of the union;

(b) a requirement to pay a sum of money to a union, branch or section of a union or to any other person;

(c) the treating as unpaid or as paid for a different purpose of any sum of money paid by a member to a union in respect of any union subscription or obligation;

(d) the deprivation or denial of access to any union benefit, service or facility which would otherwise be available to a member as a result of membership of a union, or a branch or section of the union;

(e) a recommendation to another union, or section or branch of a union that a member should not be granted membership; or

(f) the subjection of a member to any other detriment.

As to what amounts to a detriment, this is not defined by the statute and therefore falls to be resolved on a case by case basis. In *NALGO* v *Killorn and Simm* [1990] IRLR 464, a member of the appellant union was named in a list published by the union as a strike breaker so as to cause the member embarrassment. This was held by the EAT to be a detriment to the respondent.

4.2.3.3 *Unjustifiable discipline*

Unjustifiable discipline is defined exclusively in s. 65(1), (2) and (4) of TULRCA 1992. The list was extended by s. 16 of TURERA 1993 and now extends to cover any conduct or preparation towards such conduct contained within s. 65(2) or matters which are believed by a union to amount to conduct within that section on the part of a member. Any of the following types of conduct cannot now be the subject of discipline by a union:

(a) failure to participate in or support a strike or other industrial action, or an indication of a lack of support or opposition to such action whether the action is taken by the member's union or another one;

(b) failure by a complainant to contravene some requirement under a contract of employment for a purpose connected with a strike or industrial action;

(c) an assertion by a member, whether or not it is done through legal proceedings or otherwise, that a union, an official or representative of it or any trustee of union property has contravened, or is proposing or likely to contravene some rule of the union, enactment or other rule of law;

(d) encouraging or assisting other employees to either carry out lawfully imposed obligations under their contracts of employment or to make the type of claims listed in (c) above;

(e) contravening a requirement imposed by or as a result of a determination which infringes an individual's right not to be disciplined;

(f)   failing to allow an employer to deduct from the member's wages such sums as would represent an individual's subscriptions to a union pursuant to an agreement between a union and an employer for the employer to deduct the sums;

(g)   resigning or proposing to resign from a union or another union, or joining or proposing to join another union or refusing to join another union or being a member of another union;

(h)   working with, or proposing to work or not work with members of another union;

(i)   working for, or proposing to work for an employer who employs or has employed individuals who are not members of an individual's own union or union members of another union;

(j)   making a union do some act which it is required to do on a ballot of members by virtue of TULRCA 1992.

As to what amounts to 'other industrial action' in para. (a), some guidance was given by the EAT in *Fire Brigade* v *Knowles* [1996] IRLR 337. Here, two full-time firemen accepted additional part-time employment as retained part-time fire fighters. They were subsequently expelled by their union for contravening union policy on such posts. The officers claimed that the union policy amounted to industrial action but the EAT found otherwise. Keene J stated (at p. 340):

Not all things which seek to put pressure on an employer will automatically and *ipso facto* amount to industrial action, even though the employer may feel himself inhibited as a result of the pressure. The lay members of this appeal tribunal emphasise that if the industrial tribunal's approach were correct, it would lead to many negotiating sessions between employers and unions amounting to 'other industrial action', because those negotiations regularly involve the application of pressure on employers by the union side threatening to take strike action or some other form of action and the employers' freedom of action is often constrained by the knowledge of such threats.

The decision of the EAT was subsequently upheld by the Court of Appeal (at [1996] IRLR 617).

It should be noted that if a member makes any false allegation against a union or persuades another person to do so, and as a result thereof the union takes disciplinary action against the member, that action by the union is justifiable under s. 65(6).

To the extent that a member feels that he has been unjustifiably disciplined, a right of complaint lies to an industrial tribunal provided that a complaint is lodged within three months, or within such other period as the tribunal thinks reasonable in all the circumstances (s. 66(1) and (2)).

If the act of discipline lies in expelling the member, it should be noted that the remedy that must be pursued is found under s. 174 of TULRCA 1992 (the right not to be excluded or expelled from a trade union) and not under the head of unjustifiable discipline (s. 66(4) — see 4.2.2 *et seq.* above).

4.2.3.4 *Remedies for a successful complaint*
If a tribunal finds that a complaint is well-founded, it is required to make a declaration to this effect (s. 66(3)). Much will then turn upon how a union reacts to the declaration. Section 67 goes on to provide a further remedy in the form of compensation for a complainant. The hearing for a compensation award cannot be entertained until the passing of a four-week period beginning with the date of the declaration by an industrial tribunal. Further, a hearing for compensation must be sought within six months from the date of the declaration (s. 67(3)).

During the four-week period, a union is implicitly required to think about how much it wants to punish a member. If a union fails to retract disciplinary action, a compensation hearing will be heard by the EAT (s. 67(2)). The EAT can award such compensation as it thinks is just and equitable in all the circumstances of a case, subject to a statutory maximum of the total of the basic and compensatory awards for unfair dismissal, currently £18,600 (s. 67(5) and (8)). However, it must impose a minimum award of at least £5,000 (s. 67(8) and s. 176(6)).

The alternative is for a union to quash the action taken against a member within the required four-week period. Where this happens a compensation hearing will be heard by an industrial tribunal (s. 67(2)). Industrial tribunals can award to complainants such sums as they consider just and equitable in all the circumstances of a case, again being limited to the maximum of the aggregate of the basic and statutory awards (s. 67(5) and (8)). No minimum basic award can be made in such a case and the award to a complainant could therefore be nil.

Again, as with expulsion or exclusion from a union, it may be possible to award compensation for injury to feelings (see 4.2.2.3 above).

To the extent that an industrial tribunal finds that a complainant caused or contributed to disciplinary action taken by the union of which he is a member, it can reduce an award by such sum as it thinks is just and equitable (s. 67(7)).

Lastly, it should be noted that there is no power for tribunals to order that discipline taken by a union be revoked. Regard should be had to the common law methods of enforcement at 4.1.3 above.

4.2.4 The right to a ballot before industrial action

4.2.4.1 *Introduction*
The duty of a trade union to hold a ballot prior to taking industrial action will be examined in greater detail below at 7.4.2. The right of an individual union member to challenge the legality of industrial action taken or proposed to be taken by the union of which he is a member was not available until the advent of the Employment Act 1988. That right is now provided by s. 62 of TULRCA 1992.

4.2.4.2   Unlawful action

For the purpose of s. 62, industrial action will be unlawful where it is taken by a union without the support of a properly conducted ballot of union members, or where such action is taken in spite of a ballot which has resolved not to take industrial action of the type complained of (s. 62(2)).

Action will be deemed to have been taken by a union where either a union has taken the action itself, or a union is vicariously liable for the acts of any of the types of persons listed in s. 20(2) of TULRCA 1992.

A member of a union may present a complaint to the High Court that the union of which he is a member has or is likely to take action to induce members of his union (including the complainant) to take industrial action which does not have the support of a ballot (s. 62(1)). If the court finds the complaint substantiated, it may take such measures as it thinks fit under s. 62(3) to ensure that:

(a)   there is no, or no further inducement to take part in or continue the industrial action; and

(b)   no member of the union takes industrial action after the order as a result of having been induced before the order.

It is also possible for the court to grant an interlocutory injunction if it thinks necessary under s. 62(4). Under s. 109 of TULRCA 1992, it is possible to obtain assistance from the CROTUM in order to bring the proceedings.

4.2.5   The right not to suffer deductions of union subscriptions

4.2.5.1   Introduction

Deduction of union subscriptions is known as 'check off' where it is carried out by an employer. At common law, it has always been necessary for a worker to consent to the deduction at source. This could take place either through a collective agreement being incorporated into a worker's contract, or by the worker agreeing to the deduction as a term of his contract employment (see *Williams* v *Butlers Limited* [1974] IRLR 253, [1975] IRLR 120 to this end). If workers consent in writing to such deduction, no claims can arise under Pt II of the Employment Rights Act 1996 in respect of unlawful deduction of wages.

While it might initially seem that an employer derives no benefit (other than the maintenance of good industrial relations) from entering into such an arrangement, he actually receives a threefold benefit. First, an employer does not suffer 'down time' as a result of the inevitable dialogue that would occur if union representatives were to collect individual subscriptions. Secondly, an employer is able to keep an informal eye on the number of union members within the workforce. Lastly, if check off takes place, unions have reduced opportunity for contact with members. Consequently, employers have historically been happy to implement check off procedures.

The statutory position relating to deductions is contained in s. 68 of TULRCA 1992, albeit that it is now in substantially modified form from when it was originally enacted.

4.2.5.2   The right

Under s. 68 of TULRCA 1992, union members have to provide authorisation to their employers for check off deductions to take place. Under s. 68(1), an employer is not allowed to make a deduction of union subscriptions unless he has authorisation in writing from a member allowing a deduction and stating the amount of the deduction that can be made. Changes were made by TURERA 1993 which provided that unions members had to renew the authorisation every three years (s. 68(3)) and that employers had to give one month's notice to workers of any increase in subscriptions (s. 68(5)).

The reform was unpopular with unions and employers. It led to unions moving to deduction of subscriptions from members' bank accounts by means of direct debits. A proposal was put forward in the White Paper 'Fairness at Work' to amend the three-yearly renewal and notice-giving provisions. The Government has now implemented the White Paper proposal to reform the law relating to 'check-off' arrangements under s. 1 of the Deregulation and Contracting Out Act 1994 by passing the Deregulation (Deduction from Pay of Union Subscriptions) Order 1998. This provision removes the need for workers who are union members to have to confirm every three years that union-related deductions can still be made from salary. It also removes the need for employers to notify such workers one month in advance that an increase in deductions is to be made.

4.2.5.3   Remedy for unlawful deduction

In the event that an employer makes an unlawful check off deduction from a worker's wages, the worker can make a complaint to an industrial tribunal (s. 68A(1)). The complaint must be made within three months of the wrongful deduction or within such other period as the tribunal considers is reasonable.

If a tribunal finds a case to be well-founded it must make a declaration to that effect, and must also make an order for the employer to repay the amount of the unlawful deduction (s. 68A(2)).

The right is available in addition to any other rights for breach of contract, the right not to suffer unlawful deductions from wages (Pt II, Employment Rights Act 1996) or to not suffer deductions in respect of political contributions (s. 68A(3)–(4)).

4.2.6   Voting on the existence of the political fund

It has been lawful for a trade union to have a political fund since the Trade Union Act 1913. This Act overturned the House of Lords decision in *ASRS* v *Osbourne* [1910] AC 87, which held that the use of funds for political purposes was *ultra vires* the statutory objects of a trade union under the Trade Union Acts 1871–1876. When the

Trade Union Act 1984 was enacted, it sought to curb the ability of unions to have a political fund as of right on the basis that the existence and use of such funds were not necessarily representative of the wishes of the union members. The Act therefore introduced an initial ballot for the establishment of new political funds and periodic balloting for the continued existence of such funds and funds which existed at the date of enactment of the Act.

4.2.6.1   Political objects

The starting point in relation to political funds is s. 71 of TULRCA 1992, which imposes a prohibition on the use of union funds for political objects unless a political resolution has been passed by a union. Furthermore, under s. 71(1)(b) a union must draw up rules approved by the Certification Officer. Such rules must deal with the issues of the creation of a separate political fund and the ability of members to contract out of the payment into the fund if they so choose. The prohibition is widely drafted under s. 71(2) and would catch the transfer of funds to another union which had passed a political fund resolution for that other union, which would then use those funds for political ends.

Political objects are broadly defined in s. 72(1) of the 1992 Act. The definition covers expenditure on such matters as:

(a)   contributions or payments directly or indirectly made to political parties;

(b)   the provision of services or property for a political party;

(c)   the registration of electors or the candidature of any person, the selection of candidates or the holding of a ballot by the union in connection with the election of any person to a political office;

(d)   the maintenance of the holder of any political office;

(e)   the holding of any conference or meeting the main purpose of which is the transaction of business in connection with a political party; or

(f)   the production, publication or distribution of any literature, document, film, sound recording or advertisement, the main purpose of which is to persuade people to vote or not to vote for a particular political party or candidate.

Section 72(2) adds to the definition by providing that if a person attends a political conference or meeting as a delegate or otherwise as a participant, any expenditure that he incurs is deemed to be expenditure for political purposes.

Of particular importance to s. 72(1) is the extension to it provided in (f) above. If a union uses the media to highlight the need for its members' jobs, it will be outside the ambit of (f) above and expenditure can come from general union funds. However, if a union strays into the realms of seeking to influence voters in political elections, such advertisements must be paid for by the political fund. Cases on the construction of this point have been limited to but one notable exception, that being *Paul and Frazer* v *NALGO* [1987] IRLR 413. Here, the defendant union had no political fund and the plaintiffs sought to challenge the use of general union funds by the defendant for a campaign entitled 'Make People Matter'. The campaign sought to focus public attention on the treatment of public sector employees by the Conservative Government. No other government or political party was referred to in the advertisements. The defendant advanced the argument that, since the advertisements bore a disclaimer to the effect that the union was not trying to influence voters, the advertisements did not amount to a political object of the union. Browne-Wilkinson V-C took a realistic view of the situation. The advertising campaign took place immediately prior to local and general elections. To the extent that the Government had been decried in the advertisements, and to the extent that no other political party had been targeted in the campaign, then, despite the disclaimer, the effect would be to put a message to the public that the Government should not be voted for, and therefore the campaign was in reality a political one. Having said this, Browne-Wilkinson V-C concluded that if the campaign had taken place at a time when there were no elections happening, it could not have influenced voters to vote or not vote for a person or party and would not fall within s. 72(1)(f).

4.2.6.2 The political fund resolution

A political fund resolution needs to be passed under s. 73(1) of TULRCA 1992 in order to approve a political fund. Every trade union must have a fresh ballot at least once every ten years in order to maintain the political fund. If such a ballot is not held, then under s. 73(3), the previous resolution ceases to have effect on the tenth anniversary of the date of the last ballot.

If a ballot is held and a simple majority of those voting on the resolution approve it, the resolution is passed and takes effect as a substantive rule of a union and can be rescinded under a union's constitution in the same way as any other union rule (s. 73(2)). Upon the passing of a new political fund resolution, the old resolution automatically ceases to have effect. If, however, the ballot does not pass the resolution, the old resolution continues after the ballot for a further period of two weeks (s. 73(4)).

4.2.6.3 The political fund

The main rules in relation to a political fund are contained in ss. 82–83 of TULRCA 1992. By s. 82, union rules must provide for:

(a) payment for political objects out of a separate political fund;

(b) exemption from paying into the fund by those members who give notice in accordance with s. 84;

(c) non-exclusion from any union right or benefit for those members who exempt themselves from paying into a political fund; and

(d) not making contributions to a political fund a condition precedent to joining a union.

A union member who claims that he is aggrieved by a breach of the rules may complain to the Certification Officer who may make such order as he thinks is necessary to remedy any breach (ss. 82(2) and (3)).

If a union is able to create a political fund, ss. 83(1) and (2) deal with the assets of the fund. It must be a wholly independent fund which is not contingent upon any other source other than contributing members' subscriptions to the fund and other property that accrues to the fund in the course of administering the assets of the fund (interest on the capital of the fund, etc.). Further, where a political resolution is not renewed, members cannot be required to contribute to the assets of the fund.

If a union incurs liabilities as a result of its political objects, the only assets available to meet such liabilities will be the assets of the political fund (s. 83(3)). This will apply notwithstanding the fact that the liability has been contractually incurred on the basis that general union funds will be available to satisfy the liability, or that a charge has been granted over any other union asset. It is possible to recover assets improperly applied from other union funds under s. 16 of TULRCA 1992.

4.2.6.4   Voting on the resolution

Under s. 76 of TULRCA 1992, save for overseas members of the union (s. 94(1)), every member of the union is entitled to have an equal vote at the ballot for a political resolution.

A union is required to submit to, and have approved by, the Certification Officer a set of rules for the purpose of a political resolution ballot (s. 74(1)). Under s. 74(2), rules must be submitted afresh on each and every occasion that a ballot is held notwithstanding the fact that previous sets of rules have passed the Certification Officer's scrutiny. Prior to holding a ballot, s. 75 requires that a union must appoint a suitably qualified independent scrutineer which it believes to be competent and independent to oversee the whole voting process. The Secretary of State may from time to time make orders laying down the necessary qualifications for the scrutineer. In particular, regard should be had to the Trade Union Ballots and Elections (Independent Scrutineer Qualifications) Order 1988 (SI 1988 No. 2117 as amended by SI 1989 No. 31). The scrutineer's terms of appointment will include, *inter alia*, all the matters contained within s. 75(3) of TULRCA 1992 (as amended by TURERA 1993) together with any such other terms of appointment as a union may specify. This will make the scrutineer responsible for:

(a)   supervising the production, distribution and return of ballot papers;

(b)   inspecting the register of names and addresses of union members to ensure that is accurate and up-to-date. It should be noted that a member can request a scrutineer to carry out this task if the member believes that the register is out of date (s. 75(3A)).Unions are bound to comply with any request of a scrutineer to produce the register of names and allow him to inspect the same, irrespective of the format of the register (e.g., computerised or hard copy);

(c)   taking such preliminary steps as are necessary to compile a statutory report on the conduct of a ballot; and

(d)   retaining custody of voting papers and a copy of the register of members' names for a period of one year beginning on the day that the result is published.

After the result of a ballot is known a scrutineer is responsible for preparing a report (s. 78). This must state:

(a)   the number of voting papers distributed and returned to the scrutineer, together with the number of spoiled and valid votes cast;
(b)   the name of the independent person who counted the votes;
(c)   whether or not the scrutineer was satisfied that the preparation, storage, distribution and return of the ballot papers and the vote itself were carried out fairly and without contravention of any statute, and whether the scrutineer believes that he was allowed to carry out his task without interference; and
(d)   whether the scrutineer has inspected or asked to inspect the register of members' names, and whether he did so himself or was asked to do so as a result of a member's request under s. 49(3A); and, in the latter case, he must state whether or not he declined the request. If he did inspect the register he must state whether or not he believed the same to be a fair reflection of the membership of the union at the time he inspected it. (s. 78(2A)).

The vote itself is dealt with under s. 77 of TULRCA 1992. The method of voting is by a voting paper marked by a voter (s. 77(1)). Voting papers must state the name of a scrutineer on them and the date and address for return of the papers, together with an individual number from a block of consecutive whole numbers (s. 77(2)).

Voters must be able to vote without interference from any union official, member or employee and must be free to vote, as far as is reasonably practicable, without cost to the member. A ballot should be, as far as is reasonably practicable, a postal ballot, thus helping to ensure that it is secret (s. 77(3)and(4)).

Another feature of the legislation is that the counting of the ballot is undertaken by independent persons. To this end, s. 77A(1) and (2) require that unions ensure that they engage either a scrutineer or some other person whom they believe to be both competent and independent to store, distribute and count ballot papers. If the person appointed is not the scrutineer in a ballot, then it will be necessary to ensure that the person who counts the papers returns them to the scrutineer as soon as possible after the result of the ballot (s. 77A(5)).

4.2.6.5   *Remedy for failure to comply with the balloting process*
If a union fails to comply with the requirements of its balloting rules, or fails to uphold the result, then s. 79 of TULRCA 1992 allows a member to apply to either the Certification Officer (s. 80) or the High Court (s. 81) for a declaration that the union has failed to comply either with the balloting rules or with the result of the ballot as the case may be. In the case of a High Court declaration, it is also possible for the court to impose an enforcement order in such terms as it thinks fit in all the circumstances to remedy any defect (s. 81(4)).

In either case, under s. 79(3), an application must be made within one year of the ballot result being published. While the Certification Officer is not able to grant an enforcement order, an application under s. 80 does potentially have the advantage of being cost-free to an applicant. However, it should be noted that under s. 109 of TULRCA 1992 an individual member can receive legal assistance, to whatever degree is thought fit, from the CROTUM (see above at 1.2.5 with regard to the Commissioner generally).

4.2.6.6   Unspent surplus following the rejection of a political resolution
To the extent that a political ballot is resolved against the retention of a political fund, the union concerned has three options with regard to any surplus that may still remain in the fund. First, the union may carry on using the fund for political purposes for a six-month period beginning with the day on which the ballot was held. It can use this six-month period to run down the fund if it so chooses. It cannot, however, use the running down provision to incur a deficit or increase one if one already exists (s. 89(2)). Alternatively, a union has the option of transferring the remainder of the political fund to general union funds and using them for the purpose of the particular fund or funds into which they are subsequently transferred (s. 89(4)). Lastly, a union can keep the surplus frozen pending a re-ballot at some point in the future, but must ensure that no additions accrue to the fund save to the extent that they are caused as a result of normal investment activity, e.g., by way of interest or as a result of contributions that were actually collected prior to the ballot (s. 89(3)).

If a union attempts to carry on collecting subscriptions from a member, or otherwise acts other than in the manner shown above, an individual member has the right to apply to the court for a declaration as to the union's unlawful activity (s. 90(4)). If the case is found for the applicant, the court can, if it thinks it necessary to ensure that additions to the fund are stopped, make an order to that effect (s. 90(5)). It should be noted that there is no right of assistance from the CROTUM in respect of this matter.

4.2.7   Abstention for members from contributions to union political fund

4.2.7.1   Introduction
It has been lawful for a union member to contract out of paying to the union political fund since the Trade Union Act 1913. The scheme of the 1913 Act was kept substantially in place until being replaced by the Trade Union Act 1984, which is now incorporated in TULRCA 1992, Pt I, Ch. VI. The 1992 Act works on a contracting-out basis instead of those wishing to contribute to union funds being required to contract in. The TUC gave undertakings to the Government upon the implementation of the 1984 reforms to ensure that the contracting-out system was operated fairly. The necessity for these undertakings lies in the apathy to contracting out by union members who are bound by a political resolution where the use of the political funds might not necessarily accord with the beliefs of individual members

(see research to this end, Ewing, K., 'Trade union political funds: the 1913 Act revisited' (1984) 13 ILJ 227).

4.2.7.2 Substantive provisions

The main provisions under Pt I of TULRCA 1992 are to be found in ss. 84–88. Section 84(1) provides for a model form that members can use to give notice to the union of their objection to making payments to the union political fund. The form is only a model, and provided that the content is substantially the same, minor variations in individual cases will not matter. As a bare minimum, the form should contain a statement as to a member's unwillingness to pay into the political fund and the fact that the member is therefore exempt from payment into it. It should be noted that if a union has passed a new political resolution then it is required to give notice in an appropriate form to its members advising that members can contract out of contributing to the political fund, and also of the place at which a contracting out form can be obtained (this being the head office of a union, any of its branch offices or directly from the Certification Officer: s. 82(2)).

Section 84(3) specifies that the manner in which the notice is to be given to members shall be in accordance with the rules of the union as approved by the Certification Officer. Further, it goes on to state that the Certification Officer is to have regard to the existing character and status of the union on a case-by-case basis in approving the draft rules submitted.

The consequences of giving an exemption notice are that after a new political resolution has been adopted by a union, a member will be exempt from contributions from the date on which the resolution was passed, provided that he gives his notice within one month of the date of passing of the resolution (s. 84(4)(a)). If, however, a member takes longer than one month to notify his union, or notifies the union during the currency of an existing political resolution, then under s. 84(4)(b), the member will become exempt only as from 1 January in the year following the notice. In all cases, under s. 84(5), the exemption, once given and binding, will continue in force until it is withdrawn by the member.

Under s. 85 of TULRCA 1992, the exemption from contributions is all-embracing. It therefore does not matter that a union chooses to have a separate political fund levy from members, or deducts a fractional contribution from the general union subscription that each member pays. If the latter method is used, a member will be entitled to a reduced subscription to the extent of the political fund fraction of the subscription. The union rules are required to take this into account and must also, so far as is practical, show exempt members the fraction of general subscription that is put towards the political fund (s. 85(2)(b)).

4.2.7.3 Effect of contracting out upon employers

Section 86 of TULRCA 1992 applies to employers in relation to contracting out. Employers are bound by the contracting-out provisions to the extent that they are responsible for collecting political fund subscriptions either as a separate levy, or rolled up in a general union subscription. If a member wishes to contract out of a political fund, the member is required to certify in writing to his employer that he is exempt from the political fund levy and has notified his union in writing of this fact. Once this certification is provided, an employer is bound from the first day of notice (s. 86(2)).

Furthermore, an employer is not entitled to refuse to deduct any contributions from exempt members, as might occur, for example, as a result of the increased administration cost of treating contributing and non-contributing members differently. Section 86(3) effectively provides that deductions are to be an across-the-board event for all union members and, to the extent that they occur, should be correct in law for each member. This may well pose a problem to a union, since an employer would have the option of refusing to make deductions across-the-board and thereby pass the administration of deductions back to the union.

4.2.7.4   Remedy for unlawful contributions/failure to deduct

If an employer does not comply with the above requirements, individual members have a means of redress. Recovery of the exempt amount is a two-stage process and requires an aggrieved member to lodge a claim in the county court in the first instance so as to obtain a declaration that his employer has unlawfully deducted the exempt amount (ss. 87(1) and (2)). The court can also make such order as is necessary to prevent future breaches by an employer with which the employer must comply within the period specified by the order (s. 87(3)). Once a member has obtained a declaration, he may then seek to enforce recovery of the overpayment under Pt II of the Employment Rights Act 1996. Under s. 88(3) of the 1992 Act, the obtaining of a declaration is a prerequisite to the presentation of a claim under s. 23(1) of the 1996 Act.

Under s. 23(2) of the 1996 Act, the claim must be presented within the usual three-month limitation period. However, the starting point for the limitation period is the date of the county court declaration instead of the date of the last deduction as is usually the case for Pt II claims. Regard should be had to s. 88(4) of TULRCA 1992.

4.2.8   Inspection of union accounts

4.2.8.1   Introduction

A union member has wide powers to inspect the accounts of his or her trade union. The powers were increased as a result of the miners' strike of 1984–1985. This strike highlighted the inadequacies of the old accounting regime under which unions operated, which did not require proper records of assets and liabilities to be maintained. The rights are set out in TULRCA 1992, Pt I, Ch. III.

4.2.8.2   The duty to keep proper accounting records

The duty is laid down by s. 28(1) of TULRCA 1992 and requires unions to keep proper records of both assets and liabilities. Unions are also required to establish a satisfactory system of controlling accounting records, cash holdings, receipts and remittances. Records must be kept for a period of six years (s. 29(1)).

The duty to keep proper accounts is compounded by s. 32 which requires an annual return dealing with the matters set out in s. 32(3) to be filed with the Certification Officer by 1 June in the calendar year following that to which it relates (s. 32(2)). A union's annual return is available from the union to members of the public free of charge (s. 32(5)). The Certification Officer is also required to keep copies of all annual returns lodged with him, and these can be inspected by members of the public at all reasonable hours either free or on payment of a reasonable charge (s. 32(6)).

Unions are also required to provide members with a statement of the content of a return within eight weeks from the date upon which an annual return was sent to the Certification Officer (s. 32A(1)). The statement is to be either an individual statement to each member, or is to be distributed in any other way that a union commonly uses to bring matters of general interest to the attention of its members (s. 32A(2)). The statement is to deal with the matters referred to in s. 32A(3)–(5), these being:

(a)   the total income and expenditure of a union during the year;

(b)   how much of the income relates to membership subscriptions;

(c)   the total income and expenditure of any political fund;

(d)   the income received by the president, general secretary and each committee member of the union;

(e)   the report made by the auditors of the union together with their names and addresses;

(f)   any other matter that a union thinks is of importance in helping its members to reach a balanced view of a union's financial affairs; and

(g)   a statement in the form set out in s. 32A(6) advising union members that they can take up irregularities in a return with any of the union, its officials, trustees, auditors, the Certification Officer or the police. The statement should also advise members that they may receive help from the CROTUM. The Certification Officer is also required to be sent a copy of any such statement and required to make a copy of such a statement available free of charge to a union member for the period of two years after delivery (s. 32A(7)–(9)).

Unions are also required to appoint auditors under s. 33 of TULRCA 1992 and the auditors are required to report each year on the annual return (s. 36). Auditors are granted the rights of inspection set down in s. 37, those being the rights of access to records and explanations from officers of a union, and the right to attend any general meeting of a union and be heard at such a meeting.

Provisions also establish who is eligible for appointment to the post of auditor (s. 34) and for appointment to and removal from the post of auditor (s. 35).

4.2.8.3   The right of inspection

Section 30 of the 1992 Act creates a right for a union member to have access to the accounting records of his union. A former union member will also be able to take advantage of the right, in that such a person is able to inspect the records for any period when he was a member (s. 30(1)). Where a union member makes a request to inspect accounts, the union must, within 28 days from the day on which that request was made, allow the member access to the accounts. Further, the union must allow the member the right to have an accountant present if he so wishes, and allow the member to take away copies of the accounts (s. 30(2)). The right of an accountant to be present can be refused if the accountant has refused to enter into any reasonable request for confidentiality that the union may require (s. 30(5)). A union is allowed to make a reasonable administrative charge for the granting of access to records and providing copies of records. However, unions must explain to requesting members the principles upon which the charge is to be made (s. 30(6)).

4.2.8.4   Enforcement of the right
If a union fails to comply with a valid request by a member to inspect there will be two consequences. First, it will allow the member to apply to the High Court. The court can then make such order as it considers appropriate with regard to providing access to the records, and can allow an accountant to accompany the member if necessary. The court can also allow a member to take copies of or extracts from the records (s. 31(1) and (2)).

Secondly, the refusal of a valid request to inspect records is criminal offence (see 10.2.2 below) and may be dealt with as such.

4.2.8.5   Financial investigations by the Certification Officer
The Certification Officer is empowered to require unions to produce documents and may appoint inspectors from his staff to investigate the financial affairs of a union. The powers were introduced by TURERA 1993 and exist now in the form of ss. 37A–37E of TULRCA 1992.

4.2.8.5.1   Production of documents
The power of the Certification Officer to call for the production of relevant documents is contained within s. 37A of TULRCA 1992. Relevant documents are those documents relating to the financial affairs or accounts of a union (s. 37A(6)).

The power allows the Certification Officer to call for documents to be produced if he thinks that there is good cause (s. 37A(1) — see also s. 37E(1) in relation to the duty to consider the exercise of the power where an auditor does not certify the accounts to be true and fair, or where an auditor has been hindered in carrying out his functions). The power extends to production by a union, a branch or a section of a union. The order to produce should specify the documents to be produced and a time and a place for production (s. 37A(1)). There is also a power for the Certification Officer to authorise members of his staff to attend at a union and require immediate production of relevant documents on evidence of authority (s. 37A(2)). Any such production takes place without prejudice to any lien that is asserted over a relevant document (s. 37A(4)). Production includes taking copies of or extracts from documents. A person is not allowed to refuse to produce documents on the grounds that production would tend to expose the person to the risk of criminal proceedings (s. 37A(7)). This said, any such statement by a person as to this likelihood cannot be used in evidence against the maker of the statement unless in the course of a criminal investigation into a union's affairs the maker of the statement makes a further inconsistent statement dealing with the same point.

Documents that are the subject of legal professional privilege or the subject of a banker's duty of confidence cannot be required to be produced by the Certification Officer (although in relation to a banker's production at the request of a court of any record that is part of a banker's books, see the Bankers' Books Evidence Act 1879) (s. 37E(3)–(4), TULRCA 1992).

4.2.8.5.2 Investigation by inspectors appointed by the Certification Officer The power of the Certification Officer to appoint investigators is dealt with by ss. 37B–37D of the 1992 Act. Such an appointment can occur only where there are circumstances suggesting fraud or financial mismanagement on the part of a union, or where a union has failed to comply with its statutory or contractual financial obligations (s. 37B(2)).

An investigator so appointed can request production of any document relating to a union's financial affairs, or any other document that is relevant to an investigation (s. 37B(3)–(5)).

Again, as with the power to request production of documents, there is no right to withhold documents on the grounds that they tend to incriminate the producer of the document (s. 37B(6) — see 4.2.8.5.1 above on this point).

Where an inspector is appointed, the inspector has a duty to prepare a report orally or in writing (at the discretion of the Certification Officer) (s. 37C(1)). The Certification Officer can request a discontinuance of an investigation where a criminal investigation is to be conducted, or for any other reason (s. 37C(4)).

At the end of an investigation, the Certification Officer is required to publish a report and must make available a copy of the same free of charge to the union under investigation, to an auditor of the union if the auditor so requests, and to any member of a union who has caused that investigation to be undertaken by making a complaint and who requests a copy of the report (s. 37C(7)). A certified copy of a report is admissible as evidence in any legal proceedings (s. 37C(8)).

4.2.9   Elections for union officials

4.2.9.1   Introduction
Most unions have always had a provision in their rule books covering the holding of elections for union officials. To the extent that a rule book deals with this matter, it has always been possible to challenge a failure to hold elections in accordance with the strict letter of those rules (see for example, *Leigh* v *NUR* [1970] Ch 326).

The problems involved with union elections have traditionally arisen in cases where there has been a strong figurehead controlling a union. Legislation was introduced in the Trade Union Act 1984 which provided for elections to all the voting posts of a union's executive committee. However, unions were able to by-pass the election requirement by providing for non-voting membership of an executive committee, with the consequence that figureheads were not caught by the Act. Matters came to a head during the miners' strike of 1984–85 when, in 1985, the NUM, in order to remove their President from the ambit of the Act, held a vote to change the constitution of the union by making the President's position a non-voting one. The effect of this form of action by unions was to the implementation of changes in the Employment Act 1988 and the requirement that any position on an executive committee should be an elected one. These changes are now incorporated in TULRCA 1992, Pt I, Ch. IV and apply notwithstanding any rules to the contrary within the union rule book.

4.2.9.2   Election requirements

Section 46(1) of TULRCA 1992 creates a duty for unions to hold an election at least every five years for:

  (a)   membership of the executive committee;
  (b)   any position by virtue of which a person is a member of the executive committee;
  (c)   the position of president;
  (d)   the position of general secretary.

The main change is incorporated in (b) above, in that non-voting members of the executive are now caught by the 1992 Act. It should be noted that, to the extent that the office of president or general secretary is a courtesy position which cannot be occupied by an incumbent for more than 13 months, and was not so occupied by an incumbent for more than one period of 13 months, there is no requirement to hold elections for the position (s. 46(4)).

Membership of an executive committee is further defined within the legislation to cover any person who, under the rules or practices of a union, is able to attend or speak at meetings of the executive otherwise than to simply provide factual information to it (s. 46(3)). The executive is defined in s. 119 of TULRCA 1992 as being the principal committee of the union exercising executive functions.

4.2.9.3   Candidates for elections to union offices

Section 47(1) of TULRCA 1992 provides the right for each member of a union not to be unreasonably excluded from standing as a candidate for election to a union office. One matter is expressly described as being an unreasonable ground, and that is a direct or indirect requirement that a candidate should be a member of a political party (s. 47(2)). An indirect requirement would be, for example, a requirement to attend as a delegate at the annual conference of a political party. However, if a candidate is an existing member of a political party, it is perfectly possible to exclude the candidate from standing on the grounds of his belonging to that party.

A union is otherwise free to impose reasonable restrictions on candidature due to the proposed candidate's membership of a class defined by a union's rules. A class cannot be imposed on an *ad hoc* basis by a union (s. 47(3)) but can, for example, allow a union to impose restrictions on members from one particular trade in a large, multi-trade union, or allow restrictions upon candidates from a particular geographical region. Restrictions of this type will serve to make national, multi-trade unions representative of the membership as a whole.

4.2.9.4   Election addresses

An accompaniment to the right to stand as a candidate for election to union office is the right to have the election address of a candidate published (s. 48(1)). A union is allowed to limit the length of the address, but the limit cannot be less than 100 words. A union can also specify a deadline for the submission of addresses by all the candidates. Further, a union is allowed an unfettered choice in deciding what, if any, non-written matter is included in the address (s. 48(2) and (3)).

A union is not allowed to alter the copy submitted for the election address except to the extent that a candidate submitting the copy consents to the alteration, or insofar as it is necessary to make an alteration in order to print the address (s. 48(4)). Additionally, a union must ensure that the same production method is used for all candidates who stand (s. 48(5) and (6)). Unions must cover the cost of production of the election address for each candidate (s. 48(7)).

Lastly it should be noted that the only person liable for the content of a union address (whether the liability is civil or criminal) is the candidate causing the same to be published and not a union publishing the address (s. 48(8)).

4.2.9.5   Conduct of elections

If an election is uncontested, there is no requirement to hold a ballot for the election of the officials (s. 53, TULRCA 1992). However, as with the matter of a political fund ballot (noted at 4.2.6.4 above), a union is required to hold a procedurally complex ballot in order to ensure a fair and independent election process if the election is contested.

Prior to holding an election, a union is required under s. 49(1) of the 1992 Act to appoint an independent scrutineer whose task is to ensure that the election process is fairly carried out. The union must ensure that the scrutineer is fully independent, and it must believe that the scrutineering will be competently carried out (s. 49(2)). It should be noted that the functions of the scrutineer can be limited to those required by TULRCA 1992, or can be contractually expanded by a union if so chooses. The Secretary of State can, by delegated legislation, issue guidelines on the suitability of persons to act as scrutineers, and regard should be had to the Trade Union Ballots and Elections (Independent Scrutineer Qualifications) Order 1988 (SI 1988 No. 2117, as amended by SI 1989 No. 31) to this end.

The functions of a scrutineer are contained in s. 49(3) and comprise the following:

(a)   the production and, if it is the case that a scrutineer is also appointed to carry out the counting of the vote, distribution of the ballot papers. If an independent person is called upon to supervise the count of a vote the independent person will also carry out the distribution of the papers. A scrutineer is also required to provide the name of the person to whom the ballot papers should be returned by those voting;

(b)   to inspect the membership register to ensure that the same is a reasonably complete and up-to-date reflection of a union's membership;

(c)   to take such steps as appear to be reasonably necessary to compile the statutory report required by s. 52;

(d)   to retain custody of the ballot papers once they are received for a period of one year, and thereafter, if no complaint has been lodged with the High Court or Certification Officer concerning the conduct of the election, to dispose of the same.

A union, upon appointing a scrutineer, is required to ensure that each member, as far as is reasonably possible, is notified of the name of the scrutineer, and is required to supply to the scrutineer a copy of the members on the register (which should be up-to-date) in a form that is legible. If a union has a cut-off deadline by which members should have joined in order to be eligible to vote, the register should be up-to-date as at this date. A member of a union can request that a scrutineer inspects the register if the member believes the register does not accurately reflect union membership (s. 49(3A)). Unions are also required to ensure that nothing will be done so as to compromise a scrutineer's independence (s. 49(4)–(8)).

Unlike voting on the political fund, a union is free to impose restrictions on those who are eligible to vote. Therefore, while the general rule in s. 50(1) of the 1992 Act is that each member is entitled to an equal vote (subject to unions having a right to exclude overseas members by their rules under s. 60(1)), the legislation also provides for a class of excluded categories (s. 50(2)) and a class of restricted categories (s. 50(3)).

Those who can be excluded under union rules are unemployed members of a union, members who are in arrears in respect of any subscription or contribution which is lawfully due to a union, or those members of a union who are students or apprentices.

Those who can be restricted from voting are such classes as the union may have determined by reference to a trade or occupation, a geographical area or, lastly, those who, under union rules, are treated as a separate section within a union. The restrictions are therefore aimed at national and multi-trade unions in order to maintain a fair cross-section of the union voting. Restrictions are not as wide-reaching as exclusions, and it should also be noted that it is not possible to have a valid class restriction would which stop a union member from voting at all elections for political office (s. 50(4)).

Voting papers are again subject to requirements to eliminate interference in the voting process. Voting papers should be individually numbered from a series of consecutively, whole numbered papers. Each paper must bear upon it the name of the scrutineer and the address to which the paper is to be returned (s. 51(2)). The method of voting is by placing a mark upon the voting paper (s. 51(1)).

Voting should be secret so far as is possible, without cost to a voter, by post and without interference from a union, its members or employees (s. 51(3)–(5)). As regards minimal cost to members, in *Paul and Frazer* v *NALGO* [1987] IRLR 413 it was held that this requirement is satisfied by providing a reply paid envelope to a member.

The issue of applying pressure to a member, however, does not cover pressure which is brought to bear upon a voter by some third party (such as an employer), provided that the third party is not put up to the task of intimidating by a union (s. 51(3)).

The result of an election is obtained by counting the number of direct votes received for a candidate, which includes, for these purposes, a single transferable vote method of counting, i.e. ranking candidates by order of preference (s. 51(6) and (7)). In the case of *R* v *Certification Officer ex parte EPEA* [1990] IRLR 398, the House of Lords held that where a union rule book contained a restriction upon more than three members from one geographical area serving on the executive committee, this did not infringe s. 51(6). The effect of the rule was that only the first three members past the post in a particular area were entitled to seats on the executive committee, notwithstanding that a fourth member from the same area polled a greater number of votes than a candidate from another area. The restriction was introduced to stop such practices as block voting and electoral colleges.

The 1992 Act also requires that the storage, distribution and counting of the voting papers be carried out by an independent person. This can either be the scrutineer, or some other independent person with regard to whom a union has no reason to doubt either his independence or competance to carry out the task (s. 51A(1) and (2)).

An independent person is required to perform his duty so as to ensure that the procedure is carried out in a manner which is as fair as possible. In doing so, he should attempt to ensure that his function is not contravened, or subjected to malpractice or unfairness (s. 51A(3)). The independent person, if appointed separately from the scrutineer, must return the ballot papers to the scrutineer as soon as is reasonably practical after the completion of the vote count (s. 51A(5)).

Unions are not allowed to do anything that might compromise the independence of that independent person by reference to his terms of appointment, or by interfering directly or indirectly with the way in which the tasks of the independent person are to be carried out. Unions are also required to carry out any reasonable request by an independent person to enable the proper completion of the vote count (s. 51A(6)).

After a vote has been completed and the ballot papers returned to the scrutineer, the scrutineer is required to complete a report under s. 52. The report must address similar matters to those detailed at 4.2.6.4 above in relation to the ballot on political funds under s. 78 of TULRCA 1992.

Unions are not allowed to release the result of a ballot until such time as they have received a copy of the scrutineer's report. Once the result has been received, a union must take such steps as are reasonably practicable to ensure that, within three months of receipt of the report, each member of the union receives a copy of it. Alternatively, a union must distribute the content of the report by taking all such steps as it is the practice of the union to take in bringing to the attention of its members matters of general importance. A union can, in addition, on request from a member, release a copy of the report either free or upon payment of a reasonable fee (s. 52(3)–(6)).

4.2.9.6   *Remedies for failure to comply with election requirements*

The 1992 Act provides a remedy for a member, being a person who was a member at the time of an election, who feels that a union has not complied with the election requirements. Under s. 54(1), a member can make an application for a declaration stating that the union has failed to comply with this Part of the Act. The application can be made to either the Certification Officer (s. 55) or the High Court (s. 56).

The making of an application to the Certification Officer does not prevent the making of a subsequent application to the High Court in respect of the same matter (s. 54(1)), although the court is bound to have regard to any findings by the Certification Officer (s. 56(2)). No right of appeal lies from a decision of the Certification Officer, although there remains the possibility of judicially reviewing a decision.

To the extent that an application is made to the High Court, the court can back up a declaration with an enforcement order (which could require the union to re-ballot its members (s. 56(4)).

It is also possible to obtain assistance on an application to the court from the CROTUM (s. 109(1)(e) — regard should be had to 1.2.5 above with regard to the Commissioner generally).

An application to either the Certification Officer or the High Court must be made within one year of the ballot result being announced (s. 54(3)).When considering what amounts to a failure to comply, it should be noted that an error in the counting of a ballot by an independent person will not be sufficient to require a fresh ballot to be held if the error is an accidental one and would not influence the result of the election (s. 51(5)(b)). To the extent that an official is elected in an election which is subsequently found to have a material procedural irregularity, anything done by the elected official on behalf of the union between the result of the ballot and the subsequent declaration of invalidity will still be treated as a valid act of the union (s. 61(2)).

4.2.10 The right to prevent misuse of union property

4.2.10.1   *Introduction*

This head covers two discrete rights, these being the right to prevent a union from making unlawful indemnities of members and the right of a member to prevent a trustee of union property from acting improperly in relation to the same. Again, the theme in the legislation is to make unions accountable to their members. These rights are found in TULRCA 1992, Pt I, Ch. II.

4.2.10.2   The right to prevent unlawful indemnities

This right is contained in s. 15(3) of TULRCA 1992. The right covers the position where, for example, a union uses its assets to pay a fine imposed upon a union member as a result of some unlawful offence or contempt of court while the member is taking part in a union activity.

Section 15(1) provides a list of unlawful uses for union property. If a union does apply its property in a manner contrary to s. 15(1), a member so benefited becomes liable to account to the union for the value of the property used by him (s. 15(2)). To the extent that a union fails to institute proceedings to recover the property then, under s. 15(3), an individual member may institute proceedings on behalf of the union.

Further, under s. 109 of TULRCA 1992, it is possible for individual members to have assistance provided to them in such recovery proceedings by the CROTUM (see 1.2.5 above).

4.2.10.3   Right of action against trustees of union property

This right exists where an individual member claims that a union trustee either has carried out his functions so as to enable an unlawful use of union property to take place, or has complied with an unlawful direction as to how to use union property. The common law previously allowed the payment of fines incurred by a member if a union's rule book made specific provision for payment in such cases. The provision was held to cover only such fines as had actually been incurred by members, and a union was not allowed prospectively to authorise payment for offences which might be committed at some point in the future (see *Drake* v *Morgan* [1978] ICR 56 and *Thomas* v *NUM (South Wales Area)* [1985] ICR 136).

Section 16(1) of the 1992 Act now allows an application to be made to the court to determine the lawfulness of action taken by trustees. The right is available to a member who was a member at the time that the property was misapplied or when an unlawful direction to use was complied with (s. 16(2)). To the extent that the court feels a claim is justified, it can make such orders as it thinks fit for the removal of one or more of the trustees and can compel the trustees to initiate action to recover the trust property (s. 16(3)).

The right is available in addition to any other action that may exist for breach of trust on the part of the trustees (s. 16(6)). Again, under s. 109 assistance may be provided by the CROTUM (see 1.2.5 with regard to the Commissioner generally).

5 Trade Union Related Employment Rights

5.1 INTRODUCTION

This chapter will focus upon the rights that accrue to both trade union members and those wishing to abstain from union membership in respect of their employment. As with so much of recent trade union law, this area has been developed radically over the past 20 years, in particular in relation to the closed shop which once prevailed and allowed employees to be fairly dismissed for not being members of a union. Two types of right will be examined: the right to associate (or to dissociate) and the right to participate.

5.2 UNIONISED EMPLOYEES — THE RIGHT TO ASSOCIATE

5.2.1 Background

The history of trade union law has already been examined in Chapter 1. It will be recalled that the thrust of trade union law until 1979 was aimed at attempting to let unions and employers regulate their own affairs through legal abstention in the arena of industrial relations. Unions were seen as a valuable force in regulating industrial relations, and to this end the closed shop was encouraged. It will further be recalled that upon its introduction in the Industrial Relations Act 1971, the right not to be unfairly dismissed included dismissal in connection with a closed shop practice. This was then amended under TULRA 1974 so that it became automatically fair to dismiss in connection with a closed shop. While an employee dismissed due to a closed shop had a right to claim for wrongful dismissal and hope that the common law would provide him with a remedy (see, for example, *Hill* v *C. A. Parsons & Co. Ltd* [1972] Ch 305), he had no statutory rights. Employees were placed in an invidious position. They might be able to obtain damages for the loss of their notice period and, rarely, an injunction to prevent an employer breaching the contract of employment. What they were not able to do afterwards was find fresh employment if the closed shop practice was widespread in that particular industry.

As a result of legislative changes in the 1980s union membership has now become a neutral factor in the workplace through which no advantages now accrue from either belonging or not belonging to a union.

The law has moved further than just providing a right not to be unfairly dismissed, and the position as it now stands is that the following rights accrue to an individual against an employer in the context of trade unions and employment:

(a) the right not to be refused employment for a trade union related reason;

(b) the right not to have action short of dismissal taken against an employee for a trade union related reason;

(c) the right not to be unfairly dismissed for a trade union related reason; and

(d) the right not to be made redundant for a trade union related reason.

5.3 REFUSAL OF EMPLOYMENT FOR UNION RELATED REASONS

5.3.1 Introduction

The right not to be discriminated against prior to employment was one of the last changes made to the closed shop. It was introduced by s. 1 of the Employment Act 1990. With the consolidation of the trade union law in TULRCA 1992, the provision was carried over as s. 137 of the 1992 Act and reads as follows:

137.—(1) It is unlawful to refuse a person employment—

(a) because he is, or is not, a member of a trade union, or

(b) because he is unwilling to accept a requirement—

(i) to take steps to become or cease to be, or to remain or not to become, a member of a trade union, or

(ii) to make payments or suffer deductions in the event of his not being a member of a trade union.

As can be seen, the right is widely drafted. A number of points need to be considered in relation to it.

5.3.1.1 Employment

The concept of 'employment' for the purposes of the right is narrow. Under s. 143(1) of TULRCA 1992, employment means employment under a contract of employment. It is still possible to discriminate against those carrying out work under a contract for services.

For the purposes of the Act, Crown employees and those employed by the House of Commons and the House of Lords are taken to be employees (ss. 273(4) and (5), 278(4) and (5) respectively). Certain categories of workers are excluded from protection though. These are police officers (s. 280), share fishermen (s. 284) and overseas employees (s. 285(1), although see the saving in respect of workers on British registered ships in s. 285(2)).

5.3.1.2 Refusing to employ
The 1992 Act defines extensively what amounts to refusing to employ. The following, self-explanatory provisions of s. 137 deal with refusal to employ:

(5)   A person shall be taken to be refused employment if he seeks employment of any description with a person and that person—
(a)   refuses or deliberately omits to entertain and process his application or enquiry, or
(b)   causes him to withdraw or cease to pursue his application or enquiry, or
(c)   refuses or deliberately omits to offer him employment of that description, or
(d)   makes him an offer of such employment the terms of which are such as no reasonable employer who wished to fill the post would offer and which is not accepted, or
(e)   makes him an offer of such employment but withdraws it or causes him not to accept it.
(6)   Where a person is offered employment on terms which include a requirement that he is, or is not, a member of a trade union, or any such requirement as is mentioned in subsection (1)(b), and he does not accept the offer because he does not satisfy or, as the case may be, is unwilling to accept the requirement, he shall be treated as having been refused employment for that reason.

Two other subsections also deal with the concept of refusing to employ. First, s. 137(3) deals with the situation where an employer places or causes to be placed a discriminatory advertisement. It provides:

(3)   Where an advertisement is published which indicates, or might reasonably be understood as indicating—
(a)   that employment to which the advertisement relates is open only to a person who is, or is not, a member of a trade union, or
(b)   that any such requirement as is mentioned in subsection (1)(b) will be imposed in relation to employment to which the advertisement relates,
a person who does not satisfy that condition or, as the case may be, is unwilling to accept that requirement, and who seeks and is refused employment to which the advertisement relates, shall be conclusively presumed to have been refused employment for that reason.

It is not a criminal offence to place an advertisement offering employment to union or non-union employees (contrast the position under s. 38(5) of the Sex Discrimination Act 1975 and s. 29(5) of the Race Relations Act 1976, but note the similar wording under s. 9 of the Disability Discrimination Act 1995).

Secondly, where a union is given the chance to vet job applicants, regard should be had to the provision at s. 137(4) of TULRCA 1992, which makes it unlawful for a union to select on union membership grounds:

(4) Where there is an arrangement or practice under which employment is offered only to persons put forward or approved by a trade union, and the trade union puts forward or approves only persons who are members of the union, a person who is not a member of the union and who is refused employment in pursuance of the arrangement or practice shall be taken to have been refused employment because he is not a member of the trade union.

5.3.1.3   Union membership

The starting point in relation to union membership is the definition provided by s. 143(3) of TULRCA 1992. This provides that:

(3) References in sections 137 to 143 to being or not being a member of a trade union are to being or not being a member of any trade union, of a particular trade union, or of one of a number of particular trade unions. . . .

Accordingly, it is not open to an employer to argue that he has no problem with employing trade union members generally, but that he has reservations about a particular union.

One of the problems that has arisen from the drafting of the section is that, unlike ss. 146 and 152 (dealing with action short of dismissal and unfair dismissal respectively, see 5.4 and 5.5), s. 137 does not cover the concept of refusing to employ due to a person taking part in union related activities. On the face of it one might have assumed that it is possible to discriminate due to a person taking part in the activities of a union or for failing to do so, i.e., to distinguish between status as a union member and undertaking the tasks of a union member. The point has been discussed in the following cases: *Discount Tobacco and Confectionery Limited* v *Armitage* [1990] IRLR 15; *Associated Newspapers Limited* v *Wilson and Associated British Ports* v *Palmer* [1995] IRLR 28; *Harrison* v *Kent County Council* [1995] ICR 434; and *Speciality Care plc* v *Pachela* [1996] IRLR 248.

The first of these cases, *Discount Tobacco*, dealt with a trade union related dismissal as opposed to discrimination. The problem that arose was that the applicant, Mrs Armitage, enlisted the help of a union official to obtain a copy of her terms and conditions of employment. Before receiving her terms, she was dismissed for what was termed her lack of suitability. She sued her employer, claiming that she had been unfairly dismissed and that the real reason for her dismissal was her trade union membership. The industrial tribunal found that she had been dismissed on the grounds of her union membership. The employer appealed alleging that there was a difference between dismissing because of an employee's status as a union member for and taking part in the activities of a union. The EAT dismissed this argument, with Knox J holding (at p. 16):

> We find ourselves unconvinced of [the] distinction. In our judgment, the activities
> of a trade union officer in negotiating and elucidating terms of employment is, to
> use a prayer book expression, the outward and visible manifestation of trade union
> membership. It is an incident of union membership which is, if not the primary
> one, at any rate, a very important one and we see no genuine distinction between
> membership of a union on the one hand and making use of the essential services
> of a union, on the other.
>
> Were it not so, the scope of [s. 152 of TULRCA 1992] would be reduced almost
> to vanishing point, since it would be only just the fact that a person was a member
> of a union, without regard to the consequences of that membership, that would be
> the subject matter of that statutory provision and, it seems to us, that to construe
> that paragraph so narrowly would really be to emasculate the provision altogether.

The problem with this view is that in the context of s. 137, it is merely *obiter*. Further, the credibility of the EAT in this case is undermined by the decision of the House of Lords in the joint appeals of *Associated Newspapers* and *Associated British Ports* (*'Associated'*).

The facts of *Associated* concerned action short of dismissal. The House of Lords considered the decision in *Discount Tobacco*, and Lord Bridge found that the evidence in *Discount Tobacco* clearly came down in favour of the case being one of a union membership problem. He went on to hold (at p. 264) that there ought to be a distinction drawn between membership *per se* on the one hand and taking part in the activities of a union on the other hand. He stated that the decision of Knox J was, at best, an unnecessary gloss on the language of the Act and, at worst, liable to distort the meaning of the Act. Lord Slynn, though, who dissented on this point, put forward the following opinion (at p. 265):

> ... I do not consider that action 'preventing or deterring' someone from being a
> member of a trade union or penalising him for doing so is limited to action taken
> in respect of his status as a member; the fact that he has or wants to have a union
> membership card. It may include action to prevent or deter him from, or action
> penalising him for, exercising his rights as a member of a trade union. The exercise
> of such rights is not necessarily included in the phrase 'taking part in the activities'
> of a trade union, words more apt to cover such activities as attending union
> meetings or acting as an official of the union.

Lord Browne-Wilkinson, who also dissented on this point, did not express an opinion although he added that he did not share Lord Bridge's view.

The one case that has specifically dealt with the wording in s. 137 is the decision of the EAT in *Harrison* v *Kent County Council*. Here, the EAT was dealing with an appeal by the applicant against the decision of an industrial tribunal refusing his claim that he had been discriminated against prior to employment. The applicant was a social worker who had been a union member and had taken part as a union official in organising industrial action. He applied to the respondent for a job and was rejected on the ground that, because of his prior union activity, he was likely to be uncooperative given his past anti-management style. The EAT allowed the appeal holding that the industrial tribunal had misdirected itself as to the law. Mummery J held (at p. 443):

> The industrial tribunal's construction of section 137(1) of the Act of 1992 takes a narrower view of the conceptual limits of membership of a trade union than is expressed by the ordinary and natural meaning of the section. The fallacy in the tribunal's approach is to proceed, by analogy with section 146(1) and section 152(1), to draw a rigid distinction between, on the one hand, membership of a trade union and, on the other hand, taking part in the activities of a union. Although membership and activities are specified in separate paragraphs of section 146(1) and section 152(1), it does not follow that they are self-contained, mutually exclusive categories or concepts ...
>
> The construction adopted by the industrial tribunal would have a consequence inconsistent with promoting the purpose of the provision. The purpose of section 137(1)(a) of the Act of 1992 is to protect a person from being discriminated against in access to employment on grounds related to union membership. In reality, the persons most likely to be discriminated against are those who have been most active in membership.

The point that comes out of the cases is that s. 137 is indeed different to the provisions of ss. 146 and 152. While the House of Lords has, albeit *obiter*, cast doubts on the view that status and activities are one and the same, it is submitted that the purposive construction of Mummery J, which directly addresses the point at issue, is to be preferred. Indeed, in *Speciality Care plc* v *Pachela* [1996] IRLR 248 (albeit a case on trade union related dismissals), the EAT again strongly endorsed the view that the decision in *Discount Tobacco* was correctly decided and that industrial tribunals should be free to take a wide view as to when a person has been the victim of union related discrimination.

5.3.1.4   Causation

One last avenue that is open to an employer who has failed to employ a person allegedly due to a union related reason, is to allege that there is no causal link between membership and failure to employ. The union related reason must be the true cause of the failure to employ. It is therefore open to an employer to prove that another reason existed for failing to employ an applicant, e.g., that he did not employ a person because the person had lied about membership of a union and that the employer genuinely and reasonably believed that that would undermine trust in the working relationship (see *Fitzpatrick* v *British Railways Board* [1991] IRLR 376 on this point).

5.3.2   An employment agency refusing to employ on union related grounds

The duty not to discriminate against a job applicant is also extended to cover the conduct of employment agencies instructed by an employer (s. 138). This section provides that it is unlawful for an employment agency to refuse any of its services to a person because that person is or is not a trade union member, or because that person is unwilling to take steps to become or cease to be a member of a trade union (s. 138(1)).

As to when a person is taken to have been discriminated against, regard should be had to s. 138(4). This provides that an agency is taken to have refused to provide a service where:

(a)   it refuses or deliberately omits to provide the service to the applicant; or

(b)   it causes the applicant not to avail himself of the service or to cease using the service of the agency; or

(c)   it provides him with a different service or with a service on different terms to those that it would provide to others.

An agency is also taken to have discriminated against a person seeking to use its services where it makes an offer to provide services to a person but does so only on condition that one of the prohibited grounds in s. 138(1) is satisfied, and the person to whom the offer is made refuses to comply with the condition (s. 138(5)).

Additionally, where an agency publishes an advertisement that could reasonably be taken to indicate that its services would not be available to a person who is or is not a union member, or is or is not willing to take steps to become or cease to be come a member (s. 138(3)), it is deemed to have acted unlawfully to the extent that such a person applies to the agency to take advantage of its services and the agency refuses to provide the services for the reasons stated in s. 137.

It should be noted that in relation to advertisements, unlike the general requirements of s. 138(4)(b), a person claiming that he has been discriminated on the grounds of an advertisement must actually apply to an agency for the provision of its services if discrimination is to be established. However, where an agency issues an advertisement which thereby causes a person not to apply to the agency in the first place (thereby negating any claim under s. 138(3)), this will amount to causation for the purposes of s. 138(4)(b).

5.3.3 Procedure

In a case where either an employer or an employment agency unlawfully discriminates against an applicant for, respectively, employment or its services, a cause of action will lie to an industrial tribunal (s. 137(2) and s. 138(2) respectively). A complaint made in either case must be lodged within three months of the unlawful conduct, or within such further period as a tribunal considers to be just and equitable in all the circumstances (s. 139(1)).

The date of conduct giving rise to a complaint for the purposes of s. 137 is defined by s. 139(2) as being:

    (a)   in the case of an actual refusal, the date of the refusal;

    (b)   in the case of a deliberate omission—

        (i)   to entertain or process the complainant's application or enquiry, or

        (ii)   to offer employment,

the end of the period within which it was reasonable to expect the employer to act;

    (c)   in the case of conduct causing the complainant to withdraw or cease to pursue his application or enquiry, the date of that conduct;

    (d)   in a case where an offer was made but withdrawn, the date when it was withdrawn;

    (e)   in any other case where an offer was made but not accepted, the date on which it was made.

For the purposes of s. 138, the date of conduct is defined by s. 139(3) as being:

    (a)   in the case of an actual refusal, the date of the refusal;

    (b)   in the case of a deliberate omission to make a service available, the end of the period within which it was reasonable to expect the employment agency to act;

    (c)   in the case of conduct causing the complainant not to avail himself of a service or to cease to avail himself of it, the date of that conduct;

    (d)   in the case of failure to provide the same service, on the same terms, as is provided to others, the date or last date on which the service in fact provided was provided.

Where a person makes an allegation against both a prospective employer and an employment agency arising out of the same facts, the application can be made jointly against the prospective employer and the agency or against either of them (s. 141(1)). A tribunal dealing with a dispute must join the employer or agency (as the case may be) to the proceedings where a request to join is made at any time prior to the hearing of the case, although tribunals can refuse to do so after a hearing has started. A tribunal is not allowed to join a party after it has decided liability in a dispute (s. 141(2)).

It is also possible for a tribunal hearing a complaint under ss. 137 or 138 to join as a third party to the proceedings any trade union or other person who has called, organised, procured or financed a strike or other industrial action, or has threatened to do so where the purpose of that person's action is to induce an employer or employment agency to behave in a discriminatory fashion for the purposes of ss. 137 or 138. The application can be made either by the complainant or by any of the respondents to an action (s. 142(1)). As with joining employers or employment agencies, it is possible for an application to join a third party to be made at any time prior to the commencement of a hearing, whereupon the tribunal is bound to allow the application. If the application to join a third party is made after a case has commenced, the tribunal may reject the application; and if it has already decided the outcome of the case, it is bound to reject the application (s. 142(2)). A union third party in such a situation will not be immune in tort (see Chapter 7 generally and also Chapter 9 in relation to union recognition requirements in contracts for the provision of service: ss. 144 and 145).

5.3.4   Remedies

A tribunal hearing a claim under ss. 137 or 138 and finding for the complainant must make a declaration to this effect. In addition, if and to the extent that it considers it just and equitable, it can award compensation and/or make a recommendation that the respondent takes such action as is necessary, within a specified period, to reduce the adverse effect of the discrimination to the applicant (s. 140(1)).

In making an award of compensation, the tribunal is to apply the rules relating to breach of statutory duty and it may make an award to reflect injury to feelings suffered by the complainant. As to cases concerning injury to feelings in other areas of discrimination, regard should be had to cases such as *Sharifi* v *Strathclyde Regional Council* [1992] IRLR 259, which shows the minimum amount of compensation likely to be recovered, and *Orlando* v *Didcot Power Station Sports & Social Club* [1996] IRLR 262, which sets down the principles that tribunals should take into account in awarding compensation under this head. It should also be noted that, unlike cases involving sex, race and disability discrimination, trade union related discrimination cases are subject to a cap on the maximum amount of damages that can be awarded. The limit is as imposed in relation to compensation for unfair dismissal under the Employment Rights Act 1996, currently £12,000 (TULRCA 1992, s. 140(4)).

Where proceedings have been brought jointly against an employer and an employment agency, and an industrial tribunal finds in favour of a complainant, it can award compensation to be paid by either or both respondents in such amounts as it thinks fit (s. 141(3)). Likewise, where a third party has been joined to the proceedings under the provisions of s. 142, a tribunal can make an award of compensation against any or all of the employer, employment agency or third party as the tribunal thinks fit in all the circumstances of the case (s. 142(3)–(4)).

5.4 ACTION SHORT OF DISMISSAL FOR TRADE UNION RELATED REASONS

5.4.1 Introduction

The right not to be have action short of dismissal taken against an employee for a trade union related reason is one that has existed in statutory form in one shape or another since the Industrial Relations Act 1971. When it was introduced under s. 5 of the 1971 Act, the right was for an employee to either be or not be a member of a registered trade union under the Act and, if he was a member of such a union, to take part in the activities of the union at an appropriate time. The 1971 Act was repealed by TULRA 1974 and the provision under the 1971 Act was replaced by s. 53 of the Employment Protection Act 1975 (which was itself subsequently incorporated into the Employment Protection (Consolidation) Act 1978 as s. 23). As re-enacted in the form of s. 23 of the 1978 Act, the purpose of the provision changed to provide a right to take part in union activities and not to be forced into joining an employer's staff association. The provision was ultimately amended during the course of the Thatcher administration by way of, variously, the Employment Act 1980, the Employment Act 1982 and the Employment Act 1988. The last major change was incorporated into s. 146 of TULRCA 1992 by s. 13 of TURERA 1993 (discussed below at 5.4.2.1).

The formulation as it now stands in s. 146 of the 1992 Act is neutral, and is the right is not to have action short of dismissal taken against a person because he is or is not a union member or a member of a particular union.

The right is not available to police officers (s. 280), share fishermen (s. 284) or overseas employees (s. 285 — although see the savings in relation to workers on British registered ships under s. 285(2)). Crown servants, House of Lords and House of Commons staff are specifically allowed to pursue the right (ss. 273, 277 and 278 of the 1992 Act respectively).

5.4.2 The right

The right in TULRCA 1992, s. 146 provides the following:

(1) An employee has the right not to have action short of dismissal taken against him as an individual by his employer for the purpose of—

(a) preventing or deterring him from being or seeking to become a member of an independent trade union, or penalising him for doing so,

(b) preventing or deterring him from taking part in the activities of an independent trade union at an appropriate time, or penalising him for doing so, or

(c) compelling him to be or become a member of any trade union or of a particular trade union or one of a number of particular trade unions.

5.4.2.1   Action

It can be seen that the right can be breached by an employer in any of three ways. Of fundamental importance to the right, though, is the question of what will amount to 'action' for the purposes of the right. This has recently been the subject of an important House of Lords decision in the joint appeal of *Associated Newspapers Limited* v *Wilson* and *Associated British Ports* v *Palmer* [1995] ICR 406. Prior to this case, however, the legal meaning of the word 'action' for this right was set down in the case of *Ridgway* v *National Coal Board* [1987] IRLR 80.

Ridgway concerned a dispute arising out of the aftermath of the 1980s miners' strike. At the end of the strike, the NCB entered into negotiations with the newly created Union of Democratic Mineworkers (UDM) for the purposes of setting wage levels in the industry. The result was that UDM members should be paid similar wages to employees who were members of the National Union of Mineworkers (NUM). At one colliery, members of the UDM were paid enhanced salaries but members of the NUM were not. The applicant, who was an NUM member, sued for breach of the right (under s. 23 of the 1978 Act as it was then), claiming that by not giving him similar wages to employees who were UDM members, the NCB had taken action short of dismissal in order to make him become a member of the UDM. The NCB defended the action claiming that they had not taken action against the applicant but had merely omitted to grant him a pay rise. The matter reached the Court of Appeal which decided that the omission to grant a pay rise to members of the NUM amounted to action for the purposes of the right. Nicholls LJ (as he was then) stated (at p. 87):

> ... to draw the suggested distinction between action and omission would produce absurd results. Take the case of an employer who provides car parking permits for employees but not as part of the terms of their employment. If he were to give permits to only such of his employees as did not belong to a trade union, for the purpose of penalising other employees for belonging to a union, on the Coal Board's argument the failure to provide car parking permits for the union members could only constitute an 'omission' if the union members had a reasonable expectation that they too would receive the permits. But if the sequence of events were altered, and all employees had received car parking permits and then for the purpose of penalising the union members, the employer withdrew their permits, that would constitute 'action' and would be remediable under [s. 146] regardless of whether the complainants had any reasonable expectation that they would continue to hold the permits. That cannot be right.

Likewise, Bingham LJ (as he was then) stated (at p. 93):

> It is natural for lawyers to think of omissions in terms of failure to perform a duty. That is how omissions feature in the law of negligence. It is also an acceptable dictionary definition. But it is not a necessary definition. An omission need be no

more than a mere failure or neglect to act. This, I think, is the natural meaning here, where 'omission' appears as the simple converse of 'action'. No notion of duty or obligation attaches to the concept of 'action'. Nor should it, I think, to omission. If, of course, that which the employer has omitted to do is something which he would not have been expected to do and would not in the ordinary way have done, a Tribunal is unlikely to conclude that the omission was for an objectionable purpose within the subsection. I do not, however, think that there is a reason for giving this familiar word anything other than what seems to me its natural and straightforward meaning.

An important point to note is that the case was decided on the basis of the word 'action' as defined in s. 153 of the 1978 Act, which provided that 'action' included an omission. The problem was enlarged in that, due to the convoluted legislative history of s. 146 of TULRCA 1992, the 1978 Act was the first time that a definition of 'action' had been provided by the same legislation as the provision was found in. Neither the Industrial Relations Act 1971 nor the Employment Protection Act 1975 had such a definition.

The position was reviewed in the *Associated Newspapers Limited* case. The facts of the case were that the employers, the owners of a newspaper, had decided to scrap collective bargaining in their organisation and to pursue pay reviews on an individual basis. The applicant was a journalist who was a member of the National Union of Journalists (NUJ). The NUJ was one of the unions that would be affected as a result of the abolition of collective bargaining by the employers. The employers, in order to achieve their aim of individualised negotiations, offered to all those prepared to negotiate individually a 4.5 per cent pay rise. Those not accepting individual bargaining did not get the rise. The applicant contended that this was action short of dismissal. He succeeded in the industrial tribunal, lost on appeal in the EAT and further succeeded in the Court of Appeal.

After the applicant succeeded in the Court of Appeal, the Government introduced changes in the form of s. 13 of TURERA 1993, which amended the evidence that tribunals can take into account in reaching a decision. They are now allowed to look at whether an employer is seeking to further a change with a class of his employees even though this might contravene s. 146. Tribunals hearing cases are then obliged to examine the employer's reason for promoting the change and, unless it is action such that no reasonable employer would take, tribunals are to disregard the fact that it appears to be action short of dismissal (see now s. 148(3)–(5) of TULRCA 1992).

The respondent then appealed to the House of Lords. Their Lordships by a majority, held that the employer had not taken 'action' against the applicant. They so held on the basis that although reliance was placed on the meaning of the word 'act' as defined by s. 153 of the 1978 Act (now carried over as s. 298 of TULRCA 1992), which includes an omission to act in its definition, since the original enactment of the provision did not contain a definition of what amounts to 'action', the definition of 'action' provided in s. 153 of the 1978 Act could not be followed.

This was because the Act was a consolidation and would not have been expected to alter the pre-existing law. Accordingly, the majority of the House of Lords felt free to approach the question as to what amounted to 'action' as a new point of law. Their Lordships (with the lead majority judgment being given by Lord Bridge) took the view that 'action' meant positive acts and not omissions. It followed from this that since an omission rather than a positive course of action had taken place, no cause of action would arise unless the applicant could show that the purpose of the employer had been to penalise him for being a member of a trade union or to deter him from being a union member (as opposed to deterring him from making use of the services of a union), which, on the facts, he could not show.

It follows from this case that it will now be extremely difficult for an employee to succeed in a claim brought under s. 146 of TULRCA 1992 where an employer has invoked a blanket policy of derecognition (coupled with 'sweeteners' to persuade employees to deal on an individual basis) because of the combined effect of the *Associated Newspapers Limited* case and the changes incorporated in s. 148(3)–(5).

Another example of a case where the right has been unsuccessfully invoked is *Gallagher* v *Department of Transport* [1994] IRLR 231. Here, the applicant was a union official who spent between 80 and 100 per cent of his working time involved in union activity. He applied for promotion to senior executive officer, but was passed over on the grounds that he lacked management experience. Indeed, although he had apparently interviewed for the position very well, it was felt by the interview board that unless he was severely to cut back on the amount of time that he spent on union affairs it was difficult to see how he would acquire the necessary experience. The applicant therefore brought a claim under what was then s. 23 of the Employment Protection (Consolidation) Act 1978. The applicant was successful before the industrial tribunal hearing his case, who were of the view that the recommendation was intended to deter the applicant from pursuing his union activities. However, both the EAT and the Court of Appeal allowed the employer's appeal. They both took the view that the industrial tribunal had erred by looking at the effect of the employer's recommendation rather than at the purpose of the employer's action, which they took to be mere helpful guidance to an employee. Accordingly, as with *Associated Newspapers Limited*, unless the applicant was able to provide evidence showing that the intention of the employer had been to deter him from taking part in the activities of his union, his case failed.

Lastly, s. 146(3) of TULRCA 1992 provides for one particular form of action that is not allowed to be taken. This is where an employer requires a non-union employee to make a payment to another person on account of his not being a member of a union. It is expressly stated in s. 146(4) that this will be action short of dismissal.

It should be added that two proposals exist under the White Paper 'Fairness at Work' to remedy the problems created by the decision in the *Associated Newspapers Limited* case. Under the first proposal, it will be unlawful to discriminate by omission on grounds of trade union membership, non-membership or activities (i.e., a statutory reversal of the *Associated Newspapers Limited* case). Secondly, the Government is also proposing to prohibit blacklists of union members.

5.4.2.2   Action taken against employees taking part in union activity at an appropriate time
Despite 5.4.2.1 above, where action is taken against an individual employee outside the context of derecognition cases, the provisions of s. 146(1) of the 1992 Act are still important. Of particular importance are the questions of what will amount to taking part in the activities of independent trade union and what is meant by the expression 'appropriate time' in s. 146(1)(b).

5.4.2.2.1   Activities of an independent trade union   What needs to be distinguished here is the difference between action undertaken by an individual on his own account and that which has a genuine union connection. The best example of this point is the case of *Chant* v *Aquaboats Ltd* [1978] ICR 643. The case was actually decided on the basis of a similar unfair dismissal provision (in that the applicant had been dismissed for taking part in the activities of an independent trade union at an appropriate time). The applicant was a member of UCATT and had organised a petition during his work time claiming that working conditions were unsafe. His employer dismissed him for incapability due to the slowness of his work (which was slowed down by his organising the petition). His claim that he was carrying out a trade union activity was rejected by the EAT, which held that the expression 'activities of an independent trade union' did not include the applicant's activities as a trade unionist.

However, regard should be had to *Miller* v *Rafique* [1975] IRLR 70 (taking part in a union meeting), *Marley Tile Co. Ltd* v *Shaw* [1978] ICR 828 (consulting a shop steward or other union official) and *Dixon* v *West Ella Developments Ltd* [1978] ICR 856 (recruiting union members), all of which have been held to involve activities of a trade union.

By way of contrast, in *Lyon and Scherk* v *St James Press Limited* [1976] IRLR 215, the EAT held that where the applicants had been dismissed for secretly organising a chapel of the NUJ, this was still a fair dismissal since, on the facts, the act of organisation, in what was a small and informal employer, amounted to a wholly unreasonable act on the part of the members. The applicants were taken to fall outside the right. Unfortunately, the 1992 Act does not make a distinction between wholly unreasonable acts and ordinary acts of a union, and it is submitted that this case is wrong in law.

5.4.2.2.2   'Appropriate time'   The phrase 'appropriate time' in s. 146(1)(b) is defined by s. 146(2) to mean:

(a)   a time outside the employee's working hours, or
(b)   a time within his working hours at which, in accordance with arrangements agreed with or consent given by his employer, it is permissible for him to take part in the activities of a trade union;
and for this purpose 'working hours', in relation to an employee, means any time when, in accordance with his contract of employment, he is required to be at work.

Two issues arise here: first, what is meant by the 'employee's working time'; and, secondly, when an employer provides his consent.

As to the first point, one of the problems that will face an employer is whether an employee who is having a break at work is within his working hours. The matter was addressed by the EAT in *Zucker* v *Astrid Jewels Ltd* [1978] ICR 1088. Here, the case was again brought on the basis of unfair dismissal for taking part in the activities of an independent trade union at an appropriate time. The applicant had discussed union membership with fellow employees while on her lunch and tea breaks. Her employer took the view that this was not at an appropriate time since the employee was within working hours and there had been no consent provided, and so they were free to dismiss. The EAT disagreed. Its view was that an employee's working hours were those when the employee should actually be working. It followed that since the employee was not required to work during her breaks, she was outside her working hours, albeit that the breaks were a part of her working day when she was required to be at the employer's premises. Regard should also be had to the speech of Lord Reid in *Post Office* v *Crouch* [1974] ICR 378 (dealing with the now repealed s. 5 of the Industrial Relations Act 1971, but on the same point).

It should be noted that taking industrial action during the course of an employee's working hours is unlikely to be covered by the definition of taking part in activity at an appropriate time (see *Brennan* v *Ellward (Lancs) Ltd* [1976] IRLR 378).

As to the issue of consent, it seems that it is possible for consent to be implied (*Marley Tile Co. Ltd* v *Shaw* [1978] ICR 828). In such cases, it is for those asserting that implied consent exists to prove that it does, and each case will turn on its own facts on this point. Ultimately, if an employer has provided consent for employees to take part in union activities, it would seem that it must be possible (unless a binding collective agreement exists to the contrary) for an employer to terminate the right on giving either notice under the terms of a collective agreement, or reasonable notice in the event that any such agreement is silent with regard to notice or there is no such agreement.

5.4.3   Enforcing the right and procedure

Where an individual alleges that the right has been breached he has the right to complain to an industrial tribunal (TULRCA 1992, s. 146(5)). Any complaint must be presented within three months of the action or the last in any series of actions taken against the complainant, or within such other period as an industrial tribunal hearing a complaint thinks reasonable if it was not reasonably practicable to present a claim within the time limit (s. 147).

When considering a complaint, an employer is required to show the purpose of action that has been taken (s. 148(1)), and employers are not able to claim that they have been pressurised into taking action against a complainant by the threat or taking of industrial action (s. 148(2)).

As to the purpose of an employer's action, following the decision in *Associated Newspapers* v *Wilson* in the Court of Appeal, the Government introduced an amendment to s. 148 of TULRCA 1992 (by s. 13, TURERA 1993) which inserted new s. 148(3)–(5). It will be recalled that in the *Associated Newspapers* case, the employer wished to introduce individual negotiating at the expense of collective bargaining by means of enticements in the form of enhanced pay for those individually negotiating. The new subsections allow an employer to show that he wished to change his relations with either all or a class of his employees, and that he sought to do this by means of one the grounds in s. 146 (as set out in 5.4.2 above). As to what amounts to a class of employees, this is defined in s. 148(5) to include reference by grade, category, description or place of work. Employers are therefore now expressly allowed to show that they were seeking to promote individual bargaining at the expense of collective bargaining.

If action has been taken by an employer due to pressure from a third party, it is possible to join the third party to the proceedings (s. 150(1)). As seen before, where an application to join is made before the hearing of a case, an industrial tribunal must order the third party to be joined. If a hearing has begun, tribunals have a discretion to refuse the joinder, and once a case has been decided a tribunal is bound to refuse an application (s. 150(2)).

5.4.4   Remedies

When an industrial tribunal considers that an applicant has successfully proved his claim, the tribunal is required to make a declaration to that effect and may make an award of compensation (s. 149(1)). The amount of compensation that can be awarded is such sum as a tribunal considers to be just and equitable in the circumstances of a case. There is no limit to the amount that can be awarded.

Compensation must take account of the costs that have been reasonably incurred by the complainant as a consequence of the right being infringed, together with the loss of any benefits that have arisen as a result of the claim (s. 149(3)). It is not certain whether it is possible to recover for injury to feelings claimed as non-pecuniary loss. In both *Brassington* v *Cauldon Wholesale Limited* [1977] IRLR 479 and *Cheall* v *Vauxhall Motors Ltd* [1979] IRLR 253, the applicant recovered compensation for non-pecuniary loss that had been suffered in the proceedings. The correctness of the decisions was challenged in *Ridgway* v *National Coal Board* [1987] IRLR 80, but the Court of Appeal left the matter open in that case. Recently, the EAT again affirmed that it is possible to make an award under this head in the case of *Cleveland Ambulance NHS Trust* v *Blane* [1997] IRLR 332. The problem with making such an award is that it allows an employee to recover more than he would be able to in the event of his being unfairly dismissed. Following the case of *Norton Tool Co. Ltd* v *Tewson* [1972] IRLR 86, it has consistently been held that no right to compensation for injury to feelings as a result of dismissal exists. The matter is still open to doubt, despite the decisions of the EAT, in the light of *Ridgway*.

A tribunal is also bound to take account of an applicant's duty to mitigate (s. 149(4)) and may reduce the compensation that it would otherwise award due to the fact that an applicant has either caused or contributed to his own loss (s. 149(6)). It cannot take account of the fact that an employer was pressurised into taking the course of action (s. 149(5)).

If the action was taken by an employer due to pressure from a third party who has been joined to the proceedings and a tribunal finds for the applicant, it may order that the compensation to be paid is paid by the employer, or the third party or both in such amounts as it thinks fit (s. 150(3)).

5.5 THE RIGHT NOT TO BE UNFAIRLY DISMISSED FOR A TRADE UNION RELATED REASON

5.5.1 Introduction

This is another of the rights that was variously eroded and expanded during the reforms of 1979–1997. The right not to be unfairly dismissed for a trade union related reason was introduced by the Industrial Relations Act 1971. The TULRA 1974, as part of the 'Social Contract' package of measures that the Labour Government of Harold Wilson introduced, was brought in to replace the Industrial Relations Act and carried over the right. As originally enacted, if an employee was dismissed for a trade union related reason (see 5.5.2 for the current version of these reasons), the dismissal was automatically unfair. Given that the agenda of the times was the promotion of collective bargaining through means of the closed shop, it is not surprising that dismissal was automatically unfair where a person proposed to join a union, or took part in union action at an appropriate time or refused to join a body that was not an independent trade union.

This right has now been re-modelled in a number of ways. First, as a result of changes made by the Employment Act 1982, the level of compensation that may be awarded to a claimant under the right is higher than in non-union related unfair dismissal cases. Secondly, the right now acts to dissuade employers from introducing a closed shop while also paying lip service to the right to belong to a union.

This section will not focus on the principles that underpin unfair dismissal generally; regard should be had to more mainstream employment texts for these. Instead, it will focus on the ways in which unfair dismissal differs in trade union cases.

5.5.2 The right not to be unfairly dismissed for a trade union related reason

The right is contained in ss. 152 and 153 of TULRCA 1992, which provide as follows:

152.—(1)   For purposes of Part X of the Employment Rights Act 1996 (unfair dismissal) the dismissal of an employee shall be regarded as unfair if the reason for it (or, if more than one, the principal reason) was that the employee—

(a)   was, or proposed to become, a member of an independent trade union, or

(b)   had taken part, or proposed to take part, in the activities of an independent trade union at an appropriate time, or

(c)   was not a member of any trade union, or of a particular trade union, or of one of a number of particular trade unions, or had refused, or proposed to refuse, to become or remain a member.

. . .

(3)   Where the reason, or one of the reasons, for the dismissal was—

(a)   the employee's refusal, or proposed refusal, to comply with a requirement (whether or not imposed by his contract of employment or in writing) that, in the event of his not being a member of any trade union, or of a particular trade union, or of one of a number of particular trade unions, he must make one or more payments, or

(b)   his objection, or proposed objection, (however expressed) to the operation of a provision (whether or not forming part of his contract of employment or in writing) under which, in the event mentioned in paragraph (a), his employer is entitled to deduct one or more sums from the remuneration payable to him in respect of his employment, the reason shall be treated as falling within subsection (1)(c).

. . .

153.   Where the reason or principal reason for the dismissal of an employee was that he was redundant, but it is shown—

(a)   that the circumstances constituting the redundancy applied equally to one or more other employees in the same undertaking who held positions similar to that held by him and who have not been dismissed by the employer, and

(b)   that the reason (or, if more than one, the principal reason) why he was selected for dismissal was one of those specified in section 152(1),
the dismissal shall be regarded as unfair for the purposes of Part X of the Employment Rights Act 1996 (unfair dismissal).

It will immediately be noticed that there is a difference between the drafting of s. 152(1)(a) and s. 152(1)(c). It has been argued (and, indeed, accepted by the EAT in *Rath* v *Cruden Construction Ltd* [1982] IRLR 9) that they relate to different points, given that s. 152(1)(a) refers to trade unions generally whereas s. 152(1)(c) refers to a 'particular trade union'. The argument in *Rath* was that an applicant who had been dismissed as a result of failing to belong to a particular trade union (having transferred from one union to another) could not claim the right not to be unfairly dismissed because, as it was then drafted, the right only protected employees who had been dismissed by an employer who was 'anti-union' generally. Where, as in *Rath*'s case, the employer had a relationship with one union and did not want his employees to be members of other particular trade unions, the section did not apply. Following *Rath*, the Employment Act 1982 changed the formulation to its current standing, the effect of which is that it is now unlawful to dismiss because of a person's membership of a particular union or for not being a member of any union. *Rath* was criticised by the Court of Appeal in *Ridgway* v *National Coal Board* [1987] ICR 641 and is believed to be wrong in law

Those excluded from the right not be unfairly dismissed are police officers (Employment Rights Act (ERA) 1996, s. 200) shore fishermen and overseas employees (ERA 1996, s. 196 — although see the savings in relation to workers on British registered ships under s. 196(5)). Crown servants, House of Lords and House of Commons staff are specifically allowed to pursue the right (ERA 1996, ss. 191, 194 and 195 respectively)

5.5.3   The reason for the dismissal

5.5.3.1   *Union membership*
Once an employee has shown that he has been dismissed for one of the reasons in s. 152 of the 1992 Act then the dismissal will be automatically unfair. It is no defence for an employer to say that he did not intend to dismiss for a union related reason. The question to be asked is whether, objectively on all the evidence available, an employee has been dismissed for an inadmissible reason. A good example is *Dundon* v *GPT Ltd* [1995] IRLR 403. In this case, the applicant was a union representative who over the course of his 20 years' employment with the respondent had taken on more and more union related business as part of his working day. At the time of his dismissal he contributed only about 20 per cent of his working time to the business of his employer with the rest of his working time being spent on union duties. The respondent selected him for redundancy, and one of the criteria it adopted was to consider whether he produced much work. He scored very badly under this head and was dismissed. The industrial tribunal hearing the case decided that the respondent employer had not meant to select him for union related reasons and therefore the dismissal was fair. On appeal, however, the EAT decided that if the employer had selected him for redundancy because of his work output, it must be connected to his union work and therefore the reason that he had been selected was because he was a member of a particular trade union.

The main cases in relation to exercising membership rights have been looked at in relation to an employer discriminating against a job applicant for a trade union related reason and taking action short of dismissal (see above at 5.3 *et seq.* and 5.4 *et seq.* respectively), i.e., *Discount Tobacco and Confectionery Limited* v *Armitage* [1990] IRLR 15 and *Associated Newspapers Limited* v *Wilson* [1995] IRLR 258. The crucial point in relation to this section is whether someone is dismissed for taking part in the activities of a union merely because, for example, they consult a union representative as to their rights. It will be remembered from the discussion above that a distinction was drawn between the EAT judgment of Knox J in *Discount Tobacco* (who was of the view that dismissing an employee for consulting with a union representative amounted to dismissal for a membership reason since there was no genuine distinction between using the essential services of a union and being a member). In *Associated Newspapers*, the majority of the House of Lords held that a literal approach needed to be adopted when examining the issue of union membership, i.e. that quite simply membership is a status concept. However, the EAT has not followed the House of Lords in *Associated Newspapers* in cases relating to access to employment (see above at 5.3.1.3), which has left the law in the area looking distinctly disjointed. Three possible interpretations are possible:

(a)   that 'membership' for the purposes of the right not to be refused employment is distinct from 'membership' for the purposes of both the right not to have action short of dismissal taken (a broad formulation — see *Discount Tobacco* and see *Harrison* v *Kent County Council* [1995] IRLR 434) and the right not to be unfairly dismissed for a union related reason (a narrower, literal formulation — Lord Bridge's judgment in *Associated Newspapers*);

(b)   that the concept of membership of a union in the cases of *Discount Tobacco* and *Associated Newspapers* is consistent in both cases and is a narrow, literal formulation (the view of the House of Lords in *Associated Newspapers*); or

(c)   that some middle ground can be reached as to what membership of a union amounts to (the view of Lord Slynn in *Associated Newspapers*, where he stated that membership could be taken as being associated with the rights that come with membership and their usage).

The situation is not helped by the fact that the issue of membership was merely dealt with *obiter* by the House of Lords in *Associated Newspapers*. All that can be said with certainty is that this area of the law leads to a state of considerable confusion and will need to be reviewed by an appellate court at some future date.

5.5.3.2   Taking part in union activities at an appropriate time
The law in relation to this head has already been discussed above at 5.4.2.2.

5.5.3.3   Payments in lieu of membership
It will be noted that s. 152(3) makes it unfair to dismiss a person for failing to agree to a deduction from his wages in the event of his not being a union member. This provision has been in effect since the Employment Act 1980.

5.5.3.4   Selection for redundancy
Selection for redundancy on the basis of a trade union related reason is dealt with by s. 153 of TULRCA 1992. The criteria for establishing unfair dismissal under this heading are:

(a)   that a redundancy situation existed in an 'undertaking';

(b)   it applied equally to the applicant and one or more other employees in the same 'position' as the applicant; and

(c)   that the key factor in an applicant's dismissal was one of the reasons set out in s. 152(1). In establishing this ground it needs to be considered what amounts to an applicant's 'position' and what is meant by an 'undertaking'.

5.5.3.4.1   The applicant's 'position'   The 'position' of an applicant, is currently provided by s. 235 of the ERA 1996. It has a convoluted legislative history. In relation to unfair redundancies, the law used to exist as s. 59 of the Employment Protection (Consolidation) Act 1978. The 1978 Act provided a definition of 'position' (in s. 153 of that Act) in terms of status, nature of work, and terms and conditions of employment as a whole. This definition was not transposed to TULRCA 1992 when the right was consolidated as s. 153. Subsequently, the definition of 'position' was carried over into the ERA 1996 upon consolidation of the other individual employment legislation.

The meaning of 'position' was discussed in *O'Dea* v *ISC Chemicals Ltd* [1996] ICR 222. The applicant in this case was employed as a technical services operator, but in reality spent half of his time undertaking union activities and half of his time as a packing operator. His position was unique in the context of the business. He was selected for redundancy when his department closed down and was not considered for one of the other available posts with his employer. He made an application for unfair dismissal on the basis of unfair selection for redundancy under s. 59 of the 1978 Act (now s. 153 of TULRCA 1992), which the industrial tribunal rejected holding that he occupied a special position in the workforce. However, the tribunal did go on to award him compensation for unfair dismissal on the grounds that his managers had failed to inform those making the appointments to other departments that his trade union activities should be disregarded. This was then reduced by 80 per cent to take account of the fact that the applicant probably would not have been selected for one of the posts. An appeal to the EAT was unsuccessful, and finally an appeal was made to the Court of Appeal. The arguments that were presented to the Court of Appeal by the applicant were primarily that his union activities should have been disregarded in assessing his position and that the tribunal should have focused on his contractual title of technical services operator rather than on his actual work as a packing operator. Peter Gibson LJ rejected this, holding (at p. 230) that to do so:

> ... would require the industrial tribunal to ignore not merely what the applicant did as a shop steward but also what work he did as an employee as well as the terms and conditions of his employment. There is no justification for this in the language of [TULRCA 1992, s. 153 read with ERA 1996, s. 235]. Indeed it would render any meaningful comparison futile in circumstances such as the present.

Peter Gibson LJ added that what amounts to an employee's position will be a question of fact for a tribunal to determine. (See also *Britool Ltd* v *Roberts* [1993]

IRLR 481, *CGB Publishing* v *Killey* [1993] IRLR 520 and *Dundon* v *GPT Ltd* [1995] IRLR 403 for further examples in this area.)

5.5.3.4.2 Undertaking The concept of an undertaking is not defined by TULRCA 1992, but the phrase almost certainly takes on the definition of an undertaking within the meaning of TUPE 1981, reg. 2(1), and regard should be had to more mainstream employment law texts on this point.

5.5.3.5 Unfair dismissal following 'other industrial action'

5.5.3.5.1 Introduction This is another of the rights that has been heavily curtailed as a result of the trade union law reforms of the 1980s and early 1990s. The right was originally introduced under the Industrial Relations Act 1971 and covered the situation where one or more persons had been dismissed for taking part in industrial action but an employer had subsequently taken steps selectively to re-hire employees and had excluded from re-employment, for example, the ringleaders. The right was carried through into the Employment Protection (Consolidation) Act 1978 after it had been re-enacted by TULRA 1974. It was heavily modified by the Employment Act 1982, the Employment Act 1990 and TURERA 1993.

5.5.3.5.2 Unofficial industrial action The starting point in relation to this right is to consider when or what action is unofficial. This is dealt with by s. 237 of TULRCA 1992. Unofficial action is all action that is taken without the authorisation or endorsement of a union which has members engaged in the action (s. 237(2)–(3)). If an individual is not a union member and takes part in action that has union members involved in it whose union has authorised or endorsed the action then, notwithstanding that the individual is not a union member, the action will still be official as regards the individual.

The effect of the s. 237 test is to make action taken by employees at a given establishment potentially official and unofficial for different employees. For example, if an employee is a member of union X, a fellow worker is a member of union Y and a further worker is not a union member, then, to the extent that union X endorses action and union Y refuses to do so, any action taken by all three workers will be official as regards the member of union X and the non-unionised employee but unofficial as regards the member of union Y.

The result is, of course, capricious. The White Paper 'Fairness at Work' has specifically stated that the law in this particular area will not be affected. Furthermore, it cannot be avoided by the hypothetical union Y member resigning his membership of that union during the course of action. This is because s. 237(6) provides that employees who cease to be union members during the course of action are deemed to retain their membership for the purposes of determining whether action is official until the end of that action. The effect is that the only way for a person to take part in official action where his union refuses to authorise or endorse the proposed action is to resign from the union prior to taking part in the action.

It should also be noted that where employees at an organisation are not members of a union and take action, they are not dealt with by the provisions of s. 237 (unless other employees who are union members take part). Their action will neither be official nor unofficial since these are concepts relevant to unionised labour only.

5.5.3.5.3   The right to claim for industrial action related unfair dismissal
The right is now contained in ss. 237(1) and 238 of TULRCA 1992, which provide as follows:

237.   Dismissal of those taking part in unofficial industrial action

(1)   An employee has no right to complain of unfair dismissal if at the time of dismissal he was taking part in an unofficial strike or other unofficial industrial action.

. . .

238.   Dismissals in connection with other industrial action

(1)   This section applies in relation to an employee who has a right to complain of unfair dismissal ('the complainant') and who claims to have been unfairly dismissed, where at the date of dismissal—

(a)   the employer was conducting or instituting a lock-out, or

(b)   the complainant was taking part in a strike or other industrial action.

(2)   In such a case an industrial tribunal shall not determine whether the dismissal was fair or unfair unless it is shown—

(a)   that one or more relevant employees of the same employer have not been dismissed, or

(b)   that a relevant employee has before the expiry of three months beginning with the date of his dismissal been offered re-engagement and that the complainant has not been offered re-engagement.

. . .

(3)   For this purpose 'relevant employees' means—

(a)   in relation to a lock-out, employees who were directly interested in the dispute in contemplation or furtherance of which the lock-out occurred, and

(b)   in relation to a strike or other industrial action, those employees at the establishment of the employer at or from which the complainant works who at the date of his dismissal were taking part in the action.

Nothing in section 237 (dismissal of those taking part in unofficial industrial action) affects the question who are relevant employees for the purposes of this section.

The starting point is to note that under s. 237(1), if action is unofficial it matters not that an employer is selective in whom he chooses to dismiss. An employer can be as arbitrary as he wishes in such a situation, and may decide to 'shoot a few generals' as an example to the rest of the workforce. If that is the case, those employees dismissed have no recourse unless they can show that the primary reason for the dismissal is a maternity, health and safety or an employee representation reason (TULRCA 1992, s. 237(1A)).

If an employee does fall into the category of industrial action that is other than unofficial (or as the heading to s. 238 calls it, 'other industrial action') then an employer choosing to dismiss those taking part in such action is left with an all-or-nothing election and cannot pick and choose who to dismiss from amongst those taking part (s. 238(2)(a)). If an employer decides that dismissals are needed then the employer will have to recruit a completely new labour force. If an employer decides to dismiss employees taking part in industrial action, he cannot selectively re-employ from those he has dismissed unless he does so no earlier than three months after the last of the dismissals (s. 238(2)(b)).

A proposal exists, though, under the White Paper 'Fairness at Work' to amend the law relating to dismissals for properly balloted industrial action. The Government has recommended that a right of complaint for unfair dismissal will be introduced where an employer dismisses *any* employees simply because they have taken part in properly balloted industrial action. The proposal is that tribunals will not look at the merits of the industrial action; rather they will focus upon whether an employer has acted reasonably in taking into account all the circumstances of a case. Guidance is currently being sought by the Government as to how to make this proposal simple and workable.

Ultimately, at present, if an employee has been dismissed for taking part in other industrial action, unless he can show (as with those taking part in unofficial industrial action) that the reason for the dismissal is actually due to a maternity, health and safety or employee representation reason, no claim can be heard by a tribunal (s. 238(2) and (2A)).

In conclusion, it is for an employee who is dismissed to show that his employer dismissed him for an automatically unfair reason or was undertaking a lock-out. Alternatively, the employee will have to show that he was taking part in other industrial action (within the meaning of s. 238) and that his employer had either not dismissed all relevant employees' or he had done so but had then selectively re-engaged within three months of the complainant employee's dismissal. This therefore gives rise to the following questions:

(a)   What is meant by a lock-out?
(b)   When is an employee taking part in other industrial action?
(c)   At what time can an employer legitimately dismiss employees?
(d)   When does selective re-engagement occur?

(a)   *Lock-outs*   No statutory definition exists as to what is meant by a lock-out. The best judicial interpretation of the phrase is probably that provided by May LJ in the case of *Express and Star Ltd* v *Bunday* [1987] IRLR 422, where he stated (at p. 425):

... the *Shorter Oxford Dictionary* ... defines a 'lock-out' as 'an act of locking-out a body of operatives; i.e. a refusal on the part of an employer, or employers acting in concert, to furnish work to their operatives except on conditions to be accepted by the latter collectively.' For my part I would again be prepared to accept this dictionary definition as at least a reliable indication of what does constitute a lock-out in modern industrial relations. Nevertheless, I think that it would be wrong to treat the dictionary definition as if it were expressly contained in the statute and to seek to apply it word for word to any problem that may arise in this context. As has already been pointed out, each of these cases must be decided on its own facts and merits and, as will appear, subject to what I have already said, I have no doubt that the best appreciation of what is or is not a strike or lock-out will come from either an Industrial Tribunal, or on appeal the Employment Appeal Tribunal, highly experienced in these matters as these bodies respectively are.

Nothing more can usefully be added to this analysis.

(b)   *Industrial action*   Industrial action in this context is either a strike or other industrial action. The term 'strike' is defined by s. 246 of TULRCA 1992 as being a concerted stoppage of work. As to what amounts to other forms of industrial action, the law reports provide many different examples, e.g., go-slows (*Secretary of State for Employment* v *ASLEF (No. 2)* [1972] ICR 19); refusal to work overtime (*Power Packing Case Makers Ltd* v *Faust* [1983] ICR 292); and, indeed, any other form of withdrawal of goodwill (*Ticehurst* v *British Telecommunications plc* [1992] IRLR 219). It was also held in *Coates* v *Modern Methods and Materials Ltd* [1982] IRLR 318, that an employee who refused to cross a picket line for fear of harassment was involved in a strike and that her motive for refusing to cross was irrelevant. Furthermore it has been held that a strike that has been deliberately provoked by an employer is caught by the provisions of s. 238 of the 1992 Act (see *Wilkins* v *Cantrell & Cochrane (GB) Ltd* [1978] IRLR 483 and *Marsden* v *Fairey Stainless Ltd* [1979] IRLR 103).

It will of course be a question of fact as to whether a particular employee is engaged in action taking place, and a relevant employee will ordinarily need to show that he was ready, willing and able to carry out the terms of both the letter and the spirit of his contract. This said, if an employee is legitimately absent from work but takes part in industrial action, the employee still can be treated as engaged in the industrial action. The matter was dealt with by Scott J in *Bolton Roadway Ltd* v *Edwards* [1987] IRLR 392, where he held (at p. 396):

Whether an employee is taking part in strike action is, as we have said, a question of fact. Whether an employee's activity represents a breach of his obligation to attend work, may be relevant to the question whether he is taking part in a strike, but it is not in our view an essential ingredient. We would take, as an example, the case of an employee who is for the time being on holiday or away sick. That employee by reason of his holiday entitlement or his sickness would not be in breach of his contractual obligation to work; but if he associated himself with the strike, attended at the picket line or took part in the other activities of the strikers with a view to furthering their aims, he would, in our view, be capable of being held to be taking part in the strike. Any other view would be to make nonsense of the plain language of the phrase 'taking part in the strike or other industrial action'.

Therefore, where an employee does not attend for work for a reason that is unconnected with the action taking place, the prudent employer cannot simply assume that he is in breach of contract; rather, he should carry out an investigation into the reason for any non-attendance in the same way that he would for any other absenteeism (see also the comments of the EAT in *Hindle Gears Ltd* v *McGinty* [1984] IRLR 477, *Manifold Industries Ltd* v *Sims* [1991] IRLR 242, *Jenkins* v *P & O European Ferries (Dover) Ltd* [1991] ICR 652 and *Rogers* v *Chloride Systems* [1992] ICR 198, although the last case should be treated with caution).

(c) *The time of dismissal* In order for an employer to be protected from unfair dismissal actions when dismissing employees taking part in other industrial action (within the meaning of s. 238 of TULRCA 1992), the employer must dismiss only employees who are actually taking part in the relevant action *at the time* that they are taking part. This point is quite complex. To start with it needs to be shown that the employees are taking part in industrial action. If an employer 'jumps the gun' by dismissing prior to action being taken, or dismisses after action has been taken and is concluded, the dismissals will be unfair.

Two difficult examples of employers dismissing prior to action being taken are *Midland Plastics* v *Till* [1983] IRLR 9 and *Lewis* v *E. Mason & Sons Ltd* [1984] IRLR 4. As to the first of these cases, the employer had dismissed some of its union employees after they notified the employer that it was their intention to take industrial action unless certain demands were met. The employees claimed that they had been unfairly dismissed and submitted a claim to the industrial tribunal. It was alleged by the employer that the tribunal had no jurisdiction to hear the case because the employees had been dismissed for taking part in industrial action. The employer appealed to the EAT after the industrial tribunal held that it did have jurisdiction. The EAT declined the employer's appeal on the grounds that it was necessary to distinguish between a threat to take action and the taking of the action (which was the point at which what is now s. 238 operated). Browne-Wilkinson P (as he was then) held (at p. 11):

... if the employers are to succeed, as it seems to us they must be able to show that the threat of taking industrial action can itself amount to taking industrial action. We reject that view.... We cannot accept ... that because the threat to take industrial action imposed pressure on the employers, such threat itself constituted the taking of industrial action.

This said, in the *Lewis* case another division of the EAT reached exactly the opposite view and held that notice of proposed action could amount to action. It is submitted that the *Lewis* decision is wrong in law and that an employer cannot rely on action being taken until such time as the employees in question have breached the letter and spirit of their employment contracts.

As to the issue of employees being dismissed after action has ceased, regard should be had to the decisions in *Heath* v *J. F. Longman (Meat Salesman) Ltd* [1973] IRLR 214 and, more recently, in *Mainland Car Deliveries Ltd* v *Cooper* (unreported, EAT 492/96, 14 July 1997). In both cases it was held that once an employer knows that industrial action is finished and then dismisses employees, he loses the protection that would otherwise be available under s. 238 of the 1992 Act.

(d)   *Selective re-engagement*   As has been noted at 5.5.3.5.3 above, an employee will be able to claim that he has been unfairly dismissed where his employer selectively re-engages 'relevant' fellow employees who have been dismissed with the complainant for taking part in the same industrial action. This gives rise to the following questions:

(i)   Who is a relevant fellow employee?

(ii)   When do the employees take part in the same industrial action?

(iii)   At what time must it be shown that a comparitor remained in employment?

(iv)   What constitutes an offer of re-employment?

(i)   *Relevant employees*   As to this matter, the starting point is s. 238(3) of the 1992 Act. Relevant employees will include all those employees directly interested in a particular dispute and subjected to a lock-out, and all those employees taking part in a strike or other industrial action at the same establishment as the complainant. The last limb of the subsection (which ties the place of employment down to that at which the complainant works) was one of the last amendments to s. 238 and has the effect of, for example, allowing an employer with many sites to negotiate settlement terms with each different place of employment or to dismiss the workers at such establishments. It further narrows the pool of relevant employees by requiring that relevant employees are those who are taking part in the action at the date of dismissal. It follows that, if an employer issues an ultimatum to return to work which is complied with by some employees and not complied with by others, and after the date on which it expires he then dismisses those still taking action, the pool of relevant employees is those employees still taking action and does not include those employees who have returned to work prior to the deadline.

(ii)   *When does industrial action take place?*   The second question was discussed in *McCormick* v *Horsepower Ltd* [1981] ICR 535. Here, the complainant was one of a group of employees who took part in a strike for more pay. A fellow employee, B, chose not to cross the picket line and stayed away from work. In doing so, B failed to inform the employer as to his reasons for non-attendance. After a period of time B did attend for work. He was not dismissed along with the complainant who claimed unfair dismissal and submitted that B was a relevant employee taking part in action who had not been dismissed. The matter finally reached the Court of Appeal which concluded that B was not engaged in the strike and was not taking sympathy action. It followed that, since he was not taking part in the same action, he was not a relevant employee for the purposes of s. 238(3) and therefore the claim failed.

(iii)   *The time for showing that a comparitor has not been dismissed*   It was held by the Court of Appeal in *P & O European Ferries (Dover) Ltd* v *Byrne* [1989] ICR 779 that the relevant time is the end of the hearing at which the tribunal is required to consider whether it has jurisdiction. According to the Court, the purpose of the hearing is to allow an employer to know what the case is against him. Hypothetically, the by-product of the decision is that it allows an employer to defeat a claim by dismissing the comparitor employees prior to the end of the jurisdiction hearing. This said, if an employer makes offers to all employees within a three-month period of a potential claimant's dismissal, no claim can arise even if the offers of re-engagement are staggered throughout the period (*Highland Fabricators Ltd* v *McLaughlin* [1984] IRLR 482).

(iv)   *Offers of re-engagement*   When considering what amounts to an offer of re-engagement to a comparitor, it will be remembered that if a complainant is to be allowed to pursue a claim under the section, the comparitor must be offered re-engagement within three months of the dismissal of the complainant. No formal written offer is required to be made to the comparitor (*Marsden* v *Fairey Stainless Ltd* [1979] IRLR 103.

Once an offer has been made by an employer to a comparitor, it is no defence for him to say that he did not mean to make the offer. In the case of *Bigham* v *GKN Kwikform Ltd* [1992] IRLR 4, the EAT held that where an offer was inadvertently made by the employer within the three-month period, even though the employer subsequently re-dismissed the comparitor when it found out about the mistake, it was still possible to bring a claim under s. 238(2)(b) of TULRCA 1992. It was pointed out by the EAT in that case that the comparitor had no intent to defraud the employer. Where such intent is present (e.g., where an employee applies to work under a false name), it is likely that the employer will have a defence to a claim since any offer of employment would be made on the basis of a unilateral mistake and therefore acceptance by the comparitor will be of no legal effect. It would follow that the employment of the comparitor would not have been entered into and therefore the conditions of s. 238 could not be complied with.

This said, it will be possible for an employer to show that he has made an offer to all employees including the complainant even where the complainant is not individually notified by the employer. In *Marsden* v *Fairey Stainless Ltd* [1979] IRLR 103, the employer inadvertently wrongly addressed an offer to the complainant. It was held by the EAT that, given that the employee knew that an offer had been made to him in any event, the lack of formal written notice was of no importance. Likewise, it will be a defence to show that there is another potentially fair reason under s. 98 of the ERA 1996 why an offer of re-engagement has not been made to a complainant. This is because, unlike unfair dismissal under ss. 152–153 of TULRCA 1992, it is not automatically unfair to re-engage selectively. Indeed, a complainant's case locks in to the provisions of the ERA 1996 by virtue of s. 239(1) of TULRCA 1992, and therefore the full range of potentially fair reasons is available to the employer.

5.5.4 Trade union related unfair dismissal procedure

The procedural aspects of trade union related unfair dismissals are dealt with at one of two levels depending upon whether the dismissal is automatically unfair as a result of it being a dismissal within ss. 152 or 153 of TULRCA 1992, or whether it is an unfair dismissal dealt with by s. 238 of the Act. Each will be examined in turn and will assume an understanding of the basic principles of the law of unfair dismissal (see Robert Upex, *Termination of Employment*, 5th ed., Sweet & Maxwell, 1997). It should be noted generally that, in automatically unfair dismissal claims, the provisions of TULRCA 1992 lock into to those existing under the ERA 1996, Pt X, albeit in a modified form (s. 167, TULRCA 1992).

5.5.4.1 Procedure in automatically unfair dismissal claims

5.5.4.1.1 Removal of certain bars to claims   The first modification is provided by s. 154(1) of the 1992 Act, which removes the two-year qualifying period and the upper age limit of 65 in a case where the reason for the dismissal was one of those specified in s. 152(1). The normal three-month period in which claims must be brought under s. 111(2) of ERA 1996 still exists.

5.5.4.1.2 Interim continuation order   Unlike ordinary unfair dismissal claims, in the case of s. 152 unfair dismissal claims (but not claims for unfair dismissal due to unfair selection for redundancy under s. 153 of TULRCA 1992), an industrial tribunal has the power under s. 161 of the 1992 Act to make an interim continuation order so as to ensure that an employee is still employed by an employer pending the outcome of a substantive unfair dismissal claim. An application for such an order must be made to the industrial tribunal within seven days immediately following the effective date of dismissal, although it is specifically provided that an application can be made before, or after the effective date of dismissal (see s. 161(1) and (2)). The application should state why it is believed that the claim falls within s. 161 (*Stone* v *Charrington & Co.* [1977] ICR 248).

The date of dismissal is taken to be either the date on which notice was given to an employee to terminate a contract of employment, or, in any other case the effective date of termination (s. 161(6)).

It is also provided that in order for an application to be considered, under s. 161(3) a certificate in writing must be provided by an authorised official of the independent trade union to which the claimant belongs stating that:

(a)   on the date of dismissal the employee was or proposed to become a member of the union; and

(b)   there appear to be reasonable grounds for supposing that the reason or principal reason for the claimant's dismissal was the ground set out in the complaint.

There are statutory presumptions that documents purporting to be an authorisation for an official to act and to be a s. 161(3) certificate are such documents unless the contrary is proved (s. 161(5)). It is not necessary that an express appointment to a post as an authorised official exists; this can be inferred from the status of an official (*Farmeary* v *Veterinary Drug Co. Ltd* [1976] IRLR 322). To the extent that an official is challenged to prove that he is authorised and fails to do so, this amounts to a material defect in a claim and will remove an application from the jurisdiction of a tribunal hearing it (*Salemany* v *Habib Bank Ltd* [1983] ICR 60).

The whole point of the continuation procedure is to resolve the conflict at an early stage before the damage to trust and confidence caused by a dismissal becomes irreversible. To this end, when an application is made, under s. 162 of TULRCA 1992 a tribunal receiving an application for interim relief is required to determine it as soon as is reasonably practicable after receiving the application and certificate. Further, once a hearing date has been set, the date should not be postponed unless 'special circumstances' exist (s. 162(4)). A tribunal is required to give an employer not less than seven days' notice of the date, time and place of a hearing together with a copy of the application (s. 162(2)). If an action for unfair dismissal is being brought against a third party to a dispute as well as against an employer (see 5.5.4.2.3), the third party is also entitled to receive notice of the time, date and place of a hearing and a copy of the application.

At the hearing of a s. 161 claim, in the event that a tribunal finds that it is 'likely' that it will find a claimant unfairly dismissed at the substantive unfair dismissal hearing, it can then go on to make an order under s. 163 (s. 163(1)). The word 'likely' for these purposes was defined by Slynn J (as he was then) in *Taplin* v *C. Shippam Ltd* [1978] ICR 1068, at p. 1074, to mean a 'pretty good' chance of success. Slynn J accepted that the industrial tribunal chairman in the case had not erred in law by deciding that this equated to a 51 per cent or more chance of success.

A tribunal is required to announce its findings at the hearing and explain to both parties if they are present the powers that it may exercise. It is also required to ask an employer, if it is present, whether it is willing, in the period between the s. 161 hearing and the substantive unfair dismissal hearing, to reinstate or re-engage the complainant on terms not less favourable than those enjoyed prior to the dismissal giving rise to the s. 161 complaint (s. 163(2) and (3)). Where an employer is prepared to reinstate the employee the tribunal will make an order to that effect (s. 163(4)).

If an employer proposes to re-engage an employee in another job in the interim period and the employer goes on to specify the terms and conditions of the new post, the tribunal must put the proposed new working conditions to the complainant. The complainant then has the opportunity of accepting the post (whereupon the tribunal will make a continuation order in those terms) or rejecting the post. If an employee, in the opinion of a tribunal, reasonably rejects an offer made by an employer, the tribunal is bound to make a continuation order based on the terms and conditions enjoyed by the employee prior to dismissal. If the tribunal is of the opinion that a complainant has unreasonably rejected an offer, it will not make any order with regard to continuation of the employee's contract (s. 163(5)). In the event either that an employer refuses to attend, or does so but intimates to the tribunal that it is not minded to re-employ a complainant, the tribunal is bound to make a continuation order (s. 163(6)).

The provisions of continuation orders are dealt with by s. 164 of TULRCA 1992. The effect of an order is that it provides that the contract of employment in connection with which it is made, shall be taken to continue in force from the date of the initial dismissal until the determination of the substantive unfair dismissal hearing (s. 164(1)). The order is effective with regard to matters such as pay or any other benefit derived from employment, seniority, pension rights and other such matters, and also is effective with regard to determining the period of continuous employment (s. 164(1)(a) and (b)). A tribunal is specifically required to state in an order the amount of pay to be paid in a normal pay period, or part thereof, falling to be paid between the date of dismissal and a continuation order hearing (s. 164(2)). To the extent that an employer has given an employee pay in lieu of notice or a lump sum as compensation for dismissal, this must be set off against any entitlement to remuneration accruing under a continuation order (s. 164(5) and (6)).

Once an order has been made, it is possible for either party to apply to an industrial tribunal to vary or revoke the order due to a relevant change of circumstances since the making of the order (s. 165(1)). This hearing can be heard by a different industrial tribunal to that which made the continuation order (*British Coal Corporation* v *McGinty* [1988] IRLR 7). The procedure to be adopted is similar to that needed for the grant of a continuation order save that no trade union certificate needs to supplied. In the event that an employer fails to comply with the terms of a continuation order, a tribunal, upon an application being made by an employee, can award such sum as it thinks just and equitable in all the circumstances as a result of the employer's refusal to comply (s. 166).

5.5.4.2   *Remedies in automatically unfair dismissal claims*
Unlike ordinary unfair dismissal claims, a number of features have been built in to the law relating to union related dismissals under ss. 152 and 153 of TULRCA 1992 to render such dismissals extremely costly to an employer. When introduced by the Employment Act 1982, the enhanced remedies were designed to protect non-unionised employees from closed shop related dismissals. The legislation is now neutral as between those dismissed because they were union members and those dismissed because they were not members of a union or a particular union.

The usual remedies of reinstatement, re-engagement and compensation are available, but these will not be discussed in this book and regard should be had to mainstream employment law works for full treatment of this area generally. However, the two important variations to compensation will be dealt with here, i.e., first, an entitlement to receive a minimum basic award and, secondly, an entitlement to a special award in a case where an applicant has requested reinstatement or re-engagement.

5.5.4.2.1 Minimum basic award The minimum basic award is provided by s. 156 of TULRCA 1992. The award is necessary given that it is possible to claim unfair dismissal for a union related reason without an employee meeting the usual two-year qualifying period. If, for example, an employee is dismissed for a reason falling within ss. 152 or 153 and the employee has not worked for a full year, the basic award for such an employee as worked out under the usual provisions of the ERA 1996 would be nil. However, the minimum basic award under s. 156 ensures that something is paid to such a claimant, and also punishes the employer for dismissing for an unlawful reason. The amount of the award is set by s. 156(1) and is currently £2,900.

Reductions can be made from the basic award:

(a) for contributory fault on the part of an employee within the meaning of s. 122(2) of ERA 1996 (s. 156(2), TULRCA 1992);

(b) where an employee unreasonably refuses to accept an offer of reinstatement (s. 122(1) of ERA 1996);

(c) to take account of a redundancy payment (s. 122(4) of ERA 1996); and

(d) to prevent over-compensation due to an award of compensation for sexual and/or racial discrimination (s. 126 of ERA 1996).

5.5.4.2.2 Special award The special award is dealt with by ss. 157 and 158 of TULRCA 1992. The award is available only where a complainant has requested reinstatement or re-engagement (s. 157). Where an order for reinstatement or re-engagement is made in a claim under ss. 152 or 153 of the 1992 Act and is not complied with, the usual provisions of s. 117(3)(b) of ERA 1996 are specifically excluded from applying (s. 157(2), TULRCA 1992). Instead, the provisions of s. 158 of TULRCA 1992 operate. These provide that a special award shall be made amounting to the greater of either a week's pay multiplied by 104, or £14,500, but subject to a maximum of £29,000 (s. 158(1)). It should be noted that a week's pay in this instance is not capped at £220 as it is with unfair dismissal generally.

Where an employer refuses to comply with the requirements of s. 117(3)(b) of ERA 1996 by not reinstating or re-engaging an employee in defiance of an order to do so by a tribunal, the amount of the special award is increased to the greater of either a week's pay multiplied by 156, or £21,800.

It is possible for a tribunal to reduce a special award in any of the following four sets of circumstances:

(a)   where the complainant is aged over 64 under the provisions set down in s. 119(4) of ERA 1996 (a proportionate reduction of one-twelfth per month for each month that the complainant is aged over 64);

(b)   where the complainant's conduct warrants a deduction (s. 158(4), TULRCA 1992). It should be noted that the matters set down in s. 155(2) of the 1992 Act are specifically excluded from being such conduct (these being that a complainant refused to be or become a member of a union, or a particular union or unions; refused to cease to be or refrain from becoming a member of a particular union or unions; refused to take part in the activities of a union, or one or more particular unions; or objected to contributions having to be made or deductions having to be suffered in favour of a union or other person in lieu of union membership);

(c)   where a tribunal finds that a complainant has unreasonably prevented an order of reinstatement or re-engagement from being complied with (s. 158(5)(a), TULRCA 1992); and

(d)   where a complainant refuses an offer from an employer that would result in the employee being reinstated (s. 158(5)(b), TULRCA 1992).

5.5.4.2.3   Liability of third parties   As the thrust of the changes to the law in this area has been concerned with overcoming the closed shop, it is not surprising to note that a third party who induces a dismissal to take place can be brought in as a party to an unfair dismissal action. This occurs through operation of s. 160 of the 1992 Act, which applies where an employer has been induced by a third party (typically a trade union) to dismiss an employee by threat of a strike or other industrial action due to the employee's membership or non-membership of a union, or one or more particular unions (s. 160(1)). The request to join a third party can be made either by a complainant or by an employer (s. 160(1)) and must be granted if made at any time prior to a substantive unfair dismissal hearing. A request to join can be refused after the hearing has started, and must be refused after liability has been determined (s. 160(2)).

Where a third party is joined and a complaint of unfair dismissal is successful, it is possible for either or both of the employer and the third party to be held liable to pay compensation (s. 160(3)).

5.5.4.3   Procedure and remedies in s. 238 claims
The procedure and remedies for claims under this head are dealt with under s. 239(1) and (3) of TULRCA 1992, which tie into the provisions of the ERA 1996 but as a union related unfair dismissal.

This said, two caveats need to be observed, these being in relation to the time limit for presenting an application to an industrial tribunal and in relation to what amounts to contributory fault for the purposes of deductions from an award of compensation:

(a)   The time limit for a claim arising under s. 238 of TULRCA 1992 is extended from the normal period of three months (under s. 111(2), ERA 1996) to six months by s. 239(2) of the 1992 Act. The reason for this extension is to allow a dismissed employee to see whether any discriminatory re-engagement of other employees occurs in the context of s. 238(2)(b) of the Act.

(b)   The House of Lords has recently held in the case of *Crossville Wales Ltd* v *Tracey (No. 2)* [1997] IRLR 691 that when a tribunal is determining whether to make a deduction for contributory fault in the case of selective re-engagement unfair dismissals, it is to take no account of the fact that employees have taken industrial action. In the only substantive judgment in the case, Lord Nolan stated (at p. 698) that the reason for this is because of the impossibility of attaching blame individually to particular actors in collective action. This said, he went on to say that if an individual actor is shown specifically to have engaged in conduct over and above the industrial action generally then the particular fault can be used to reduce an award of compensation.

5.6   PARTICIPATION RIGHTS

5.6.1   Introduction

Participation rights in the activities of a trade union are contingent upon a union being independent and recognised by a particular employer (see 2.1.4 *et seq.*). The rights cannot exist without this important qualification. There are two participation rights: (i) the right of a union official to have paid time off to carry out union duties; and (ii) the right for members of a union to have time off to take part in the activities of a union. The statutory rights are also supplemented by the ACAS Code of Practice on Time Off.

5.6.2   Paid time off for union officials

5.6.2.1   *The right*
The provisions relating to the right for union officials to have paid time off is set out in ss. 168–169 of TULRCA 1992. The right to time off itself is set out in s. 168(1)–(2), which provide as follows:

(1)   An employer shall permit an employee of his who is an official of an independent trade union recognised by the employer to take time off during his working hours for the purpose of carrying out any duties of his, as such an official, concerned with—
(a)   negotiations with the employer related to or connected with matters falling within section 178(2) (collective bargaining) in relation to which the trade union is recognised by the employer, or
(b)   the performance on behalf of employees of the employer of functions related to or connected with matters falling within that provision which the employer has agreed may be so performed by the trade union.

(2)   He shall also permit an employee to take time off during his working hours
for the purpose of undergoing training in aspects of industrial relations—

(a)   relevant to carrying out of such duties as are mentioned in subsection
(1), and

(b)   approved by the Trades Union Congress or by the independent trade
union of which he is an official.

It can be seen immediately that the right is a tightly prescribed one turning, first,
on the matter for which a union official employee is to be released being related to
or connected with collective bargaining (see 3.7 *et seq.* above). If that aspect is
satisfied, there are two sets of circumstances in which the right can be exercised,
essentially for 'performance' (s. 168(1)) and for 'educational' purposes (s. 168(2)).

It should be noted that prior to the implementation of s. 14 of the Employment Act
1989, the right was wider in scope and allowed an official time off for any duties
connected generally with industrial relations. Any cases prior to the commencement
of this amendment are therefore of limited help in defining the modern scope of the
right.

5.6.2.1.1   The 'performance' purpose   The performance limb of the right allows a
union official time off to prepare and take part in the negotiation of collective
agreements falling within s. 178 of TULRCA 1992 on behalf of employees, or to
exercise functions granted by such collective agreements on behalf of fellow
employees.

The right applies only where a union has granted an official authority to act in
respect of the matters contained in or connected with a s. 178 collective agreement.
This is a matter to be sorted out between a relevant official and his union. An official
cannot claim paid time off if he usurping a duty which does not fall within the
authority granted expressly or impliedly by his union. In *Ashley* v *Ministry of
Defence* [1984] IRLR 57, the EAT held that attendance by a union official at an
unofficial meeting of union representatives to ensure a common approach on pay and
allied terms prior to an official meeting did not to fall within the right. The EAT
concluded that unless the official's union had authorised the meeting (which on the
facts it had not), it could not be said that the official was acting within his duty.

This said, it follows that where a union has authorised an official to act and he is
preparing for that action, this will ordinarily be caught within s. 168(1)(a) by virtue
of its being 'connected with' the matter. An example of this point is *London
Ambulance Service* v *Charlton* [1992] IRLR 510 (which approved a number of the
pre-1990 cases, notably, *Sood* v *GEC Elliot Process Automation Ltd* [1979] IRLR
416, *Beal* v *Beacham Group Ltd* [1982] IRLR 192 and *British Bakeries (Northern)
Ltd* v *Adlington* [1988] IRLR 177).

5.6.2.1.2   The 'educational' purpose   The educational purpose of the right allows
a union official time off for training either in aspects of industrial relations connected

with s. 178 collective agreements, or in respect of matters approved by the TUC or by the official's own union. Again, it is necessary that the duties performed or to be performed by the official fall within the express or implied authority granted by his union. It follows from this that the right to paid time off for this purpose will turn on the circumstances and status of a particular official. For example, in *Menzies v Smith and McLaurin Ltd* [1980] IRLR 180, an application for time off was correctly refused according to the EAT. In this case the applicant had asked for paid time off to attend a course on job security. At the time of his request, his employer was negotiating redundancies. However, the Scottish EAT held that the course was too general in nature and would not have had any direct impact on his ability to negotiate in the particular circumstances. It was also felt that it was designed for a higher level of official than the applicant. It follows from this latter point that although approval may be granted to a course either by the TUC or by a particular union, it is still necessary for the course to be relevant to the applicant's circumstances.

5.6.2.2   The amount of time off

The provision dealing with the amount of time off to be granted is s. 168(3) of TULRCA 1992. This states that an employee is entitled to such time off as is reasonable in all the circumstances for the purposes of s. 168 having regard to the relevant provisions of the ACAS Code of Practice on Time Off. Two points arise: (1) what are the employee's working hours; and (ii) who is to decide what is reasonable time off?

5.6.2.2.1   The employee's working hours

The right in s. 168(1) and (2) allows an employee to take time off for union duties during his working hours (defined in s. 173(1) as being any time that an employee is required by his contract of employment to be at work). It follows that if, for example, an employee attends a course or a meeting outside his working hours, he will have no right to claim a corresponding amount of time off from his working hours. This said, if the course or meeting is outside his working hours but he is required to travel in working hours to get to it, the member will be allowed time off for the travelling since this will be 'reasonable' within the context of s. 168(3) of TULRCA 1992.

The best illustration of this point is the case of *Hairsine v Kingston-Upon-Hull City Council* [1992] IRLR 211. Here the applicant was required to work on a shift basis. He was allocated an afternoon and evening shift by his employer on a day when he was due to attend a course in the morning and afternoon. As the applicant was rostered to attend at work for the afternoon and evening shift, and worked the latter shift only, he argued that he should have been paid on the basis that he had worked a full day during the morning and afternoon and was entitled to pay for a full day for that session (i.e., his evening shift was effectively overtime). His employer paid him for the afternoon and evening shift only. He made a claim under s. 169(5) of the 1992 Act claiming that he was entitled to pay for the morning shift in addition to afternoon and evening pay. The claim was refused by both the industrial tribunal and the EAT. In the EAT, Wood P stated (at p. 214) that the time off must be part of his 'working hours', i.e., it is to be given a literal meaning. Since the applicant had not been working during the morning, he had no right to payment for it.

5.6.2.2.2 Time off to be reasonable   The Act 1992 requires that the time off must be reasonable. In assessing the question of the reasonableness of a request, an employer can take into account the amount of time off that is being requested, the purpose for which it is being taken and the occasions on which it is being requested, together with any conditions that have been laid down by the employer (s. 168(3)).

The question arises as to what test is to be applied to the question of reasonableness in this context. Should it be a subjective view of reasonableness from the point of view of the employer at the time of refusal, or an objective view determined by a tribunal subsequently? In *Ministry of Defence* v *Crook* [1982] IRLR 488, the EAT took the view that the test was to consider whether the employer had behaved within a band of reasonable responses to the request for time off (i.e., the same test as that for unfair dismissal). The problem with this decision is that the test in s. 168(3) of TULRCA 1992 is phrased differently to that in Pt X of the ERA 1996, and requires that account must be taken of 'all the circumstances' of the case. This view has been endorsed, albeit *obiter*, in *Wignall* v *British Gas Corporation* [1984] IRLR 493 and in the *Hairsine* case.

5.6.2.3   Refusal of time off
Where an employer refuses an employee time off, the employee is left with a difficult choice. The employee must either forego the course etc. and then claim under s. 168(4) of the Act, or take the time off and make a claim under s. 169 (which allows an employee to be paid for the time off, 5.6.2.4) if his employer subsequently refuses to pay him. In the event that the employee does take time off in defiance of an employer's instruction, the result may well be a breach of contract on the employee's part. This said, it may be possible to show that the employer has behaved so unreasonably as to undermine trust and confidence in the working relationship. If the employer were to dismiss in such circumstances, it would be automatically unfair by virtue of s. 104 of the ERA 1996, although this may well be small consolation to the employee who has been dismissed. In such circumstances, employees are best advised to (say) miss a course and make a claim for compensation to an industrial tribunal under s. 168(4) of TULRCA 1992.

5.6.2.4   Right to pay for time off
Where an employee has taken time off under s. 168 of TULRCA 1992, an employer is bound to pay the employee for the time so taken under s. 169(1). The amount of remuneration is dealt with by s. 169(2)–(4) and is to be such sums as an employee would ordinarily be paid for the working time during which the employee is absent. If an employee is entitled by his contract of employment to be paid for time off, the sums that he would be entitled to under the statutory right are set off under s. 169(4).

5.6.2.5 *Enforcing the rights*
As has been stated in 5.6.2.3 above, to the extent that an employer unreasonably refuses to allow an employee to take time off or unreasonably refuses to pay for the working time that has taken been taken off, a claim can be made to an industrial tribunal under TULRCA 1992, ss. 168(4) and 169(5). A claim must be made within three months of the date on which the failure occurred, or within such other period as the tribunal thinks fit where it has decided that it was not practicable to present the claim in three months (s. 171).

Where a claim is made under s. 168 and upheld by a tribunal, the tribunal is bound to make a declaration to that effect and may award compensation of such sum as is just and equitable taking into account any fault on the part of the complainant (s. 172(1) and (2)). Where a claim is made under s. 169, the remedy is again a declaration but shall also comprise compensation, being the wages that have not been paid (s. 172(3)).

5.6.3 Time off for trade union activities

5.6.3.1 *The right*
The right to time off to take part in trade union activities is set out in s. 170 of TULRCA 1992, which provides as follows:

(1) An employer shall permit an employee of his who is a member of an independent trade union recognised by the employer in respect of that description of employee to take time off during his working hours for the purpose of taking part in—
(a) any activities of the union, and
(b) any activities in relation to which the employee is acting as a representative of the union.
(2) The right conferred by subsection (1) does not extend to activities which themselves consist of industrial action, whether or not in contemplation or furtherance of a trade dispute.

The right is very widely defined and (subject to the following) covers 'any activities'. The only excluded activity is industrial action, whether official or otherwise. This said, the EAT has sought to limit the scope of the right. In *Luce* v *London Borough of Bexley* [1990] IRLR 422, the applicant sought time off to attend a union lobby of Parliament. His employer refused the time off, whereupon the applicant lodged proceedings in the industrial tribunal claiming that he should have been allowed to attend. The industrial tribunal rejected his claim on the grounds that it was necessary to consider whether it was a reasonable activity, which it found it was not. The EAT rejected an appeal, with Wood P holding (at p. 425) that: '... although we do not consider that the phrase [any activities] should be understood too restrictively, we are satisfied that it cannot have been the intention of Parliament to have included any activity of whatever nature'.

It is submitted that neither the view of the industrial tribunal nor that of the EAT
is correct. The 1992 Act simply requires that an employee takes part in any of the
activities of an independent trade union recognised by his employer. It has no
qualification apart from that relating to industrial action, and as such the above
decision must be wrong in law. Indeed, for either an employer or a tribunal to second
guess what a union believes is necessary for its members would seem to extend the
law far beyond that.

As with the right to time off for union duties, an employer can consider whether
the request is reasonable (s. 170(3)) and regard should be had to 5.6.2.2.2 above on
this point.

5.6.3.2   Enforcing the right

As with the right to time off for union duties, it is possible to lodge a complaint with
an industrial tribunal within three months of the refusal (ss. 170(4) and 171). If a
claim is held to be proved by a tribunal, the tribunal must grant a declaration and,
where appropriate, make an order for compensation. Regard should be had to 5.6.2.5
above generally these points.

5.7   REFORM

A further right has been proposed by the White Paper 'Fairness at Work' in relation
to union members. The suggested right is for employees to be accompanied by a
fellow employee or trade union representative of their choice at grievance or
disciplinary procedures. The proposed right stops short of imposing a duty for such
a nominated representative to attend. Protection against unfair dismissal or action
short of dismissal will be available for nominated representatives. As with all the
suggestions in the White Paper, the time frame for implementation is some way off.

6 Industrial Action 1 — The Industrial Torts and Breach of Contract

6.1 INTRODUCTION

6.1.1 Background

Industrial action has long been the means that unions have adopted as a last resort to bring about change. As was seen in Chapter 1, it has been an accepted part of the industrial negotiating machinery since the last quarter of the 19th century. It places two collectives against each other (capital and labour) and allows the collectives to engage in a process of attrition to bring about a new industrial order. Up until the start of the 1970s, it was accepted that this was the natural order of industrial negotiation. Various judgments over the course of the 20th century reflected the importance of the right to strike. In *Crofter Hand Woven Harris Tweed Co. Ltd* v *Veitch* [1942] AC 435, Lord Wright stated (at p. 463):

> In commercial affairs each trader's rights are qualified by the right to compete. Where the rights of labour are concerned, the rights of the employer are conditioned by the rights of the men to give or withhold their services. The right of workmen to strike is an essential element in the principle of collective bargaining.

The statement is very much the high point of the collective *laissez-faire* school of thought.

The current view of the law, however, is that there is no right to strike, merely immunity from the tortious consequences of action taken. Further, individuals withdrawing their labour will breach their contracts (although the law, in the form of s. 216 of ERA 1996, does recognise that the continuity of employment of an employee who chooses to strike will be maintained during the course of such action until such time as the employee either returns to or is dismissed from the work that he is employed to do). To the extent that an employee does take industrial action and his wages are reduced to reflect the value of services lost by his employer as a result of the strike, no claim for the lost wages exists under Pt II of the 1996 Act. Other statutory employment rights that can be lost are the right to receive a redundancy payment (ERA 1996, s. 140) and the right to receive guarantee payments (ERA 1996, s. 29). Furthermore, the question of entitlement to social security benefits is also tied into the issue of industrial action, and the absence of a right to strike is reflected in the fact that it is not possible to claim jobseeker's allowance during the course of industrial action (Jobseekers Act 1995, s. 14) or statutory sick pay (Social Security Contributions and Benefits Act 1992, sch. 11, paras (2) and (7)).

6.1.2   Formulation of claims in tort in respect of industrial action

The purpose of industrial action is to appeal to an employer's interest, capital. Deliberately harming the legitimate interests of another can amount to tortious conduct, and there is no doubt that in most cases industrial action can be seen as a deliberate attempt to harm the legitimate interests of an employer (even if this view is held only by any employers affected by such action). In order for an employer to claim a remedy against a union taking or organising action, the employer must show that a recognised tort has been committed against him. The problem for employers, however, is that when considering the legality of industrial action, it must be remembered that, as shown in Chapter 1, unions can enjoy a degree of immunity in tort when they take industrial action. This said, in certain circumstances, the immunity enjoyed by union can be removed. What needs to be considered when contemplating legal action against a union arising out of industrial action are the following questions:

(a)   Has a tort been committed in the course of the action taken?
(b)   Does an immunity exist in law for the tort committed?
(c)   Has the immunity been removed?
(d)   Does a remedy exist, to any extent, against the union?

This chapter will focus on the first of those questions, Chapter 7 will focus on questions (b) and (c) and Chapter 8 will discuss the issue of remedies.

6.1.3   The industrial torts

A number of torts have evolved over the years, some or all of which may be committed during the course of industrial action. They are as follows:

(a)   conspiracy, both simple and by using unlawful means;
(b)   inducing breach of contract directly or indirectly;

(c)   interfering with a contract, trade or business using unlawful means;
(d)   intimidation;
(e)   harassment;
(f)   torts committed during picketing.

Each of the torts will be examined in turn.

6.2   CONSPIRACY

6.2.1   Simple conspiracy

6.2.1.1   *Introduction*
After the introduction of the Conspiracy and Protection of Property Act 1875, s. 3 of which stated that 'An agreement or combination by two or more persons to do or procure to be done any act in contemplation or furtherance of a trade dispute ... shall not be indictable as a conspiracy if such act committed by one person would not be punishable as a crime', it was assumed that it was no longer possible for a union to be thwarted in its attempts to bring about change in the workplace by means of a concerted withdrawal of labour. The problem was that the 1875 Act expressly dealt with the concept of criminal conspiracy only. It did not address conspiracy as it arose in the form of the law of tort, for a good reason, namely, that it was a little used tort. Indeed, as Oliver J stated in *Midland Bank Trust Co. Ltd v Green (No. 3)* [1979] Ch 496, at p. 523:

> As regards the tort of conspiracy, however, very little is heard of it until the 19th Century when it was brought into prominence as a result of the legislature having, in 1875, enacted that combinations in furtherance of trade dispute should not be indictable ...

After the 1875 Act, however, a number of cases were brought using the tort of conspiracy as a cause of action, the three most prominent of which were *Mogul Steamship Co. Ltd v McGregor, Gow & Co.* [1892] AC 25, *Allen v Flood* [1898] AC 1 and Quinn v *Leathem* [1901] AC 495.

In *Mogul*, the case concerned a shipowners' trade association. The association had decided that, in order to protect the interests of its members, its members should reach an agreement on the number of ships to be sent to particular ports, the rates that would be charged for cargo and the rebates that would be given to cargo owners who agreed to use associated members exclusively as their shipping agent. The plaintiff was a shipowner who had been excluded from the association. It sent its ships to ports at which the defendant operated in order to procure cargoes. The defendant discovered that the plaintiff was operating in one of its ports and promptly sent more of its members' ships to the port. It underbid the plaintiff at prices which were uneconomic for the journeys being undertaken. Further, it instructed agents operating for it that they would be dismissed if they gave cargoes to the plaintiff, and told customers that the rebates that were provided would be removed from customers who insisted on using the plaintiff. The plaintiff launched an action claiming that the concerted action of the association amounted to a conspiracy to injure the plaintiff. The matter reached the House of Lords. Lord Watson stated (at p. 41):

> As the law is now settled, I apprehend that in order to substantiate their claim, the appellants must shew, either that the object of the agreement was unlawful, or that illegal methods were resorted to in its prosecution. If neither the end contemplated by the agreement, nor the means used for its attainment were contrary to the law, the loss suffered by the appellants was *damnum sine injuria*.

The House of Lords went on to hold that a combination to trade and offer discounts for doing so, even if it might be harmful, did not amount to a conspiracy in law.

This decision was followed in 1898 by *Allen*. The importance of *Allen* can be seen by the length of the case (189 pages of the Appeal Cases) and by the fact that it was argued twice before the House of Lords (the second occasion being in front of nine Law Lords and an advisory body of eight High Court judges). The facts of the case were, of themselves, quite simple. The plaintiffs were shipwrights who had been employed to carry out work on the repair of a ship. The defendant was an ironworker and union official. The union to which he belonged operated a closed shop at the Glengall Iron Company's shipyard. The defendant informed the employer that, unless the plaintiffs were dismissed, his union would call a strike of its members at Glengall. The consequence of this threat was that the employer duly dismissed the plaintiffs, who sued the defendant claiming that he had conspired with members of the union to injure the interests of the plaintiff. At trial, the claim was rejected by Kennedy J who held that there was no evidence of conspiracy, coercion, intimidation or breach of contract on the part of the defendant. However, a jury found that the defendant had maliciously caused the employer to dismiss the plaintiffs and awarded damages of £40. The decision was then affirmed by the Court of Appeal. On appeal to the House of Lords, though, a majority decision (6:3), found in favour of the defendant. Lord Watson (in the majority) stated (at p. 98):

> It is, in my opinion, the absolute right of every workman to exercise his own option with regard to the persons in whose society he will agree or continue to work. It may be deplorable that feelings of rivalry between different associations of working men should run ever so high as to make members of one union seriously object to continue their labour in company with members of another trade union; but so long as they commit no legal wrong, and use no means which are illegal, they are at perfect liberty to act upon their own views.

The majority of the House also went on to add that the conduct of the defendant was not actionable even if it was motivated by malice or bad motive. There had been no conspiracy. To put the matter in a different way, if no tort had been committed, the defendant was perfectly entitled to do something that he had a lawful right to do and to do it with bad grace.

Allen was followed shortly by the third of the cases in the simple conspiracy trilogy, *Quinn v Leathem*. In *Quinn*, the plaintiff was a Belfast butcher who employed the defendants. They were members of a union. One of the union's objects was to help promote the interests of other members of the union at the expense of non-members. To this end, the defendants organised a closed shop. The plaintiff also employed a non-union butcher. The plaintiff was visited by the defendants who informed him that if the non-union employee continued to be employed they would cause one of his clients not to take meat from him any more by informing the customer that their members in the customer's employment would refuse to handle the meat delivered by the plaintiff. The result was that the plaintiff lost the customer and, additionally, was put on black lists in the Belfast area by the union. As a result of the action taken by the union, the plaintiff sued for damages caused by the conspiracy and the matter ultimately reached the House of Lords. The House of Lords found for the plaintiff and, in doing so, distinguished *Allen v Flood*. According to their Lordships, the chief distinction between the two cases was that in *Allen*, the mere presence of threats existed which were not carried into effect by the defendants. However, in *Quinn*, the defendants had gone further in their actions. They had threatened the plaintiff with a potential loss of business and then carried the threat into effect. The matter was addressed in this fashion by Lord Brampton (at p. 528):

A conspiracy consists of an unlawful combination of two or more persons to do that which is contrary to law, or to do that which is wrongful and harmful towards another person. It may be punishable criminally by indictment, or civilly by an action on the case in the nature of conspiracy if damage has been occasioned to the person against whom it is directed. It may also consist of an unlawful combination to carry out an object not in itself unlawful by unlawful means. The essential elements, whether of a criminal or actionable conspiracy, are, in my opinion, the same, though to sustain an action special damage must be proved.

At first glance, the decisions in *Mogul*, *Allen* and *Quinn* are irreconcilable in that they appear to decide the same point in differing fashions. However, the accepted point of reconciliation between the three cases appears to be that *Mogul* decided that it is not unlawful to carry out acts that harm another where the acts complained of are not unlawful in themselves and will further the interests of those combining; *Allen* decided, on the other hand, that an act that is not carried into effect in the form of a conspiracy and which is of itself lawful is not actionable; and *Quinn* holds that a combination to injure another, which is not in the trade interests of those combining, can be actionable where it is spiteful action aimed at the victim, assuming that special damage can be proved by the victim. This viewpoint has been echoed in a number of judgments, notably, *Ware and De Freville* v *Motor Trade Association* [1921] 3 KB 40, *Sorrell* v *Smith* [1925] AC 700 and *Crofter Hand Woven Harris Tweed Co. Ltd* v *Veitch* [1942] AC 435.

6.2.1.2   Elements of a simple conspiracy
The elements of the tort of simple conspiracy are that a plaintiff must show the following:

(a)   a combination of two or more persons;

(b)   an agreement between the members of the combination to do an act or cause an act to be done to the victim of the conspiracy;

(c)   an intention to injure the plaintiff;

(d)   a predominant purpose of injuring the plaintiff.

6.2.1.2.1   The combination   One of the problems that is thrown up in relation to trade unions is whether the union itself can count as a person for the purposes of establishing a conspiracy. As was seen at 2.1.5.2 *et seq.* above, a union does not have legal personality save to the extent that it is granted status by s. 10 of TULRCA 1992. Regard should be had to the debate above generally on this point. However, as regards a union's ability to be a conspirator, it must be doubtful that the alleged conspirators in an action could be both an official of the union (e.g., a shop steward) and the union itself. Indeed, if the language of s. 20 of TULRCA 1992 (the section attaching liability in tort to a union) is examined, s. 20(1)(b) states that:

(1)   Where proceedings in tort are brought against a trade union—

   (b)   in respect of an agreement or combination by two or more persons to do or to procure the doing of an act which, if it were done without any such agreement or combination, would be actionable in tort on such a ground,

then, for the purpose of determining in those proceedings whether the union is liable in respect of the act in question, that act shall be taken to have been done by the union *if, but only if* [emphasis added], it is to be taken to have been authorised or endorsed by the trade union in accordance with the following provisions.

The provisions that follow on in s. 20(2) require that another person or group of persons, who hold positions of authority in the union, act to make the union liable. It is submitted that since the 1992 Act requires the conspiracy to have taken place before liability can attach to the union, the union cannot itself be a conspirator.

   Another more fundamental problem exists in any event, and that is the question of how one is to determine whether a body that is, at best, quasi-corporate has the will to enter into a conspiracy. This said, it has been held that corporate bodies can conspire with directors of corporations (see, for example, *Belmont Finance*

Corporation v *Williams Furniture Ltd (No. 2)* [1980] 1 All ER 393 and *Prudential Assurance Co. Ltd* v *Newman Industries (No. 2)* [1982] Ch 204).

6.2.1.2.2 The agreement   An agreement for the purposes of a conspiracy can be express or implied. It must, however, be present. It is not enough for the purposes of the law that the parties alleged to be conspirators have independently done the same thing to the victim. An agreement may, however, be implied from the circumstances of the action taken against the plaintiff, e.g., as where all unionised employees at an establishment walk out on strike at the same time. A conspiracy will not take place though where, say, individuals break their contracts of employment by refusing to cross an unlawful picket line.

This said, it is not necessary for conspirators to reach agreement at the same time. It is possible for a person to become a conspirator after a harmful common venture has been embarked upon by a group of tortfeasors where the wrongful act is still continuing, e.g., as with an employee joining an unlawful strike after it has begun.

Further, it is possible to have a conspiracy where one of the parties taking part in the conspiracy could not actually carry the conspiracy into effect himself. In *Rookes* v *Barnard* [1964] AC 1129, industrial action was threatened to enforce a closed shop, the result of which was the dismissal of the plaintiff, a non-union employee. Part of the plaintiff's claim alleged a conspiracy. One of the conspirators involved in the threat to break contracts of employment was a union official not actually employed by the employer, but the House of Lords held, nonetheless, that he could be involved in the conspiracy.

Once the conspiracy has been established, the law treats an act done by one of the conspirators as an act of them all if the act is in furtherance of the objects of the conspiracy (*per* Evershed MR in *D. C. Thomson & Co. Ltd* v *Deakin* [1952] Ch 646, at p. 674).

6.2.1.2.3 Intention to injure   One key feature of every conspiracy is that there must be an intention to cause wrongful harm to the plaintiff (*per* Lord Diplock in *Lonrho Ltd* v *Shell Petroleum Co.* [1982] AC 173, and see also the further decision of the House of Lords in *Lonrho plc* v *Fayed* [1992] 1 AC 448). In the case of a simple conspiracy, the wrongful harm is found in the malicious purpose, being the doing of the act to the plaintiff (*per* Lord Wright in *Crofter Hand Woven Harris Tweed Co. Ltd* v *Veitch* [1942] AC 435).

As to what amounts to intention on the part of the tortfeasors, it would appear to amount to the same test as intention under the criminal law, i.e. that wrongful harm to the plaintiff is the natural and probable consequence (*R* v *Hancock* [1986] AC 455).

6.2.1.2.4 Predominant purpose   As has been seen from the discussion in 6.2.1.1 above, the key distinction between the cases of *Allen* v *Flood* [1898] AC 1 and *Quinn* v *Leathem* [1901] AC 495 is that in order for liability to attach against conspirators, an act must actually be done — a threat will not suffice. The most obvious form of act will be a withdrawal of labour on the part of the conspirators.

Moreover, it is the manner in which act is performed which is important. The conspirators must behave maliciously towards the victim; they must know what they are doing, know that they are behaving oppressively towards the victim, and must do so in the absence of a lawful defence. To the extent that a lawful defence can be established, no tort will have been occasioned (*Mogul Steamship Co. Ltd* v *McGregor, Gow & Co.* [1892] AC 25).

6.2.1.3 Defences

A defence does exist to a claim for simple conspiracy. The tort requires a predominant purpose on the part of the conspirators to injure the interests of the plaintiff. This predominant purpose was rather taken for granted by the courts in earlier cases where a simple conspiracy was alleged, until the landmark case of *Crofter*, above. In this case, the plaintiff was a manufacturer of tweed cloth on the Scottish mainland. Members of the defendant union were dockers on the island of Lewis. Millowners on the island had agreed with the union to operate a closed shop if the union could stop the import of cloth from the Scottish mainland. The dockers managed to do this by refusing to handle the plaintiff's cloth, which needed to be finished on the island in order to be sold as Harris tweed. The plaintiff sued claiming an injunction and damages for the alleged simple conspiracy that had taken place. The matter reached the House of Lords who took the view that, when one is looking at industrial disputes, the issue of enforcing a change in the terms and conditions of employment for the benefit of union members will usually be the predominant purpose of a union. A union may well intend to cause harm to an employer to achieve that purpose; but that is a side issue. To this end, a union will have a defence in most cases.

Regard should also be had to *D. C. Thomson & Co. Ltd* v *Deakin* [1952] Ch 646, *Scala Ballroom (Wolverhampton) Ltd* v *Ratcliffe* [1958] 1 WLR 1057 and *J. T. Stratford & Son Ltd* v *Lindley* [1965] AC 269. The *Thomson* case revolved around an attempt made by the printing union, NATSOPA, to make an employer abandon its policy of employing non-union labour. This was held to be a legitimate purpose. Likewise, in the *Stratford* case, an attempt to gain union bargaining rights was also held to be a valid primary purpose. A case that shows how flexible is the concept introduced by *Crofter* is *Scala*. Here, the removal of a colour bar at a ballroom was the object of a boycott by the Musicians' Union. This was held to be a justification for the action even though it did not translate into detailed financial benefits for the union's members. However, in *Huntley* v *Thornton* [1957] 1 WLR 321, judgment was granted against the defendant union. The case turned on a decision to expel the plaintiff union member who had refused to support a 24-hour strike over a wage claim. Initially, the union was intent merely on disciplining the plaintiff. The plaintiff, convinced that he was right, left the disciplinary meeting before its conclusion. The local committee of the union therefore decided to recommend the expulsion of the plaintiff to the executive council, which refused to endorse the decision. The plaintiff in the meantime had left his original employment and was seeking fresh employment. The local committee was successful in blocking this. The plaintiff tried to make amends with the local committee but they refused to bury the hatchet. Indeed, they resolved to expel him, which, under their rules, they did not have a power to do. Ultimately, the plaintiff sued for conspiracy and succeeded. The trial judge, Harman J, held that the predominant purpose in this case was not the interests of the union but an attempt to appease the local committee's 'ruffled dignity'.

6.2.1.4   Burden of proof
The burden of proof in a simple conspiracy case will lie on the plaintiff, who must establish all elements of the tort including the predominant purpose on the part of the tortfeasors (*per* Lord Wright in *Crofter Hand Woven Harris Tweed Co. Ltd* v *Veitch* [1942] AC 435, at pp. 471–72). It will commonly be the case that, as to the issue of purpose, the defendants will adduce evidence in rebuttal by showing that while they may be taken to have intended to harm the plaintiff, their purpose was to secure a legitimate aim (see, for example the view of Lord Cave LC in *Sorrell* v *Smith* [1925] AC 700, at p. 712).

6.2.1.5   Problems with simple conspiracy
It has been suggested that the tort of simple conspiracy is an anomaly. The problem lies in the comparison between *Allen* v *Flood* and *Quinn* v *Leathem*, in that if one takes the view that the determining factor in *Allen* was that it involved an individual acting on his own as opposed to a conspiracy, the cases are otherwise indistinguishable. If that is the case, the question arises as to why it is unlawful to do a thing in concert with another which would, if done by an individual actor, be lawful. This issue was addressed by the House of Lords in *Lonrho Ltd* v *Shell Petroleum Co. Ltd (No. 2)* [1982] AC 173. Lord Diplock referred to the above problem in the nature of the cause of action, but concluded (at p. 189) that the tort was 'too well established to be discarded however anomalous it may seem today'.

6.2.1.6   Summary
While the law relating to the tort of simple conspiracy is plentiful, the importance of the tort in the context of trade disputes is relatively minor following the decision in *Crofter Hand Woven Harris Tweed Co. Ltd* v *Veitch* [1942] AC 435.

   In nearly every case it will possible for a union to establish that it is attempting to put forward the interests of its members, and therefore unless a union loses sight of those interests (as in *Huntley* v *Thornton* [1957] 1 WLR 321), the effect of the *Crofter* decision has been to remove simple conspiracy from the raft of torts open to a plaintiff who has suffered loss at the hands of a union.

6.2.2   Conspiracy using unlawful means

6.2.2.1   Introduction
Whereas the tort of simple conspiracy focuses upon a wrongful motive for the doing
of an act, conspiracy using unlawful means focuses upon the means adopted to cause
harm. As a result of this the composition of the tort is different and the matters that
need to be pleaded are:

(a)   a combination of two or more persons;
(b)   an agreement between the members of the combination;
(c)   an act which is itself unlawful committed by or at the behest of the members
of the combination for the purpose of injuring the plaintiff;
(d)   an intention to injure the plaintiff.

As regards matters (a), (b) and (d), regard should be had to 6.2.1.2.1–6.2.1.2.3
respectively.

6.2.2.2   Unlawful acts
Unlawful acts can essentially be broken down into three categories, these being (i)
acts which are themselves criminal, (ii) acts which consist of other torts, and (iii) acts
that consist of a breach of contract on the part of the tortfeasor.

6.2.2.2.1   Criminal acts   The generally accepted view is that where a combination
of workers addresses an act which is criminal in its own right against another, the
combination will be actionable as a conspiracy in tort. However, this view is reached
against the background of the difficult decision in *Lonrho Ltd* v *Shell Petroleum Co.
Ltd (No. 2)* [1982] AC 173. Prior to *Lonrho*, the House of Lords had accepted that a
conspiracy which had at its root a criminal act aimed at the plaintiff, could be
actionable under the tort of conspiracy using unlawful means (see, e.g., Lord Devlin
in *Rookes* v *Barnard* [1964] AC 1129 at p. 1206, and see also *Sorrell* v *Smith* [1925]
AC 700, Viscount Cave at p. 714 and Lord Dunedin at p. 719).

The *Lonrho* case itself arose out of the economic blockade of the former Southern
Rhodesia, which was implemented by the British Government. The blockade was
imposed by an Order in Council and it was to be enforced under pain of criminal
sanctions against any person who broke the boycott. The plaintiff, as part of its
trading operations, carried out the business of suppliers of oil. It brought proceedings
against the defendants claiming that Shell and BP had conspired between them to
carry on supplying oil to Southern Rhodesia in breach of the boycott. Further, the
plaintiff alleged that this directly affected its business interests.

While it was clear that, to the extent that a conspiracy arose it must do so out of
the form of using unlawful means, there were problems for the plaintiff. First, while
the defendants had indeed conspired to commit criminal acts, the acts were not aimed
at the plaintiff. Therefore the plaintiff was not able to establish a conspiracy.

However, of far greater concern was the only judgment given by the House of Lords, that being the judgment of Lord Diplock, who stated (at pp. 185–86), that it is not possible to frame a civil action out of the breach of a criminal statute unless the statute provides for enforcement through the civil courts, or because the plaintiff is someone who suffers particular harm as a result of a breach of the statute. Since the plaintiff did not satisfy either category, the injunction was refused.

A further example is the case of *Gouriet* v *Union of Post Office Workers* [1978] AC 435. Here, the plaintiff was a member of the Freedom Association. He objected to a threatened boycott of mail to South Africa by postal workers and claimed that the boycott would contravene s. 58 of the Post Office Act 1953 (see 10.3.3.2). He therefore sought injunctive relief. The case reached the House of Lords where the injunction was refused. The House of Lords affirmed the general view of the civil law, this being that the courts would not grant civil remedies to uphold penal statutes unless either the claim was brought by the Attorney-General, or because the plaintiff would suffer personal hardship as a result of the criminal action. Since the plaintiff had not been able to persuade the Attorney-General to take action and would not suffer himself, the injunction was refused.

After *Lonrho* v *Shell*, it seemed that it would not be possible to use criminal wrongdoing as a ground for launching a civil conspiracy claim unless the plaintiff fell into either or both of Lord Diplock's categories. However, in *Lonrho plc* v *Fayed* [1992] 1 AC 448, the House of Lords reviewed the law relating to conspiracy using unlawful means. Lord Bridge took the view that all that is decided by *Lonrho* v *Shell* is that in every conspiracy an intent to injure the plaintiff must be shown. It follows that Lord Diplock's two categories of cases are *obiter* and that the long-standing views of the House of Lords in *Rookes* v *Barnard* and *Sorrell* v *Smith* still hold good.

6.2.2.2.2 Tortious acts It is perfectly possible to allege that a combination of workers has agreed to commit other torts against a plaintiff. In such a case, there is a genuine question as to whether or not the allegation of conspiracy actually adds anything to a claim, or amounts to 'belt and braces' litigation. Certainly, the view of Lord Dunedin in *Sorrell* v *Smith* was that an allegation of conspiracy in such circumstances added nothing to a plaintiff's case (see [1925] AC 700, at p. 716).

6.2.2.2.3 Breach of contract It is still debatable whether a breach of contract amounts to unlawful means for the purposes of this form of conspiracy. Two cases on the point are pertinent, these being *Rookes* v *Barnard* [1964] AC 1129 and *Barretts & Bairds (Wholesale) Ltd* v *IPCS* [1987] IRLR 3. In *Rookes* v *Barnard*, the plaintiff sued the defendants on account of his dismissal by an airline. The dismissal had been brought about due to the fact the airline operated a closed shop. The plaintiff was not a member of the union in question and, as a result, officials of the union threatened the airline with a strike unless the plaintiff was dismissed. This duly happened, whereupon the plaintiff sued, alleging, *inter alia*, a conspiracy using unlawful means (the threat to break contracts). The House of Lords left the point open as to whether a conspiracy to break contracts of employment was actionable. Lord Devlin stated (at p. 1210):

> I am not saying that a conspiracy to breach a contract amounts to the tort of conspiracy; that point remains to be decided. I am saying that in the tort of intimidation a threat to break a contract would be a threat of an illegal act. It follows from that that a combination to intimidate by means of a threat of a breach of contract would be an unlawful conspiracy; but it does not necessarily follow that a combination to commit a breach of contract simpliciter would be an unlawful conspiracy.

With the point left open by the House of Lords as to whether a breach of contract could amount to unlawful means, it was not until 1987 that the point was revisited in *Barretts & Bairds*. This case is, regrettably, only a decision at first instance. It concerned a dispute involving fatstock officers staffing private abattoirs. A dispute arose between the officers and their employer, the Meat and Livestock Commission. An abattoir owner affected by the dispute launched proceedings in the High Court for an injunction. One of the issues was whether a conspiracy using unlawful means was taking place. Although the case was decided on other grounds, Henry J took the view that there was an arguable case for finding that a breach of contract could amount to unlawful means.

As the law currently stands, it is uncertain whether breach of contract does amount to unlawful means. For the sake of consistency with other torts, there is a strong argument that it should do. Against this view is the problem that arose in *Lonrho* v *Shell*. In Lord Diplock's unreconstructed view, using breach of a penal statute constituted unlawful means only either if it gave an individual a right specifically to enforce the statute in the civil courts under the provisions of the statute itself, or if the wrong perpetrated specifically affected the plaintiff. In other words, it would be possible to use breach of the statute as unlawful means only if the statute gave rights to an individual.

If this argument is transposed to the context of using breach of contract as unlawful means, the same problem arises. Where a breach of contract occurs, it confers rights only on the parties to the contract (see, for example, Lord Haldane in *Dunlop Pneumatic Tyre Co.* v *Selfridge* [1915] AC 847, at p. 853). If breach of contract can constitute unlawful means, it makes substantial in-roads into the principle of privity of contract. If this is so, the only person who could use the breach of contract as unlawful means would be an employer. However, there would then be a powerful argument against the employer being able to use the tort since he would be electing to sue in tort rather than contract and should, presumably, use the law of contract where a choice arises (*per* Lord Scarman in the Privy Council decision of *Tai Hing Cotton Mills Ltd* v *Liu Chong Bank Ltd* [1985] 2 All ER 947, at p. 957).

6.2.2.3 *The mental element — predominant purpose or intention to harm?*

In relation to conspiracy using unlawful means, the matter of the conspirators' state of mind in the commission of the tort was addressed in *Lonrho plc v Fayed* [1992] 1 AC 448. The case arose out of the aborted take-over of the House of Fraser by the plaintiff. The plaintiff had been prevented from assuming control of the group pending the outcome of a Monopolies and Mergers Commission (MMC) investigation, which would, in all probability, have released the plaintiff from undertakings that it had given to the Secretary of State once the Secretary had accepted the report. In the meantime, House of Fraser attracted a rival bid from the defendants. Allegedly, the defendants, in order to avoid having themselves referred to the MMC, made various untrue representations to the Secretary of State dealing with such matters as their source of funding and commercial background. The result of the alleged statements was that they induced the Secretary of State not to refer them to the MMC, and the sale was allowed to go ahead. The plaintiff therefore sued, claiming that the defendants had conspired using unlawful means to injure its business interests. The House of Lords was asked to consider as an interlocutory point whether it was necessary to show that the defendants had a predominant purpose of injuring the plaintiff. Their Lordships held that, in a case of conspiracy to use unlawful means, the motive (i.e., the predominant purpose) of the conspirators was irrelevant. All that was necessary was that an intention of harming the plaintiff be shown.

6.2.2.4 *Summary*

In order to establish the existence of a conspiracy to use unlawful means, a plaintiff will have to show that a conspiracy did exist, that it involved the use of unlawful means to harm the interests of the plaintiff, and that there was an intention on the part of those combining (i.e., there was a moral certainty) that the act would harm the legitimate interests of the plaintiff.

A problem exists with the tort in relation to the form of unlawful means that can be used to establish the tort; it is by no means clear that it is possible to use the commission of a crime as the basis of a tort, and neither is it clear that it is possible to use breach of contract to establish it.

6.2.3 Damage

It appeared to be settled as early as *Quinn v Leathem* [1901] AC 495 that in order to establish a conspiracy (of either variety) a plaintiff is required to establish that he has suffered pecuniary loss. The point was challenged though in *Lonrho plc v Fayed (No. 5)* [1994] 1 All ER 188. Here, the Court of Appeal drew a distinction between being able to assess financial loss arising to a plaintiff as a result of a conspiracy, which could be assessed with some degree of precision, and that which arose in a more general fashion (in that case, damages for loss of reputation). In the latter case, it was held that conspiracy is not the proper cause of action. In *Lonrho*, Stuart-Smith LJ stated, *obiter*, that he would usually expect to see a calculation of loss being pleaded. The Court of Appeal also went on to hold that on the facts of the particular case, the appropriate cause of action would be to sue in defamation for the damage to reputation.

6.3   INDUCING BREACH OF CONTRACT

6.3.1   Introduction

Inducing breach of contract has existed as a known tort since the case of *Lumley* v *Gye* (1853) 2 E & B 216. The tort owes its origins to the old law of master and servant, and was derived from employers' status in society rather than from any more rational explanation. The historical view of the relationship was that a servant was essentially a chattel of his master, and therefore the law ought to protect the relationship in favour of a master by preventing outside interference (see the judgment of Lord Sumner in *Commissioner for Executing the Office of Lord High Admiral* v *SS Amerika* [1917] AC 38, at p. 60). The action has now been re-rooted in modern times to cover a right not to have contracts generally interfered with by outsiders, and it matters not whether the plaintiff is an employer, an employee or is suing to prevent a wrong arising in relation to some other genus of contract.

The tort can be committed in two forms, i.e., by means of a direct inducement, or by indirectly inducing a breach.

6.3.2   Direct inducement

6.3.2.1   Introduction

Direct inducement is the oldest and simplest form of the tort. Its origins, as stated above, lie in the case of *Lumley* v *Gye*. The case concerned a theatre manager who had contracted to hire the services of an opera singer for a fixed period of three months. One of the terms of the singer's contract was that she would not sing elsewhere during the currency of the agreement without the consent of the plaintiff. During her contractual term, she was approached by the defendant, the owner of a rival music hall, who offered her the chance to sing at his establishment on better terms. The result was that the singer duly left the plaintiff's establishment, and the plaintiff sued the defendant for procuring a breach on the part of the singer. The Queen's Bench found by a majority of three to one that the plaintiff could succeed in the action brought. The judges in the case reshaped the existing law that a master could sue a person who procured a servant of his to leave the master's employment. The action did not require that there should be a strict relationship of employment. As Erle J put the matter (at p. 231):

... the class of cases referred to me rests upon the principle that the procurement of [a] violation of [a] right is a cause of action, and that, when this principle is applied to a violation of a right arising upon a contract of hiring, the nature of the service contracted for is immaterial. It is clear that the procurement of the violation of a right is a cause of action in all instances where the violation is an actionable wrong ...

Lumley v *Gye* was viewed at the time as a massive extension of union liability and the tort was vigorously used (the reason being that organisers of a strike will invariably cause employees to abstain from working in breach of the notice term of their contract and, in doing so, commission of the tort is inevitable).

The tort was ultimately addressed by the Trade Disputes Act 1906, which created an immunity in tort in the form of s. 3 of the 1906 Act.

6.3.2.2   Elements of the tort

In order to establish direct inducement to breach a contract, a plaintiff is required to prove a number of points. These are derived from the judgment of Jenkins LJ in *D. C. Thomson & Co. Ltd* v *Deakin* [1952] Ch 646, at p. 697, and are as follows:

(a)   the existence of a contract;

(b)   knowledge of the existence of the contract to be breached on the part of the tortfeasor;

(c)   an intention on the part of the tortfeasor to procure a breach of contract to the detriment of the plaintiff;

(d)   an inducement by the tortfeasor to the person contracting with the plaintiff to break the contract;

(e)   a breach of the contract arising causally as a result of the inducement of the tortfeasor.

6.3.2.2.1   Existence of the contract   The tort generally occurs only where a contract is currently in existence. It had been suggested at the inception of the tort that it could be committed where a person induced another not to enter into a contract with a person in the first place. Regard should be had to *Temperton* v *Russell* [1893] 1 QB 715, in particular the judgment of Lord Esher MR (with whom Lopes LJ concurred) who dealt with the point (at p. 728):

The next point is, whether the distinction ... between the claim for inducing persons to break contracts already entered into with the plaintiff and that for inducing persons not to enter into contracts with the plaintiff can be sustained, and whether the latter claim is maintainable in law. I do not think that the distinction can prevail. There was the same wrongful intent in both cases, wrongful because malicious. There was the same kind of injury to the plaintiff. It seems a rather fine distinction to say that, where a defendant maliciously induces a person not to carry out a contract already made with the plaintiff and so injures the plaintiff, it is actionable, but where he injures the plaintiff by maliciously preventing a person from entering a contract with the plaintiff, which he would otherwise have entered into, it is not actionable.

However, A. L. Smith LJ in the case expressly left the question open.

In *Allen* v *Flood* [1898] AC 1, Lord Herschell, on the question of extending liability to cases where a contract has not yet been entered into, stated of the observations in *Temperton* v *Russell* (at p. 120):

> It seems to have been regarded as only a small step from the one decision to the other, and it was said that there seemed to be no good reason why, if an action lay for maliciously inducing a breach of contract, it should not equally lie for maliciously inducing a person not to enter into a contract. So far from thinking it a small step from the one decision to the other, I think there is a chasm between them. The reason for a distinction between the two cases appears to me to be this: that in the one case the act procured was the violation of a legal right, for which the person doing the act that injured the plaintiff could be sued as well as the person who procured it; whilst in the other case no legal right was violated by the person who did the act from which the plaintiff suffered ...

This view was endorsed by Megarry J in *Midland Cold Storage Ltd* v *Steer* [1972] Ch 630, at p. 644.

This said, it has been held that an action will lie in a case where no contract exists but a tortfeasor has indicated that if one comes into existence he will induce breach of it. In *Torquay Hotel Co. Ltd* v *Cousins* [1969] 2 Ch 106, the plaintiff owned a hotel that was affected by secondary industrial action brought by the Transport and General Workers Union. In order to further its cause (gaining a union foothold at the plaintiff's hotel), the union asked its members at Esso not to supply fuel oil to the hotel. The hotel therefore decided to contact another fuel supplier to arrange delivery. Prior to a contract with the new supplier and the plaintiff being concluded, the defendants found out about the proposed contract and told the supplier that the plaintiff had been 'blacked' and that there would be serious repercussions if it dealt with the plaintiff. The plaintiff therefore sought injunctions preventing the union from inducing the breach of contract with Esso and the alternative, unfinished agreement with the secondary supplier. The Court of Appeal held for the plaintiff in respect of both the existing contract with Esso and the arrangement with the alternative supplier, notwithstanding that the existence of a contract had not been proved in the latter case. The defendants had shown by their conduct that they would have attempted to breach the contract, and that was enough for the purposes of granting an injunction.

Therefore, in summary, the accepted view now is that an action will lie only where a contract has or will be breached at the behest of a tortfeasor.

6.3.2.2.2 Knowledge of the contract on the part of the tortfeasor It has consistently been held by the courts that knowledge of the contract to be breached has to exist on the part of the tortfeasor if an actionable inducement is to be established. For example, Lord Devlin, in *Rookes v Barnard* [1964] AC 1129, stated (at p. 1212) that 'An act of inducement is not by itself actionable'. Further, in *British Industrial Plastics Ltd v Ferguson* [1940] 1 All ER 479, Lord Russell of Killowen stated (at p. 483) that knowledge of the contract 'is an essential ingredient to the cause of action'. Further still, in *Associated British Ports v Transport and General Workers Union* [1989] IRLR 305, Stuart-Smith LJ stated (at p. 315): 'It is clear, however, that the [tort] must derive from a legally enforceable contract.' A number of points arise in relation to knowledge.

6.3.2.2.2.1 Knowledge of the precise terms of the agreement or simply the agreement? First, it needs to be asked whether the knowledge to fix liability is knowledge of the precise terms of the contractual agreement, or simply knowledge of the existence of a contract between the plaintiff and another. The answer is now clearly the latter of these two formulations. However, this was not always so. As recently as 1964 it was argued that a tortfeasor would be liable only where he had precise knowledge of the existence of a contract and the terms to be breached under it. This proposition was finally put to rest in *J. T. Stratford & Son Ltd v Lindley* [1965] AC 269. In this case, the plaintiff company was associated with another company, Bowker and King Ltd (Bowker) via a controlling third party. The plaintiff carried on the activities of repairing and hiring barges. Bowker was approached by two unions for the purposes of recognition (the Transport and General Workers (TGWU) and the watermens union). Bowker rejected the recognition requests of both unions initially. Ultimately, it gave recognition to the TGWU. The result of this was that the watermen's union decided to 'black' the boats of the plaintiff after off-loading any cargoes that they might be carrying. The effect of this call from the union was to cause serious problems to the plaintiff since it would effectively immobilise the company's barges. The plaintiff sued, claiming the union had induced breaches of the barge charterers' contracts and that this had adversely impacted upon its business. It was also argued that no immunity was available to the union since the breaches of contract were not breaches of contracts of employment committed in contemplation or furtherance of a trade dispute (see Chapter 7). An argument was advanced by the defendants that they did not have knowledge of the precise terms of hire and therefore they could not have committed the tort. An interlocutory injunction was initially granted in favour of the employer, but the Court of Appeal quickly overturned this. Lord Denning MR stated (at p. 288):

> [The] breaches were due, no doubt, to the embargo imposed by the union. But are the defendants guilty of the tort of inducing the breaches of contract? For this purpose it must be shown that the defendants knew of the relevant terms of the contract and intended to procure breaches of them . . .

The majority of the Court of Appeal then went on to hold that it had not been shown that the union in question did have knowledge of the relevant terms.

If this requirement had subsisted, the tort would quickly have become redundant as regards inducing breaches of sale or supply contracts. In most cases a union will not know the detailed content of a contract between an employer and a customer or supplier, and to have such a precise formulation of liability would act substantially to the detriment of an employer. As it happened, the reversal of fortune was swift. The House of Lords in the appeal in *Stratford* v *Lindley* swiftly reversed the knowledge requirement and went on to hold that all that was necessary to attach liability to a union was knowledge of the existence of the contract, not the terms of it. Lord Reid said (at p. 323):

> The respondents knew that barges were always returned promptly on completion of the job for which they had been hired, and it must have been obvious to them that this was done under contracts between the appellants and the barge hirers. It was argued that there was no evidence that they were sufficiently aware of the terms of these contracts to know that their interference would involve breaches of these contracts. But I think at this stage that it is reasonable to infer that they did know that.

Lord Pearce added (at p. 332):

> Did the defendants have sufficient knowledge of the terms of the hirers' contracts? It is no answer to a claim based on wrongfully inducing a breach of contract, to assert that the defendants did not know with exactitude all the terms of the contract. The relevant question is whether they had sufficient knowledge of the terms to know that they were inducing a breach of contract.

This position has been followed consistently since *Stratford* v *Lindley*.

While the courts require there to be knowledge of the contract, it seems at times that they pay mere lip service to the requirement. For example, in *Associated Newspapers Group* v *Wade* [1979] ICR 664, it was held that action taken to enforce union recognition by means of refusing to handle advertisements from particular advertisers would amount to inducing breach of contract. The argument that the defendant, who had caused the advertising contracts to be breached, had no knowledge of them, was dealt with in short order by the Court of Appeal who concluded that as a union representative who had dealt in the plaintiff's line of business for many years, he must be taken to have known that advertising contracts were secured well in advance of publication.

6.3.2.2.2 Actual or constructive knowledge? The second point to be dealt with is whether knowledge of the existence of a contract can be inferred in the case of a tortfeasor who claims that he is ignorant of the existence of a contract that is being breached. The answer to this question is that in an appropriate case knowledge will be imputed to such a person. As can been seen from, say *Associated Newspapers Group* v *Wade* (above), in some cases it simply defies belief that a person cannot have knowledge. However, if a person were to choose to avoid the existence of a contract coming to his attention then this would give him an advantage that would not be available to more straightforward tortfeasors.

The matter was dealt with in *Emerald Construction Co. Ltd* v *Lowthian* [1966] 1 WLR 691. Here, a large power station was to be built using a particular contractor. The contractor had sub-contracted out the work to the plaintiff who operated a policy of labour only sub-contracting. The contractor was visited by an official of the Amalgamated Union of Building Trade Workers, who informed the contractor that, unless the sub-contract was terminated, the union's bricklayer members would not operate on the site. The plaintiff therefore sought an injunction preventing the defendants from inducing a breach of contract. The defendants admittedly knew of the existence of the contract but not the precise terms. On the issue of the union's knowledge, Lord Denning MR said (at p. 700):

> If the officers of the trade union, knowing of the contract, deliberately sought to procure a breach of it, they would do wrong ... Even if they did not know of the actual terms of the contract but had the means of knowledge — which they deliberately disregarded — that would be enough. Like the man who turns a blind eye. So here, if the officers deliberately sought to get this contract terminated, heedless of its terms, regardless whether it was terminated by breach or not they would do wrong. For it is unlawful for a third person to procure a breach of contract knowingly, or recklessly, indifferent whether it is a breach or not.

Regard should also be had to *Merkur Island Shipping Corporation* v *Laughton* [1983] 2 AC 570; *NWL Ltd* v *Woods* [1979] 1 WLR 1294; *Express Newspapers Ltd* v *McShane* [1980] AC 672; and *Dimbleby & Sons* v *NUJ* [1984] 1 WLR 427, all of which show the ease of inferring knowledge on the part of union officials.

It should also be noted that that since many cases will seek to injunct a tortfeasor at an early stage in a dispute where a tort is being committed and is not protected by a statutory immunity, an interlocutory injunction will often be sought. Since the case of *American Cyanamid Co.* v *Ethicon Ltd* [1975] AC 396, it has been necessary only to prove that a serious question exists to be tried. This, of course, will be established on affidavit evidence, which does not reveal as much as cross-examination. Given the ready inferences that courts make as to the knowledge of union officials, the hurdle of establishing liability on the part of a tortfeasor is a relatively low one for the plaintiff to cross.

6.3.2.2.2.3 Genuine and honest ignorance of a contract   The corollary of the above point is that where a defendant is ignorant of a contract that is being breached, no liability in tort can attach. The point was taken to its logical conclusion in *Smith* v *Morrison* [1979] 1 WLR 659, where the question at issue was whether a defendant had an honest doubt as to the existence of a contract. According to the trial judge, where an honest doubt does exist no liability can attach. However, to escape liability, doubt must exist as to the fact of the contract and not as to the effect of breach (*Pritchard* v *Briggs* [1980] Ch 338, at p. 413, and *Metropolitan Borough of Solihull* v *National Union of Teachers* [1985] IRLR 211).

6.3.2.2.3   Intention to harm the plaintiff   It has been said that the requirement of intention to injure the plaintiff is tied up with knowledge of the contract to be breached (see, for example, the comments of Lord Diplock in *Merkur Island Shipping Corporation* v *Laughton* [1983] 2 AC 570, at pp. 608–609). However, it is still uncertain just how far this requirement extends. A debate exists as to whether the intention is to be defined in the 'wilful blindness' sense of the criminal law (see, for example, *R* v *Hancock* [1986] AC 455), or whether the tort can be committed only where the predominant purpose of the tortfeasor is to cause injury to the plaintiff.

As to the first of these propositions, regard should be had to *Falcolner* v *ASLEF and NUR* [1986] IRLR 331. This case concerned an action brought by the plaintiff as a passenger of British Rail against the defendant railway unions, on the grounds that they had not complied with ss. 10 and 11 of the Trade Union Act 1984 in calling a strike. The plaintiff had been stranded in London as a result of the strike and was forced to incur the expense of a hotel room as well as suffering general inconvenience. The action was brought before the introduction of s. 235A of TULRCA 1992 ('Industrial action affecting supply of goods or services to an individual'). In defence to a claim of inducing British Rail to breach contracts with its passengers, the defendant unions alleged, *inter alia*, that they had not intended to harm the plaintiff, rather they wished to put pressure on British Rail. The matter was heard in the county court before His Honour Judge Henham. In response to the union claim that they had not intended to harm the plaintiff, Judge Henham stated (at p. 333):

As to the need to prove the defendants intended to procure a breach of, or interference with the performance of, those contracts, I find no sympathy for the argument that the plaintiff was not the object or instrument of the action taken when the strike was called. Undoubtedly it was the intention of the defendants to cause the BR Board to be rendered incapable of performing its contractual obligations with the plaintiff and other passengers but to suggest that the effect upon them (i.e. the passengers) was merely consequential is, in my view, both naive and divorced from reality. It was clearly the intention of the defendants in calling the strike to direct its effect upon the plaintiff and others and thus to induce the Board to accede to the defendants' wishes.

In other words, the only possible effect of the action would have been to harm people in the position of the plaintiff, and the defendant unions had been deliberately blind to this point.

Against this view, though, is a decision of the High Court in *Barretts & Bairds (Wholesale) Ltd* v *Institution of Professional Civil Servants* [1987] IRLR 3. Henry J, in refusing to continue an interlocutory injunction, held that in order to establish liability under the tort it was necessary to show a predominant purpose of injuring the plaintiff on the part of the tortfeasor. In so holding, he based his decision on the House of Lords authority in *Lonrho Ltd* v *Shell Petroleum Co. Ltd (No.2)* [1982] AC 173.

Both decisions have their weaknesses. As to *Falconer*, it is a first instance decision in the county court, albeit one that was argued by very able counsel on both sides. *Barretts & Bairds*, while being a first instance decision of the High Court, does not refer to *Falconer*, and must also lose some of its authority following the decision at the Court of Appeal stage in *Lonrho plc* v *Fayed* [1990] 2 QB 479 which doubted whether it was necessary to show in a case of interfering with a business (the tort on which *Barretts & Bairds* was decided) a predominant purpose of harming the plaintiff. While one possible solution to the problem is that different requirements do exist in relation to the two torts, there is no logical reason why this should be the case. Further, if one examines s. 235A of TULRCA 1992 (which effectively codifies the principle in *Falconer*), it can be seen that Parliament opted for a similar formulation to Judge Henham's simply by requiring that a plaintiff prove that the effect or a likely effect of the action taken is to affect the plaintiff. It is submitted that the totality of the law in the area supports the view put forward in *Falconer*, although the matter still awaits resolution by a higher court.

6.3.2.2.4 Inducement   The third element that has to be proved in the tort is that of inducement. According to Evershed MR in *D. C. Thomson & Co. Ltd* v *Deakin* [1952] Ch 646 at p. 686, inducement can take effect in essentially three ways, these being pressure, persuasion or procuration.

6.3.2.2.4.1 Pressure   Numerous examples exist of what amounts to pressure on the part of a tortfeasor. Pressure essentially consists of threats made to a contracting party that some undesirable consequence will happen in the event of continuing to deal with a plaintiff. In *D. C. Thomson* v *Deakin* (above), the pressure consisted of informing a supplier of the plaintiff that it might experience labour troubles of its own if it carried on dealing with the plaintiff. As a result, the supplier stopped supplying the plaintiff. In that case an interlocutory injunction was not granted, on the grounds that the affidavit evidence did not establish evidence of direct procurement of a wrongful act on the part of the supplier. However, in *J. T. Stratford & Son Ltd* v *Lindley* [1965] AC 269, a minority of the House of Lords held that pressure had been applied to a trade association to which barge hirers belonged which informed them of the possibility of the barges being 'blacked'. Although the language of the letter from the union was couched in neutral language, the clear inference from it was that there was an embargo on the boats which would be enforced. That could amount to pressure according to Lord Pearce. Regard should also be had to *Torquay Hotel Co. Ltd* v *Cousins* [1969] 2 Ch 106.

Pressure must be distinguished from the mere giving of advice to a person not to deal with another. It has been commented that it will be very difficult to draw a line between the giving of advice and pressure (see Coleridge J in *Lumley* v *Gye* (1853) 2 E & B 216, at p. 252, *Camellia Tanker Ltd SA* v *International Transport Workers Federation* [1976] ICR 274 and *Timeplan Education Group Ltd* v *NUT* [1997] IRLR 457).

6.3.2.2.4.2 Persuasion   Persuasion will commonly occur where a union asks its members to go out on strike in breach of the notice requirements provided for by their contracts of employment. Again, as with pressure, a distinction needs to be drawn between persuasion and advice. Advising as to the consequences of a continued course of dealings with a person is not unlawful. However, there is again a thin line between advice and persuasion. In the *Torquay Hotel* case (above), the 'advice' given by the Transport and General Workers Union to its members, as to the existence of a dispute with the plaintiff, was held to amount to persuasion.

It should be noted that it is no defence to an allegation of persuasion that the party who has been persuaded to break the contract was easily persuaded. In *Thomson* v *Deakin*, Jenkins LJ dealt with the point (at p. 694) in the following way:

> But the contract breaker may himself be a willing party to the breach, without any persuasion by the third party, and there seems to be no doubt that if a third party, with knowledge of a contract between the contract breaker and another, has dealings with the contract breaker which the third party knows to be inconsistent with the contract, he has committed an actionable interference . . . The inconsistent dealing between the third party and the contract breaker may, indeed, be commenced without knowledge by the third party of the contract thus broken; but, if it is continued after the third party has notice of the contract, an actionable interference has been committed by him . . .

Other cases which deal with parties willing to breach a contract include *British Motor Trade Association* v *Salvadori* [1949] Ch 556 and *Sefton* v *Tophams Ltd* [1965] Ch 1140, later reversed by the House of Lords on other grounds.

6.3.2.2.4.3 Procuration   The third way in which inducement can occur is by giving some form of consideration to the contract breaker not to fulfil his obligations. Examples of this have included *Lumley* v *Gye* (1853) 2 E & B 216, where money was paid to an opera singer to induce her to breach her contract, and *British Motor Trade Association* v *Salvadori* (above), where money was paid to car dealers to supply cars to a secondhand car dealer in breach of a re-sale agreement.

6.3.2.2.5 Breach of the contract   As was seen above at 6.3.2.2.1, in most cases it is necessary that the contract is actually breached before all elements of the tort are finally established (see, for example, *Midland Cold Storage Ltd* v *Steer* [1972] Ch

630, at pp. 644–45). An exception does exist to this rule where a tortfeasor threatens to breach a contract as soon as it is concluded, as was seen above in the case of *Torquay Hotel Co. Ltd* v *Cousins* [1969] 2 Ch 106 and in *Brekkes Ltd* v *Cattel* [1972] Ch 105.

Further, to the extent that a contract is caused to be breached in circumstances where a clause allowing suspension or termination of the contract exists could have been validly operated, it is no defence to say that the contract could lawfully have been terminated (see, e.g., *Emerald Construction Co. Ltd* v *Lowthian* [1966] 1 WLR 691). This will commonly occur where unionised labour is called upon to take industrial action, since although an individual's contract can lawfully be brought to an end upon the giving of proper notice, a call to such action, while possibly being accompanied by strike notice, will not usually be accompanied by notice of termination. This is true even where the strike notice is of equivalent length to the notice required to terminate the contract of employment lawfully. Lord Devlin in *Rookes* v *Barnard* [1964] AC 1129, said of this point at p. 1204:

It is not disputed that the notice constituted a threat of breach of contract by the members of AESD. It is true that any individual employee could lawfully have terminated his contract by giving seven days' notice and if the matter is looked at in that way, the breach might not appear to be a very serious one. But that would be a technical way of looking at it. As Donovan LJ said in the Court of Appeal, the object of the notice was not to terminate the contract either before or after the expiry of seven days. The object was to break the contract by withholding labour but keeping the contract alive for as long as the employers would tolerate the breach without exercising their right of recession.

The matter was put more succinctly in *Barretts & Bairds* (above), where Henry J stated (at p. 8) that 'no one today gives their notice before striking...'.

6.3.2.3 Defences

To the extent that a plaintiff can establish the above, and assuming that no immunity is available to a defendant, the next question to be addressed is whether or not a defence is available. Only one defence appears to exist to the tort of directly inducing breach of contract, and that is justification.

To the extent that the defence does still exist today, it has only ever been successfully raised in one case, and that was not a typical trade union dispute. In *Brimelow* v *Casson* [1924] 1 Ch 302 the plaintiff was a theatre manager who was suing the defendant for inducing breach of contract. The plaintiff had organised a number of reviews at different theatres. The defendant, in his capacity as a union official, had discovered that because of the very low wages that were being paid by the plaintiff, female members of the theatre's chorus line were turning to prostitution. The defendant contacted the venues that the plaintiff had booked and requested that they refuse to honour the agreements that they had with the plaintiff, which they duly did. The case was heard at first instance by Russell J, who held that the defendant was justified in procuring the breach as a result of a duty that was owed to his profession to prevent the chorus girls from being corrupted through of their insufficient income. The case derived its authority from the judgment of Bowen LJ in *Mogul Steamship Co. Ltd v McGregor, Gow & Co.* (1889) 23 QBD 598, where he stated (at p. 618) that in relation to the issue of justification: 'The good sense of the tribunal which had to decide would have to analyse the circumstances and decide on which side of the line each case fell.'

In the House of Lords in *South Wales Miners Federation v Glamorgan Coal Co.* [1905] AC 239, their Lordships held that there was no justification involved in a union trying to obtain better wages for members of the union, even where the union believed that higher wages would ultimately benefit the employer as well.

Indeed, in cases that have followed *Brimelow*, judges have gone to extreme lengths to show that the defence succeeded only on the basis of a moral duty that was owed to the members of the chorus line (see, for example, the judgment of Stuart-Smith LJ in *Edwin Hill & Partners v First National Finance Corporation* [1988] 3 All ER 801, at p. 806).

In most cases it would seem that there will be no common law defence available to a defendant in the context of industrial relations.

6.3.3   Indirect inducement to breach a contract

6.3.3.1   Introduction
Unlike the simpler form of action, indirect inducement to breach a contract requires that a defendant, with knowledge of the existence of a contract between a third party (T1) and the plaintiff, induces another (T2, commonly an employee of T1) to do an unlawful act to T1 thereby causing T1, as a necessary consequence of the unlawful wrong, to break the contract that T1 has with the plaintiff. Further, the defendant must intend to cause harm to the plaintiff as a result of the act of inducement.

6.3.3.2   Development of the tort and the concept of unlawful means
The first case on the tort of indirect inducement was *D. C. Thomson & Co. Ltd v Deakin* [1952] Ch 646, where union officials called for the plaintiff company to be the subject of an embargo (the aim being to introduce a closed shop within the plaintiff company). In order to enforce the boycott, the defendant officials contacted lorry drivers within their union who handled supplies of paper from Bowaters to the plaintiff. They warned their members that the plaintiff had been blacked and that they were not to carry out further deliveries. Bowaters refused to allow their drivers to handle the paper deliveries (fearing reprisals if they carried on supplying the plaintiff). The plaintiff sued for an injunction preventing breach of the commercial contract. An injunction was refused at first instance and then again in the Court of Appeal, where it was held that in order to establish the tort it was necessary to prove that the contracts of the lorry drivers at Bowaters had actually been breached.

However, since the drivers were ordered not to load lorries of the defendant by Bowaters, no liability could attach.

Nevertheless, the House of Lords was to develop the tort a short time later in *J. T. Stratford & Son Ltd* v *Lindley* [1965] AC 269. The facts of this case are set out above at 6.3.2.2.2.1. The case concerned a refusal by watermen to return barges to the owner after cargoes of goods had been delivered. The action was to ensure that union recognition took place at a company associated with the plaintiff. In this case, however, the House of Lords, after first having redefined what was meant by knowledge of a contract on the part of a tortfeasor, went on to find that the watermen were in breach of their contracts of employment and that this constituted unlawful means for the purposes of the tort. The decision was subsequently followed in the 1980s by the House of Lords in *Merkur Island Shipping Corporation* v *Laughton* [1983] 2 AC 570, where the principle was used to pin liability on the defendants for instructing tugmen to refuse to service ships operated under flags of convenience, and also in *Dimbleby & Sons Ltd* v *National Union of Journalists* [1984] 1 WLR 427. In this case, liability was extended to cover journalists who would not supply news copy to their employer due to the employer's insistence on using a particular printer. It was held that a refusal to supply copy amounted to a breach of contract.

What is now beyond doubt is that it is necessary to establish unlawful means if the tort is to be proved (*per* Lord Diplock in the *Merkur Island* case, at pp. 607–10). It is, however, this requirement that has provided a small degree of salvation to unions faced with the reforms of the Conservative Governments of 1979–1997, as was shown in the case of *Middlebrook Mushrooms Ltd* v *Transport and General Workers Union* [1993] IRLR 232. The case concerned a mushroom grower who was involved in a dispute with staff over overtime payments. Industrial action ensued and the defendant union, through its regional officer, announced that it would cause its members to attend at supermarkets supplied by the plaintiff and would instruct the members to hand out leaflets informing the public of the dispute. The leaflets concluded with a call from the union for the public to boycott the plaintiff's mushrooms. The plaintiff sued claiming that the defendant union was inducing the supermarkets it supplied to breach their contracts with the plaintiff. An interlocutory injunction was granted by the High Court preventing the action. On appeal, the Court of Appeal reversed the decision. It held that the High Court had incorrectly treated the case as one of direct inducement.

The Court of Appeal took the view that, unlike, cases such as *Merkur Island Shipping or Stratford* v *Lindley*, the defendant in this case probably had no knowledge of any mushroom supply contracts. Mushrooms were oversupplied and had a very short shelf life. It was probably the case that no long-term supply contracts existed and contracts were more likely to be *ad hoc*. If this was the case, it was difficult to see how the defendant could have knowledge of the contracts.

In any event, the facts did not support the allegation of direct inducement since it was supermarket shoppers and not the supermarkets themselves who were being targeted. The tort was therefore one of indirect inducement if it was anything at all.

It followed that if customers were being targeted then, in the ordinary course of things, they would be able to make up their own minds whether or not to buy mushrooms (unless unlawful means were used against them, which would have to be proved by the plaintiff). Ultimately, the plaintiff did not have evidence of this. The handing out of leaflets amounted to nothing more than free speech and could not be considered to be unlawful. Hoffmann LJ (as was then) stated (at p. 237):

> The fact that the defendant has communicated to the contracting party the information that consequences will follow if he does not break his contract does not necessarily mean that the communication is the cause of the contract being broken. That is the equivalent of killing the messenger. I suppose there may be a case in which the defendant's force of personality is such that his mere communication of a request not to perform the contract, unaccompanied by any express or implied intimation of favourable consequences if he does so, or adverse consequences if he does not, is in itself sufficient to cause the contract to be broken. It is more usual, however, for the contracting party to be told expressly or impliedly that some action will be taken if or unless he breaks the contract. In such a case it is the occurrence or apprehension of that action which causes the contract to be broken, not the communication. To decide whether the inducement was direct or indirect, one therefore has to ask whether the actual or apprehended action was on the part of the defendants or persons for whom they were in law responsible.

It followed that since the leafleting was not directly aimed at the supermarket no direct inducement had been made out, and it was impossible to make out a case of indirect inducement since the customers were able to make up their minds whether they wanted to enter into contracts to buy mushrooms.

6.3.3.3 Remoteness of damage

In order for the plaintiff to prove the tort, causation must be established. In *D. C. Thomson & Co. Ltd* v *Deakin* [1952] Ch 646, Jenkins LJ stated that breach of contract must follow as a 'necessary consequence' of the breach. He added (at p. 697):

> I should add that by the expression 'necessary consequence' used here and elsewhere in this judgment, I mean that it must be shown that, by reason of the withdrawal of the services of the employees concerned, the contract breaker was unable, as a matter of practical possibility, to perform his contract; in other words, I think the continuance of the services of the particular employees concerned must be so vital to the performance of the contract alleged to have been interfered with as to make the effect of their withdrawal comparable, for practical purposes, to a direct invasion of the contractual rights of the party aggrieved under the contract alleged to have been interfered with, as for example (in the case of a contract for personal services), the physical restraint of the person by whom such services are to be performed.

It follows that if the contract breaker has a free choice in the matter (e.g., as in *Middlebrook Mushrooms*, where the supermarkets might have responded to perceived commercial pressure from their customers), no causation can be established and therefore neither can the tort.

6.3.3.4 Defence

As with the direct version of the tort, it is conceivably possible that the defence of justification, to the extent that it still exists in the context of contracts of employment (see above at 6.3.2.3), is available in the case of the indirect version.

6.3.4 Proof of loss

In both versions of the tort of inducing a breach of contract it will be necessary for the plaintiff to show that loss has actually been occasioned as a result of the tort.

6.4 INTERFERING WITH A CONTRACT, TRADE OR BUSINESS USING UNLAWFUL MEANS

6.4.1 Introduction

The tort of interfering with a contract, trade or business is an evolutionary one that has come into being through refinement of the tort of inducing breach of contract (in both of its forms). The tort was unheard of until 1969, when it was first promulgated in the case of *Torquay Hotel Co. Ltd* v *Cousins* [1969] 2 Ch 106. The facts are fully stated above at 6.3.2.2.1, but it will be remembered that the plaintiff's supplier of fuel oil had been told by the Transport and General Workers Union that the hotel had been 'blacked'. There existed in the contract of supply between Esso and the plaintiff a *force majeure* clause which included prevention of the contract due to industrial action as one of its 'triggers'. One of the questions facing the Court of Appeal was whether or not there had been a breach of contract which could give rise to liability under the tort. The decision of the Court of Appeal was that the union which had engineered the strike could not take advantage of the clause so as to deny the existence of the tort which it had itself committed. The Court of Appeal was therefore prepared to hold that the tort that had in fact been committed was one of indirect inducement to breach. Lord Denning MR was prepared, albeit *obiter*, to go further. He stated (at p. 138):

> The principle of *Lumley* v *Gye* . . . is that each of the parties to a contract has a right to the performance of it: and it is wrong for another to procure one of the parties to break it or not to perform it. That principle was extended a step further by Lord MacNaghten in *Quinn* v *Leathem* . . . so that each of the parties has a right to have his 'contractual relations' with the other duly observed. 'It is . . . a violation of

legal right to interfere with contractual relations recognised by law if there be no sufficient justification for the interference.' ... The time has come when the principle should be extended further to cover 'deliberate and direct interference with the execution of a contract without that causing any breach.' That was a point left open by Lord Reid in *Stratford* v *Lindley* ... But the common law would be seriously deficient if it did not condemn such interference.

Lord Denning's *obiter* remarks were used in the subsequent cases of *Hadmor Productions Ltd* v *Hamilton* [1983] 1 AC 191 (where the House of Lords confirmed the existence of the tort) and, more importantly, in *Merkur Island Shipping Corporation* v *Laughton* [1983] 2 AC 570.

The *Merkur Island* case concerned a blockade of a ship operating under flags of convenience. The plaintiff was a shipowner who operated a ship, the *Hoegh Apapa*, and had registered it in Liberia. The boycott arose due to the International Transport Workers Federation (ITF) receiving a complaint of low wages from one of the workers on the ship. Prior to the complaint the ITF was already pursuing a campaign against ships that operated under flags of convenience.

The plaintiff chartered the ship prior to the dispute, and it was then subsequently sub-chartered. One of the clauses of the charter provided that payment under the charter should cease for time lost due to boycotts, and that if more than ten days were lost the master of the ship would have the option of terminating the charter altogether. The ITF discovered that the *Hoegh Apapa* had been chartered and was due to load at Liverpool in 1982. It instructed its members in Liverpool not to take the ship out to sea, at which point the plaintiff sued alleging interference with its contracts, trade or business.

The case eventually reached the House of Lords which had to decided whether or not an interlocutory injunction could be granted. Lord Diplock (who gave the only substantive judgment in the case) adopted further remarks of Lord Denning MR in the *Torquay Hotel* case. In that case, Lord Denning had stated (at p. 138, whilst defining the elements of the tort):

> ... there must be *interference* in the execution of a contract. The interference is not confined to the procurement of a *breach* of contract. It extends to a case where a third person *prevents* or *hinders* one party from performing his contract, even though it be not a breach.

(the emphasis is that of Lord Denning). Lord Diplock approved this comment and also went on to approve the five-stage classification put forward by Jenkins LJ in *Thomson* v *Deakin* in relation to inducing breach of contract (see above at 6.3.2.2). Lord Diplock stated that the tort of interfering with a contract, trade or business had the same ingredients as inducing breach of contract, but that instead of having as one of its central elements a requirement that a tortfeasor should intend breach of contract, there should be substituted a requirement that the tortfeasor induced interference with performance of the contract, trade or business, thereby covering acts that fell short of breach of contract. This substitution, he added, would not apply in cases where the wrongdoing consisted of employees breaking their own contracts of employment and thereby having a knock-on effect of interfering with the performance of a plaintiff's contract.

The tort was also used in the case of *Falconer v ASLEF and NUR* [1986] IRLR 331 (see above at 6.3.2.2.3).

6.4.2 Elements of the tort

As has been seen above at 6.4.1, the tort has the same elements as for inducing breach of contract (but for the substitution of a requirement for the tortfeasor to intend to interfere with performance as opposed to breach a contract). It can be committed both directly and indirectly. If the tort is committed indirectly, unlawful means must be used in its commission.

One issue remains to be resolved (as with inducing breach of contract), and that is whether the intention to injure on the part of the tortfeasor is wilful blindness or a predominant purpose. This debate is discussed at 6.3.2.2.3. One final comment on it, though, is that as Lord Diplock treats the two torts as being 'cut from the same cloth' in *Merkur Island*, it seems inconceivable that different standards of intention apply to the two torts.

6.4.3 Scope of interfering with trade or business

It is uncertain exactly how wide the tort is. To this end, each case must proceed very much on its own particular facts while attempting to derive help from the cases already handed down. Other examples of cases where the tort has been used are *Hadmor Productions Ltd v Hamilton* [1983] 1 AC 191 (where the plaintiff claimed a right to be able to have its films transmitted without interference from a film technicians union — although the House of Lords recognised the existence of the tort, their Lordships felt that it had not been established that the defendants were not protected by statutory immunity from the consequences of the tort that they had committed); *Messenger Group Newspapers Ltd v NGA (1982)* [1984] IRLR 397 (writing letters to potential advertisers in a free newspaper discouraging them to advertise — damages awarded) *Meade v Haringey London Borough Council* [1979] ICR 494 (inducing breach of statutory duty); and *Lonrho plc v Fayed* [1992] 1 AC 448 (see above at 6.2.1.2 *et seq.*).

6.4.4 Proof of loss

As with the other economic torts, it is necessary for a plaintiff to establish that he has in fact suffered loss as a result of the commission of the tort.

6.4.5   Defences

It would appear that the defence of justification should be available here, in the same way that it is available to other torts within the group of inducing and interfering with contracts, trades or business. Regard should be had to 6.3.2.3 above.

6.5   INTIMIDATION

6.5.1   Introduction

The tort of intimidation is probably the oldest of the recognised industrial torts. This said, it took some surprising detective work in the 1960s to establish that the tort still existed, since it was unheard of between 1793 and 1964 when the House of Lords confirmed that the tort had not lapsed in *Rookes* v *Barnard* [1964] AC 1129.

In 1793, the case of *Tarleton* v *McGawley* (1793) 1 Peake 270 was the last reported occurrence of the tort. The case concerned two ships attempting to carry out trades off the coast of Cameroon. One of the ships, the *Tarleton*, had sent out a smaller vessel to trade with the local inhabitants who had come out to meet the boat in a canoe. Seeing this, the captain of the other ship fired a cannon across the bow of the canoe with the result that one of its occupants was killed. The rest of the crew of the canoe turned the canoe around and headed back for the coast, with the result that no trade took place. The owners of the *Tarleton* sued for the loss of the value of the trade. They recovered damages, with Lord Kenyon holding that it was unlawful for the defendants to threaten those lawfully undertaking trade.

It may be wondered how firing cannons at canoes can provide a cause of action to a plaintiff in the context of industrial action. In *Rookes* v *Barnard*, the House of Lords showed how the tort operated in the industrial arena. The case concerned a designer working for BOAC. He was a non-union employee (having recently resigned from his union because of his views as to the union's conduct). One of the facts was that BOAC had an informal agreement with the union under which a closed shop was established. As a result of the planitiff's resignation and in order to ensure that closed shop was maintained, the defendants (who were union officials) informed BOAC that unless the plaintiff was dismissed, the other members of the design office would withdraw their labour. As a result of this pressure, BOAC duly suspended the plaintiff and then, after having given him notice, terminated his employment. The plaintiff sued, claiming amongst other things that he had been the victim of the tort of intimidation. At first instance he was successful in his claim and damages were awarded against the defendants (it being accepted that the immunity in tort provided by the Trade Disputes Act 1906 did not cover intimidation). On appeal, the Court of Appeal refused to recognise that the tort covered threats relating to industrial action and held that, to the extent that it existed, it was confined to cases where the wrongful action was a threat of physical violence. Indeed, it was labelled by Pearson LJ at the

Court of Appeal stage ([1963] QB 623, at p. 688) as 'a rare and peculiar cause of action'.

On appeal to the House of Lords, the notion that threats of physical violence only provided the basis for the action was rejected. Indeed, the judgments in the case went to great lengths to disprove this contention. Lord Reid stated (at p. 1169):

Intimidation of any kind appears to me to be highly objectionable. The law was not slow to prevent it when violence and threats of violence were the effective means. Now that subtler means are at least equally effective I see no reason why the law should have to turn a blind eye to them.

Lord Hodson, on the type of threat needed to establish the tort, added (at p. 1201):

It would be strange if threats of violence were sufficient and the more powerful weapon of a threat to strike were not, always provided that the threat is unlawful. The injury and suffering caused by a strike is very often widespread as well as devastating, and a threat to strike would be expected to be certainly no less serious than a threat of violence.

Lord Devlin added further (at p. 1209):

I find therefore nothing to differentiate between a threat of a breach of contract from a threat of physical violence or any other illegal threat. The nature of the threat is immaterial ... All that matters to the plaintiff is that, metaphorically speaking, a club has been used. It does not matter what the club is made of — whether it is a physical club or an economic club, a tortious club or an otherwise illegal club. If an intermediate party is improperly coerced, it does not matter to the plaintiff how he is coerced.

Lord Pearce concluded the judgment by saying (at p. 1234):

Businesses are run on the basis of contracts. The threat by an important supplier to withhold the supplies under a long term contract on which a manufacturer relies might be tantamount to a threat of ruin and compel him to the supplier's demands. It would seem strange if the law should disregard intimidation by such potent contractual weapons, while taking cognisance of less potent tortious weapons.

It is clear from the speeches that the nature of a threat made to a person is immaterial. It follows that in almost every single case where economic pressure is exerted by unionised labour, the tort of intimidation will be committed.

6.5.2   Elements of the tort

According to Lord Denning MR in *Morgan* v *Fry* [1968] 2 QB 710, at p. 724, the essential elements of the tort of intimidation are:

(a)   a threat by a person;

(a)   to use unlawful means;

(b)   with the intention of compelling a person to obey the tortfeasor's wishes;

(c)   causing loss to the plaintiff as a result of the person at whom the threat is aimed submitting to the same in order to prevent the threat being carried into effect.

6.5.2.1   Threats

The nature of threats has been discussed above at 6.5.1. In short, as Lord Devlin stated in *Rookes* v *Barnard*, the nature of the threat is immaterial. The threat can be either express, or it can be implied from a reasonable man's expectation of a tortfeasors's likely conduct (*per* Lord Devlin in *Rookes* at p. 1209).

To qualify as a threat a demand must contain an element of compulsion. Templeman J in *Camellia Tanker Ltd* v *ITWF* [1976] ICR 274 took the view that the threat should be designed so as to compel an employer to 'come to his senses'. It follows from this that, in the absence of a threat, where all that is present is the mere communication of information, no liability can attach (see for example, Lord Donovan in *J. T. Stratford & Son Ltd* v *Lindley* [1965] AC 269, at p. 340). The problem of the distinction between threats and communication lies in the fact that it is very difficult to divorce the reality of a situation from the way in which a comment relating to it is delivered. In other words, what might be perceived as information by a trade unionist might be construed as a threat by an employer (see *Beaverbrook Newspapers Ltd* v *Keys* [1978] ICR 582, where the alleged 'information' amounted to a comment by a union official to the effect of 'You have the law on your side, but I have common sense on mine. If you go down that road, I will close you down' — this was held to amount to a threat; and also *News Group Newspapers Ltd* v *SOGAT (No. 2)* [1986] IRLR 337, the 'Wapping dispute'). The courts seem to have taken a harsh line on when information will be construed as a threat and look at the innuendo behind the delivery of a statement.

6.5.2.2   Unlawful means

In order for a threat to be actionable, it must contain an intimation that unlawful means will be used against the victim so as to procure a benefit to the tortfeasor. A threat to carry into effect lawful action cannot amount to a threat for the purpose of establishing the tort. The view that it could provide the basis for a tort was dismissed in the case of *Sorrell* v *Smith* [1925] AC 700, where Lord Dunedin described it (at p. 719) as 'the leading heresy'. Lord Reid took the matter further in *Rookes* v *Barnard*. His view (at p. 1168) was:

So long as the defendant only threatens to do what he has a legal right to do he is on safe ground. At least if there is no conspiracy he would not be liable to anyone for doing the act, whatever his motive may be, and it would be absurd to make him liable for threatening to do it but not for doing it. But I agree with Lord Herschell (*Allen* v *Flood* [1898] AC 1, 121) that there is a chasm between doing what you have a legal right to do and doing what you have no legal right to do, and there seems to me to be the same chasm between threatening to do what you have a legal right to do and threatening to do what you have no legal right to do.

Unlawful means now covers threats to commit a breach of contract (*per* Lord Devlin in *Rookes* v *Barnard*, at p. 1209); a tort (*per* Lord Reid in *Rookes* v *Barnard*, at p. 1167; see also *Morgan* v *Fry* [1968] 2 QB 710); a crime (*per* Lord Evershed in *Rookes* v *Barnard*, at p. 1182, and *Tarleton* v *McGawley* (1793) 1 Peake 270); and it probably covers a threat to breach an equitable obligation (see *Prudential Assurance Co. Ltd* v *Lorenz* (1971) 11 KIR 78).

On the other hand, it has been held in *Morgan* v *Fry* [1968] 2 QB 710 that where workers give notice to their employer in the form of 'strike notice' equivalent in length to that properly required to terminate their contracts of employment, that will not amount to unlawful means. This decision is hard to reconcile with subsequent cases such as *Simmons* v *Hoover* [1977] ICR 61, and the better view is probably that workers do not mean to give notice to terminate their contracts and therefore must simply be taken as giving notice to an employer of a wrong that is to be committed by them.

6.5.2.3   Intention of coercing the victim of the threat

The tort of intimidation is quite clearly one of intention (see Lord Evershed in *Rookes* v *Barnard*, at p. 1183 and also Lord Devlin, at p. 1205). The usual problem arises in relation to this tort as in the other industrial torts based on intention, namely, whether the intention must rank as the tortfeasor's predominant purpose, or whether it is enough that the tortfeasor is wilfully blind to the consequences of his action. A full discussion of this point has already taken place at 6.3.2.2.3 above.

6.5.2.4   Loss

As a result of the threat, the plaintiff must show that he has suffered a loss and that the same is causally related to the threat. In *Messenger Newspapers Group Ltd* v *NGA (1982)* [1984] ICR 345, the plaintiff incurred substantial costs in attempting to stave off potential unlawful action, which, it was threatened, would shut down a printing works and result in phone calls to the establishment being cut off. Despite the fact that the threat had not yet been brought into effect (and attempts were subsequently made to enforce it), the plaintiff was able to recover damages for the costs involved in preventing the threat becoming a reality as they were causally related to the threat.

6.5.2.5   Defences

As with the other torts having a basis of intention, it appears possible to allow the defendant to justify the conduct that has led to the threat. It is doubtful to what extent (if at all) the defence exists today and regard should be had to 6.3.2.3 above for a full discussion of justification.

6.6   HARASSMENT

6.6.1   The discovery of the tort

Harassment is one of the newer industrial torts and is a product of the courts dealing with violent industrial conflict in the 1980s. Disputes such as the mineworkers' strike and the Wapping dispute resulted on each occasion in a barrage of both abuse and missiles being thrown at those that dared to cross picket lines. As a result of this, action was taken to stop the violence. This relied upon the Code of Conduct on Picketing issued by the Secretary of State. As will be recalled from 1.1.2.5, the Code was issued under s. 3 of the Employment Act 1980, which gave the Secretary of State a power to issue Codes where it was necessary to give guidance to promote industrial relations. The effect of the Code (and its successor) was not law, but it did provide evidence as to what good industrial practice amounted to (in much the same way as the Highway Code provides evidence of what amounts to good practice on the road). Paragraph 31 of the Code stated:

> Large numbers on a picket line are also likely to give rise to fear and resentment amongst those seeking to cross that picket line, even where no criminal offence is committed. They exacerbate disputes and sour relations not only between management and employees but between the pickets and their fellow employees. Accordingly, pickets and their organisers should ensure that in general the number of pickets does not exceed six at any entrance to a workplace. Frequently a smaller number would be appropriate.

One of the first cases to test the effect of the Code and to attempt to define the boundaries of the tort of harassment was *Thomas* v *NUM (South Wales Area)* [1985] IRLR 136 (see 1.2.1.2). The case involved picketing at a number of collieries in Wales during the miners' strike. The conduct of the pickets in the case was both abusive and violent towards strike-breakers. Further, the houses of the non-strikers were picketed by those on strike. An action was brought claiming that the plaintiffs were the victims of harassment and nuisance (the nuisance being in respect of picketing at their homes). The defendants claimed that they were immune from an action being brought against them under the statutory immunity granted for peaceful picketing. The matter was heard by Scott J. who had to consider whether the case was an appropriate one for the grant of an interlocutory injunction. He dealt first with the contention that the union was immune from action in tort by questioning whether the presence of such large number of pickets was reasonably necessary for the purposes of peacefully communicating with people entering the workplace (see 7.3.3). He concluded that there was no need for such large numbers to have congregated; the communication could easily have taken place with the recommended six pickets (or fewer). He then went on to consider the issue of how the acts that were being carried out could conceivably be dealt with under the banner of tort. He rejected claims that the actions of the pickets amounted to assault, obstruction of the highway, unlawful interference with the contracts of the working miners and intimidation (not in the *Rookes* v *Barnard* sense of the tort, but in attempting to compel employees not to work). Scott J did, however, consider that a variation on the tort of nuisance might have been committed by the pickets. He said (at p. 149):

> The working miners are entitled to use the highway for the purpose of entering and leaving their respective places of work. In the exercise of that right they are at present having to suffer the presence and behaviour of the pickets and demonstrators. The law has long recognised that unreasonable interference with the rights of others is actionable in tort. The law of nuisance is a classic example ... It is, however, not every act of interference with the enjoyment by an individual of his property rights that will be actionable in nuisance. The law must strike a balance between conflicting rights and interests ... Nuisance is strictly concerned with, and may be regarded as confined to, activity which unduly interferes with the use of land or of easements. But there is no reason why the law should not protect on a similar basis the enjoyment of other rights. All citizens have the right to use the public highway. Suppose an individual were persistently to follow another on a public highway, making rude gestures or remarks in order to annoy or vex. If continuance of such conduct were threatened no one can doubt but that a civil court would, at the suit of the victim, restrain by injunction the continuance of the conduct. The tort might be described as a species of private nuisance, namely unreasonable interference with the victim's right to use the highway. But the label for the tort does not, in my view matter ... A decision whether in this, or in any other similar case, the presence or conduct of pickets represents a tortious interference with the right of those who wish to go to work to do so without harassment must depend on the particular circumstances of the particular case. The balance to which I have earlier referred must be struck between the rights of those going to work and the rights of the pickets.

Having found that the rights of the plaintiffs were being interfered with under the tort he had just defined and in respect of the nuisance that they were suffering at their homes, Scott J then went on to grant an interlocutory injunction limiting the number of pickets in attendance to six, notwithstanding that the plaintiff could not show that harm was being suffered over and above the volley of abuse.

6.6.2   Criticism of the tort

After *Thomas* v *NUM* had been decided, the next case to deal with the point was *News Group Newspapers Ltd* v *SOGAT (No. 2)* [1986] IRLR 337, a case arising out of the Wapping printers' dispute. In deciding the case, Stuart-Smith J was asked to consider whether he would grant an injunction to prevent the disputes occurring at Wapping on, *inter alia*, the grounds of harassment. He addressed the paragraph from *Thomas* v *NUM* quoted above at 6.6.1 and stated (at p. 348):

> The defendants criticise this statement of law. They submit that Scott J should not have invented a new tort and that it is not sufficient to found liability that there has been an unreasonable interference with the rights of others, even though when a balance is struck between conflicting rights and interests the scale comes down heavily in favour of the plaintiffs, unless those rights are recognised by the law and fall within some accepted head of tort. I am bound to say that, with all respect to Scott J, I think there is force in these criticisms, especially where it does not appear that damage is a necessary ingredient of the tort. If, of course, damage peculiar to the plaintiff is established, then the tort is that of nuisance.

Stuart-Smith J went on to conclude that nuisance had been made out in the case he was dealing with, and intimidation had been threatened. There was therefore no need to deal with the tort of harassment.

In the only other case to have discussed the tort and its existence, *Khorasandjian* v *Bush* [1993] 3 All ER 669 (a case concerned with harassment by persistent telephone calls), Peter Gibson J (sitting as a judge of the Court of Appeal) agreed with the comments of Stuart-Smith J. However, the comments are merely *obiter* as he went on to hold that there was no need to decide the case before him on the basis of the alleged tort (neither Dillon LJ nor Rose LJ addressed the matter).

It would appear that the weight of judicial opinion seems to be against the existence of a common law tort of harassment.

6.7   OTHER TORTS COMMITTED DURING PICKETING

6.7.1   Introduction

Since the main focus of this book is trade union law, this section will do no more than briefly examine the other torts that can be committed during the course of picketing, and regard should be had to more mainstream works on the law of tort. The other torts that could be committed are the following:

(a)   trespass to the highway;
(b)   private nuisance;
(c)   public nuisance.

6.7.2 Trespass to the highway

In relation to picketing, trespass to the highway can be committed by a person who uses a highway for any purpose outside that which he has a right to. Public highways provide a right for the public to pass along them for the purposes of travel (*per* Lopes LJ in *Harrison* v *Duke of Rutland* [1893] 1 QB 142). To the extent that they are used for purposes other than this, the persons so misusing them may be liable in tort for either damages or an injunction.

The main problem that arises in relation to this tort in that most highways are these days owned by local authorities who have little interest in claiming for damages or an injunction.

In *Hubbard* v *Pitt* [1975] ICR 77 (aff'd [1975] ICR 308), the plaintiff was an estate agent who was being picketed by local residents. An action was brought by the agent to prevent the picket which, it was alleged, was causing harm to the plaintiff's business. Forbes J granted an interlocutory injunction (on the grounds of nuisance) and stated (at p. 91):

> The law appears to me to be clear: At common law, the use of the highway for picketing is illegal as it is a use not responsive to the purposes for which the highway was dedicated. It is, therefore, at least a trespass. It may also be an unreasonable user of the highway and therefore a common law nuisance. This will always be a question of fact, and what is or is not a reasonable user of the highway will be determined by reference to the purposes for which the highway was dedicated. As picketing is a use of the highway wholly unconnected with the purposes of dedication and is, in fact, designed to interfere with the rights of an adjoining owner to have unimpeded access from the highway, it is likely to be found to be an unreasonable user unless it is so fleeting and so insubstantial that it can be ignored under the *de minimis* rule ... Put shortly, therefore, the use of the highway for picketing is illegal unless — (1) it is in contemplation or furtherance of a trade dispute in the circumstances set out in the statute, or (2) it is found as a fact to be insubstantial in the sense that I have mentioned.

Since the only person who has a legitimate interest in enforcing an injunction for trespass to the highway is the owner of the sub-soil (a local authority), the tort will be of little use to a plaintiff in the context of industrial action unless the tort is committed on a private highway.

6.7.3 Private Nuisance

The tort of private nuisance is committed where a person is caused by another to suffer an unreasonable and unlawful interference with the use or enjoyment of his property (see, e.g., *Cunard* v *Antifyre Ltd* [1933] 1 KB 551).

In the context of industrial disputes this can occur where, for example, pickets congregate outside a workplace in such numbers as to provide an unreasonable obstruction to an employer's business.

Various cases have shown that an employer may use the tort to prevent picketing. In *Hubbard* v *Pitt* (discussed above at 6.7.2), an injunction was awarded on the point of a nuisance being occasioned by the pickets. Likewise, in *News Group Newspapers Ltd* v *SOGAT (No. 2)* [1986] IRLR 337, Stuart-Smith J was prepared to hold that the activity of pickets in the Wapping dispute amounted to nuisance on account of their obstruction of and abusive behaviour on the highway. This misuse of the highway by the pickets prevented the plaintiff from being able reasonably to use its land and thereby established a private nuisance.

Regard should also be had to *Mersey Dock and Harbour Co.* v *Verrinder* [1982] IRLR 152, *Norbrook Laboratories Ltd* v *King* [1982] IRLR 456 and *Thomas* v *NUM (South Wales Area)* [1985] IRLR 136.

In *Hubbard* v *Pitt* [1975] ICR 308, Lord Denning MR in the Court of Appeal gave a strong dissenting judgment attacking the view that picketing will of itself be a nuisance. He said (at p. 317):

Picketing is not a nuisance in itself. Nor is it a nuisance for a group of people to attend at or near the plaintiff's premises in order to obtain or communicate information or in order to peacefully persuade. It does not become a nuisance unless it is associated with obstruction, violence, intimidation, molestation or threats.

Most cases since *Hubbard* v *Pitt* have tended not to follow Lord Denning's view as to the legality of picketing and have instead focused on the view of the majority of the Court of Appeal.

It follows that in most disputes where picketing takes place, there is a good chance that the tort of private nuisance will be committed, but it needs to be remembered that if the picketing is lawful within the definition in s. 220 of of of TULRCA 1992 (see 7.3.3) the action will be protected. Much will depend upon the conduct of the pickets and, if there is large number of pickets involved, on the effect of the Code of Practice, especially para. 51.

6.7.4 Public Nuisance

The tort of public nuisance is committed where an act or omission takes place which unreasonably causes harm or potential harm to a class of Her Majesty's subjects (*per* Denning LJ in *Southport Corporation* v *Esso Petroleum Co. Ltd* [1954] 2 QB 182, who added at p. 196 that it is an idea that 'covers a multitude of sins, great and small').

In order for a plaintiff to establish liability for the tort, he must show that he has suffered special damage himself over and above that suffered by the public generally as a result of the tort being committed.

In *News Group Newspapers Ltd* v *SOGAT (No. 2)* [1986] IRLR 337, Stuart-Smith J held that the tort had been committed by pickets unreasonably obstructing the highway and causing the plaintiff substantial expense in the form of having to arrange buses to bring journalists and other employees into the plants affected.

Public nuisance is also a crime at common law.

6.8 INDUSTRIAL ACTION AND BREACH OF CONTRACT

6.8.1 Introduction

Where employees take industrial action, the action so taken may amount to a breach of contract on the part of the employees involved in the action. In deciding whether or not this is so, much will depend upon the nature of the action that is taken. This section will focus on the particular quirks of the law of contract when applied to industrial action. As to the position in relation to contracts of employment generally, regard should be had to a more general work on employment law.

Breach of contract is an action available to employers and employees alike. It follows that if action is taken in response to the unreasonable action of an employer, those affected by the employee's action may be able to sue for breach of contract.

6.8.2 Action taken by employees

In determining whether or not employees have committed a breach of contract, the nature of the action that has been taken by the employees involved needs to be considered. Action can basically be divided into two categories: (i) cases where employees totally deny the benefit of their services to an employer; and (ii) cases where employees provide services less than the employer is entitled to expect under the terms of the contract of employment.

6.8.2.1 Total denial of service
The most common situation is a strike. A strike for the purposes of TULRCA 1992 is defined as 'any concerted stoppage of work' (s. 246). It was once thought that provided employees gave notice equivalent in length to that which would lawfully bring about the termination of their contract, they were committing no breach. Such notice was termed 'strike notice'. Lord Denning MR discussed the concept of strike notice in *Morgan* v *Fry* [1968] 2 QB 710, at p. 725: 'It has been held for over 60 years that workmen have a right to strike ... provided that they give sufficient notice beforehand: and a notice is sufficient if it is as least as long as the notice required to terminate the contract.' This view has been eroded, though. The notice given, it has come to be thought, did not operate to terminate the contract of employment when those on strike took up the strike. As was said by Lord Reid in *Rookes* v *Barnard* [1964] AC 1129, at p. 1204: 'The object of the notice was not to terminate the

contract either before or after the expiry of the seven days. The object was to break the contract by withholding labour but keeping the contract alive for as long as the employers would tolerate the breach without exercising their right of rescission.'

The matter was subsequently taken further by Phillips J in *Simmons* v *Hoover Ltd* [1977] ICR 61, who said (at p. 76): '. . . a settled, confirmed and continued intention on the part of the employee not to do any of the work which under his contract he had engaged to do; which was the whole purpose of the contract . . . appears . . . to be repudiatory of the contract of employment.'

The position therefore appears to be that workers who strike will themselves commit a breach of contract and open themselves to the potential for action by their employer to be taken against them (see 6.8.4), unless it is the case that either:

(a)   they are striking in response to a breach of contract on the part of their employer; or
(b)   they have a term in their contract allowing them to suspend the contract through the giving of strike notice.

6.8.2.2 Denial of particular benefits under the contract of employment by employees

Where employees decide to carry on working for their employer but to deny him the benefit of a particular function of their employment, they may commit a breach of contract. In deciding whether or not this is the case, it needs to be considered whether the benefit that is being denied is contractual or non-contractual. Much will turn on the facts of the dispute.

Examples of cases where a contractual benefit has been denied to an employer are *Secretary of State for Employment* v *ASLEF (No. 2)* [1972] ICR 19 (a withdrawal of labour in a work to rule — held to be a breach of the implied term of trust and confidence); *Cresswell* v *Board of Inland Revenue* [1984] IRLR 190 (where employees refused to adapt to computerised working methods requested by the employer and simply operated in accordance with the way in which they had traditionally carried on their employment — held to be a breach of contract); *Miles* v *Wakefield Metropolitan District Council* [1987] ICR 368 (worker who failed to work $^3/_{37}$ths of his monthly hours while involved in a dispute — held to be a breach of contract); and *Ticehurst* v *British Telecommunications plc* [1992] IRLR 219 (refusal to give an undertaking to work normally and not take part in further industrial action — held to be a breach of the implied term of trust and confidence).

In order to escape liability for failing to provide a benefit, the activity must genuinely be a voluntary one. This point was considered in *Metropolitan Borough of Solihull* v *National Union of Teachers* [1985] IRLR 211. The case concerned the refusal of teachers engaged in industrial action to provide cover for staff who were ill, to supervise pupils during lunch periods or provide lunchtime activities. The High Court found that, on the facts, the action taken by the staff amounted to a breach of contract since the staff received free lunches for the supervision and, accordingly, an injunction could be issued against the staff taking action (since no ballot had been taken prior to the action).

What will amount to voluntary activity will depend upon the facts of any particular case, but could, for example, cover such matters as teachers refusing to supervise after-school sports activities. It should be noted that where an employee holds a position of responsibility, e.g., as a manager, it will probably be no defence for the employee to finish work according to the stipulated hours of his contract and claim that any extra services are voluntary. There is undoubtedly expected to be some flexibility in a working relationship (working on the basis of the implied term of trust and confidence), and the higher up a person is in an organisation, the greater is the degree of flexibility that can be expected of the employee.

6.8.3 Breach by an employer

In the same way that employees can commit breaches of contract, employers may also commit breaches. In the context of industrial action, this may take the form of a lock-out on the part of the employer with the intent that it will induce employees to accept changes imposed upon them against their will. Lock-outs are a rare luxury for employers in the 1990s and are very much a tactic of days gone by. In *Express Newspapers Ltd* v *Bunday* [1987] IRLR 422, lock-outs were defined by Glidewell LJ (at p. 427):

> Since their is no [statutory] definition of the word 'lock-out'..., it must be given its ordinary meaning ... What is material is that in my view the ordinary meaning of the word 'lock-out' comprehends not merely the act of the employer in refusing to allow his employees to work, but the reason why he refuses.

Lock-outs may amount to a breach of contract on the part of an employer who instigates such action if the lock-out is effected without giving employees their proper notice entitlement (see *Saunders* v *Neale* [1974] ICR 565); or they may amount to a reasonable response by an employer to breaches of contract that have been perpetrated upon him by his employees (see *Express Newspapers* v *Bunday*).

It follows that there may well be a considerable overlap between a strike and a lock-out, and deciding what the action amounts to will ultimately lie in the hands of a court or tribunal hearing a claim arising out of a dispute.

If an employer stages a lock-out in breach of contract, he may open himself to the usual remedies available to an employee, *viz.*, damages for breach of contract, an injunction to prevent breach or a claim for unfair dismissal. However, if employees are seeking to bring an action for damages arising out of their loss of salary during the period when a lock-out takes place, it is incumbent upon them to show that they were ready and willing to work for the employer if had let them into the workplace (see *Henthorn* v *Central Electricity Generating Board* [1980] IRLR 361).

6.8.4   Action open to an employer faced with a breach of contract

An employer faced with industrial action amounting to a breach of contract has a number of remedies and courses of action open to him. These are considered more fully in Chapter 8.

7 Industrial Action 2 — Immunity, Loss of Immunity and Collective Responsibility

7.1 INTRODUCTION

This chapter will focus upon the issues of when a union is immune from the consequences of industrial action taken in its name and when it can be held liable for the consequences of industrial action. The final issue that will be addressed is vicarious liability — in particular, when a union can be liable for the actions of its officials.

7.2 ESTABLISHING IMMUNITY

7.2.1 Introduction

The immunities in relation to tort are granted by ss. 219–220 of TULRCA 1992. A number of points can be made about the immunities. The first is that immunity, to the extent that it exists, is available only in respect of the *tortious* consequences of industrial action. This means that there is no defence to an action for breach of contract that may be taken against an individual employee.

The second point to be made in relation to trade union immunity is that it can exist irrespective of whether or not a defence exists for a tort or torts that have been committed during the course of industrial action.

The third point to make is that it in order to be immune from the consequences of tort, those seeking the immunity must show that they have complied with a precise formulation of what the law takes to be protected industrial action. It is not enough that a union or group of employees claim that they are involved in industrial action with their employer. As was seen in Chapter 1, this formulation has changed over the years during the course of the Conservative Government of 1979–1997. Therefore care needs to be taken when relying on old case law in this regard as such cases might not be decided the same way today in the light of the more restrictive immunities that exist.

7.2.2 The 'golden formula'

This expression is used to describe the statutory formulation adopted before the immunities granted by ss. 219 and 220 of TULRCA 1992, and is believed to have been coined by Professor Lord Wedderburn (see K. W. Wedderburn, *The Worker and the Law*, Penguin, 1965, p. 222). Under the formula, liability in tort will be excluded where the torts to which the sections apply are committed wholly or mainly 'in contemplation or furtherance of a trade dispute'. What amounts to a 'trade dispute' is defined by s. 244(1) of TULRCA 1992, which provides:

(1)   In this Part a 'trade dispute' means a dispute between workers and their employer which relates wholly or mainly to one or more of the following—

(a)   terms and conditions of employment, or the physical conditions in which any workers are required to work;

(b)   engagement or non-engagement, or termination or suspension of employment or the duties of employment, of one or more workers;

(c)   allocation of work or the duties of employment between workers or groups of workers;

(d)   matters of discipline;

(e)   a worker's membership or non-membership of a trade union;

(f)   facilities for officials of trade unions; and

(g)   machinery for negotiation or consultation, and other procedures, relating to any of the above matters, including the recognition by employers or employers' associations of the right of a trade union to represent workers in such negotiation or consultation or in the carrying out of such procedures.

As will be seen in the course of this chapter, a summary of the immunities is that:

(a)   an act done by a person;

(b)   at a relevant time;

(c)   to a legitimate target;

(d)   predominantly;

(e)   for legitimate purposes

will be protected.

Each limb of the golden formula needs to be examined.

7.2.2.1 *The person committing the act*

The formulation of the legislation is completely neutral for a deliberate purpose, that being to allow the protection to be claimed by any one of the potential tortfeasors (employee, union official or union) who may commit a tort and then seek to rely on the immunity.

7.2.2.2   Relevant time

The formulation places a temporal limit on the availability of immunity by requiring that the immunity can be claimed only where it is 'in contemplation or furtherance' of a dispute. Lord Loreburn, speaking of the provisions relating to immunity under the Trade Disputes Act 1906, in the case of *Conway* v *Wade* [1909] AC 506, said of this requirement (at p. 512): '... either a dispute is imminent and the act is done in expectation of and with a view to it, or ... the dispute is already existing and the act is done in support of one side to it.' In that case, the plaintiff sued his former union in respect of its inducing his former employer to dismiss him for failing to pay union dues. In defence of the action, the union put forward the argument that it was acting in contemplation or furtherance of a trade dispute and that it was therefore immune from action in tort. The House of Lords found in the case that no trade dispute existed or was contemplated. The action taken by the union was vindictive and aimed at ensuring that the plaintiff paid his union dues. It followed that as the action taken was not within the formula, it could not be the subject of the immunity.

This said, each case will turn very much on its own facts. If one is seeking to establish that a trade dispute is contemplated, it is not necessary that battle lines should be drawn. As Lord Denning put it in *Beetham* v *Trinidad Cement Ltd* [1960] AC 132, at p. 143: 'By definition a trade dispute exists wherever a "difference" exists; and a difference can exist long before the parties become locked in combat. It is not necessary that they should have come to blows. It is sufficient that they should be sparring for an opening.' Therefore, when looking to the question of a proposed dispute, it will be necessary for the person claiming immunity to show that there was a sufficiently proximate relationship between the tort committed and the contemplated trade dispute. Another example is the case of *Bent's Brewery Co. Ltd* v *Hogan* [1945] 2 All ER 570. The case concerned a questionnaire sent out by a union official to pub managers in Liverpool, requesting details of their working conditions so as to enable the union to plan a programme for obtaining better wages and conditions for its members. The plaintiff brewery claimed that the letter constituted an inducement to their managers to breach their contracts of employment since many of them contained confidentiality clauses. The defendant claimed that the information was being collected in contemplation of a trade dispute and therefore he was immune from action in tort. At trial, Lynsky J stated (at p. 579):

> The next question I have to decide is whether the document was sent out by the defendant, or on his behalf, in contemplation or furtherance of a trade dispute ... No demand has been made for either better conditions or increased wages by any manager to any of the plaintiff brewery companies. No such demands had been made by the plaintiff, or his union on behalf of such managers ... In my opinion, a dispute cannot exist unless there is a difference of opinion between two parties

as to some matter. There is no evidence before me that any dispute existed. The highest that can be put on the evidence in favour of the defendant is that the document was sent out to obtain information which, after consideration of the information obtained, might lead to a request which, if not granted, might result in a dispute.

It follows that a dispute must be objectively ascertainable on the facts, i.e., within the contemplation of both parties on the evidence available, if the immunity is to be claimed on the basis of contemplating a trade dispute.

A case that illustrates the point the other way is *Health Computing Ltd* v *Meek* [1980] IRLR 437. Here, NALGO had issued notices to its members operating in the National Heath Service instructing them not to work with the plaintiff company. The plaintiff had been requested to advise local health authorities on the installation of computerised medical services. At the time of their instruction, no jobs were directly threatened. The plaintiff took action seeking an injunction and the matter was heard in the High Court by Goulding J. The evidence upon which the application was based showed that some of the health authorities might tend to use the services of the plaintiff, and as a result this could bring the defendant union into dispute with the plaintiff. As a result, it was objectively reasonable to infer that a dispute was contemplated.

A comparison between the two cases shows that they are materially different in nature. In *Bent's Brewery*, the information was requested to see if a dispute *might* arise if pub managers' conditions were not as they should have been (in the opinion of the union). Any dispute was two steps away (the receipt of information and then deciding whether to act upon it). However, in *Health Computing*, the possibility of job losses had already been foreseen (although not confirmed) and the dispute was therefore only one step away (i.e., the likelihood of conflict) and was therefore proximate.

In *Conway* v *Wade*, Lord Shaw said of the meaning of the words 'in contemplation or furtherance' that:

> ... they do not cover the case of coercive interference in which the intervener may have in his own mind that if he does not get his own way he will thereupon take ways and means to bring a trade dispute into existence. To 'contemplate a trade dispute' is to have before the mind some objective event or situation with those elements of fact or probability to which I have adverted, but it does not mean a contemplation, mediation or resolve in regard to something as yet wholly within the mind and of a subjective character.

This said, once the facts giving rise to the dispute have been objectively established, it does not matter that the person acting takes a decision which he thinks will help further his objectives but which in reality would not do so. Thus the test as to whether the action taken is in contemplation or furtherance of the dispute is a subjective one.

This was shown by *Express Newspapers Ltd* v *MacShane* [1980] IRLR 35. The facts of this case were that the NUJ was in dispute with certain regional newspapers and called on journalists who were with the Press Association to join the dispute. When the call to arms was not fully complied with, the NUJ asked its members working for national newspapers (including the plaintiff) to boycott Press Association copy. In the Court of Appeal, an interlocutory injunction was granted against the union on the ground that the activity of the union would not be reasonably capable of helping it reach its stated objectives. The problem with the decision of the Court of Appeal was that it made the action of trade union officials reviewable by the courts, and therefore also the decision as to what action could be taken by a union. The Court's decision was appealed to the House of Lords.

Lord Diplock (with whom a majority of the House of Lords agreed) analysed the position and concluded that the test of whether action was likely to further a person's position in the course of a trade dispute was subjective. He was of the view that in some cases, action taken by trade union officials might tend to be out of proportion to the benefit that was provided by the taking of the action. It was this position, in his view, that caused the subjective test to 'stick in judicial gorges' (at p. 39). He added (at p. 40) that the effect of the statute on a plain and literal reading meant that the words 'an act done by a person in furtherance or contemplation of a trade dispute' were to refer to the state of mind of the doer of the act. His analysis of the position (at pp. 39–40) was as follows:

> My Lords, ... [the objective test] [has] ... the effect of enabling the court to substitute its own opinion for the *bona fide* opinion held by the trade union or its officers, as to whether action proposed to be taken or continued for the purpose of helping one side or bringing pressure to bear upon the other side to a trade dispute is likely to have the desired effect. Granted *bona fides* on the part of the trade union or its officers this is to convert the test from a purely subjective to a purely objective test and for the reasons I have given I do not think the wording of the section permits of this. The belief of the doer of the act that it will help the side he favours in the dispute must be honest; it need not be wise, nor need it take account of the damage it will cause to innocent and disinterested third parties.

Another issue that needs to be addressed in relation to the formula is when action will be taken to further a dispute. It is clear that once a dispute has been settled by agreement, subsequent action cannot be related to that resolved dispute (see, for example, *Stewart* v *AUEW* [1973] IRLR 57). One issue that could possibly allow an old dispute to be re-opened is, as with the common law generally, where the resolution of the dispute has been achieved by fraud or misrepresentation.

This said, in the absence of a written agreement, it may be difficult to point to the precise time when a trade dispute has ceased. It is in these grey area cases that the courts could potentially intervene so as to decide whether there is, objectively, a dispute (see *J. T. Stratford & Son Ltd* v *Lindley* [1965] AC 269 and *Newham London Borough Council* v *NALGO* [1993] IRLR 83 in this regard).

The final point in relation to action taken in contemplation or furtherance of a trade dispute is to consider the position of action taken by a person where he knows that the other side to a potential dispute will cave in at the possibility of pressure being exerted. The position at common law was that such action was not regarded as being taken in contemplation of a trade dispute. As Buckley LJ put it in *Cory Lighterage Transport Ltd* v *Transport and General Workers Union* [1973] IRLR 152: 'How can an act be done in contemplation of a trade dispute where the actor knows that no dispute will arise?' However, the law is now clear that such action will be deemed to be in contemplation of a trade dispute, and regard should be had to s. 244(4) of TULRCA 1992, which provides:

(4)   An act, threat or demand done or made by one person or organisation against another which, if resisted, would have led to a trade dispute with that other, shall be treated as being done or made in contemplation of a trade dispute with that other, notwithstanding that because that other submits to the act or threat or accedes to the demand no dispute arises.

In other words, a trade dispute is not prevented from being so simply because the other party does not want a dispute.

7.2.2.3   The target of the action

Section 244(1) of the 1992 Act requires that where action is taken it should be in support of a dispute 'between workers and their employer'. It should be noted that the definition of 'worker' in s. 296 excludes the police (s. 280) and armed services (s. 296(1)(c)). Further, in the context of a trade dispute, the general definition of 'worker' is restricted by s. 244(5) which provides that a worker:

... in relation to a dispute with an employer, means—
    (a)   a worker employed by that employer; or
    (b)   a person who has ceased to be so employed if his employment was terminated in connection with the dispute or if the termination of his employment was one of the circumstances giving rise to the dispute.

Therefore, workers are those who are in employment or who were in employment with the employer immediately before the dispute. It is not possible to protest about a prospective employer (as, for example, where a transfer of an undertaking is mooted and it causes resentment among the workforce). In such a situation it will be possible to be in dispute with the transferring employer but not with the prospective transferee employer.

In considering the statutory definition, it is also necessary to take account of the fact that under s. 244(2) of the 1992 Act, a Minister of the Crown is treated as being an employer where the dispute arises from the Minister's portfolio of responsibility, notwithstanding that the Minister is not a *de facto* employer of those taking part in the action.

Other than this, questions as to whether the parties fall into the protected relationship are questions of fact. Two issues need to be examined in looking at this relationship. The first is whether it is possible for a union to take action so as to further its own causes, or whether it must do so genuinely on behalf of the workers of a particular employer. The second is whether a union can pierce the veil of incorporation in determining whether a group of companies, of which one has a genuine trade dispute, can be the subject of action.

7.2.2.3.1   Action taken by a union to further its own causes   Generally, it will be impossible to distinguish the objects of a union from those of its members. In some recognition disputes, the courts have held that the action of a union is independent to that of its members and is therefore outside the immune relationship (see, for example, *J. T. Stratford & Son Ltd* v *Lindley* [1965] AC 269). Another example of action that the courts have on occasion held to be that of a union rather than of its members is that of a union seeking to promote its own political purpose (see, for example, *Mercury Communications Ltd* v *Scott-Garner* [1983] IRLR 494, concerning a union's objection to the privatisation of British Telecommunications; and *Associated British Ports* v *Transport and General Workers Union* [1989] IRLR 399, a case concerned with the abolition of the Dock Labour Scheme).

7.2.2.3.2   Piercing the veil   The question whether or not the courts will allow a union to pierce the veil of incorporation depends upon whether the veil is being used as a sham device to defeat a union's claim to immunity, or whether the employer that has been the target of action has a legitimate commercial reason for having a number of companies. Regard should be had to *Examite Ltd* v *Whittaker* [1977] IRLR 312 and *The Marabu Porr* [1979] 2 Lloyd's Rep 331, where it was held possible to take industrial action against a company other than that at which the dispute had originated.

A case supporting the contrary proposition is *Dimbleby & Sons Ltd* v *National Union of Journalists* [1984] IRLR 161. In *Dimbleby*, action was taken by the union against a printing company, T. Bailey Foreman Ltd (TBF). At the time of the dispute, secondary picketing was still lawful against the customers of a party in a dispute. The union in the case found out that, apparently, the plaintiff company had their printing carried out by TBF. However, the reality was that a subsidiary, T. Bailey Foreman (Printers) Ltd, carried out the work. The union caused its members at the plaintiff company not to send copy to T. Bailey Foreman, thereby inducing them to breach their contracts of employment. The result of this action was that the plaintiff company sued and the union claimed immunity. The claim was ultimately rejected, even after the House of Lords was asked to pierce the veil. Their Lordships refused to hold that a dispute with T. Bailey Foreman necessarily meant one with T. Bailey Foreman (Printers) Ltd.

7.2.2.4   Predominant purpose
The law requires that in order for action to be protected, it must be wholly or mainly for the purposes set out in s. 244(1) of the 1992 Act. The problem will lie for a union where it has an ulterior motive. The motive can be anything, but the case law in existence has provided two examples, those being cases which are aimed at government policy and those where a union is seeking to gain revenge on an employer or another person.

7.2.2.4.1   Political strikes   The starting point in this area is what amounts to a political strike. In *Sherrard* v *AUEW* [1973] IRLR 188, Roskill LJ (as he was then) said:

> Although the phrase 'political strike' has from time to time been used in reported cases, it is to my mind a phrase which should be used, at any rate in a court of law, with considerable caution, for it does not lend itself to precise or accurate definition. It is all too easy for someone to talk of a strike as being a 'political strike' when what that person really means is that the object of the strike is something that he as an individual subjectively disapproves.

It follows from this that whether or not a strike is aimed at attempting to change policy rather than influencing matters within the workplace is something that has to be judged from the facts of a given case.

A good example is the case of *Mercury Communications Ltd* v *Scott-Garner* [1983] IRLR 494. Here, the second defendant was the Post Office Engineering Union. It opposed the idea put forward by the Conservative Government to privatise the telephone system in the United Kingdom, and therefore instructed its members not to help the plaintiff by connecting it to the telephone network. The plaintiff sued, and the union defended on the basis that it was involved in a trade dispute and was therefore immune from the consequences of its action. The defence was based upon concerns that the union apparently had regarding job losses. The Court of Appeal held that a dispute could exist between British Telecommunications and the defendant but that it did not do so on the facts. These showed that the objections of the union actually related to the principle of privatisation rather than to imminent job losses. It was shown that British Telecommunications anticipated that any job losses that were likely to arise would have occurred anyway either through natural wastage or through retirements. A fundamental problem for the union was that it knew this and, as such, immunity was not available to the union.

Other examples of actions that have been held to be prompted by political objects rather than by reasons connected with a trade dispute *Associated Newspaper Group Ltd* v *Flynn* (1970) 10 KIR 17 (action taken in defiance of the introduction of the Industrial Relations Act 1971); *BBC* v *Hearn* [1977] IRLR 273 (a union's dissatisfaction over the South African Government's apartheid policy); and *Express Newspapers Ltd* v *Keys* [1980] IRLR 247 (a protest over the Government's economic policy). However, regard should also be had to *London Borough of Wandsworth* v *National Association of Schoolmasters/Union of Women Teachers* [1983] IRLR 344. Here, the plaintiff sought an injunction against the defendant union on the ground that it had induced teacher employees of the plaintiff to breach their contracts. The dispute between the parties arose as a result of a ballot which had asked the following question of the union's members: 'In order to protest against the excessive workload and unreasonable imposition made upon teachers, as a consequence of the national curriculum and testing, are you willing to take action, short of a strike?' The question was the result of the union's protest at the hours that were being requested of school teaching staff. The union had also voiced concerns about the educational quality of the proposed new national curriculum. In response to the ballot question, an 88 per cent majority was returned which resulted in a boycott of all elements of the national curriculum that were deemed to be unnecessary. The union defended the action on the basis of immunity from action.

Both the High Court and the Court of Appeal upheld the union's claim to immunity. In the Court of Appeal, Neill LJ stated:

> We have come to a clear conclusion in this case ... It seems to us to be quite clear that looking at the history since 1990 there has been increasing concern expressed by the union on behalf of its members with regard to working time. This concern came to a head as the date for the key stage 3 testing approached. It is quite clear that members of the union have criticisms to make of the national curriculum educational grounds. This was recognised by Mr de Gruchy in paragraph 3 of his affidavit, but he added: 'Of most concern to the union in relation to its members is the excessive and unnecessary workload that the national curriculum imposes on teachers'.
>
> That statement, which remains uncontradicted, is to be read in the context as referring primarily to the extra time which teachers have to work. Furthermore, we attach considerable importance to the wording of the question posed in the ballot paper ... In our judgment the dispute does mainly relate to the terms and conditions of employment of the union's members and is a trade dispute ...

Therefore, it is not enough that a union has expressed concern over Government policy; it is important to remember that the key question to be addressed is whether the dispute relates mainly to the matters set down in s. 244(1) of TULRCA 1992. If this question is properly considered then it does not matter that a union has a dispute with the Government as an employer, even though the dispute may appear to arise out of a matter connected with Government policy. For example, in *Sherrard* v *AUEW* [1973] IRLR 188, the plaintiff sought an injunction to prevent his union from taking strike action in protest over what might have appeared to be Government prices and incomes policy. The protest was launched by members of the union employed by the Government who objected to a pay freeze arising under the Counter Inflation (Temporary Provisions) Act 1972. The injunction was refused. The Court of

Appeal ultimately held that there was enough evidence to suggest that the dispute arose as a consequence of a protest about wage fixing. That was enough to bring the dispute within the golden formula.

Other examples of disputes that have been held to be non-political are *NWL Ltd* v *Nelson* [1979] IRLR 478 (allegation that a union was embarking upon a political crusade against ships bearing flags of convenience rather than caring for its members' wages — this argument was rejected by the House of Lords, who took the view that a connection with an external political purpose was irrelevant); *Hadmor Productions Ltd* v *Hamilton* [1982] IRLR 102 (where the defendant union was found to have a genuine concern about possible job losses for its members if independent television companies were used to produce television programmes); and *Associated British Ports* v *Transport and General Workers Union* [1989] IRLR 291 (union held to be acting correctly in a dispute over collective bargaining rather than seeking to protest over the abolition of the National Dock Labour Scheme — affirmed on different grounds [1989] IRLR 399).

7.2.2.4.2   Revenge sought by a union   The other common example of cases held not to be predominant connected with a trade dispute as defined by s. 244 of TULRCA 1992 is where a union has acted out of a desire for revenge. Examples of this are *Torquay Hotel Co. Ltd* v *Cousins* [1969] 2 Ch 106 (see Chapter 6 generally) and *Universe Tankships Inc. of Monrovia* v *ITWF* [1982] IRLR 200. This latter case arose from the ITWF's campaign against ships operating under a flag of convenience. The facts were that the union had agreed to release the plaintiff's ship from being blacked on condition that the plaintiff paid a sum of money to the union's welfare fund. Having paid the money over, the plaintiff sought to recover the money under the law of restitution. The case raises an interesting point as to when hard bargaining on the part of a union becomes economic duress. The House of Lords was prepared to find that this amounted to a case of duress. The reasoning adopted was that although the immunities will not apply to an action in restitution, the point at which the boundary between teaching an employer his place and hard bargaining is reached is the same as that at which a person would lose his immunity in tort. Their Lordships found by a 3:2 majority that the union had crossed the boundary.

7.2.2.5   Legitimate purposes
Industrial action will be carried out for legitimate purposes if it seeks to address any of the matters in s. 244(1) of TULRCA 1992 (see 7.2.2). It should be noted that if the action relates to a matter in s. 244(1) and takes place between workers and their employer in contemplation or furtherance of a trade dispute then, notwithstanding that the matter to which the dispute relates takes place outside the United Kingdom, the action is still protected (see s. 244(3)).

7.3   THE SCOPE OF THE IMMUNITIES

7.3.1   The immunities in tort: ss. 219 and 220 of the 1992 Act

The immunities work by protecting only primary industrial action, i.e. disputes between workers and their employer. This said, in the case of lawful picketing, it is possible for the secondary consequences to be protected. This section will examine the scope of the immunities provided by ss. 219 and 220.

7.3.2   Protection from certain tort liabilities

The starting point in relation to the immunity provided by s. 219 of TULRCA 1992 is its scope. It provides that:

(1)   An act done by a person in contemplation or furtherance of a trade dispute is not actionable in tort on the ground only—
    (a)   that it induces another person to break a contract or interferes or induces another person to interfere with its performance, or
    (b)   that it consists in his threatening that a contract (whether one to which he is a party or not) will be broken or its performance interfered with, or that he will induce another person to break a contract or interfere with its performance.
(2) An agreement or combination by two or more persons to do or procure the doing of an act in contemplation or furtherance of a trade dispute is not actionable in tort if the act is one which if done without any such agreement or combination would not be actionable in tort.

It can be seen that the section essentially provides a list of the characteristics of torts that are protected under it. It follows that if a claim is either:

(a)   not brought in tort against a union (e.g., *Universe Tankships Inc. of Monrovia* v *ITWF* [1982] IRLR 200 — *claim brought in restitution; or Prudential Assurance Co. Ltd* v *Lorenz* (1971) 11 KIR 78 — claim based upon the equitable duty to account); or
(b)   brought under a tort to which the provision does not apply (e.g., *Thomas* v *NUM (South Wales Area)* [1985] IRLR 136 — tort of harassment, to the extent that it exists; or historically, *Rookes* v *Barnard* [1964] AC 1129, tort of intimidation, now covered by s. 219(1)(b));

the action taken will not be protected by immunity.
    The torts that have the benefit of the immunity (assuming that they are committed in contemplation or furtherance of a trade dispute) have one characteristic in common, i.e., they all require lawful means to be used against the victim of the tort, or have a potentially unlawful element about them removed by operation of the Act. Thus the torts that are themselves immune under the Act are as follows:

(a) *Inducement to breach a contract* (direct covered by s. 219(1)(a), indirect usually covered by s. 219(1)(a) or (b)). It should be noted that if the means used against the third person are unlawful and not protected by the immunities, it is possible for liability to attach to the tortfeasor. See 6.3.3.2 above in relation to unlawful means.

(b) *Interfering with a contract, trade or business.* Again, liability for the direct form of the tort is removed under s. 219(1)(a), and to the extent that unlawful means are not used against a third party the tortfeasor will be protected under s. 219(1)(b).

(c) *Intimidation.* Covered by s. 219(1)(b) provided, again, that the threats relate solely to breaches of contract and not to other unlawful means of obtaining an outcome to the dispute in progress.

(d) *Simple conspiracy* (covered by s. 219(2)).

(e) *Conspiracy using unlawful means.* Provided that the unlawful means are the torts already discussed and are committed in a lawful fashion, this would make the tort 'not actionable' for the purposes of the s. 219(2) definition and would therefore mean that the tort of conspiracy was immune as a consequence. If, however, the conspiracy is to commit a tort that does not enjoy the benefit of statutory immunity, e.g., to the extent it exists, harassment, then since the primary tort's unlawful means are not protected, the conspiracy cannot be protected either.

Section 219(3) goes on to add that if a tort is committed in the course of picketing, the tortfeasor will be immune only if the tort is committed in the context of the immunity for peaceful picketing.

7.3.3   Liability in connection with peaceful picketing

7.3.3.1   Scope of the immunity
Section 220(1) of TULRCA 1992 provides as follows:

(1) It is lawful for a person in contemplation or furtherance of a trade dispute to attend—
(a) at or near his own place of work, or
(b) if he is an official of a trade union, at or near the place of work of a member of the union whom he is accompanying and whom he represents,
for the purpose only of peacefully obtaining or communicating information, or peacefully persuading any person to work or abstain from working.

Section 220 provides a complex set of hurdles to be overcome if the immunity is to be obtained.

7.3.3.2   Geographical restriction

The first point to note about the immunity is the geographical restriction that accompanies the temporal restriction ('contemplation or furtherance' — see 7.2.2.2 above). This requires physical proximity to an employee's 'place of work'. An expanded definition of this phrase is provided for employees who have a number of potential places of employment and for ex-employees who have been dismissed. This allows the former to claim any place from which they work, or from which their work is administered to be their place of work (s. 220(2)). The latter can claim as their place of work the place that they used to work at prior to their employment terminating.

In all cases, 'place of work' is exactly as defined by the statute (at s. 220(2)). Stuart-Smith J, in *News Group Newspapers Ltd v SOGAT (No. 2)* [1986] IRLR 337, was asked to consider whether ex-employees can picket their ex-employer's new place of business. His view was that it was not possible to transfer a picket line since pickets would not have worked at the new plant and this was not covered by the literal reading of the immunity. A similar decision was reached in *Union Traffic Ltd v Transport and General Workers Union* [1989] IRLR 127.

Where, however, in order to avoid trespassing, employees set up a picket at the nearest point to an employer's business that they are able without going on to private land, the use of the words 'at *or near* his own place of work' will come to the aid of the employee (see the Court of Appeal in *Rayware Ltd v Transport and General Workers Union* [1989] IRLR 134. 'Or near' is used in this context to expand upon the permissible geographical area.

The definition, it can be seen, also allows union officials to claim the benefit of the immunity if they are accompanying members of the union. Again, the same geographical and temporal restrictions apply.

7.3.3.3   Purpose of the picket

The second point to note about picketing is that an immunity will be provided only for limited purposes. These will be where the purpose of the picket is peacefully to communicate and receive information, or peacefully to attempt to make people work or prevent them from doing so. The courts have taken a hard line down the years as to when these purposes have been exceeded. In *Tynan v Balmer* [1967] 1 QB 91, the Divisional Court held that the purposes had been exceeded by union members who, in the course of a picket, had attempted to seal off a public highway. The case shows the link between the immunity, which if complied with is a full immunity in tort only, and the powers of the police. Since the police enjoy a considerable discretion in moving pickets on to prevent *criminal* consequences arising from picketing (see Chapter 9), the right to attend is a limited one. Furthermore, there is the possibility that, simply through weight of numbers, a picket line may be unlawful (see, for example, *Thomas v NUM (South Wales Area)* [1985] IRLR 136).

The result, then, is that picketing, if carried out at or near an employee's place of work, for the limited purposes provided for by the Act, will be immune from the consequences of any tort that occurs.

7.4   REMOVING THE IMMUNITIES

7.4.1   Introduction

Once a tortious act has been afforded immunity by the statute, it does not follow that the person committing the tort will always remain protected from the consequences of tort. The 1992 Act has a number of measures built into it that operate to disapply the immunities that would otherwise be granted. Many of the disapplying sections are used to enforce duties that are owed by a union to an employer. The immunities will be removed where:

    (a)   no strike ballot takes place;
    (b)   no notice of industrial action is given to an employer;
    (c)   action is taken by a workforce to enforce union membership;
    (d)   action is taken to support dismissed unofficial strikers;
    (e)   secondary action is taken;
    (f)   action is taken to enforce recognition of a union in a supply contract; and
    (g)   action is taken by pickets acting otherwise unlawfully.

7.4.2   No strike ballot takes place

The starting point in relation to strike ballots is that a union is obliged to hold them if it wants to bring lawful pressure to bear on an employer. The requirement was introduced by the Trade Union Act 1984, which provided that secret postal ballots must be held if a union was to keep the benefit of the immunities. It was not until the Employment Act 1988 that members of the union were given the right to demand that a ballot be held.

If a union does not hold such a ballot, it can be stopped from taking action by any one of three interested parties, these being an employer (as a necessary consequence of the immunity being removed under s. 226 of TULRCA 1992), a union member (who has the right to have a ballot before industrial action under s. 62, see 4.2.4) and any third party who suffers as a result of the unlawful action (under s. 235A, see 9.3 below). Section 226 reads as follows:

    (1)   An act done by a trade union to induce a person to take part, or continue to take part, in industrial action
        (a)   is not protected unless the industrial action has the support of a ballot, and
        (b)   where section 226A falls to be complied with in relation to the person's employer, is not protected as respects the employer unless the trade union has complied with section 226A in relation to him.
    In this section 'the relevant time', in relation to an act by a trade union to induce a person to take part, or continue to take part, in industrial action, means the time at which proceedings are commenced in respect of the act.

(2)   Industrial action shall be regarded as having the support of a ballot only if—

   (a)   the union has held a ballot in respect of the action—

      (i)   in relation to which the requirements of section 226B so far as applicable before and during the holding of the ballot were satisfied,

      (ii)   in relation to which the requirements of sections 227 to 231A were satisfied, and

      (iii)   in which the majority voting in the ballot answered 'Yes' to the question applicable in accordance with section 229(2) to industrial action of the kind to which the act of inducement relates;

   (b)   such of the requirements of the following sections as have fallen to be satisfied at the relevant time have been satisfied, namely—

      (i)   section 226B so far as applicable after the holding of the ballot, and

      (ii)   section 231B; and

   (c)   the requirements of section 233 (calling of industrial action with support of ballot) are satisfied.

Any reference in this subsection to a requirement of a provision which is disapplied or modified by section 232 has effect subject to that section.

(3)   Where separate workplace ballots are held by virtue of section 228(1)—

   (a)   industrial action shall be regarded as having the support of a ballot if the conditions specified in subsection (2) are satisfied, and

   (b)   the trade union shall be taken to have complied with the requirements relating to a ballot imposed by section 226A if those requirements are complied with,

in relation to the ballot for the place of work of the person induced to take part, or continue to take part, in the industrial action.

(4)   For the purposes of this section an inducement, in relation to a person, includes an inducement which is or would be ineffective, whether because of his unwillingness to be influenced by it or for any other reason.

In short, the requirements that need to be complied with for the purposes of ensuring that industrial action is lawful are:

(a)   the union needs to have called the action properly;

(b)   the ballot paper must be correct in all material respects;

(c)   those being balloted must be the correct community of the total union membership; and

(d)   the ballot itself must be properly conducted.

This said, the requirements do not need to be observed where either the number of members entitled to vote in the ballot, or, if separate workplace ballots need to be held under s. 228(1), the aggregate number of members entitled to vote in each of them, is less than 51 (TULRCA 1992, s. 226C).

Over and above this, the union should also attempt to comply with the Code of Practice on Industrial Action Ballots and Notice to Employers (1995) issued by the Secretary of State. The Code, as with other Codes of Practice, is supposed to be mere guidance for those subject to it, but inevitably it will weigh heavily on the minds of any court hearing disputes arising out of a failure to follow the provisions of the Code as it is admissible as evidence of good industrial relations practice under s. 207 of TULRCA 1992.

The White Paper 'Fairness at Work' has recommended that the law and Code of Practice relating to balloting should be overhauled because of their excessive complexity. It has asked for suggestions as to how this reform should be implemented.

7.4.2.1   Calling action

The most notable features of the changes to the law concerning industrial action are, first, that it is now necessary to specify on the ballot paper a person who is authorised (either actually, or as a result of being deemed authorised by s. 20(2) of TULRCA 1992) to call industrial action on behalf of the union (s. 233(1) and (3)(b)), and, secondly, the ballot cannot be called to validate retrospectively action that has been taken without the support of a ballot (s. 233(3)(a)). If these requirements are not complied with, any action taken is deemed to be unauthorised and those taking part will not enjoy the immunity that might otherwise have been available.

It should be noted that is that the action must be called within the time allowed before the ballot becomes stale and a fresh ballot is required (s. 233(3)(b) and s. 234). That time limit is four weeks (s. 234(1)) beginning with the date of the ballot and ending at midnight on the last night of the fourth week (see *RJB Mining (UK) Ltd* v *NUM* [1995] IRLR 556).

7.4.2.2   The ballot paper

The ballot paper must contain a number of key points in order to comply with the requirements of TULRCA 1992, s. 229. First, it must contain the name of an independent scrutineer (who will oversee the balloting process) and the address to which the paper is to be returned. It must also state the number of the ballot paper, which must be one of a number of consecutive whole numbers (s. 229(1A)). If the voters are merchant seamen, the address to which the paper should be returned is taken out of the requirements and the name of the ship to which the crew belongs is inserted instead (s. 229(1A)).

Next, the paper must contain a question that can be answered in the form of 'Yes' or 'No'. The question can be to a formulation of a union's own devising, but it must deal with the issue of whether those voting wish to take part in a strike, or whether they are prepared to take part in industrial action short of a strike (s. 229(2)). To the extent that a union is putting forward both options as alternatives, it must ask both questions. This point was dealt with in *Post Office* v *Union of Communication Workers* [1990] IRLR 143. Here the union had asked the two questions rolled up in the form of one question, namely whether its members were 'willing to take industrial action up to and including strike action'. An injunction was sought by the plaintiff alleging that the proposed action (which had the support of 51 per cent of those voting) was illegal. The Court of Appeal granted an injunction to prevent the action. It held that TULRCA 1992 required that, if action was to be taken and both courses were suggested by the union, the questions had to be asked in full as alternatives so as to give a purposive construction to the Act.

Further the ballot paper must disclose the identity of the person authorised to call the action. This person need not be one who is allowed to call action under the union rules, but under s. 229(3) he must be capable of making the union responsible for the consequences of his actions under s. 20(2) of TULRCA 1992 (see 7.5.1.2 for who such persons are).

The final matter to be included on the ballot paper is the following statement: 'If you take part in a strike or other industrial action, you may be in breach of your contract of employment.' This requirement is laid down by s. 229(4). It is not possible to qualify or comment upon the statement in any way on the ballot paper. This is true even if the action proposed does not go to an employee's contractual obligations. If a union is minded to comment on the content of the statement, as a matter of good practice it should do so on a separate publication that is not sent with the ballot paper. This will then avoid the possibility of an invalid ballot.

7.4.2.3   The proportion of the union to be balloted

Those entitled to vote on industrial action are dealt with under s. 227 of TULRCA 1992. This states (s. 227(1)) that entitlement to vote must be accorded equally to all members of the union who it is reasonable at the time of the ballot for the union to believe will be induced to take part in or continue with the action proposed or commenced. The requirement is supported by s. 227(2), which states that if a member who was entitled to vote has been denied the right to do so, and his union then calls upon him to take part in action, the ballot will fail to comply with the Act.

It is up to the union to decide the class of members that it is seeking to canvass. It can therefore choose between different classes of members at one employer, provided that it makes reasonable efforts to approach all employees in that class. It can also choose to ballot all employees of a particular description at different employers nationally if there is genuinely a trade dispute with all the different employers (*University of Central England* v *NALGO* [1993] IRLR 81). A union may also ballot all members of a national workforce. In doing so, strict adherence to s. 227 of the 1992 Act is required. If a sizeable proportion of a union's membership within a national workforce is omitted from a ballot, the ballot will fall outside the statutory requirements and will be invalid (see, for example, *RJB Mining (UK) Ltd* v *NUM* [1997] IRLR 621).

When considering whether a union has attempted to take proper account of those entitled to vote, regard should be had to s. 230(4). This requires that a ballot is to be conducted so as to ensure that it is fair and accurate, and that any minor errors in counting are to be disregarded if they are accidental and would not make a significant difference to the result.

A complication arises in the form of members who have joined an employer after the holding of a ballot and who are then asked to take part in action which they have not had the opportunity to vote on. In such a situation, is the ballot valid? The matter was addressed by the Court of Appeal in three cases, *British Railways Board* v *NUR* [1989] IRLR 349, *Post Office* v *Union of Communication Workers* [1990] IRLR 143 and *London Underground* v *National Union of Rail, Maritime and Transport Workers* [1995] IRLR 636. In the *Post Office* case, Lord Donaldson MR stated (at p. 147):

> The union clearly cannot identify and ballot those of its members who are not employees of the employer at the time of the ballot, but who will, in the event, join the workforce at a later date. It would seem to follow that any call for industrial action following a ballot should be expressly limited to those who were employed by the employer, and given an opportunity of voting, at the time of the ballot.

In the *London Underground* case, the defendant union had enjoyed a large increase in membership after a call for action and subsequent ballot (692 new members). It called on these members to take part in industrial action against the plaintiff employer. The plaintiff took the view that, given the upturn in membership, the defendant did not have a ballot that had a majority of its membership in favour of action. It therefore sought an injunction. In the High Court, Mance J granted the injunction requested, but this decision was overturned by the Court of Appeal. Millett LJ stated (at p. 639):

> There is nothing in the very detailed requirements which Parliament has laid down for the conduct of the ballot which compels the union to restrict its call for industrial action to those of its members who were members at the date of the ballot and were given the opportunity to take part in it. Parliament must be taken to have appreciated that there would be constant changes in the membership of a large union, and that by normal accretion alone significant numbers of new members might join the union between the date of the ballot notice given to the employer ... and the holding of the ballot, and between the holding of the ballot and the taking of industrial action. In the case of a lengthy dispute, the numbers in the latter case could be very large indeed.

He went on to consider the position of extending the action to a new class of union members at the employer (at p. 639): 'If [the union] changes its mind and decides to extend the industrial action to members *who were members of the union at the time when the ballot was held* but who were not balloted, then it must hold a fresh ballot.'

While these cases apparently conflict, they can be reconciled in that, as Millett LJ himself points out in the *London Underground* case, Lord Donaldson appears to be discussing changes to an employer's workforce rather than to union membership and is therefore presumably dealing with persons who were members of the union taking action at the time of the action although not initially employed by the employer, but subsequently came to be employed by the employer against whom the action was taken. In such a situation, those members should be balloted. As Millett LJ also points out, no reference is to be found in s. 227 to the employer against whom action is taken. Further, since Lord Donaldson was not supported by the other members of the Court of Appeal in the *Post Office* case, the better view is that his remarks were merely *obiter*.

It should be added that the *British Railways Board* case makes the point that if changes to membership between a ballot and subsequent action are *de minimis*, they will not be allowed to invalidate the ballot.

Section 228(1) requires that unions have separate workplace ballots at each different workplace that an employer has. A union only has to invite to vote at a workplace such of its members as it reasonably believes work at a particular workplace. A supplemental point arises here in relation to the place of work of employees who have no fixed place of work, e.g., lorry delivery drivers. If they are consistently on the road and load their vehicles from a number of different loading points, where is their place of work? The answer is provided by s. 228(4), which states that it will be the place of work with which such an employee has the closest connection. Where exactly this will be is a question of fact to be decided in each particular case.

Section 228(4) goes further than this, though. In defining a place of work, it talks in terms of the 'premises occupied by his employer' from which an employee works as being his place of work. It is conceivable that this phrase is capable of meaning that an employer may occupy more than one set of premises on a particular site, and therefore there may be a duty on a union to hold more than one ballot at each such site. This point was tested in *InterCity West Coast Ltd* v *National Union of Rail, Maritime and Transport Workers* [1996] IRLR 583. The facts of the case were that the plaintiff was a wholly-owned subsidiary of the British Railways Board and operated trains out of Manchester Piccadilly Station. The operating part of the station was owned by Railtrack Ltd, and this company entered into formal access agreements with the plaintiff to allow them to use offices on the station concourse. A dispute arose involving train conductors and the plaintiff, and a ballot was called asking for industrial action to be taken. The plaintiff took the view that there should have been separate ballots at its different operating points around the station. An injunction was granted by the High Court, but was subsequently overturned by the Court of Appeal by a majority decision. Neill LJ stated of s. 228(4) (at p. 585):

This section is part of legislation dealing with industrial relations and the conduct of trade unions, and in particular the way in which ballots are to be conducted before industrial action is taken. It seems to me therefore that one has got to look at the word 'occupation' in that context. It is not to the point that if one was looking at the word for some different purpose one might construe the word 'occupy' more narrowly ... It seems to me that once one accepts that the licence is a licence for the staff to use Manchester Piccadilly for the purpose of business, then, having regard to the nature of the business of this operating railway company, that the station is indeed premises occupied ... for the purposes of this subsection.

The upshot of this decision is that, although other cases may be differently decided, one should avoid straying too far into the realms of property law to work out what are 'premises' and should instead take a purposive approach to the construction of the subsection by looking at the reality of the nature of an employer's occupation of premises.

The final point to be considered is the issue of the majority. In deciding what amounts to a majority, two questions need to be asked: (i) whether the majority is of all those entitled to vote, or whether it is a majority of valid votes cast; and (ii) whether account should be taken of spoiled ballot papers. Both matters were addressed by the Court of Appeal in *West Midlands Travel Ltd* v *Transport and General Workers Union* [1994] IRLR 578. Here, a majority of just over 50 per cent had been achieved on the basis of valid votes cast, but if spoiled ballot papers had been taken into account, only 48 per cent of those 'voting in the ballot' would have voted in favour of action. The Court of Appeal held that those voting in the ballot under s. 226(2)(a)(iii) meant those validly casting votes. As such, a majority had been achieved.

7.4.2.4   The conduct of the ballot
The conduct of the ballot is dealt with by s. 230 of TULRCA 1992. This provides that every person entitled to vote is allowed to do so free from constraint or interference by the union or anyone acting for it (although it is conceivably possible for an employer to attempt to interfere with the outcome of a ballot), and the ballot is required to be at minimal cost to the member (s. 230(1)). Further, since s. 230(2) requires that a ballot is to be by post, it follows that this will require the union to send pre-paid envelopes for the use of the voter. If the union has members who are merchant seamen special provisions apply allowing them to vote on their ship if the ship is likely to be at sea or outside Great Britain during the period in which votes may be cast (see s. 230(2A) and (2B)).

7.4.2.5   Independent scrutineers
The voting procedure, as with nearly all other forms of vote in relation to trade unions (see Chapter 4), requires that an independent scrutineer be appointed (TULRCA 1992, s. 226B) and that the scrutineer observes the conduct of the ballot. The scrutineer is required to prepare a report stating whether or not he is satisfied that the balloting procedure was properly carried out; that appropriate arrangements were made for handling the voting papers right the way through to counting them; and that he was not interfered with in any way by the union, its officials or employees

(s. 231B(1)). To the extent that the scruntineer is not able to confirm these points, he is required to particularise the problems that he incurred.

The scrutineer is required to make available to any person entitled to vote in the ballot, or to the employer of such a person, a copy of the report at any time up to six months after the ballot and is able to charge a reasonable fee for doing so (s. 231B(2)).

Provided that a union complies with the foregoing requirements, it will have validly called industrial action.

7.4.3 Failure to give notice of industrial action to an employer

7.4.3.1 Introduction

The strike notice provisions arose as a result of a campaign of industrial action taken in connection with the London Underground. The requirements were introduced by s. 21 of TURERA 1993 and are now to be found in s. 234A of TULRCA 1992. As a result of the changes, an employer is required to be given written notice of the fact that industrial action will be taken against it. The effect of the strike notice provision is to give an employer a chance to notify its customers of impending industrial action, to warn its employees of the consequences of industrial action that will face them and, if it is able to do so, to employ temporary workers so as to minimise the effect of action taken.

The immunity in tort that would otherwise be available in respect of a properly balloted strike is removed by s. 234A(1) where a union fails to take such steps as are reasonably necessary to ensure that the employer receives relevant notice within the 'appropriate period'.

7.4.3.2 Notice

Notice is required to be in writing and must identify the employees that the union has induced to take action so that the employer can 'readily ascertain them' (TULRCA 1992, s. 234A(3)(a)). This requirement was discussed in *Blackpool and the Fylde College* v *National Association of Teachers in Further and Higher Education* [1994] IRLR 227. In this case, the words 'readily ascertain them' were taken to mean that an employer must be able to 'identify' the employees who are to take part in the action. It was said in this case by the Master of the Rolls, Sir Thomas Bingham, that he sympathised with the view that this construction would cause unease in the field of industrial relations, although he thought that the construction was 'inescapable'.

The employer must also be informed whether the action to be taken is to be continuous or discontinuous, and the date or dates of the action (s. 234B(3)(b)).

This is another of the areas that has been earmarked for reform under the White Paper 'Fairness at Work'. The proposal under the White Paper is that the class of workers taking action is all that should be identified and that individual workers will not have to be specified in future.

7.4.3.3 The 'appropriate period'

The length of notice to be given is seven days, commencing with the date that an employer is informed of the result of a ballot on the holding of industrial action (a requirement imposed under s. 231A) and ending on the seventh day before the first action day (s. 234A(4)). If given at an the appropriate time, the notice will then comply with the requirements of the Act and the immunity will be maintained.

If the action taken by a union is continuous but is subsequently called off by the union, the union must give fresh notice to the employer to recommence action (s. 234A(7)).

7.4.4 Action taken to enforce the closed shop

7.4.4.1 Introduction

As was seen in Chapter 1, much of the thrust of the Conservative reforms of the 1980s was aimed at bringing to an end the practice of the closed shop, which was seen as uncompetitive and responsible for setting wages above the market level. Now, if a union uses tortious means to ensure that a closed shop is established, no immunity will be available in respect of that action by virtue of TULRCA 1992, s. 222.

7.4.4.2 Scope of the removal of immunity

Section 222 reads as follows:

(1) An act is not protected if the reason, or one of the reasons, for which it is done is the fact or belief that a particular employer—

(a) is employing, has employed or might employ a person who is not a member of a trade union, or

(b) is failing, has failed or might fail to discriminate against such a person.

(2) For the purposes of subsection 1(b) an employer discriminates against a person if, but only if, he ensures that his conduct in relation to—

(a) persons, or persons of any description, employed by him, or who apply to be, or are, considered by him for employment, or

(b) the provision of employment for such persons,

is different in some or all cases, according to whether or not they are members of a trade union, and is more favourable to those who are.

(3) An act is not protected if it constitutes, or is one of a number of acts which together constitute, an inducement or attempted inducement of a person—

(a) to incorporate in a contract to which that person is a party, or a proposed contract to which he intends to be a party, a term or condition which is or would be void by virtue of section 144 (union membership requirement in contract for goods or services), or

(b) to contravene section 145 (refusal to deal with person on grounds relating to trade union membership).

As can be seen, the removal is all-embracing and covers situations where pressure is brought to bear upon an employer who does not want to have a closed shop (s. 222 (1) and (2)), and the situation of extending the union's influence to suppliers of the employer (s. 222(3)).

It is significant to note that action is not protected if the union seeks to make an employer discriminate in favour of union members (s. 222(2)). However, it would seem that the immunity will not be removed where a union is protesting about pay increases awarded to non-union employees and the union is merely seeking to obtain parity, as opposed to gain an advantage, with the non-union members.

Essentially, action will not be protected where it seeks to put union members in a better position than non-union members working for an employer or for the employer's suppliers.

7.4.5 Support of employees dismissed for taking unlawful industrial action

The main thrust of removing the immunity here is to discourage unofficial action. The measure was introduced by the Employment Act 1990 and is now found in s. 223 of TULRCA 1992. Section 223 removes the immunity where the commission of a tort, or one of the reasons for its commission, is to support workers who have been dismissed for taking unlawful industrial action. It should be noted that any notion that action has been taken to support dismissed unlawful strikers is enough to remove the immunity (even though a union might have other legitimate grievances that would otherwise be protected).

7.4.6 Secondary action

7.4.6.1 Introduction
The removal of immunity under this head was introduced as one of the first reforms of employment law by the Thatcher Government in 1980. Prior to this, it was potentially lawful to take action against another employer who might not be connected with a dispute. The first attempt to reform was found in s. 17 of the Employment Act 1980, which allowed some secondary action to be carried out in relation to commercial contracts in three situations, these being:

(a)   where there was a direct contractual relationship between the victim of the secondary action and the victim of the primary action. It therefore allowed action to be taken against suppliers of a party involved in a trade dispute;

(b)   where the victim of the secondary action was an associated employer of the victim of primary action, or was a customer or supplier of the associated employer;

(c)   where the action was taken by a person lawfully picketing at his own place of work, or by a trade union official accompanying such a person (see now s. 220(4) of TULRCA 1992 as to this last point).

Section 4 of the Employment Act 1990 did away with the first two of those exceptions and replaced them with what is now s. 224 of TULRCA 1992. This provides as follows:

(1)   An act is not protected if one of the facts relied on for the purpose of establishing liability is that there has been secondary action which is not lawful picketing.

(2)   There is secondary action in relation to a trade dispute when, and only when, a person—

(a)   induces another to break a contract of employment or interferes or induces another to interfere with its performance, or

(b)   threatens that a contract of employment under which he or another is employed will be broken or its performance interfered with, or that he will induce another to break a contract of employment or to interfere with its performance, and the employer under the contract of employment is not the employer party to the dispute.

(3)   Lawful picketing means acts done in the course of such attendance as is declared lawful by section 220 (peaceful picketing)—

(a)   by a worker employed (or, in the case of a worker not in employment, last employed) by the employer party to the dispute, or

(b)   by a trade union official whose attendance is lawful by virtue of subsection (1)(b) of that section.

(4)   For the purposes of this section an employer shall not be treated as a party to a dispute between another employer and workers of that employer; and where more than one employer is in dispute with his workers, the dispute between each employer and his workers shall be treated as a separate dispute. . . .

7.4.6.2   Scope of the immunity

The reason for the change to the above was largely the complexity of the legislation that preceded it (for a failed attempt to take advantage of the old immunity see *Dimbleby & Sons Ltd* v *National Union of Journalists* [1984] IRLR 161). The legislation in its old form allowed for a degree of balance between the interests of the union in being able to make a point and the right of third parties not to become embroiled in a dispute which was nothing to do with them. The new formulation has the advantage of simplicity over its predecessor (all secondary action is unlawful save for peaceful picketing at an employee's own place of work where the employer being picketed is a legitimate party to a trade dispute). Thus all that is protected now in the form of secondary action is essentially the secondary effect of primary action (i.e., attempting to persuade the suppliers, customers and other employees of the employer in dispute not to deal with him and using lawful means to do so).

Lastly, it should be noted that the immunity could be lost under s. 17 of the Employment Act 1980 only where commercial contracts were being targeted by a union. The new s. 224 does not distinguish between commercial and non-commercial contracts.

7.4.7   Action taken to impose union recognition at suppliers

The provision was initially introduced in the Employment Act 1982, and the immunity is now removed under this head pursuant to s. 225 of TULRCA 1992, which reads as follows:

(1)   An act is not protected if it constitutes, or is one of a number of acts which together constitute, an inducement or attempted inducement of a person—

(a)   to incorporate in a contract to which that person is a party, or a proposed contract to which he intends to be a party, a term or condition which is or would be void by virtue of section 186 (recognition requirement in contract for goods or services), or

(b)   to contravene section 187 (refusal to deal with person on grounds of union exclusion).

(2) An act is not protected if—

(a)   it interferes with the supply (whether or not under a contract) of goods or services, or can reasonably be expected to have that effect, and

(b)   one of the facts relied upon for the purposes of establishing liability is that a person has—

(i)   induced another to break a contract of employment or interfered or induced another to interfere with its performance, or

(ii)   threatened that a contract of employment under which he or another is employed will be broken or its performance interfered with, or that he will induce another to break a contract of employment or to interfere with its performance, and

(c)   the reason, or one of the reasons, for doing the act is the fact or belief that the supplier (not being the employer under the contract mentioned in paragraph (b)) does not or might not—

(i)   recognise one or more trade unions for the purpose of negotiating on behalf of workers, or any class of worker, employed by him, or

(ii)   negotiate or consult with, or with an official of, one or more trade unions.

As can be seen, the provision is again a mirror image of the duty not to attempt to impose recognition requirements in supply contracts (dealt with below at 9.2.3). The removal of immunity does not cover the position where a union is seeking to gain a foothold of recognition at the place of employment of the workers taking the action, provided that the employees taking the action confine it to seeking recognition for themselves only.

7.4.8   Ancillary unlawful action taken by pickets

Over and above all of these possible grounds for the loss of immunity will be the loss of immunity where any ancillary action taken by pickets is unlawful. For action to be lawful, not only must the action be properly called and for a proper purpose, it must be properly carried out. The requirement is contained in s. 219(3) of TULRCA 1992, which provides:

> (3)   Nothing in subsections (1) and (2) prevents an act done in the course of picketing from being actionable in tort unless it is done in the course of attendance declared lawful by section 220 (peaceful picketing).

Sections 219(1) and (2), it will be remembered, establish the general immunity in tort (see 7.3.2). It follows that if the picket line does not behave itself in an orderly fashion then liability will attach under this provision.

7.4.9   Summary of the disapplying legislation

The changes to the old-style blanket immunity have come about largely as a result of union misconduct during industrial action in the 1980s. The whole thrust of the law as it now stands is to provide a narrow channel of immunity for unions provided that they ensure that their members are in favour of action, that they take steps to inform an employer of the action and that they then carry out the action properly. If a union operates outside the channel then it will lose immunity.

7.5   ESTABLISHING COLLECTIVE RESPONSIBILITY

7.5.1   Introduction

The law relating to the liability of unions and employers' associations operates by making such bodies liable for their own wrongs, for the acts of their officials and also, potentially, for acts of the members of such bodies. The rules relating to the liability of a union for its members are essentially a function of 'good housekeeping'. A union should operate so as to keep its members in line or risk the taking the consequences (which can be a liability in damages of up to £250,000).

This section will focus upon, first, trade union liability and, secondly, the liability of employers' associations.

7.5.2   Trade union liability

7.5.2.1   Introduction
The history of trade union liability has been extensively dealt with in Chapter 1. Essentially, it has been possible to take legal proceedings against a trade union in its own name since the case of *Taff Vale Railway Co.* v *Amalgamated Society of Railway Servants* [1901] AC 426. This position has been codified by statute, most recently in s. 10 of TULRCA 1992. Once it is established that a union can potentially be sued,

the next question to consider is the nature of the harm that has been committed. This will determine whether the general common law rules relating to the attachment of liability will operate, or whether special statutory rules apply.

7.5.2.2 Harm committed by a union

In the context of industrial action, torts fall into two categories, those being the industrial torts (for which unions have *prima facie* immunity in tort) and other torts which amount to unlawful acts in their own right.

7.5.2.2.1 Liability in respect of the industrial torts

As regards the first category, liability can be incurred either by a union itself acting unlawfully, or by the law deeming a union liable for the acts of its officials or making it vicariously liable for the acts of its members.

As regards primary liability, this will occur where the union has rules which authorise the taking of tortious activity in its name (TULRCA 1992, s. 20(2)(a)). The union rules for these purposes are defined as being a union's written rules, or any other written provisions forming part of the membership contract. It follows from this that it is not possible to have an oral rule agreed by members that would have the effect of binding a union by way of primary liability.

Secondly, it is possible for a union to be liable for the acts of its officials, they being defined as the principal executive committee, the president or the general secretary (TULRCA 1992, s. 20(2)(b)). This remains the case even if the union rulebook or a contract purports to exclude liability for unlawful acts taken by such persons (s. 20(4)).

Thirdly, the union can be made vicariously liable for the acts of either a committee of the union or any other official of the union, whether or not the official is employed by the union, e.g., it can include shop stewards and other branch level officials (s. 20(2)(c)). A union committee for the purposes of s. 20(2)(c) is defined in s. 20(3)(a) as meaning 'any group of persons constituted in accordance with the rules of the union'. It should also be noted that an act is taken to be done, authorised or endorsed by an official if it was carried out by any committee constituted for the purposes of industrial action of which the official was a member (s. 20(3)(b)).

Section 20(2)(c) is potentially the most damaging to unions and is the one that requires the greatest diligence in policing. In order to ensure that this is done, a union is left with the option of either taking the responsibility for acts of these persons (which as will be seen below, can be costly), or repudiating any such acts of minor officials or committees (s. 20(4)).

Repudiation must take place according to the statutory formula set out in s. 21 of TULRCA 1992. It must be effected by the executive committee, president or general secretary of a union and must happen as soon as reasonably practicable after an unlawful act comes to the attention of any such persons (s. 21(1)). Constructive knowledge is not enough to attach liability for these purposes.

The form of repudiation is dealt with by s. 21(2). This requires that written notice of repudiation must be given to the official or committee without delay. It also requires a union to do its best to ensure that written notice is given to each member of the union who is taking part, or might want to take part, in the action and to the employer of such persons. Again, the notice must be given without delay.

The notice is required to be drawn up with a specific form of wording included (s. 21(3)). This reads as follows:

> Your union has repudiated the call (or calls) for industrial action to which this notice relates and will give no support to unofficial industrial action taken in response to it (or them). If you are dismissed while taking unofficial industrial action, you will have no right to complain of unfair dismissal.

To the extent that the repudiation is not carried out in this fashion, it is ineffective and a union will be liable notwithstanding that it has attempted to repudiate in other ways (s. 21(4)).

Furthermore, even if a union does comply with the letter of the law, it cannot attempt to defeat the spirit of it. If at any time after the repudiation has taken place, the executive committee, president or general secretary behaves in a manner inconsistent with the repudiation, the repudiation is treated as being ineffective (s. 21(5)). Likewise, if the tortious act consists of the interfering with a commercial contract (as defined in s. 21(7) as to exclude contracts of employment or for the personal performance of work or services) and a party to the contract has not received written notice of the repudiation within three months of requesting it, the repudiation is deemed to be ineffective (s. 21(6)).

7.5.2.2.2   Other tortious acts committed by unions   To the extent that torts are committed by a union other than *prima facie* immune industrial torts, the ordinary law of vicarious liability will apply in determining whether a union is responsible for consequential loss. The leading case on the point is *Heaton's Transport (St Helens) Ltd* v *Transport and General Workers Union* [1972] IRLR 25. In this case the defendants had adopted a policy of ensuring that sea containers should be loaded and unloaded only by persons registered under the statutory dock labour scheme. If firms refused to honour this policy, their lorries were to be blacked by the union. Shop stewards at two ports established unofficial committees to ensure that the blacking took place. When the plaintiffs sued, the defendant union contended that it was not liable for the acts of the unofficial committees. The House of Lords rejected this claim, with Lord Wilberforce stating (at p. 28):

> No new development is involved in the law relating to the responsibility of a master or principal for the act of a servant or agent. In each case the test to be applied is the same: was the servant or agent acting on behalf of, and within the scope of authority conferred by the master or principal ... Usually a servant, as

compared with an agent, has wider authority because his employment is more permanent and he has a larger range of duties as he may have to exercise discretion in dealing with a series of situations as they arise. The agent in an ordinary case is engaged to perform a particular task on a particular occasion and he has authority to do whatever is required for that purpose but has no general authority.

The House of Lords went on to add that unless the union had gone on to take action that could objectively be construed as forbidding the members concerned from taking action (e.g., withdrawing their credentials), the union would be bound by the action taken (see also *Thomas* v *NUM (South Wales Area)* [1985] IRLR 136 and *News Group Newspapers Ltd* v *SOGAT 82 (No. 2)* [1986] IRLR 337).

7.5.3 Torts committed by employers' associations

Employers' associations can be sued in the same way as any other company (if they are incorporated), or (in the case of an unincorporated association) by virtue of s. 127(2)(b) of TULRCA 1992. No special rules exist with regard to affixing liability. Furthermore, although there is no limit on the amount of damages that can be awarded against an employers' association (see Chapter 8 for the position relating to trade unions), if damages are awarded against such an association then they can be enforced only against the property of the association. In the case of an unincorporated association, the personal property of its members is specifically excluded from being subject to enforcement (TULRCA 1992, s. 130).

8 Remedies Against Trade Unions

8.1 INTRODUCTION

This chapter will focus upon the remedies that can be awarded against a trade union in the context of industrial disputes. The rules relating to remedies are modified in certain respects, both in the way that common law remedies can be awarded and also in relation to equitable remedies. The general position with regard to remedies will be examined initially, and thereafter the particular modifications that exist in the context of industrial relations will be discussed.

8.2 EQUITABLE REMEDIES

8.2.1 Specific performance

Specific performance is an order of the court compelling a party in breach of contract to honour its obligations under the terms of the contract. As it is a final remedy, it will inevitably be inappropriate in labour disputes where a remedy may be needed quickly to prevent an unlawful strike adversely affecting an employer.

The general position in relation to specific performance is that, as with all equitable remedies, it is discretionary; and the discretion will be granted only in relation to a contract having a specific, as opposed to a general, purpose. Further, it will not be granted where damages are an adequate remedy. In most employment cases, since it will generally be possible to find adequate replacement labour, specific performance will not ordinarily lie as a remedy. Over and above this, though, the courts have taken the view that specific performance should not lie as a remedy in employment cases, the reasoning being set down in *De Francesco* v *Barnum* (1890) 45 Ch D 430, where Fry LJ stated (at p. 438):

I should be very unwilling to extend decisions the effect of which is to compel persons who are not desirous of maintaining continuous personal relations with one another to continue those personal relations. I think the courts are bound to be jealous lest they should turn contracts of service into contracts of slavery; and . . . I should lean against the extension of the doctrine of specific performance and injunction in such a manner.

In the case of *C. H. Giles & Co. Ltd* v *Morris* [1972] 1 WLR 307, Megarry J (as he then was) did not think that the proposition put forward in *De Francesco* was an absolute one, and his view was that:

[T]he reasons why the court is reluctant to decree specific performance of a contract for personal services (and I would regard it as a strong reluctance rather than a rule) are, I think, more complex and more firmly bottomed on human nature. If a singer contracts to sing, there could no doubt be proceedings for committal if, ordered to sing, the singer remained obstinately dumb. But if instead the singer sang flat, or sharp, or too fast, or too slowly, or too quietly, or too loudly, or resorted to a dozen of the manifestations of temperament traditionally associated with some singers, the threat of committal would reveal itself as a most unsatisfactory weapon: for who could say whether the imperfections of perform-ance were natural or self-induced? To make an order with such possibilities of evasion would be vain; and so the order will not be made.

Ultimately, given the views put forward by Megarry J in *Giles* v *Morris* (and subsequently followed in, e.g., *Hill* v *C. A. Parsons & Co. Ltd* [1972] Ch 305), the law was changed by statute, most recently in the form of s. 236 of TULRCA 1992, which provides as follows:

236. No court shall, whether by way of—
(a) an order for specific performance or specific implement of a contract of employment, or
(b) an injunction or interdict restraining a breach or threatened breach of such a contract,
compel an employee to do any work or attend at any place for the doing of any work.

The position now is that specific performance does not lie as a remedy in employment cases.

8.2.2 Injunctions

8.2.2.1 General
An injunction is an order of the court preventing a state of affairs being carried into effect or from continuing in effect where, in either case, the state of affairs amounts or would amount to an actionable civil wrong. The power of the courts to grant

injunctions is now derived from s. 37 of the Supreme Court Act 1981, which provides that: 'The High Court may by order (whether interlocutory or final) grant an injunction . . . in all cases in which it appears to the court to be just and convenient to do so.'

Injunctions can therefore be either interlocutory or final in nature. The principles applicable to each will be dealt with in turn.

8.2.2.2   Interlocutory injunctions

The starting point in relation to interlocutory injunctions is to consider their use in the context of industrial disputes. The big advantage of an interlocutory injunction is the speed with which it can obtained. This may well be of importance in the context of threatened industrial action, or action which has taken place without notice.

8.2.2.2.1   Ex parte *interlocutory injunctions*

In general, it is possible to obtain an interlocutory injunction *ex parte*, thus making it an extremely effective remedy for an employer threatened with a trade dispute. When an application is made *ex parte* it involves only one party being heard. Such an injunction can be granted only where full and frank disclosure is made by the party seeking the order, and will be granted only where the case is an urgent one in which the plaintiff would suffer irreparable harm if forced to go through the procedure for obtaining a normal interlocutory injunction (which, in unabridged form, requires that at least two clear days' notice is given to the defendant). (Regard should be had to *Bates* v *Lord Hailsham* [1972] 1 WLR 1373 and to *Practice Direction* [1983] 1 WLR 433 with regard to the procedure for obtaining such an order.)

While an application using this procedure would involve the plaintiff putting both sides of the case, an application in such circumstances will be made, inevitably, with the 'spin' of the plaintiff being placed on the facts. The general rule in relation to *ex parte* injunctions is that they are granted until the next motion day (every weekday during term being a motion day in the Chancery Division, see *Practice Direction* [1980] 1 WLR 741). It should also be noted that injunctions can be granted in the Queen's Bench Division by a judge in chambers. Regard should also be had to s. 38 of the County Court Act 1984, which deals with the power of the county court to grant injunctions.

The problem with using *ex parte* injunctions in the context of labour disputes arises under s. 221(1) of TULRCA 1992. This states that:

(1)   Where—
    (a)   an application for an injunction or interdict is made to a court in the absence of the party against whom it is sought or any in representative of his, and
    (b)   he claims, or in the opinion of the court would be likely to claim, that he acted in contemplation or furtherance of a trade dispute,

the court shall not grant the injunction or interdict unless satisfied that all steps which in the circumstances were reasonable have been taken with a view to securing that notice of the application and an opportunity of being heard with respect to the application have been given to him.

It should be noted that the formulation allows the court to consider whether a union would be likely to make a claim of immunity, in the absence of the union being represented in court due to the speed with which the remedy has been sought. Further, there is no requirement for the claim to immunity to be a justifiable claim under s. 221(1).

If a union does make such a claim (or the court is satisfied that it would), the net result of s. 221(1) is that, in the ordinary course of things, an *ex parte* injunction will not lie in a case involving a trade dispute, save to the extent that all reasonable steps have been taken to bring the matter to the attention of the union to try and draw them into the proceedings. Regard should be had to, e.g., *United Biscuits (UK) Ltd* v *Fall* [1979] IRLR 110 and also to *Barretts and Bairds (Wholesale) Ltd* v *IPCS* [1987] IRLR 3.

Obviously, this has profound consequences for an employer seeking to gain a tactical advantage over workers taking action, since he will not be able to spike the guns of potential strikers in the same way that he could with an ordinary tortfeasor.

8.2.2.2.2 General interlocutory injunctions TULRCA 1992 also builds upon the general position at common law in relation to the grant of interlocutory injunctions. The grant of such injunctions was dealt with by the House of Lords in the now famous case of *American Cyanamid Co.* v *Ethicon Ltd* [1975] AC 396. In this case, Lord Diplock stated (at p. 406):

My Lords, when an application for an interlocutory injunction to restrain a defendant from doing acts alleged to be in violation of the plaintiff's legal right is made upon contested facts, the decision whether or not to grant an interlocutory injunction has to be taken at a time when *ex hypothesi* the existence of the right or the violation of it, or both, is uncertain and will remain uncertain until final judgment is given in the action. It was to mitigate the risk of injustice to the plaintiff during the period before that uncertainty could be resolved that the practice arose of granting him relief by way of interlocutory injunction; but since the middle of the 19th century this has been subject to his undertaking to pay damages to the defendant for any loss sustained by reason of the injunction if it should be held at the trial that the plaintiff had not been entitled to restrain the defendant from doing what he was threatening to do. The object of the interlocutory injunction is to protect the plaintiff against injury by violation of his right for which he could not be adequately compensated in damages recoverable in the action if the uncertainty were resolved in his favour at the trial; but the plaintiff's need for such protection must be weighed against the defendant's corresponding need to be protected against injury resulting from his having been prevented from exercising his own legal rights for which he could not be adequately compensated under the plaintiff's undertaking in damages if the uncertainty were resolved in the defendant's favour at the trial. The court must weigh one need against the other and determine where the 'balance of convenience' lies.

His Lordship then went on to consider how to assess the strength of a case on the evidence available at an interlocutory hearing, stating (at p. 407):

Hubbard v *Vosper* [1972] 2 QB 84 was treated by Graham J and the Court of Appeal in the instant appeal as leaving intact the supposed rule that the court is not entitled to take account of the balance of convenience unless it has first been satisfied that if the case went to trial upon no other evidence than is before the court at the hearing of the application the plaintiff would be entitled to judgment for a permanent injunction in the same terms as the interlocutory injunction sought.

Your Lordships should in my view take this opportunity of declaring that there is no such rule. The use of such expression as 'a probability,' 'a *prima facie* case,' or 'a strong *prima facie* case,' in the context of the exercise of a discretionary power to grant an interlocutory injunction leads to a confusion as to the object sought to be achieved by this form of temporary relief. The court no doubt must be satisfied that the claim is not frivolous or vexatious; in other words that there is a serious question to be tried.

It is no part of the court's function at this stage of the litigation to try to resolve conflicts of evidence on affidavit as to facts on which the claims of either party may ultimately depend nor to decide difficult questions of law which call for detailed arguments and mature considerations.

His Lordship then addressed the issue of granting an injunction at the request of a plaintiff (at p. 408):

... the governing principle is that the court should first consider whether, if the plaintiff were to succeed at trial in establishing his right to a permanent injunction, he would be adequately compensated by an award of damages for the loss he would have sustained as a result of the defendant's continuing to do what was sought to be enjoined between the time of the application and the time of the trial. If damages in the measure recoverable at common law would be an adequate remedy and the defendant would be in a financial position to pay them, no interlocutory injunction should normally be granted, however strong the plaintiff's claim appeared to be at that stage. If, on the other hand, damages would not provide an adequate remedy for the plaintiff in the event of his succeeding at the trial, the court should then consider whether, on the contrary hypothesis that the defendant were to succeed at the trial in establishing his right to do that which was sought to be enjoined, he would be adequately compensated under the plaintiff's undertaking as to damages for the loss he would have sustained by being prevented from doing so between the time of the application and the time of the trial. If damages in the measure recoverable under such an undertaking would be an adequate remedy and the plaintiff would be in a financial position to pay them, there would be no reason upon this ground to refuse an interlocutory injunction.

It is where there is doubt as to the respective remedies in damages available to either party or to both, that the question of balance of convenience arises. It would be unwise to attempt even to list all the various matters which may need to be taken into consideration in deciding where the balance lies, let alone to suggest the relative weight to be attached to them. These will vary from case to case.

Where other factors appear to be evenly balanced it is a counsel of prudence to take such measures as are calculated to preserve the status quo.

Lord Diplock went on to add that only in the last resort should regard be had to the relative strength of the parties' cases as revealed in the affidavit evidence.

The position generally, therefore, is first to consider the implications of damages. If that is not conclusive, it is necessary to consider the balance of convenience and then, and only then, the court should consider the relative strength of each side's case on paper.

The position is modified in relation to injunctions in the context of industrial action by s. 221(2) of TULRCA 1992. This provides:

> (2) Where—
> (a) an application for an interlocutory injunction is made to a court pending the trial of an action, and
> (b) the party against whom it is made claims that he acted in contemplation or furtherance of a trade dispute,
> the court shall, in exercising its discretion whether or not to grant the injunction, have regard to the likelihood of that party's succeeding at the trial of the action in establishing any matter which would afford a defence to the action under section 219 (protection from certain tort liabilities) or section 220 (peaceful picketing).

This provision, together with the law as stated in *American Cyanamid*, raises a number of issues in the context of industrial action injunctions.

The first issue is the question of whether damages awarded against a union for tort (see 8.3 *et seq.*) will be adequate to compensate an employer for the harm that occurs to him as a result of torts committed against him. Given that damages are capped under the provisions in s. 22 of TULRCA 1992, it is conceivable that in, for example, a long-running trade dispute with a large union, or, for that matter, a short dispute with a small union, damages may not be adequate to compensate an employer. This factor ought to weigh on the mind of a court hearing an application for an injunction (see *Dimbleby and Sons Ltd* v *NUJ* [1984] IRLR 161 on this point and also the reasoning of Sir John Donaldson MR in *Mercury Communications Ltd* v *Scott-Garner* [1984] IRLR 494).

Secondly, there is the issue of the modification made to the law by s. 221(2) of TULRCA 1992. This requires the court to consider the likelihood of the defence to action provided under the 'golden formula' (see 7.2.2). This requirement has been considered by the House of Lords in *NWL Ltd* v *Nelson* [1979] IRLR 478 and in the *Dimbleby* case, on each occasion by Lord Diplock. In *NWL* v *Nelson*, his Lordship was of the view that, if a defendant could show that it was likely that immunity would be established, an application for an injunction should be refused. However, this view was revisited in *Dimbleby* in the light of the significant changes that had been made which allowed an action to be brought in damages (albeit that the quantum of damages was capped by statute). Here, Lord Diplock took the view that now that cases could proceed to trial it was unlikely that actions would be disposed of at the interlocutory stage. His Lordship appears to be saying that as a consequence of the foregoing injunctions should be granted more readily.

The third issue to be considered is whether, over and above s. 221(2) of the 1992 Act, there is a power for the court to grant an injunction even if it were possible to establish immunity under the golden formula. The answer appears to be that there is such a power. In *Duport Steels Ltd* v *Sirs* [1980] 1 WLR 142, the House of Lords granted an interlocutory injunction to prevent a strike of steelworkers on the ground that their activity was potentially threatening to the national economy. Lord Fraser said (at p. 166) that an injunction could be granted where the industrial action would cause 'immediate serious danger to public safety or health'. His Lordship went on to add that such cases would rarely arise since it is the preserve of Government to act in times of national crisis, not the courts. However, in *Express Newspapers Ltd* v *MacShane* [1980] AC 672, Lord Scarman said (at p. 695) that such an injunction could be granted where the action 'endangers the nation or puts at risk such fundamental rights as the right of the public to be informed and the freedom of the press'. With respect to his Lordship (and indeed to Lord Denning MR in *Beaverbrook Newspapers Ltd* v *Keys* [1978] IRLR 34), the need of the nation to have its daily newspaper hardly seems to come into the same league as a strike that could have paralysed the economy. Further, as Lord Wedderburn has pointed out, the result is that the granting of injunctions so as to protect the public interest is a way of by-passing the statutory immunities that exist (Lord Wedderburn, *The Worker and the Law*, Penguin, 3rd edn, 1986).

Fourthly, over and above the position of the law as stated in *American Cynamid* and modified by s. 221(2) of TULRCA 1992 , there is a question whether a harsher principle does, in any event, apply. This is due to the fact that the effect of the decision in *American Cyanamid* has been watered down by subsequent cases. In many cases involving industrial action, it is unlikely that a dispute will go to trial. In such situations it was held by the Court of Appeal in *Cayne* v *Global Natural Resources plc* [1984] 1 All ER 225 that the better view of the law is that of the House of Lords in *NWL Ltd* v *Nelson*, i.e. that the relative strength of the parties' cases should be looked at. The Court of Appeal was of the view in this case that *American Cyanamid* was mere guidance from the House of Lords and was not to be rigidly applied in every case. Regard should also be had to *Lansing Linde Ltd* v *Kerr* [1991] IRLR 80 and to *Cambridge Nutrition Ltd* v *BBC* [1990] 3 All ER 523 to like effect.

Lastly, it needs to be borne in mind that s. 221(2) applies only to the industrial torts. If other torts are alleged to have been committed in the course of industrial action, s. 221(2) does not apply and a court is free to determine any dispute on the basis of the general common law principles.

8.2.2.2.3 Mandatory interlocutory injunctions   Due to the difficulty in enforcing them and the problems that such orders create in the context of industrial relations, the general rule in relation to mandatory injunctions is that they should be awarded in exceptional cases only (see, for example, *Austin Rover Group Ltd* v *AUEW (TASS)* [1985] IRLR 162, *Parker* v *Camden London Borough Council* [1986] Ch 162, *Kent Free Press* v *NGA* [1987] IRLR 267 and *Jakeman* v *South West Thames Regional Health Authority* [1990] IRLR 62).

8.2.2.3 Final injunction
A full discussion of the law relating to the grant of final injunctions is beyond the scope of this work and reference should be made to specialist works on the law of equity. However, by way of summary, in the context of industrial action, it is rarely the case that an injunction will be sought as a final measure at trial since most disputes will either be effectively curtailed upon the grant of an interlocutory injunction or will settle through negotiation in the fullness of time in the event that an injunction is refused. Even if a matter does proceed to trial the award of damages may in any event be more appropriate as a remedy. If trial does occur with an injunction being sought as the final remedy, it would be granted upon the basis of the general principles of the law of equity in either a prohibitive or mandatory form.

8.2.2.4 Who to injunct
When considering whether to pursue a claim for an injunction in the context of industrial action, regard should be had to the question of who to injunct. If action undertaken against a person is taken by a union and various of its members and/or officials of the union, the question arises whether it is possible to request an injunction restraining a class or classes of the potential defendants from committing tortious acts. The answer to the question is still undecided. The Court of Appeal in *M. Michaels (Furriers) Ltd* v *Askew* (1983) SJ 597, held that it was possible to allow a representative action against a group of unnamed pickets protesting about cruelty in the fur trade. However, in the context of industrial action, the High Court has held that this is not correct. In *News Group Newspapers* v *SOGAT 82* [1986] IRLR 337, Stuart-Smith J stated that members of the defendant union could not be the subject of a representative action since individual members of the union might well have

different defences to a claim alleging tortious misconduct on their part. He added that the reason for this was that some of the members might have actively participated in the tortious action, while others might have condemned it. It was therefore inappropriate to grant a blanket injunction.

Lastly, it needs to be borne in mind that the only people who can be the subject of an injunction are people who are directly involved in the commission of the civil wrong (albeit that this might cover the servants, officers or agents of a union though). Regard should be had to *Attorney-General* v *Newspaper Publishing plc* [1988] Ch 333 on this point.

In short, it appears that it is possible to injunct collectively only where the allegations of separate interests are a sham device put forward by defendants who in reality know that an application for such an order has substance to it.

8.2.2.5   Injunctions and the proper plaintiff

A fundamental principle relating to the grant of an injunction is that the plaintiff must have a legal interest that can be protected by the injunction being sought. In short, the plaintiff must be facing loss or harm as a result of a threatened wrong at the hands of a tortfeasor. Generally, this will be evident from the circumstances surrounding an application. However, one problem does arise in the form of a plaintiff seeking to enforce the criminal law by means of an injunction.

As has been seen above in relation to the industrial torts (Chapter 6), and as can be seen below in relation to the commission of criminal offences in the context of industrial action (Chapter 10), a number of criminal offences can be committed in the course of industrial action that may give rise to civil consequences. The question arises whether a plaintiff can use the civil courts to enforce the criminal law and thereby minimise the consequences of industrial action. The leading case on the point is *Gouriet* v *Union of Post Office Workers* [1978] AC 435. Here, the plaintiff was a public spirited private individual who objected to a boycott of post to South Africa by the defendant union which was acting on the grounds of that country's apartheid policy. The plaintiff initially contacted the Attorney-General to seek his permission to bring a relator action on the basis that the postal workers were contravening s. 58 of the Post Office Act 1953, which makes it an offence wilfully to delay or detain any postal packet. This was refused. He therefore commenced proceedings to obtain an injunction. This was refused at first instance but then granted on appeal by the Court of Appeal. One of the unions subjected to the injunction was joined *ex parte* on the grounds that, since the conduct of the union was outside the golden formula, s. 221(1) of TULRCA 1992 (as it now is) did not apply. The matter was appealed to the House of Lords by the Attorney-General.

Their Lordships took the view that the plaintiff, in order to establish a cause of action in tort, would have to show that he was personally suffering special damage as a result of the defendant's conduct. As he was not personally suffering, his action could not succeed in tort. The only alternative for him was to enforce the criminal law through the civil courts, which would require the Attorney-General's permission (which had already been refused). Furthermore, their Lordships considered that it would be an exceptional case that allowed the Attorney-General to use an injunction to protect the public interest since a failure to follow the court's direction would allow the court to use its civil jurisdiction to enforce the criminal law through committal proceedings (see 8.2.2.5).

Gouriet currently reflects the state of the law with regard to the award of injunctions in criminal cases.

8.2.2.6   Enforcing injunctions

Injunctions are remedies that are aimed against a particular person or persons. An injunction must be obeyed by the defendant to whom it is addressed; and to the extent that a defendant breaches the terms of an injunction, he will be in contempt of court. Contempt of court is a criminal offence under the Contempt of Court Act 1981. A person who commits a contempt may be sent to prison for a period not exceeding two years (s. 14(1), 1981 Act).

The criminal standard of proof (i.e., proof beyond a reasonable doubt) is applicable by the court before a plaintiff can succeed in establishing that a contempt of court has occurred (*Attorney-General* v *Newspaper Publishing plc* [1988] Ch 333). The Court of Appeal has held that the *mens rea* for the crime in the context of breaching a civil order is that the defendant knowingly breached the terms of that order (*Director General of Fair Trading* v *Smiths Concrete Ltd* [1992] ICR 229).

It is possible for a defendant to breach an order in a number of different ways. These are:

(a)   simple breach by the person to whom the order is addressed;
(b)   vicarious liability on the part of the defendant;
(c)   liability arising from interference by third parties.

8.2.2.6.1   Breach by the defendant   The starting point is that a defendant is bound by an order from the moment that he has knowledge of its existence. In *Kent Free Press* v *NGA* [1987] IRLR 267, a mandatory injunction had been served on the defendant union to prevent them 'blacking' the plaintiff's work at a typesetter unconnected with the dispute in progress between the plaintiff and the defendant union. The defendant union was informed of the content of the order by a telephone call, but did not comply with the order until two days after receiving a copy of the order. At the contempt hearing, Henry J held that by not following the terms of the order as soon as the union had received notice, they were, on the facts of the case, committing a contempt of court. He added that in an appropriate case, it may be possible for a defendant to wait until he has sight of an order before acting upon the same, but this will not usually be the case where a defendant is an experienced litigant (e.g., a large union), well used to the content of injunctive orders and the implications of failing to comply with them.

The second issue that arises is the way in which the contempt takes place. Contempt of court will occur where a defendant fails to follow a court order to the letter of the order. In *Howitt Transport Ltd* v *Transport and General Workers Union* [1973] IRLR 25, Sir John Donaldson dealt with the forms in which contempt may occur (at p. 26), stating that:

> It may, at the top end of the scale, consist of a flat defiance of the court's authority. Going down the scale, it may not amount to flat defiance but rather to a passive ignoring of the court's order. Going down the scale further, it may amount to a half-hearted or, perhaps, colourable attempt to comply with the court's order, and at the bottom end of the scale, there may have been a genuine, whole hearted use of the best endeavours to comply with the order which, nevertheless, has been unsuccessful. In each case there is a breach of the court's order. In each case, to use the technicalities of the law, there is 'contempt of court', but the quality of the non-compliance varies over an enormous range.

In *Express and Star Ltd* v *National Graphical Association* (1982) [1986] ICR 589, the defendant union was found to be in contempt of court for failing to support the substance of an injunction. The defendant had allowed industrial action to continue in the face of a court order despite making a sham attempt at compliance with the order by issuing instructions to its members to comply but then failing to distribute the instructions. There must be compliance with the full terms of an order and the spirit of the order, not the paying of mere lip service to the same.

As Sir John Donaldson stated in *Howitt Transport*, any failure to comply is technically a contempt of court. This gives rise to the question of what happens to a defendant who has attempted substantially to comply with the terms of a court order. In *Express Newspapers Ltd* v *Mitchell* [1982] IRLR 465, the defendants had threatened to take industrial action in support of workers in the health service. The action amounted to unlawful secondary action and an injunction was issued which required the defendants to desist from taking such action and to ensure that their members were contacted to prevent them from taking part in the action. One of the defendants issued a statement to the members of his union that 'strongly recommended' that industrial action should not be taken. The union had some 1,300 members employed in the area of the dispute at the time that the statement was issued. The acts of the official were still held to be inadequate to comply with the terms of the order, although it was accepted that his conduct amounted to a form of mitigation when considering the penalty to be imposed upon him.

In *Austin Rover Group Ltd* v *AUEW (TASS)* [1985] IRLR 162, the defendant union failed to comply with the terms of a mandatory interlocutory injunction made against it which prevented it from taking industrial action without first holding a strike ballot. The union advanced the claim that it was not bound to hold a ballot on account of the fact that the order against it was defective and it could not comply with it. Hodgson J held that the proper course of action in such a situation was to appeal the terms of the order, not to protest by failing to comply. As such, the union was found to be in contempt.

It seems that a court hearing an application in relation to contempt will assume that the original order was valid when made. Regard should also be had to *Richard Read (Transport) Ltd v National Union of Mineworkers (South Wales Area)* [1985] IRLR 67 and *Isaacs v Robertson* [1985] AC 97 on this point.

8.2.2.6.2   Vicarious liability   A defendant union can be made vicariously liable for the acts of it members. The test will be that adopted under s. 20 of TULRCA 1992 in relation to the torts committed by the union or in its name (see 7.5.2.2 *et seq.*). A union may be able to disown the actions of minor officials provided that it acts in accordance with the requirements set out generally in s. 21 of the 1992 Act. See *Heatons Transport (St Helens) Ltd v Transport and General Workers Union* [1973] AC 15 and *Richard Read (Transport) Ltd v National Union of Mineworkers (South Wales Area)* [1985] IRLR 67 on this point.

8.2.2.6.3   Liability attaching to third parties   A third party can be made liable for committing acts that are the subject of an injunction where that third party has knowledge of the injunction. The principle is best illustrated by the case of *Attorney-General v Newspaper Publishing plc* [1988] Ch 333. The case arose out of the infamous 'Spycatcher' litigation in the 1980s. During the litigation, the Attorney-General was granted an injunction against the *Observer* and the *Guardian* newspapers, preventing them from printing extracts of the book *Spycatcher* which breached the Official Secrets Act 1911. Other national newspapers later printed extracts from the book, although they were not themselves parties to the injunction. The Attorney-General subsequently brought contempt proceedings against the other newspapers. At first instance, Browne-Wilkinson V-C held that, since the news-papers were not parties to the initial action, they could not be the subject of committal proceedings brought in respect of the publications. However, the Court of Appeal overturned the decision and held that a third party could be liable for breaching the terms of an injunction even though it was not itself a party to the order, provided that the third party had knowledge of the order being breached and knew that it would be interfering with the administration of justice by committing the breaches complained of.

The point about liability under this head is that, if a third party acts at the request of a defendant union, the third party itself can be liable for the act as a *criminal* contempt (rather than a civil one), since the third party is not a party to the order but has nevertheless carried out the defendant's bidding for him.

8.2.2.7   Penalties for contempt
To the extent that a union or an official of a union commits a contempt, much will turn upon the circumstances of the case in deciding how the contempt will be punished. The power of the court to punish for contempt is found under RSC Ord.

45, r. 5. A court has three ways in which to punish for contempt, these being by either a fine or imprisonment in the case of an individual, or, in the case of a union or a corporate body, by sequestrating the assets of that person. In the case of sequestration, assets are returned to the contemnor, less the cost of the sequestration and any fine that is imposed, upon the contempt being purged. Costs are usually substantial.

It should be noted that where sequestration does take place, sequestrators are entitled to receive information relating to assets to be sequestrated from third parties, notwithstanding that the third party does not personally hold any of the contemnor's assets. The law was set out by Sir John Donaldson in the NIRC in the case of *Eckman* v *Midland Bank Ltd* [1973] ICR 71, at p. 80, where he said:

> In our judgment, the position of a third party in relation to a writ of sequestration is analogous to that of a third party in relation to an injunction, namely, that he is subject to a duty not knowingly to take any action which will obstruct compliance by the sequestrators with the terms of the writ of sequestration which require them to take possession of the assets.

This approach was confirmed by the Court of Appeal in *Messenger Newspapers Group Ltd* v *National Graphical Association (1982)* [1984] ICR 345.

Lastly, it should be noted that only the specific assets of the contemnor (not those jointly owned with others) can be sequestrated. For an example of this point, see *News Group Newspapers Ltd* v *SOGAT 82* [1986] IRLR 227.

8.2.2.8   Enforcing contempt — a power or a duty?

In relation to civil contempt, there is a question as to whether a party having the benefit of a court order has a discretion as to whether or not to enforce that order through contempt proceedings, or whether the matter can be enforced by the Attorney-General or, indeed, by the court itself. The general view is that, since a civil contempt suit enforces a matter between the parties, it is up to the plaintiff to enforce a court order in his favours and refusal to do so can allow the contempt to go unpunished. In *Attorney-General* v *Times Newspapers Ltd* [1974] AC 273, Lord Diplock stated (at p. 307):

> ... the mere disobedience by a party to a civil action of a specific order of the court made on him in that action ... is classified as 'civil contempt'. The order is made at the request and for the sole benefit of the other party to the civil action. There is an element of public policy in punishing civil contempt, since the administration of justice would be undermined if the order of any court of law could be disregarded with impunity; but no sufficient public interest is served by punishing the offender if the only person for whose benefit the order was made chooses not to insist on its enforcement.

This view has been rejected in cases where the public interest is at stake over and above a trade dispute, or where the matter is urgent, when either the Attorney-General or the court can enforce the contempt.

In the case of the court enforcing contempt proceedings, it is generally thought that the court will exercise this power sparingly (*per* Megarry V-C in *Clarke v Chadburn* [1984] IRLR 350, at p. 353). However, see the views expressed in *Con-Mech (Engineers) Ltd v Amalgamated Union of Engineering Workers* [1974] IRLR 2, which suggest that the parties ought not to be the ones to decide whether to enforce a deliberate refusal to follow the orders of the court.

8.2.2.9   *Purging contempt*

The method of purging contempt will vary according to the nature of the penalty that has been imposed by the court. Usually the contemnor will be required to apologise to the court for its actions. Indeed, the court may refuse to hear any applications made by the contemnor until such time as it is satisfied that the contemnor recognises the authority of the court (see, for example, *Clarke v Heathfield* [1985] ICR 203 and *Clarke v Heathfield (No. 2)* [1985] ICR 606). An apology must amount to an admission of wrongdoing on the part of the contemnor. An apology that is phrased as a non-admission of liability will be ineffective (see *Mirror Group Newspapers Ltd v Harrison* (November 1986, unreported)).

A fine can be levied as punishment for contempt. If a fine has been imposed by the court, it does not matter that it is not paid *by the contemnor*. All that matters is that the fine has been paid. It should be noted that fines are not subject to the cap on damages that can be awarded against a union under s. 22 of TULRCA 1992.

In a case where an apology is not forthcoming, imprisonment for contempt may be appropriate. In such a situation, it is possible to release a contemnor notwithstanding that he does not apologise, since it has to be remembered that the purpose of the imprisonment is punishment. This is as true of committal to prison as it is in the case of a union failing to apologise before having its assets returned (see, for example, the comments of Scott J in *Richard Read (Transport) Ltd v National Union of Mineworkers (South Wales Area)* [1985] IRLR 67).

8.3   DAMAGES

8.3.1   Introduction

The final remedy that may be sought against a union is damages. When looking at the law relating to damages, TULRCA 1992 again modifies the common law position as to the quantum that can be awarded. This part of the chapter will focus upon the general common law rules before going on to consider the modified position under the 1992 Act.

8.3.2   The general common law position

In the ordinary course of things, the quantum of damages in tort will be assessed by reference to the rule set out by Lord Blackburn in *Livingstone* v *Rawyards Coal Co.* (1880) 5 App Cas 25 (at p. 39, where he stated that the damages to be awarded were: '... that sum of money which will put the party who has been injured, or who has suffered, in the same position as he would have been in if he had not sustained the wrong for which he is now getting his compensation or reparation.'

The potential plaintiffs that might bring an action against a union will usually fall into one of four categories, these being:

(a)   employers;
(b)   workers suffering at the hands of a closed shop;
(c)   commercial third parties; and
(d)   third party consumers.

The loss that each group may suffer will vary, but the following are typical of the types of harm that may occur:

(a)   loss of profit;
(b)   consequential loss;
(c)   injury to feelings;
(d)   damages for loss caused by contempt of court.

In addition, it needs to be considered whether exemplary damages can be awarded to make an example of a union in a particular case. Each of these points will be considered in turn.

8.3.2.1   *Loss of profit*
In most industrial tort actions, it will be necessary to show that the plaintiff has suffered a loss. If the loss is profit-based, a problem may lie in attempting to show the amount of profit lost, such a course of action being potentially speculative. The courts have consistently been ready to infer that profit loss to a commercial party will be suffered as a necessary consequence of unprotected tortious conduct on the part of a defendant involved in a commercial dispute. For example, in *Goldsoll* v *Gregory* [1914] 2 Ch 603, Nevile J stated (at p. 615):

The damage may be inferred, that is to say, that if the breach which has been procured by the defendant has been such as must in the ordinary course of business inflict damage upon the plaintiff, then the plaintiff may succeed without proof of any particular damage which has been occasioned to him.

Regard should also be had to the comments of Kay LJ in *Exchange Telegraph Co.* v *Gregory* [1896] 1 QB 147, at p. 156, and to those of Slesser LJ in *British Industrial Plastics* v *Ferguson* [1938] 4 All ER 504, at p. 511, both of whom provide support for this contention.

In the case of *Bent's Brewery Co.* v *Hogan* [1945] 2 All ER 570, the High Court was prepared to hold that loss of profit could arise as a result of unlawfully disclosed information revealed by questionnaires that related to pub managers' salaries and which were used by the defendant union to exert pressure on the plaintiff in order to raise salaries. This had the effect of reducing the plaintiff's profit as a consequence of the extra wages. Lynskey J was prepared to find for the plaintiff in this case even though loss had yet to be incurred, since it was sufficient to infer that loss would arise.

Loss of profit can be claimed by an employer who is the victim of unlawful industrial action, or by a commercial third party who suffers as a result, e.g., as a result of the loss of a supply contract.

8.3.2.2 Consequential loss

As a general statement, any consequential loss that flows as a result of tortious misconduct on the part of a defendant can be recovered provided that it is not too remote.

In *British Motor Trade Association* v *Salvadori* [1949] Ch 556, the defendant induced breaches of covenants not to re-sell cars at a premium to persons such as the defendant. In the course of litigation, the plaintiff claimed from the defendant the cost of an inquiry system set up to investigate the breaches of covenant that had been induced. In granting the claim, Roxburgh J stated (at p. 569) that 'I can see no reason for not treating the expenses so incurred which could not be recovered as part of the costs of the action as directly attributable to their tort or torts. That these expenses cannot be precisely quantified is true, but it is also immaterial'.

More recently, in *Messenger Newspapers Group Ltd* v *National Graphical Association (1982)* [1984] IRLR 397, the plaintiff, so as to keep on producing its newspapers, was forced to ferry staff across a picket line in the course of unlawful industrial action. The defendant was found liable to pay damages for these costs and for the costs incurred in order to protect the plaintiff's business generally. The trial judge, Caulfield J, awarded substantial damages for the loss occasioned under this latter head.

8.3.2.3 Injury to feelings

It has been consistently held that in order to ground an action for one of the economic torts, financial loss must be shown by a plaintiff. Further, it seems that while mere injury to feelings is not, of itself, enough to ground an action, if injury to feelings has been occasioned over and above financial loss, it too may be the subject of a claim. In *Pratt* v *British Medical Association* [1919] 1 KB 244, McCardie J stated (at p. 281):

The plaintiffs are not limited to actual pecuniary damages suffered by them. The court or jury, once actual financial loss be proved, may award a sum appropriate to the whole circumstances of the tortious wrong inflicted ... I cannot ignore the deliberate and relentless vigour with which the defendants sought to achieve the infliction of complete ruin. I must regard not merely the pecuniary loss sustained by the plaintiffs but the long period for which they respectively suffered humiliation and menace.

Likewise, in *Quinn* v *Leathem* [1901] AC 495, the trial judge provided a note of the evidence (at p. 498), which stated:

I told the jury that pecuniary loss, directly caused by the conduct of the defendants, must be proved in order to establish a cause of action, and I advised them to require to be satisfied that such loss to a substantial amount had been proved by the plaintiff. I declined to tell them that if actual and substantial pecuniary loss was proved to have been caused to the plaintiff by the wrongful acts of the defendants, they were bound to limit the amount of damages to the precise sum so proved. I told them that if the plaintiff gave the proof of actual and substantial loss necessary to maintain the action, they were at liberty in assessing damages to take all the circumstances of the case, including the conduct of the defendants, reasonably into account.

The upshot of this is that the court can take account of deliberate malice in the way that industrial action is taken by awarding aggravated damages (see, for example, the comments of Caulfield J in *Messenger Newspapers Group Ltd* v *National Graphical Association (1982)* [1984] IRLR 397). Furthermore, this head can clearly be used by an individual who is the victim of unlawful tortious conduct committed by a trade union, as *Pratt* v *BMA* shows.

8.3.2.4   Damages arising from a contempt of court

It is not possible for damages to be awarded for contempt of court. The proper method of enforcing court orders is through committal proceedings (see above at 8.2.2.6). Regard should also be had to *Re Hudson* [1966] Ch 207.

8.3.2.5   Exemplary damages

The purpose of exemplary damages is to provide an award over and above that merely compensating a victim of a tort. The purpose of such an award is to punish a tortfeasor for the way in which he has gone about committing a tort. To this end, such an award deviates from the general aim of the law of tort stated in *Livingstone* v *Rawyards Coal Co.*, that being to compensate and to put the plaintiff in the position he would have been in if the tort had not been committed.

Prior to *Rookes* v *Barnard* [1964] AC 1129, an apparently common feature of the law of tort was the willingness of the courts determining cases to award a sum to a

plaintiff for the way in which a tort had been committed. The House of Lords in
Rookes v *Barnard* decided that, except in three specific categories of cases, no award
of exemplary damages would be allowed. The categories are:

(a)   where such an award is expressly authorised by statute;

(b)   where the award is to punish oppressive conduct by a government official; or

(c)   where the conduct of the tortfeasor is intended to produce a profit for the
tortfeasor as a result of the tort.

As Lord Devlin said (at p. 1230), the decision would:

... remove from the law a source of confusion between aggravated and exemplary
damages which has troubled the learned commentators on the subject. Otherwise,
it will not, I think, make much difference to the substance of the law or rob the law
of the strength which it ought to have. Aggravated damages in this type of case can
do most, if not all, of the work that can be done by exemplary damages. In so far
as they do not, assaults and malicious injuries to property can generally be
punished as crimes.

The decision of the House of Lords in *Rookes* v *Barnard* subsequently came under
assault from the Court of Appeal in *Broome* v *Cassell & Co.* [1971] 2 QB 354. This
was a libel case, where the Court tried to reverse the decision in *Rookes* v *Barnard*
on the ground that it had been arrived at *per incuriam* and that the three categories
propounded by Lord Devlin were illogical, arbitrary and restrictive. The House of
Lords then reviewed the decision of the Court of Appeal in *Broome* (at [1972] AC
1027) and confirmed the decision in *Rookes* v *Barnard*. Lord Hailsham of St
Marylebone stated (at p. 1082):

It follows from what I have said that I am not prepared to follow the Court of
Appeal in its criticisms of *Rookes* v *Barnard*, which I regard as having imposed
valuable limits on the doctrine of exemplary damages as they had hitherto been
understood in English law and clarified important questions which had previously
been undiscussed or left confused.

He went on (at p. 1083): 'We cannot depart from *Rookes* v *Barnard* here. It was
decided neither *per incuriam* nor *ultra vires* this House.'

The question thus arises whether or not exemptary damages can be awarded in
industrial disputes. In *Messenger Newspapers Group Ltd* v *National Graphical
Association (1982)* [1984] IRLR 397, Caulfield J made an award of damages against
the defendant union under this head and expressly relied on Lord Devlin's speech in
Rookes v *Barnard* for his ability to do so (see Caulfield J's analysis (at p. 407).

The position, it seems, is that provided a union has deliberately taken steps in the
form of an unprotected tort to further the interests of itself and/or its members, and

provided further that a plaintiff is the victim of such behaviour, and that an award when made is moderate, exemplary damages can be awarded against a union.

8.3.3   The modifications imposed by TULRCA 1992

8.3.3.1   Introduction
The 1992 Act modifies the common law position in two ways. First, it imposes a cap on the amount of damages that can be awarded against a union committing a tort not having the benefit of statutory immunity. Secondly, it limits the assets that can be the subject of enforcement proceedings. Each will be looked at in turn.

8.3.3.2   The cap on damages
Damages awarded against a union in tort are limited by s. 22 of TULRCA 1992. This section applies where any proceedings are brought in tort against a union save for:

(a)   proceedings for personal injury as a result of negligence, nuisance or breach of duty imposed by either the common law or statute;
(b)   proceedings for breach of duty in connection with the ownership, occupation, possession, control or use of property; or
(c)   proceedings brought in respect of defective products under Pt I of the Consumer Protection Act 1987 (TULRCA 1992, s. 22(1)).

The capping provision works according to the size of membership that a union has. The following limitations apply:

Number of members of union	Maximum award of damages
less than 5,000 members	£10,000
5,000 or more but less than 25,000	£50,000
25,000 or more but less than 100,000	£125,000
100,000 or more	£250,000

Two things should be noted. First, the cap applies only to damages that are awarded against the union and does not apply to interest on damages, or to fines made against a union (see, for example, *Messenger Newspapers Group Ltd* v *National Graphical Association (1982)* [1984] IRLR 397, where both were included in the order made against the defendant).

Secondly, the Secretary of State retains a power to vary the sums of damages that can be awarded against a union (s. 22(3)).

8.3.3.3   Restrictions on enforcing awards against certain property of a union
Not only is there a cap on the amount of damages that can be awarded against a trade union, there is also a limit on the property that can be attached to enforce a judgment. The restriction is dealt with under s. 23 of TULRCA 1992. The first part of the

section establishes that any in proceedings brought against a union, an amount cannot be awarded against protected property of the union, whether the action be in tort or otherwise, and whether the amount represents damages, costs or expenses (s. 23(1)). The definition of where an amount is awarded against the union is wide and covers the situation where an amount is awarded against the union itself, against trustees of a union holding property on trust for the union, or where the the the amount is awarded against members or officials of a union who are sued in a representative capacity for the union generally.

As to what amounts to protected property, this is defined in s. 23(2) of TULRCA 1992 and comprises:

(a)   property belonging to trustees otherwise than in their capacity as trustees;

(b)   property belonging individually to members of a union;

(c)   property belonging to an official of a union who is neither a member nor a trustee;

(d)   property that is comprised in a union's political fund where there is a restriction in the union rules preventing the fund from being used to finance strikes and it was in force at the time of the action that is subject to the complaint;

(e)   property that is comprised in a union's provident benefit fund.

It should be noted that although such property is protected as regards judgment debts, it can still be sequestrated.

8.3.3.4   Employers' Associations

In respect of categories (a)–(c) in 8.3.3.3 above, employers' associations enjoy a similar (although more limited) protection as to the property that can be safeguarded against enforcement proceedings. (*per* s. 130 of TULRCA). However, they do not receive the benefit of the cap on damages.

9 Trade Unions and Third Parties

9.1 INTRODUCTION

This chapter will focus upon the relationships that exist between a union and third parties other than an employer. These relationships may be divided into three categories, these being:

(a)   relations with an employer's suppliers;
(b)   relations with individuals affected as a consequence of industrial action; and
(c)   relations with other unions.

9.2 RELATIONS WITH AN EMPLOYER'S SUPPLIER

9.2.1 Introduction

This aspect of the law was one of the most heavily modified during the Conservative era of 1979–1997. Prior to the reforms, the law was largely abstentionist in its attitude towards trade unions. It allowed unions to put pressure on employers who recognised a particular union to extend recognition to the employer's suppliers. The effect of this extension was to promote closed shops at the suppliers in one of two ways, either through the use of recognition clauses in supply contracts or through the device of a union labour only clause contained in the supply contract. The purpose of such clauses was to make sure that either suppliers recognised particular unions for the purposes of collective bargaining, or that all employees working for an employer's supplier were members of one or more particular unions.

The Employment Act 1980 made in-roads into the practice by removing immunity in tort and providing the right not to be unfairly dismissed as a worker at a supplier who was forced to adopt such policies. The Employment Act 1982 followed this up by providing that union labour only clauses and recognition clauses were to be treated as void in supplier contracts. The Employment Act 1988 took the matter further, and its provisions (discussed below) are now contained in TULRCA 1992. Effectively, any action taken to enforce union membership has no immunity in tort.

9.2.2   Union labour only requirements

The law relating to union labour only requirements comprehensively acts to defeat such clauses on all fronts. First, the clauses are deemed to be void under s. 144 of TULRCA 1992, which provides:

> A term or condition of a contract for the supply of goods or services is void in so far as it purports to require that the whole, or some part, of the work done for the purposes of the contract is done only by persons who are, or are not, members of trade unions or of a particular trade union.

It is important to note that the section is phrased neutrally, so that if an employer were to stipulate that no union labour was to be engaged by his suppliers, this would be unlawful in the same way as a requirement that union labour only should be used.

The second way in which the Act operates is that s. 145 makes it actionable to refuse to deal with a person on account of that person's failure to operate in accordance with a union labour clause. Refusal to deal is defined in s. 145(2)–(4) and essentially sets up three types of unlawful refusal to deal. The first of these is where a person operates an approved suppliers list and fails to enter a supplier or prospective supplier of goods or services on the list on account of that person's failure to comply with union membership grounds (s. 145(2)).

Secondly, in relation to a proposed contract for the supply of goods or services, a refusal to deal will occur where a person is either:

(a)   excluded from a group of persons tendering for a contract;
(b)   refused permission to tender for goods or services; or
(c)   otherwise not dealt with in relation to a proposed contract;

and that in any of these three cases the reason for the refusal is a union membership requirement (s. 145(3)).

Thirdly, if a person terminates a supply contract with another on account of a union membership requirement, since such a requirement is void under s. 144 of the Act, termination of the supply contract will amount to a breach (s. 145(4)). In the case of a contract which lapses and is not renewed on account of a union membership requirement, this will probably fall under s. 145(3)(c) above rather than being a breach of contract.

In relation to s. 145(2) and (3), the cause of action will arise under s. 145(5) and amounts to a breach of statutory duty. The usual defences and other legal incidents that would otherwise apply to claims for breach of statutory duty are expressly maintained under s. 145(5).

Trade Unions and Third Parties

It should be noted that the action will be commenced against an employer who submits to pressure to impose such a clause rather than against a union, since an employer has ample opportunity to prevent the clause coming into effect through effective negotiation or can seek an injunction to prevent the clause being imposed through pressure of industrial action. Any action taken by a union to persuade an employer would not have the benefit of immunity due to s. 222 of TULRCA 1992. For further discussion on this point, see 7.4.1 *et seq.* above.

9.2.3 Union recognition requirements

As with union labour only clauses, it is now unlawful for a union to attempt to impose a union recognition clause on an employer's suppliers. The provisions are similar in scope to those already looked at in 9.2.2. Any such clause that is purportedly included in a supply contract can be avoided under s. 186 of TULRCA 1992, which provides as follows:

> A term or condition of a contract for the supply of goods or services is void in so far as it purports to require a party to the contract—
> (a)   to recognise one or more trade unions (whether or not named in the contract) for the purpose of negotiating on behalf of workers, or any class of worker, employed by him, or
> (b)   to negotiate or consult with, or with an official of, one or more trade unions (whether or not so named).

Where an employer wishes to include such a clause and then refuses to deal with a supplier on account of the supplier's reluctance to include such a term, this amounts to refusal to deal with a person due to union recognition grounds which is made actionable by s. 187 in the same way as a union labour requirement (see 9.2.2 above). The cause of action will either be a breach of contract due to termination by reliance upon a void union recognition clause, or an action for breach of statutory duty, which will exist under s. 187(3). The usual defences, etc. in relation to breach of statutory duty will apply.

The cause of action lies against an employer who has tried to impose the requirement and not against a union demanding the inclusion of such a clause. Any action taken by a union to make an employer demand such a clause is not protected under the immunities in ss. 219 and 220 of the 1992 Act due to s. 225, which removes that immunity (see 7.4.6 above).

9.2.4 Local government contracts and union labour recognition requirements

Over and above the general duties that exist under TULRCA 1992, it should also be remembered that a local authority cannot take account of non-commercial considerations when putting out to tender commercial contracts under the provisions of s. 17(1) of the Local Government Act 1988. Union labour or recognition requirements are both caught under s. 17(5)(a) and (f) of the Act as non-commercial matters.

9.3   RELATIONS WITH INDIVIDUAL CUSTOMERS OF AN EMPLOYER

9.3.1   Introduction

This type of relationship is relatively new in terms of the duties that a union owes. The concept of the duty here emerged at common law in the 1980s as a result of the case of *Falcolner* v *ASLEF* [1986] IRLR 331. It will be remembered that this case establishes the common law right of a customer of an employer involved in a trade dispute not to have a contract to which he is a party interfered with by a third party, such as a trade union (see above at 6.3.2.2.3). The right was incorporated into TULRCA 1992 as ss. 235A–235C (as inserted by s. 22 of TURERA 1993).

The starting point is s. 235A(1) and (2) which create the right:

(1)   Where an individual claims that—

(a)   any trade union or other person has done, or is likely to do, an unlawful act to induce any person to take part, or to continue to take part, in industrial action, and

(b)   an effect, or a likely effect, of the industrial action is or will be to—

(i)   prevent or delay the supply of goods or services, or

(ii)   reduce the quality of goods or services supplied,

to the individual making the claim,

he may apply to the High Court or the Court of Session for an order under this section.

(2)   For the purposes of this section an act to induce any person to take part, or to continue to take part, in industrial action is unlawful—

(a)   if it is actionable in tort by any one or more persons, or

(b)   (where it is or would be the act of a trade union) if it could form the basis of an application by a member under section 62.

The first point to note about the provision is that it applies where an individual suffers loss. Thus it is not a right that can be exercised by commercial customers of an employer. Further, in order to be able to claim under the right, an individual must show one of two things:

(a)   that the matter complained of is actionable in tort. This will require an individual being able to prove that not only is a tort being committed, but that there is no immunity or defence available to the tortfeasor; or

(b)   that an actionable failure to hold a ballot prior to industrial action by a union has taken place.

The statute requires liability on the part of a union which, according to s. 235A(6), will be determined in accordance with the rules set out in s. 20 of TULRCA 1992 (see 7.5 *et seq.* above on this point).

It should be noted that in determining whether an individual may make an application under s. 235A, 'it is immaterial whether or not the individual is entitled to be supplied with the goods or services in question' (s. 235A(3)). What must be shown under s. 235A(1) is that the consequence of the action affects, or is likely to affect, the claimant. The term 'likely' to is clearly capable of covering a wide range of meanings; and as to when a likelihood will occur, this will be a question of fact in a particular case.

9.3.1.1 Orders to enforce the right
To the extent that a claimant in proceedings can show that the right is available to him and that it has been breached, a court can make an order to stop the action continuing, or to stop threatened action occurring in the first place (s. 235A(4)).

9.3.1.2 Assistance in enforcing the right
Under s. 235B of TULRCA 1992, it is possible for an individual to claim assistance from the CPAUIA. In providing assistance, the Commissioner is required to consider whether the matter is complex and substantially in the public interest (s. 235B(3)). The Commissioner can provide assistance in the form of advice by a solicitor or counsel, and even representation in the same way as the CROTUM (s. 235B(5) and (6)). Regard should be had to 1.2.5 and 1.2.6 above generally in relation to the functions of the Commissioner.

9.4   MERGERS AND DE-MERGERS

9.4.1   Introduction

This area is substantially the largest of the three areas to be examined. In this section the issue of mergers and de-mergers will be discussed, together with the rules relating to employers' associations on these points.

9.4.2   Mergers

Legislation concerning union mergers has been in effect since 1876 when the Trade Union Act was introduced. The old procedural requirements were complex and had the effect of deterring unions from merging. The procedure now, although simplified, is still quite complex and is contained within TULRCA 1992. Union mergers can take place in one of two ways:

  (a)   by amalgamation of the unions in question; or

(b)   by transferring the engagements of one union to another.

The provisions are dealt with by statute in ss. 97–108 of TULRCA 1992 and apply to all trade unions. Each of the methods will be examined in turn.

9.4.2.1   Amalgamation

9.4.2.1.1   General   Amalgamation is the process whereby two or more interested unions pool their collective assets and lose their individual identities to take on a new merged form covering the interests of all their constituent members. The process of amalgamation is overseen by the Certification Officer. A free booklet has been produced by the Certification Officer covering the process of merger, *Mergers — A guide to the statutory requirements for transfers of engagements and amalgamations*. The procedure to be adopted during the course of an amalgamation starts in s. 97 of TULRCA 1992, which requires that an instrument of amalgamation is approved, that notice is given to members, and that a ballot is held and passed with a majority in favour of the amalgamation (s. 97(1)).

9.4.2.1.2   The instrument of amalgamation   An instrument of amalgamation must be approved by the Certification Officer. The instrument must be submitted to him for approval prior to a ballot being held in relation to the amalgamation (s. 98(l)). The instrument of amalgamation is required to comply with any regulations that exist relating to the content of the instrument. Currently, these are to be found in sch. 1 of the Trade Union and Employers' Associations (Amalgamations etc.) Regulations 1975 (SI 1975 No. 536). This requires that the following matters be contained within the instrument:

(a)   a statement that the document is an instrument of amalgamation, together with the names of the organisations to be amalgamated and the fact that the merged body will comply with the rules of the new body;
(b)   either

(i)   the rules of the proposed new body, or
(ii)   a summary of the rules, having particular regard to the name and principal purposes of the body, the conditions of admission to membership, the methods of appointing its governing body and principal member and of changing its rules, and the contributions and benefits available to its members;

(c)   the property held for the benefit of members of the merging bodies that is not going to be applied in the new body, and a statement of what is to happen to it;
(d)   the proposed date of the amalgamation.

The matters set out above are the minimum that needs to be included and, obviously, it is possible for the instrument to include more than the statutory requirements.

Once the instrument has been drawn up, it must then be sent to the Certification Officer having been signed by three members of the committee of management and the secretary of each of the merging bodies. The instrument must be sent on any form that the Certification Officer issues from time to time (reg. 6(1)) and must be accompanied by the appropriate fee from time to time in force. When all of these requirements have been met, the Certification Officer must approve the instrument (TULRCA 1992, s. 98(2)).

9.4.2.1.3 Notice to members   The notice to be given to members is dealt with in s. 99 of TULRCA 1992. Every voting paper sent out for the purposes of the ballot must be accompanied by a written notice approved by the Certification Officer (s. 99(1)). The content of the notice must either include the full instrument of amalgamation, or give a sufficient account of the instrument for members of the union to make a reasonable judgment as to the effects of the transfer (s. 99(2)). To the extent that the full terms of the instrument are not set out, the notice must state where the instrument can be inspected by interested parties (s. 99(3)). The notice is not allowed to contain any views as to the desirability or otherwise of a merger (s. 99(3A)).

Upon the notice being submitted to the Certification Officer, provided that it complies with the terms of the Act, the Certification Officer is bound to approve the notice (s. 99(5)). The Certification Officer has provided guidance as to the appropriate content of notices in the booklet on mergers previously referred to at 9.4.2.1.1. The booklet states that a notice is likely to be approved where it contains the following matters:

(a)   a heading stating clearly that the document is a Notice to Members;

(b)   a reference to the 1992 Act, which imposes the requirement of notice, either as a subheading to the document or otherwise clearly at the forefront of the document;

(c)   a reference to the amalgamation and the statutory requirement to hold a ballot in relation to the amalgamation;

(d)   a statement providing that all that is needed to approve the ballot is either a simple majority, or such majority as the union rules require together with a statement of the majority required if it is greater than the statutory requirement;

(e)   a statement to the effect that the instrument and the notice have both been received by the Certification Officer and approved by him;

(f)   the dates of the voting period and a statement that, in the case of voting papers sent out before the voting period, papers received prior to the commencement of that period shall be deemed to have been received during the voting period. It should be noted that the guide purports to add to the statutory requirements by requiring that the start of the voting period is declared on the notice.

9.4.2.1.4 The balloting requirements   As with most trade union voting require-ments, the 1992 Act sets down detailed provisions for the casting of votes. The starting point is s. 100(1), which requires that a resolution approving the proposed transfer must be passed by ballot of the members in accordance with ss. 100A–100E. These new requirements were inserted by s. 4 of TURERA 1993. The 1992 Act merely requires a simple majority unless union rules expressly require a greater majority in favour of merger (s. 100(2)). Those entitled to vote are dealt with in s. 100B, which provides: 'Entitlement to vote in the ballot shall be accorded equally to all members of the trade union.'

A preliminary point needs to be addressed, and that is to decide who are the members that are entitled to vote on a resolution; in particular, where a union has more than one class of members, whether all members of the union are entitled to vote or whether it is simply such classes as the union allows to vote. The point was addressed in *National Union of Mineworkers (Yorkshire Area)* v *Millward* [1995] IRLR 411. Here, the EAT was required to consider whether or not members of the union who had limited membership (they were unemployed members who had the right to become full members again in the future if they found work) were entitled to vote in the election. The Certification Officer agreed that not all members had been allowed to vote since the limited members had been denied a right to vote. According to Mummery P in the EAT (at p. 415), the correct approach is 'to ask how the language of [s. 100B] would be reasonably understood in the particular case by those to whom the section is addressed and whose affairs are to be affected by it'. He added:

> The crucial point in this case is that there is more than one class of persons described as members in the union rules: does section 100B include all of them or only some of them? To determine the scope of the section it is necessary to examine the relationship between each class of members and the union with other members. Although they all belong to or form part of the union, there are significant differences between the different classes of members — in particular between the full members, on the one hand, and the rest of the members on the other hand, as well as between the different classes of other members.

The EAT went on to conclude that, on the facts of the case, the limited members were entitled to some fringe benefits of membership but not an entitlement to vote. The practical implications of this decision are that, first, it is the union itself that determines who has the right to vote, and the Certification Officer should consider a particular union, and not unions generally, in determining whether all the members have had a chance to vote. Secondly, it follows from this that it is possible for a union to have different classes of members, some of whom may be entitled to have a greater say in the running of the union than others. It is therefore prudent to ensure that the rules of a union are drawn up so as to define who will have voting rights in relation to the continued existence of the union and to exclude from voting those who have a lesser capacity (e.g., retired, student or honorary members).

Turning now to the new requirements introduced by TURERA 1993, the first of these is that an independent scrutineer is required to be appointed under s. 100A to oversee the running of the ballot. His brief is set down in s. 100A(1), which is to comply with such statutory and additional requirements as are necessary in the ballot. It follows from this that a union can request additional functions to be performed by the scrutineer. The scrutineer is required to be 'suitably qualified'. This requires him to comply with any requirements set down by the Secretary of State. Further, the union holding the ballot must have no grounds to doubt his suitability to carry out the function (s. 100A(2)). The scrutineer is required to carry out the following tasks under s. 100A(3):

(a)   to supervise the production and distribution of the voting papers;

(b)   to examine the register of members' names to ensure that the same is up-to-date and accurate for the purposes of distributing the ballot papers;

(c)   to take such steps as are necessary for the making of a report (in line with the requirements set out in s. 100E of TULRCA 1992) and to make the report as soon as possible after the last day for voting in the ballot; and

(d)   to retain custody of the ballot papers for a year after the ballot.

The union also has certain functions to fulfil in relation to the appointment of the scrutineer. These are:

(a)   to ensure that it does nothing to compromise the scrutineer's independence in the terms of his appointments (s. 100A(7));

(b)   to ensure that it takes steps to either individually notify the members of a union of the appointment of the scrutineer, or use the usual method that a union would adopt to bring matters of importance to the attention of members of that union (s. 100A(8));

(c)   to supply the scrutineer with a copy of the register of members' names and comply with any requests that the scrutineer may have with regard to inspecting the register (s. 100A(9)); and

(d)   to ensure that the scrutineer carries out his functions and that there is no interference with him during the carrying out of those functions which might compromise the scrutineer's independence.

The second of the new requirements is set out in s. 100C and covers the matter of voting. Voting is carried out by the marking of a ballot paper by the person voting (s. 100C(1)). The voting papers are required to state the name of the scrutineer and the address to which the paper is to be returned, together with the date by which it must be returned. The paper must be one of a series of consecutively whole numbered papers and be marked with a number (s. 100C(2)). The vote must, as with all formal union ballots, be conducted with minimal cost to the members of the union and be carried out by post. This will usually require the provision of a reply paid envelope (s. 100C(3) and (4)). Further still, the voting paper must not have sent with it any direction or opinion as to how to vote (s. 100C(5)). If the ballot paper is supplied with any other documents (other than the reply paid envelope or the s. 99 notice) the ballot will be invalid. Lastly in relation to the conduct of a ballot, it is to be carried out so as to ensure, so far as is possible, that it is secret and fairly and accurately counted. Minor errors which could not materially affect the outcome of a ballot are to be disregarded (s. 100C(6)).

The third of the major changes is that, under s. 100D, the ballot papers are to be stored, distributed and counted by an independent person (who can be the scrutineer or such other person meeting the requirements of independence). If the independent counter is not the scrutineer then he is obliged to return the papers to the scrutineer as soon as reasonably practicable after counting the papers (s. 100D(5)). Again, a union is not allowed to compromise the independence of the independent person, it is required to ensure that he carries out his tasks, and a union should also ensure that it complies with any reasonable requests made of it by the independent person (s. 100D(6)).

9.4.2.1.5 Registering the instrument of amalgamation An instrument of amalgamation takes effect only when it is registered in line with s. 101 of TULRCA 1992. There is no duty to register the amalgamation if the parties to the merger decide that they do not wish it to go through.

Section 101(2) goes on to provide that a merger is not to take effect until the expiry of six weeks from the date on which an application is made to the Certification Officer for registration of the amalgamation. This provision allows the Certification Officer to see whether any challenges are mounted against the merger under the provisions of s. 103. Applications for registration cannot be made to the Certification Officer until such time as the independent scrutineer's report has been received by the union.

9.4.2.1.6 Complaints arising out of the amalgamation procedure A complaint can be made that a union has failed to comply with any of the requirements of ss. 99 to 100E, or in relation to a union's own rules in connection with amalgamations. The complaint is made under s. 103(1) to the Certification Officer. Indeed, s. 103(5) establishes that a complaint to the Certification Officer is the only way that an amalgamation can be initially contested. A complaint must be made within six weeks beginning with the date on which an application to register a merger was sent to the Certification Officer (s. 103(2)). Where the Certification Officer feels that the complaint is justified, he must make a declaration to that effect and is required to make an order specifying the steps to be taken before an application for registration will be entertained by him (s. 103(3)). The Certification Officer is required to provide an order, either orally or in writing, setting out the reasons for his decision (s. 103(4)).

Appeals lie from a decision of the Certification Officer to the EAT on a question of law only (s. 104).

9.4.2.2   Transfers of engagements

9.4.2.2.1   Introduction   The second method of merging a union is by transfer of engagements. This occurs where one union transfers its business to another which undertakes to carry out the engagements of that union (TULRCA 1992, s. 98(2)). In the case of transfers of engagements, the procedure is less time-consuming in that only the transferring union needs to ballot its members. This therefore makes it a more popular way of merging. The right to transfer is dealt with by s. 97(2) of the 1992 Act, which provides that a union may transfer its engagements to another on condition that an instrument of transfer is drawn up in accordance with s. 98 and that notice is given to members prior to a ballot being held of the members.

9.4.2.2.2   The instrument of transfer   The instrument of transfer must comply with sch. 2 of the Trade Union and Employers' Associations (Amalgamations, etc.) Regulations 1975 (SI 1975 No. 536). This requires that the following matters be incorporated into the instrument of transfer:

(a)   a statement that the document is an instrument of transfer of the engagements of the transferring union and, that upon the transfer taking effect the members of the transferee organisation will become members of the transferee union and will become subject to its rules;

(b)   a statement as to:

(i)   what contributions and benefits will be applicable to members being transferred to the transferee union under that union's rules,

(ii)   the branch or section of the union that members are to be assigned to (if any),

(iii)   whether or not the transferee union's rules are to be changed prior to joining, and

(iv)   the effect of the changes and the date on which the transfer is to take effect.

The instrument is also required to specify any property that is not going to be transferred and must state what is to happen to that property. It must be signed by three management committee members of the transferor union and by the secretary of each of the organisations.

Usually, an instrument will have more clauses, including an undertaking on the part of the transferee organisation to the effect that it will carry out the engagements of the transferor (which thereby provides evidence that the requirement of s. 98(2) will be complied with).

The instrument is required to be submitted to the Certification Officer before a ballot of members and must be approved by him prior to the ballot taking place (s. 98(1)). The Certification Officer is bound to approve the instrument if it meets with the above criteria (s. 98(2)).

9.4.2.2.3 Notice to members Notice is required to be given to members of the transferor union under s. 99 of TULRCA 1992 in the same way as with a merger by amalgamation, and regard should be had to 9.4.2.1.3 above on this point.

9.4.2.2.4 Balloting requirements The same balloting requirements must be observed (by a transferor union only) as in the case of a union that merges by amalgamation under ss. 100–100E of TULRCA 1992. Regard should be had to 9.4.2.1.4 above on this point generally.

9.4.2.2.5 Alteration of the transferee union's rules A power exists under s. 102 of TULRCA 1992 for a transferee union to alter its rules in relation to a forthcoming transfer where it is necessary to give effect to the transfer. The power is to be exercised by the committee of management or other governing body of the transferee union, and an alteration is required to take place in the form of a written memorandum setting out the way in which the rules have been changed (s. 102(1)). The power under s. 102 is to be exercised only where there is no express power in the transferee union's rules preventing the operation of s. 102(1).

The change of rules takes effect at the time the transfer becomes operative (s. 102(2)) and the power in s. 102(1) applies notwithstanding any general provision to the contrary in the rules of the transferee union (s. 102(3)). The amended rules should be sent to the Certification Officer for approval as a matter of good practice since he will be unable to review the transfer instrument otherwise.

9.4.2.2.6 Registration Once a union has complied with all the requirements and has a majority of members in favour of the change, it is possible to register the change with the Certification Officer under s. 101(1) of TULRCA 1992. The same restrictions apply in relation to registration as apply in the case of an amalgamation (including the six-week delay between receipt by the Certification Officer and registration coming into effect under s. 101(2)). Regard should be had to 9.4.2.1.5 above with regard to registration generally.

9.4.2.3 Practical effect of mergers
When registration of a merger takes place a number of points need to be borne in mind. First, if the body has a new name, it will need to be listed with the Certification Officer. If a body ceases to exist, then under s. 4(3) of TULRCA 1992 it will have to be removed from the list.

Secondly, where, as a result of a merger, a union ceases to exist, final accounts will have to be returned to the Certification Officer. In the case of a newly formed body, it will not have to submit a return as to its financial affairs until such time as it has been in existence for 12 months (TULRCA 1992, s. 43).

Thirdly, the rules relating to leadership elections are changed. Where a person holding office in a union that is to be amalgamated is appointed to an office in the new union, he is excused from having to submit to the usual union election requirements for a period of five years (s. 46(1) — see further 4.2.9.2 *et seq.* above). This period can be extended under s. 57(1) of of the Act due to the fact that an amalgamated union is not required to hold elections for its leadership in the first year of its formation. This said, under the union rulebook, a duty may exist to hold elections at an earlier point in time. The same is true of a union official who has taken an electable office in a transferee union on the occurrence of a transfer of engagement, where s. 57(3) applies.

Fourthly, the list of members must be brought up-to-date where unions merge, under s. 24(1) of TULRCA 1992. An extension is granted in the case of an amalgamated union, and the new union will have a period of one year in which to organise the new list of members names (s. 43(2)).

Fifthly, in the case of an amalgamation, where both of the unions combining had in place a valid political resolution, the political resolution in effect in the amalgamated union will be deemed to be that resolution passed first in time by either of the combining unions (TULRCA 1992, s. 93). In the case of a transfer of engagements, if the transferee union has in existence a political resolution, the members of the transferor union are bound by it.

Lastly, in relation to the property of merging unions, this is automatically transferred in the case of either an amalgamation or a transfer of engagements under the provision of s. 105 of the 1992 Act. This section does not apply, however, to property that is expressly excluded from the operation of a transfer by means of the instrument of amalgamation or transfer. Nor does the section apply to government issued securities (TULRCA 1992, s. 105(4)).

9.4.2.4   Employers' associations and mergers

The rules relating to the mergers of unincorporated employers' associations are similar to those relating to unions (TULRCA 1992, s. 133(1)). However, some differences do exist in relation to balloting, since there is a duty to have a ballot only where all members of the association have an equal entitlement to vote, with voting taking place in the manner set down in s. 100C. There is no obligation to appoint a scrutineer or to comply with the statutory reporting obligations affecting unions (s. 133(2)).

In the case of an employers' association that is incorporated, any mergers taking place will do so under the provisions of the Companies Acts 1985–1989.

9.4.3   De-mergers and other break-ups

9.4.3.1   Introduction

The point at issue here is what happens to a union either which has formed an alliance with another union which turns out to be unsuccessful, or where there is a large number of disaffected members who are seeking to break away and form their own union. Three possibilities exist in such a situation, these being:

(a)　that the union is subject to a breakaway;
(b)　that a de-merger takes place; or
(c)　that the union decides to wind itself up.

Each of these possibilities will be examined below.

9.4.3.2　Breakaways from a union

When members of a union become dissatisfied with the way in which a union is being run, they may decide to 'go it alone' and set up a rival union. This possibility no longer poses problems to unionists in the same way that it did in the days when the closed shop was prevalent. An example was the formation of the Union of Democratic Mineworkers by breakaway members of the National Union of Mineworkers in the aftermath of the 1980s miners' strike. The law on the position of breakaway members is very simple. The 1992 Act does not include any special provisions for large-scale defections of members. What it does provide is for an individual to leave a union by means of resignation from that union upon the giving of reasonable notice and compliance with reasonable conditions in relation to leaving (see s. 69). Where this occurs with disaffected members, there is no difference between one member resigning and a group of members resigning together. In circumstances where this happens, the members will have no right to claim a share of the union property, as the property is held collectively for the union and the members have a mere contractual right to enjoy the property during the currency of their membership. This right terminates on their leaving the union (see 2.1.5.3.3 above on this point).

9.4.3.3　De-merger

A de-merger of a union can take place for any number of reasons. In considering whether it is possible to de-merge, the starting point, given the absence of statutory provisions, is the union rule book. The rule book is the contract that sets down the rights of members or groups of members, and it is therefore necessary to consider whether it makes express contractual provision for de-mergers. If rules do exist, these must be followed to the letter. A failure to do so can result in members seeking to stop the de-merger by applying for an injunction to prevent breach of contract (regard should be had to, e.g., *AUEW (TASS)* v *AUEW (Engineering Section)* [1983] IRLR 108 on this point). In the absence of an express rule, it is unlikely that a rule will be implied into the contract of membership allowing de-merger, especially given the existence of the statutory right to resign from a union. Given that this is so, the only other way of seeking a de-merger would be to bring about a change in union rules using any power that a union has within its existing rules, or, if there is no such power, by reaching a consensus of all union members who will then be able to bring about such a change (see the common law position set down in *Dawkins* v *Antrobus* (1881) 17 Ch D 615).

　　As to the property of a union on a de-merger, the starting point is again to consider the rules of the union. If these provide for property to be granted to a section of the union upon its devolution, then the rules simply have to be followed by that part of the union claiming the property in dispute. If, however, the rules do not provide for a division of property then, unless the de-merger is a friendly one (in which case the rules can be amended as above), that part of the union de-merging may well have to do so without property. In *Burnley Nelson Rossendale and District Textile Workers Union v Amalgamated Textile Workers Union* [1986] IRLR 298, the plaintiff union wished to de-merge from the defendant union and claimed that it was entitled to an equitable proportion of the defendant union's funds. Tudor Price J held that in the case of a hostile de-merger, the court had no inherent jurisdiction to rewrite the rules of a union where the junior partner to the rulebook wanted to leave and the remainder of the union did not want to provide it with funds. He concluded that to hold otherwise would be 'an unjustified intervention into the affairs of the union'.

9.4.3.4   Dissolving a union

Again, as with the two preceding heads of de-merging, this head raises two fundamental questions, these being:

(a)   whether a union can dissolve itself; and
(b)   what will happen to the property of the union in the event of dissolution.

9.4.3.4.1   Dissolution   As to the first point, if the union has within its rules a power allowing the union to be dissolved, the rules should be followed. However, if no such power exists, the next question is whether the body can be wound up in any other way. It would appear that there are in fact three possible methods. First, if all of the current members of an unincorporated association unanimously vote in a properly constituted meeting to dissolve the society to which they belong, it would appear that there is nothing to stop the society bringing itself to an end (*Dawkins v Antrobus* (1881) 17 Ch D 615).

Secondly, in any event, the High Court has an inherent jurisdiction to wind up an unincorporated association where no rules exist allowing this to be done by the members of the association. Regard should be had on this point to the decision of Megarry J in *Keys v Boulter (No. 2)* [1972] 1 WLR 642.

Thirdly, the association can dissolve itself where there are fewer than two members left in it. This proposition was postulated by Walton J in *Re Bucks Constabulary Widows' and Orphans' Fund Friendly Society (No. 2)* [1979] 1 WLR 936. The reason for this is that the very nature of an association is that it provides a facility for people to associate with others. If there are no others members in the association, who is a sole surviving member to associate with?

9.4.3.4.2   Distribution of funds   Upon dissolution, assuming that a union is wound up by its members, where do the proceeds go? This depends primarily on the rules of the union. If an express provision exists, this should be followed. However, where no provision exists, two possibilities arise. The first is that a resulting trust is created in favour of all subscribers to the union in proportion to the contributions that they have made during their membership. It would also allow any donations that have been received from external sources to be returned to those sources to the extent that they have not been exhausted by the union (see, for example, *Re Gillingham Bus Disaster* [1958] Ch 300 and *Davis* v *Richard & Wallington Ltd* [1990] 1 WLR 1511).

Problems exist with the resulting trust analysis. It poses huge administrative difficulties in determining who has contributed to the funds and in what proportions over the years. The disposal of the surplus to long-dead members whose next-of-kin may be difficult to trace is an additional problem even if the contributions and proportions can be determined. Furthermore, the resulting trust model was rejected by the High Court in *Re Bucks Constabulary Widows' and Orphans' Fund Friendly Society (No. 2)* [1979] 1 WLR 936. This case decided that the better view is that, during membership, a member of an unincorporated association will usually have a simple contractual relationship with the association and a right to use the facilities of the association but no right to claim a severable share of association assets (see also *Hughes* v *TGWU* [1985] IRLR 382 to this end). Therefore, upon winding up, an individual member will become entitled on the basis of an equal share in the assets with all other members at the time of dissolution (this assumes the absence of any provision in the rules of the society to the contrary — *per* Megarry J in *Re Sick and Funeral Society of St John's Sunday School Golcar* [1973] Ch 51). Other cases to like effect include *Tierney* v *Tough* [1914] IR 142, *Re St Andrew's Allotment Association* [1969] 1 WLR 229 and *Re GKN Bolts and Nuts Ltd Sports and Social Club* [1982] 1 WLR 774. To the extent that a union is moribund on termination then, assuming that it is governed by the usual contractual principles in relation to membership, the property falls to the Crown as *bona vacantia* (*per* Walton J in *Re Bucks Constabulary (No. 2)*).

10 Trade Unions and the Criminal Law

10.1 INTRODUCTION

Trade union law has had a long history of regulation by the criminal law. Chapter 1 describes how unions have become legally accepted entities. This said, there is still a large amount of criminal law that has potential consequences for trade unions and their members. The legislation exists to ensure that regulatory matters and the provisions of TULRCA 1992 are complied with, and for the protection of the public at large. This chapter will focus upon potential offences, and will also examine restrictions that can be imposed on bail for those charged with offences committed in the context of industrial action.

10.2 REGULATORY MATTERS

10.2.1 Introduction

To ensure that a defined duty existing under trade union law is carried into effect, the following offences are created:

(a) failure to keep proper records; and
(b) an employer's failure to notify the Secretary of State of a collective redundancy.

10.2.2 Record-keeping offences

A number of offences exist in relation to record-keeping duties under s. 45 of TULRCA 1992 (see Chapter 4 with regard to record-keeping duties generally). The number of offences was increased by TURERA 1993, which was implemented partially as a result of the unsuccessful prosecution of National Union of

Mineworkers officials for what the Crown alleged was a failure to keep proper accounts. As a result of the changes made by TURERA 1993, certain strict liability offences have been introduced. Each of the offences under s. 45 of TULRCA 1992 (as amended by TURERA 1993) will be examined first.

10.2.2.1   Refusal to comply with record-keeping duties
The first of the offences exists in relation to failure to perform record-keeping duties and is contained in s. 45(1)–(3), which reads as follows:

(1)   If a trade union refuses or wilfully neglects to perform a duty imposed on it by or under any of the provisions of—
  section 27 (duty to supply copy of rules),
  sections 28 to 30 (accounting records),
  sections 32 to 37 (annual return, statement for members, accounts and audit),
or
  sections 38 to 42 (member's superannuation schemes),
it commits an offence.
(2)   The offence shall be deemed to have been also committed by—
  (a)   every officer of the trade union who is bound by the rules of the union to discharge on its behalf the duty breach of which constitutes the offence, or
  (b)   if there is no such officer, every member of the general committee of management of the union.
(3)   In any proceedings brought against an officer or member by virtue of subsection (2) in respect of a breach of duty, it is a defence for him to prove that he had reasonable cause to believe, and did believe, that some other person who was competent to discharge that duty was authorised to discharge it instead of him and had discharged it or would do so.

10.2.2.1.1   Actus reus   The *actus reus* of the offence is the failure to perform any of the duties mentioned or referred to in s. 45(1).

10.2.2.1.2   Mens rea   The *mens rea* of the offence is either intentional refusal, or wilful neglect. As to intention, this will bear the meaning set out by the House of Lords in *R* v *Hancock* [1986] AC 455. In that case, Lord Scarman, in formulating the concept of intention, was of the opinion that intention would be present where a defendant acted in a way that made it virtually certain that a particular thing would occur.
A refusal in this context is capable of being an outright rejection of one of the duties in s. 45(1) of the Act, or a failure to act which would give the impression that the union was refusing to act.
The alternative form of *mens rea* is wilful neglect. According to the Court of Appeal in *R* v *Newington* (1990) 91 Cr App R 247, this will be present where a defendant either has knowledge that the wrongdoing is being committed, or is reckless as to the commission of the wrongdoing.

10.2.2.1.3   Potential defendants

Persons capable of committing the offence will be the union itself as the primary defendant and also, under s. 45(2), officers of the union contractually bound by the union rules to carry out the function, or all members of the general management committee of the union. It should be noted that if a lower level employee of the union refuses to comply with the duty, such a person does not commit the offence. The offence is therefore specifically drafted to ensure that good housekeeping prevails on the part of a union and its officials.

10.2.2.1.4   Defences

A defence does exist for an officer or member of a management committee, but not for a union itself. The defence is provided by s. 45(3) if an officer or committee member has reasonable cause to believe, and did believe, that the duty imposed would be carried out by another person competent to discharge it.

To prove the defence, a defendant must establish that he had reasonable grounds to believe that the duty would be performed by another person. This will obviously vary from case to case, but is capable of covering such situations as the union having a compliance officer who is ordinarily responsible for the duties set down in s. 45(1). In addition, a defendant will have to show subjectively that he did believe that the duty was being carried out by that other person. Again, how he will show this will turn on the facts of a given case.

10.2.2.1.5   Penalty

To the extent that a person is convicted of an offence under this section, he will be liable to a fine not exceeding level 5 on the standard scale (s. 45A(1)(a)).

10.2.2.1.6   Time limit for prosecuting the offence

Time limits are laid down in s. 45A(2) and (3) of TULRCA 1992 for the prosecution of an offence under s. 45. In order for a prosecution to be brought in relation to an offence of failing to send annual returns to the Certification Officer, it is possible to bring proceedings at any time within a three-year period commencing with the date that the offence was committed (s. 45A(2)). If the offence is any of the other offences under s. 45(1), proceedings can be commenced either within six months beginning within the date that the offence was committed, or within 12 months beginning with the date that the Certification Officer had sufficient evidence to justify the proceedings. The time limits are subject to the requirement that proceedings must, in any event, be brought within three years beginning with the date of the offence being committed (s. 45A(3)). The Certification Officer is allowed to sign a certificate stating the date on which he had sufficient information to prosecute the offence, and this is conclusive proof of that fact (s. 45A(4)).

10.2.2.2   Wilful alteration of documents with intent to falsify

This offence is created under s. 45(4) of TULRCA 1992:

(4)   A person who wilfully alters or causes to be altered a document which is required for the purposes of any of the provisions mentioned in subsection (1), with intent to falsify the document or to enable a trade union to evade any of those provisions, commits an offence.

10.2.2.2.1   Actus reus   The *actus reus* requires the commission of a number of acts:

(a)   either altering, or causing a document of the type set out in s. 45(1) (accounting records) to be altered. This limb of the *actus reus* is therefore capable of being committed by any person (whether or not they are members or officials of the union, or whether they are third parties or are acting at the request of the union, e.g., an accountant).
(b)   that the document is falsified as a result of the alteration.

10.2.2.2.2   Mens rea   The *mens rea* of the offence comprises two limbs, the first being wilful knowledge of an alteration and the second an intention to falsify the document. Wilful knowledge and intention have both been discussed above at 10.2.2.1.2.

10.2.2.2.3   Potential defendants   The crime can be committed by anyone who carries into effect the falsification.

10.2.2.2.4   Defences   The 1992 Act provides no specific defence to the offence.

10.2.2.2.5   Penalty   To the extent that a person is convicted of an offence under s. 45(4) he will be liable to either a maximum term of six months' imprisonment, or a fine not exceeding level 5 on the standard scale or both (s. 45A(1)(b)).

10.2.2.3   Hindering the Certification Officer in the investigation of financial affairs
The offence under this head is aimed at persons who prevent the Certification Officer from carrying into effect a financial investigation into the affairs of a union (see 4.2.8.5 above on this point). The offence is created by s. 45(5) of TULRCA 1992, which provides as follows:

If a person contravenes any duty, or requirement imposed, under section 37A (power of Certification Officer to require production of documents etc.) or 37B (investigations by inspectors) he commits an offence.

10.2.2.3.1   Actus reus   The *actus reus* of the offence is to not carry into effect a request from the Certification Officer or one of his officers to produce a relevant document.

10.2.2.3.2   Mens rea   The offence is one of strict liability, and as such no *mens rea* is needed to commit the offence.

10.2.2.3.3   Potential defendants   Section 45(5) makes it an offence for any person to fail to comply with the requirements.

10.2.2.3.4   Defence   A defence is provided under s. 45(6), which requires a person charged with the offence to prove two things (i) that he did not have a relevant document that he has been requested to supply; and (ii) that it was not reasonably practicable to expect him to comply with the requirement.

10.2.2.3.5   Penalty   To the extent that a defendant is found guilty, he is subject to a fine not exceeding level 5 on the standard scale.

10.2.2.4   Destroying, mutilating or falsifying documents relating to the financial affairs of a union
The offence here is created under s. 45(7) of TULRCA 1992, which provides as follows:

> (7)   If an official or agent of a trade union—
>   (a)   destroys, mutilates or falsifies, or is privy to the destruction, mutilation or falsification of, a document relating to the financial affairs of the trade union, or
>   (b)   makes, or is privy to the making of, a false entry in any such document,
> he commits an offence unless he proves that he had no intention to conceal the financial affairs of the trade union or to defeat the law.

10.2.2.4.1   Actus reus   The *actus reus* can be committed in a number of different ways, i.e., either by the defendant destroying, mutilating or falsifying relevant documents, or where the defendant simply has knowledge of the destruction, etc. of a relevant document.

Documents that are relevant are any documents that relate to the financial affairs of a union.

10.2.2.4.2   Mens rea   Again, this is an offence of strict liability and a defendant will be presumed guilty unless he can show the defence provided for by the subsection.

10.2.2.4.3   Potential defendants   The persons who are liable to prosecution under s. 45(7) are any officials or agents of the union. Officials and agents are defined by s. 119 of TULRCA 1992 to mean:

(a)   in the case of an official, an officer of a union (including any member of a union's governing body or a trustee of unions funds) or of a branch or section thereof, or a person elected or appointed in accordance with the rules of the union to be representative of union members to some degree;

(b)   in the case of an agent, a banker or solicitor of, or any person employed as an auditor by, the union or any branch or section of it.

It should be noted that if the destruction etc. is carried out by someone who is not in such a position but at the bidding of an official or agent, the official or agent will be privy to the act and therefore liable.

10.2.2.4.4   Defence   A defence does exist for a defendant charged under s. 45(7) who is able to show that he had no intention (again, to be construed in the light of *R v Hancock* [1986] AC 455 — see 10.2.2.1.2) to conceal the financial affairs of the union or to defeat the law.

10.2.2.4.5   Penalty   If convicted of this offence, a person is liable either to a term of imprisonment not exceeding six months, or to a fine not exceeding level 5 on the standard scale or both.

10.2.2.5   Fraudulent alteration or deletion of documents relating to the financial affairs of a union
This offence is created under s. 45(8) of TULRCA 1992, which provides as follows:

(8)   If such a person fraudulently—
(a)   parts with, alters or deletes anything in any such document, or
(b)   is privy to the fraudulent parting with, fraudulent alteration of or fraudulent deletion in, any such document,
he commits an offence.

10.2.2.5.1   Actus reus   The *actus reus* of this offence requires that any document relating to the financial affairs of a union be parted with, altered or deleted by or with the connivance of an official or agent of a union (as defined in s. 119 of TULRCA 1992).

10.2.2.5.2   Mens rea   The *mens rea* that has to be shown is fraud on the part of a defendant. Fraud in this context amounts to the definition of dishonesty as set down by the Court of Appeal in *R v Ghosh* [1982] QB 1053, which requires the application of a two-stage test:

(a)   whether according to the standards of honest people the conduct which the defendant was charged with was dishonest; and
(b)   if so, whether the defendant subjectively knew this to be the case.

10.2.2.5.3   Potential defendants   Again, as with the offence under s. 45(7), those who can be charged are officials or agents of a union (see 10.2.2.4.3).

10.2.2.5.4   Defence   No specific defence is provided under s. 45(8).

10.2.2.5.5   Penalty   If convicted by magistrates, it is possible for the defendant to receive either a sentence of up to six months' imprisonment, or a fine not exceeding level 5 on the standard scale or both.

10.2.2.6   False or misleading statements in the course of financial investigations
This is the final offence created under s. 45 of the 1992 Act and arises under s. 45(9). The offence is as follows:

> (9)   If a person in purported compliance with a duty, or requirement imposed, under section 37A or 37B to provide an explanation or statement—
>   (a)   provides or makes an explanation or statement which he knows to be false in a material particular, or
>   (b)   recklessly provides or makes an explanation or statement which is false in a material particular,
> he commits an offence.

10.2.2.6.1   Actus reus   The *actus reus* of the offence is to make a statement or provide an explanation to a question during the course of a financial investigation into the affairs of a union which is materially inaccurate.

10.2.2.6.2   Mens rea   The *mens rea* can be satisfied either with knowledge that the statement is incorrect (i.e., a moral certainty in the same light as *Hancock*), or by being reckless as to the truth or otherwise of the statement. Recklessness was defined by the House of Lords in the appeal of *Caldwell* [1982] AC 341 as the doing of an act that is obviously likely to result in the crime that the defendant is charged with, or the doing of the act where it was obvious to the defendant, on addressing his mind to it, that it would result in the crime with which he is charged.

10.2.2.6.3   Potential defendants   Any person can be charged with the offence under s. 45(a).

10.2.2.6.4   Defence   The 1992 Act does not provide any specific defence for this offence.

10.2.2.6.5   Penalty   If convicted of this offence, it is possible for a defendant to be sentenced either to six months' imprisonment, or to a fine not exceeding level 5 on the standard scale or both.

10.2.2.7   Additional civil consequences of a conviction
As well as being convicted under any of the offences above and having the resultant criminal consequences accrue to a defendant, it should also be noted that conviction

will result in the disqualification of a person from holding a senior position in a union. If the conviction is under s. 45(1) or (5), a person so convicted is not allowed to hold a senior position for a period of five years starting with the point in time immediately preceding the conviction (s. 45B(1)(a)). If the conviction is under s. 45(4), (7), (8) or (9), the period of disqualification is ten years (s. 45B(1)(b)). The restricted posts are defined in s. 45B(5) as any of the following:

(a)   member of the executive (including any person who is entitled to attend at a union executive meeting for any reason other than the mere provision of information, or professional or technical advice);

(b)   any position by virtue of which a person is a member of the executive;

(c)   the president of a union;

(d)   the general secretary of a union.

As to the last two categories, if these are purely nominal in nature and cannot last for a period of more than 13 months, it may still be possible to hold office in these positions (s. 45C(4)).

10.2.2.8   Employers' associations

Employers' associations are caught by similar restrictions in relation to the information that they are bound to provide publicly where they are unincorporated employers' associations (TULRCA 1992, s. 131(1)). However, unlike trade unions, where a person is convicted of an offence under s. 45, there is no restriction placed on the offender preventing him from holding office within the association.

10.2.3   Failure to provide information relating to collective redundancies

10.2.3.1   Introduction

This offence has been looked at briefly in the context of Chapter 3. The offence is created under s. 194 of TULRCA 1992 and arises where an employer fails to notify the Secretary of State of a collective redundancy situation as set out under s. 193. The offence is one of strict liability and is committed where an employer fails to give the appropriate period of notice of at least 90 days where it is proposed to make redundant 100 or more employees, or 30 days where more than 20 employees are to be so dismissed. Upon commission of the offence, an offender can be punished on summary conviction by a fine not exceeding level 5 on the standard scale (s. 194(1)).

10.2.3.2   Issuing of proceedings

Only the Secretary of State or a person authorised by him may prosecute the offence, and such an authorised person is expressly authorised appear in the magistrates' court (s. 194(2)).

10.2.3.3   Possible defendants
Where an offence is committed by a body corporate under s. 194, it is also deemed
to have been committed by any director, manager, secretary or other similar officer
who consents to, connives in or is otherwise similarly neglectful as regards
commission of the offence (s. 194(3)).

10.3   GENERAL CRIMINAL OFFENCES

10.3.1   Introduction

The offences that can be committed by a trade union during the course of industrial
action are many and varied. However, they can be broadly divided up into the
following three categories:

(a)   offences existing under TULRCA 1992;
(b)   industry specific offences; and
(c)   general public order offences.

The offence of harassment will be discussed at the end of this section.

10.3.2   Offences under TULRCA 1992

10.3.2.1   Introduction
The offences under TULRCA 1992 are consolidated in ss. 240–241. They were
originally enacted under the Conspiracy and Protection of Property Act 1875, but
have been modified over the years to their current form. Two offences are created
under the two sections. The first involves breaching a contract of service or hiring
where to do so could endanger human life or seriously damage valuable property.
The second offence is, broadly speaking, criminal intimidation.

10.3.2.2   Breach of contract involving risk of injury to persons or property
This offence was originally enacted under s. 5 of the 1875 Act. Section 240 of
TULRCA 1992 now reads as follows:

(1)   A person commits an offence who wilfully and maliciously breaks a
contract of service or hiring, knowing or having reasonable cause to believe that
the probable consequences of his so doing, either alone or in combination with
others, will be—
(a)   to endanger human life or cause serious bodily injury, or
(b)   to expose valuable property, whether real or personal, to destruction or
serious injury.

(2) Subsection (1) applies equally whether the offence is committed from malice conceived against the person endangered or injured or, as the case may be, the owner of the property destroyed or injured, or otherwise.

It appears that the offence has never actually been used since its introduction under the 1875 Act.

10.3.2.2.1 Actus reus The *actus reus* of the offence occurs where as a result of breaching a contract of service or hiring its probable consequence is the risk of serious injury to persons or property as described. It should be noted that only a probable consequence is required (i.e., greater than 50 per cent chance, *per* Lord Diplock in *R* v *Sheppard* [1981] 3 All ER 899) and not that it has actually occurred.

10.3.2.2.2 Mens rea The *mens rea* is twofold. It requires, first, that a contract is breached either wilfully or maliciously. The concept of a wilful act has been discussed above at 10.2.2.1.2. As to malice, this was defined in the case of *R* v *Cunningham* [1957] 2 QB 396, at p. 399, to mean:

... (1) an actual intention to do the ... harm ...; or (2) recklessness as to whether such harm should occur or not (i.e., the accused has foreseen that the particular type of harm might be done yet has gone on to take the risk of it).

Secondly, the defendant must know or have reasonable grounds to believe (i.e., it must be obvious to an honest and reasonable man) that the consequences of his action will be to cause damage to persons or property as defined.

10.3.2.2.3 Potential defendants As stated above, the offence has never actually been prosecuted. It would seem that those most likely to commit the offence are in the emergency services, hospital workers or in those employed in the privatised utility companies.

Further, it is difficult to see how this offence could be prosecuted privately. In order for a member of the public to prosecute the crime, he would have to be specifically affected by the crime or be granted the right to prosecute in the name of the Attorney-General (see *Gouriet* v *UPOW* [1978] AC 435 on this point).

The offence cannot be committed by seamen (s. 240(4)).

10.3.2.2.4 Defences No specific defence is created by statute.

10.3.2.2.5 Penalty If a person is convicted of the offence, he is liable to either a three-month term of imprisonment, a fine not exceeding level 2 on the standard scale or both (s. 240(3))

10.3.2.3   Criminal intimidation
The offence of criminal intimidation was originally enacted under s. 7 of the 1875
Act and is now reproduced in s. 241 of TULRCA 1992. It has been extensively used
as a means of controlling offenders in industrial action. It was used 275 times alone
in the miners' strike of 1984/5. The offence is specifically declared to be arrestable
in the absence of a warrant (s. 241(3)).

The offence covers a multitude of sins on the part of those engaged in industrial
action (though it should be noted that it is not confined solely to industrial action: see
Todd v *Director of Public Prosecutions* [1996] Crim LR 344). Section 241 provides:

(1)   A person commits an offence who, with a view to compelling another
person to abstain from doing or to do any act which that person has a legal right to
do or to abstain from doing, wrongfully and without lawful authority—
(a)   uses violence to or intimidates that person or his wife or children, or
injures his property,
(b)   persistently follows that person about from place to place,
(c)   hides any tools, clothes or other property owned or used by that person,
or deprives him or hinders him in the use thereof,
(d)   watches or besets the house or other place where that person resides,
works, carries on business or happens to be, or the approach to any such house or
place, or
(e)   follows that person with two or more other persons in a disorderly
manner in or through any street or road.

10.3.2.3.1   Actus reus   The *actus reus* of the offence can be committed in a variety
of different ways. It is important for all of the variations of the offence that they be
committed wrongfully and without lawful authority. This point was considered by
Scott J in *Thomas* v *National Union of Mineworkers* [1985] IRLR 136, at p. 147,
where he concluded (after having reviewed *Ward, Lock & Co. Ltd* v *OPAS* (1906) 22
TLR 327), that in order for the conduct to be wrongful, it would have to be tortious.
The section is intended to provide criminal consequences for acts that were at least
tortious in nature prior to the 1875 Act. As to the remainder of the potential forms of
the *actus reus*, these will be considered separately.

10.3.2.3.1.1   Intimidation   The courts have consistently stressed that what
amounts to intimidation is a question of fact to be decided on the basis of common
sense in a particular case. In *Connor* v *Kent* [1891] 2 QB 545, the defendant was a
member of a different trade union to that of the victim. The victim had been told that
a strike would occur unless he left his union and joined that to which the defendant
belonged. No violence was threatened, but upon his refusing to join the union he was
dismissed by his employer. A summons was brought alleging that the defendant had
committed the offence of intimidating the victim. The victim claimed that he was
intimidated from working anywhere where members of the defendant's union were

numerically superior to his own union. An acquittal was the result in the magistrates' court and on appeal. At the appeal, Lord Coleridge CJ stated (at p. 559): ''Intimidate'' is not ... a term of art — it is a word of common speech and everyday use; and it must receive, therefore, a reasonable and sensible interpretation according to the circumstances of the cases as they arise from time to time.'

More recently, in *R* v *Jones* (1974) 59 Cr App R 120, the Court of Appeal did attempt partially to define 'intimidate', and stated (at p. 125): '... intimidate in this section includes putting persons in fear by the exhibition of force or violence or the threat of force or violence, and there is no limitation restricting the meaning to cases of violence or threats of violence to the person.'

10.3.2.3.1.2 Persistent following Again, as with the previous head, the circumstances in which this part of the *actus reus* can be committed are many. In *Smith* v *Thomasson* (1890) 62 LT 68, Hawkins J stated that it would be 'impossible' to provide a definition. Each case therefore turns very much on its own facts.

10.3.2.3.1.3 Deprivation of property This element of the offence was considered by the Court of Appeal in *Fowler* v *Kibble* [1922] 1 Ch 487. Here, the defendants were unionised miners who objected to working with other non-union miners. In order to prevent the non-union miners from working, they asked an employee of the mine owner not to give the non-union miners a safety lamp (the effect of which was to deny them the ability to work). The non-union miners complained that they had been denied their property and the offence had therefore been committed. The Court of Appeal, however, took the view that because the action taken was to promote a closed shop (a lawful act at that time), nothing unlawful was being done in preventing the miners from being given a safety lamp and therefore no offence was being committed.

It is worth noting that the important element of this case was that the lamps belonged to the employer and not to the miners themselves. If the lamps had belonged to the miners, a trespass would have been committed (tortious); and since that is itself unlawful, criminal consequences could have been visited on the defendants.

10.3.2.3.1.4 Watching or besetting The *actus reus* of watching or besetting is to be construed in line with the ordinary everyday meaning of the words (*J. Lyons & Sons* v *Wilkins* [1899] 1 Ch 811 and *Ward, Lock & Co. Ltd* v *OPAS* (1906) 22 TLR 327).

Again, as with the other forms of committing the offence, any watching or besetting must be unlawful *per se* for the offence to be committed. If this is the case, it does not matter that the place that is watched or beset is that of a person who is not employed or who is not working for a particular employer. For example, in *Charnock* v *Court* [1899] 2 Ch 696, a prosecution was successfully brought under the section when unionised labour watched for potential non-union labour at railway stations around the country.

10.3.2.3.1.5 Following a person in a disorderly manner What amounts to a disorderly manner will vary from case to case. In *R* v *McKenzie* [1892] 2 QB 519, it was stated that, procedurally, the conduct amounting to the offence must be specified in the charge before the magistrates. It is not enough to state simply that a person has been followed. The full particulars of how the following is said to be disorderly must also be provided.

10.3.2.3.2 Mens rea The *mens rea* of the offence is committed where a defendant has the objective purpose of compelling a person to do or refrain from doing that which he has a right not to do or to do. This, according to the Divisional Court in *Director of Public Prosecutions* v *Fidler* [1992] 1 WLR 91, means more than merely attempting to persuade. The prosecutor does not have to show that the compulsion was effective, merely that it was attempted (*Agnew* v *Munro* (1891) 18 R (J) 22).

10.3.2.3.3 Potential defendants No specific person is defined as being a defendant under s. 241 and the offence can therefore be committed by anyone.

10.3.2.3.4 Defences No specific defence is provided to the offence, save that the conduct on the part of those taking part in the action may be protected from the consequences of tort in the first place. It follows that, if a defendant is able to claim the protection provided by peaceful picketing under s. 220 of TULRCA 1992, and if the same is not removed for other reasons (see Chapter 7 generally), the action will not be unlawful (one of the required elements of the *actus reus*) and the offence cannot be committed. Therefore, while s. 220 does not of itself provide a defence to criminal action, complying with the requirements of s. 220 will inevitably avoid successful criminal proceedings being brought under s. 241 for criminal intimidation (see *Tynan* v *Balmer* [1967] 1 QB 91, *Broome* v *DPP* [1974] ICR 84 and *Kavanagh* v *Hiscock* [1974] ICR 282 on this point).

10.3.2.3.5 Penalties The offence was relatively lightly used up until the miners' strike. Because of its utility in that conflict it was amended by s. 40(2) of the Public Order Act 1986 so that offenders could be punished by means either of a period of imprisonment not exceeding six months, or a fine not exceeding level 5 on the standard scale or both (now s. 241(2)).

10.3.3 Industry specific offences

10.3.3.1 Introduction
A small number of industry specific offences are created by statute that are capable of being committed in the course of industrial action. They exist in relation to variously, postal workers, merchant seamen and the police force. None of the offences (with the exception of the police force) is specifically created to prevent industrial action taking place.

10.3.3.2   Postal workers

The offence exists in relation to postal workers under s. 45 of the Telegraph Act 1863 and s. 58 of the Post Office Act 1953.

The 1863 Act makes it an offence for persons employed by the Post Office wilfully or negligently to omit or delay to transmit or deliver a message sent by telegraph. It is possible to be punished by a fine not exceeding level 3 on the standard scale.

The 1953 Act makes it an offence for a person employed in the business of the Post Office wilfully to delay or detain, or to procure or suffer the wilful delay or detainment of, a postal packet contrary to his duty. It is possible for such a person to be imprisoned for up to two years, or to receive a fine or both.

An argument exists that both offences are capable of being committed when industrial action is waged by postal workers. This argument was tested in the case of *Gouriet* v *UPOW* [1978] AC 435. In this case a relator action was sought by Mr Gouriet against postal workers involved in industrial action consisting of a boycott of post to South Africa in protest at the apartheid regime. The Attorney-General refused to sanction the proposed action and subsequently a civil action was launched by the plaintiff seeking an injunction to prevent the postal workers offending under s. 58 of the 1953 Act. The claim failed ultimately in the House of Lords on the ground of the plaintiff's lack of *locus standi* as he ultimately was not affected by the action. Nevertheless, the case has not laid to rest the possibility that the offences could be committed during the course of action by postal workers in an appropriate case.

10.3.3.3   Merchant seamen

Under s. 58 of the Merchant Shipping Act 1995, a person employed as a merchant seaman commits an offence if, while on board or in the immediate vicinity of his ship, he deliberately does or omits to do an act the effect of which is likely to cause death or serious injury to persons, or damage to the machinery, structure or safety equipment, on his or another ship.

The offence is clearly capable of being committed where members of a union take industrial action. All that is necessary for the commission of the offence is that the prohibited forms of harm are *likely* to occur (see *R* v *Sheppard* [1981] 3 All ER 899 on this point).

To the extent that the offence is committed, it is possible to be sentenced on summary conviction to the maximum fine and, if convicted on indictment, to a term of imprisonment not exceeding two years, a fine or both (Merchant Shipping Act 1995, s. 58(5)).

10.3.3.4   Police officers

In relation to the police force, the position with regard to industrial action is dealt with by legislation at two levels under the Police Act 1996. First, under s. 64 of the 1996 Act, it is not possible for a police officer to be a member of a trade union that has, as one of its objects, the desire to control or influence the pay, pensions or conditions of service of a police force (s. 64(1)). If, however, a person was a member of a union prior to joining the police, it is possible for that person to remain within the union with the consent of the Chief Officer of police (s. 64(2)). If permission is granted under this subsection, the overriding criteria in s. 64(1) must still be observed.

Secondly, it is possible to be convicted of an offence where a person causes or attempts to cause, or does any act calculated to induce, any member of a police force to withhold his services (Police Act 1996, s. 91(1)). This is obviously capable of covering a call to strike action. If convicted of an offence under this section, it is possible upon summary conviction to be imprisoned for a term not exceeding six months, or fined to the extent of the statutory maximum or both. If convicted on indictment the penalty can be increased to imprisonment for a term not exceeding two years, or a fine or both.

10.3.4   General public order offences

10.3.4.1   Introduction
This section will only highlight the public order related offences that can be committed generally in the course of industrial action. Regard should be had to specialist criminal law reference works when looking in detail at these offences.

Offences exist both at common law in the form of breach of the peace and under statute (in the form of the Criminal Law Act 1977, the Highways Act 1980, the Public Order Act 1986 and the Police Act 1996).

10.3.4.2   Breach of the peace
The utility of prosecuting pickets for breaching the peace was highlighted during the miners' strike 1984/5 when over 4,100 charges were made concerning the offence.

The offence of breach of the peace was defined in *R* v *Howell* [1982] QB 416, where Watkins LJ stated of it (at p. 427):

> We are emboldened to say that there is a breach of the peace whenever harm is actually done or is likely to be done to a person or in his presence to his property or a person is in fear of being so harmed through an assault, an affray, a riot, unlawful assembly or other disturbance. It is for this breach of the peace when done in his presence or the reasonable apprehension of it taking place that a constable, or anyone else, may arrest an offender without warrant . . .

The power to arrest for breaches of the peace was not removed by s. 26 of the Police and Criminal Evidence Act 1984.

The usefulness of the offence can be seen in cases such as *Piddington* v *Bates* [1960] 3 All ER 660 and *Kavanagh* v *Hiscock* [1974] ICR 282, where it was used to restrict the numbers of pickets in attendance on a picket line. It was also used in the infamous case of *Moss* v *McLachlan* [1985] IRLR 76, where police officers used the power to arrest so-called 'flying pickets' who travelled from Kent to coal mines in the Nottingham area during the miners' strike in order to picket. At the time of the arrests, the pickets were several miles from the collieries. Their convictions were upheld by the Divisional Court. In arresting the strikers the police were held to be able to take into account their knowledge of the violent nature of the dispute. The proximity of the striking miners to the collieries undoubtedly helped the police in that case. However, arrest for the offence was also used as a deterrent by police officers in turning back miners at the Dartford Tunnel. It is submitted that it is doubtful whether a conviction for breach of the peace could be obtained where a person is arrested in such circumstances due to the lack of proximity by the alleged offender to the place of industrial action.

10.3.4.3   Statutory offences

10.3.4.3.1   Criminal conspiracy   Criminal conspiracy is regulated by the Criminal Law Act 1977. The offence of criminal conspiracy will be committed where two or more persons combine to commit, or to attempt to commit another substantive offence.

Limitations do exist in relation to conspiracy in the context of industrial action. First, in order to prosecute conspiracy on indictment for a substantive offence that would be of itself only summary in nature, it is necessary to have the consent of the Director of Public Prosecutions under s. 4(1) of the Criminal Law Act 1977 (although an ordinary Crown Prosecutor can exercise this function on his behalf under s. 1(6) of the Prosecution of Offences Act 1985). Secondly, the maximum sentence that can be handed down is limited to that of the substantive offence (s. 3 of the 1977 Act).

Additionally, s. 242 of TULRCA 1992 creates restrictions on criminal conspiracy. Where the substantive offence is summary in nature and not punishable by imprisonment, it cannot be prosecuted as a criminal conspiracy.

10.3.4.3.2   Obstructing the highway   The offence here is created under s. 137 of the Highways Act 1980, which provides:

> If a person, without lawful authority or excuse, in any way wilfully obstructs the free passage along a highway he is guilty of an offence and liable to a fine not exceeding level 3 on the standard scale.

Wilful obstruction requires that an act is done deliberately and not through inadvertence (*R* v *Senior* [1899] 1 QB 283). This is capable of occurring where, for example, pickets prevent free passage in and out of an employer's buildings for either persons or vehicles. In *Broome* v *DPP* [1974] ICR 84, the defendant was convicted for refusing to allow a lorry along a highway during the course of a strike by standing in front of it. The defendant appealed, unsuccessfully, to the House of Lords on the grounds that he was exercising his peaceful right to picket (under what is now s. 220 of TULRCA 1992). In dismissing the appeal, their Lordships were of the view that the peaceful picketing immunity did not provide a lawful right to obstruct the highway during the course of picketing. As Lord Salmon said (at p. 96):

> [The] words make it plain that it is nothing but the attendance of the pickets at the places specified that is protected; and then only if their attendance is for one of the specified purposes. The section gives no protection in relation to anything the pickets may say or do whilst they are attending if what they say or do is itself unlawful. But for the section, the mere attendance of pickets might constitute an offence under ... the [Highways Act 1980] or constitute a tort, for example, nuisance. The section therefore gives a narrow but nevertheless real immunity to pickets. It clearly does no more.

10.3.4.3.3   Offences under the Public Order Act 1986   The Public Order Act 1986 was brought in as a response to various high profile public order disturbances of the 1980s (including the miners' strike). The Act is indeed aimed at industrial action in its control over processions and static demonstrations. It has two main angles of attack as far as industrial action is concerned. These are, first, the specific public order offences that are created under ss. 1–5 of the Act and, secondly, the control over processions and assemblies in ss. 11–16.

10.3.4.3.3.1   Public Order Act offences   The offences in ss. 1–5 were introduced to repeal the existing common law offences of riot, rout, unlawful assembly and affray, and also the offence under s. 5 the Public Order Act 1936 of causing a breach of the peace by the use of threatening, abusive or insulting words or behaviour. In their place a graduated series of offences was created covering various forms of public disorder. These are as follows:

(a)   *Riot.* This offence is created by s. 1 of the 1986 Act and is the most serious of the public order offences. It requires that 12 or more persons who are present together, intentionally or recklessly (s. 6(1)), use or threaten unlawful violence (whether or not this occurs simultaneously) for a common purpose (which can be inferred from the conduct of the actors (s. 1(3)). The conduct of the actors when taken together must be such as to cause a notional person of reasonable firmness present at the scene to fear for his personal safety (s. 1(1)). Riot can be committed in public or in private places (s. 1(5)).

Riot is punishable on conviction on indictment by a maximum sentence of ten years (s. 1(6)). A prosecution for riot may not be brought without the permission of the Director of Public Prosecutions (s. 7(1)).

(b)   *Violent disorder.* This offence is created under s. 2 of the 1986 Act. In order to establish the offence, it is necessary to show that three or more persons who are present together, intentionally or recklessly (s. 6(2)), use or threaten unlawful violence, and that the conduct of them (taken together) is such as to cause a notional person of reasonable firmness present at the scene to fear for his personal safety

(s. 2(1)). It is immaterial whether the use or threat of violence is simultaneously carried into effect by the offenders for an offence under s. 2(1) to be committed (s. 2(2)). The offence can again be committed in public as well as in private places (s. 2(4)). A person found guilty of violent disorder can, if convicted on indictment, be sentenced to up to five years' imprisonment, a fine or both. Alternatively, if convicted in a summary trial that person may be imprisoned for up to six months, fined to the statutory maximum, or both (s. 2(5)).

(c) *Affray*. The offence of affray is committed where a person, intentionally or recklessly, uses or threatens unlawful violence towards another and his conduct is such as would cause a notional person of reasonable firmness present at the scene to fear for his safety (s. 3(1)). Threats cannot be made by words alone if a defendant is to be charged with affray (s. 3(3)).

Affray can be committed in public and private places alike (s. 3(5)) and a power of arrest without a warrant is available to a constable (s. 3(6)). The penalty upon conviction on indictment is a term of imprisonment not exceeding three years, or a fine or both. If the conviction is in summary form, the maximum sentences are a term of imprisonment not exceeding six months, a fine up to the statutory maximum or both (s. 3(7)).

(d) *Fear or provocation of violence*. This offence is committed where a person either intentionally or recklessly uses threatening, abusive or insulting words or behaviour towards another, or distributes or displays to another any writing, sign or other visible representation that is threatening, abusive or insulting. In order for the crime to be fully constituted, it is necessary that the intention of a defendant should be such as to cause the person perceiving the communication to believe that immediate unlawful violence will be used against him or against a third party, or would provoke it to be used (s. 4(1)). The offence can be committed in public or in private (s. 4(2)). It replaced the old offence under s. 5 of the Public Order Act 1936. Again, a power of arrest without warrant is expressly provided (s. 4(3)). The offence may be the subject of a summary trial only. A maximum sentence is provided of six months' imprisonment, a fine not exceeding level 5 on the standard scale or both (s. 4(4)).

(e) *Intentional harassment, alarm or distress*. This offence was introduced into the 1986 Act by s. 154 of the Criminal Justice and Public Order Act 1994. The offence consists of intentionally causing harassment, alarm or distress by using threatening, abusive or insulting words or behaviour, or by distributing or by displaying any written or visible representation that is threatening, abusive or insulting and that would cause harassment, alarm or distress (s. 4A(1)). The offence can be committed in public or in private (s. 4A(2)) and a power of arrest is again provided (s. 4A(4)). The offence may be the subject of a summary trial only and has a maximum sentence of six months' imprisonment, a fine not exceeding level 5 on the standard scale or both (s. 4A(5)).

(f) *Harassment, alarm or distress*. This offence occurs where a person, within the sight or hearing of another, intentionally or recklessly uses threatening, abusive or insulting words or behaviour, or distributes or displays any written or visible representation that is threatening, abusive or insulting and would cause harassment, alarm or distress (s. 5(1)). The offence can again be committed in public or in private (s. 5(2)), and a power of arrest is provided if a person refuses to desist from the behaviour after having been warned by a constable (s. 5(4)). The maximum penalty is a fine on summary conviction not exceeding level 3 on the standard scale (s. 5(6)). The offence probably adds nothing to the powers that constables already have to arrest for breach of the peace. A defence is provided under s. 5(3) where a person shows that either, (a) he had no reason to believe that any person was within sight or hearing who might be harassed, alarmed or distressed, or, (b) that the person was inside a dwelling and had no reason to believe that his conduct could be observed by sight or sound or (c) that the conduct was reasonable.

10.3.4.3.3.2 Public Order Act controls The controls that exist arise at two levels — those relating to demonstrations and those relating to assemblies. As to the first category, these are dealt with under ss. 11–13 of the 1986 Act. The powers allow the police to receive written notice of public processions intended to demonstrate support for a particular view, to publicise a cause or campaign or to mark a particular event (s. 11(1)). The notice must inform the police of the route, the time and the date of the procession, and also of the name and address of the organiser of the procession (s. 11(3)). Generally, six clear days' notice is required s. 11(5). An exception does exist in relation to spontaneous processions, but it is unlikely to arise in the context of unions who are now required to comply with a clearly defined course of conduct if they are to be immune from the tortious consequences of action that they might take (see Chapter 7 generally).

Upon receiving notice, a Chief Officer of police can impose conditions on a procession, including refusing to allow the same to go ahead (ss. 12–13, Public Order Act 1986).

Failure to comply with the requirements imposed amounts to an offence which can lead to imprisonment for a period of up to three months, or a fine not exceeding level 4 on the standard scale. Any person committing an offence by taking part in such a procession is liable to a fine not exceeding level 3 (ss. 12(5)–(6) and 13(7)–(9)).

The second of the requirements exists in relation to assemblies. Unlike processions, assemblies are static bodies and therefore provide less of a problem as regards their likely impact in the community since they will affect a much smaller proportion of it. As a consequence of this, the requirements are less detailed than in the case of processions. Section 14 of the 1986 Act deals with this area. It should be noted that new provisions were introduced in relation to trespassory assemblies under the Criminal Justice and Public Order Act 1994, but these are unlikely to apply industrial disputes and are aimed at 'raves'.

The provisions of s. 14 allow a senior police officer to impose conditions on an assembly where he reasonably believes that an assembly may either result in serious public disorder, serious damage to property or serious disruption to the life of the community. Conditions may also be imposed where he reasonably believes that the purpose of those organising is to intimidate people into doing something that they have a right not to do, or to do that which they have a right to abstain from doing.

Where the conditions are satisfied, the senior police officer may make directions concerning the place at which the assembly is being, or is to be, held, its duration and the maximum number of people who may take part in the assembly in order to minimise the potential disorder, damage, disruption or intimidation (s. 14(1)).

The practical implications of these sections are obvious given that the whole point of industrial action is to make a person do that which he does not want to do. Further, given that the Code of Conduct on Picketing (1992) makes express reference to the powers of the police (paras 45–47) and then follows on with Section E, entitled 'Limiting Numbers of Pickets' (which includes para. 51, recommending a maximum number of six pickets per workplace entrance), the potential for the police to exercise discretion so as to dilute the effectiveness of a picket line is obvious.

10.3.4.3.4   Offences under the Police Act 1996   Two offences can be committed under the 1996 Act, i.e., the offences of assaulting an officer in the execution of his duty and of wilfully obstructing a police officer in the execution of his duty (s. 89(1) and (2) respectively). As to what will amount to an assault, regard should be had to *Fagan* v *Metropolitan Police Commissioner* [1969] 1 QB 439 and to *Donnelly* v *Jackman* [1970] 1 All ER 987.

A wilful obstruction will occur where it is an intentional obstruction without lawful excuse, for example, refusing to follow directions issued by a police officer during the course of a picket (*R* v *Senior* [1899] 1 QB 283).

If convicted on a summary trial of assaulting a police officer, it is possible to be imprisoned for up to six months, or to receive a fine up to level 5 on the standard scale or both (s. 89(1)). If convicted of obstructing a police officer in the execution of his duty, it is possible to be imprisoned for a term not exceeding one month, or to receive a fine not exceeding level 3 on the standard scale or both (s. 89(2)).

10.3.5   Harassment

10.3.5.1   Introduction
The offence of harassment was introduced by the Protection from Harassment Act 1997 to combat the problems faced by victims of 'stalking'. The Act creates criminal offences in relation to stalking, and also provides for civil remedies in the form of both damages and an injunction. Unlike normal injunctions, if the offender shows contempt by failing to obey the terms of an injunction, committal proceedings can be undertaken or the offender can be convicted of an offence under s. 3(6). Both forms of proceedings can result in either imprisonment for a term not execeeding five years, or a fine or both where the offence is tried on indictment; or, if the offence is tried summarily, the offender can be sentenced to a term of imprisonment not exceeding six months, or a fine up to the statutory maximum or both. It is not possible

to be committed for contempt and convicted of an offence in relation to failing to
obey an injunction (s. 3(8)).

No definition of harassment is provided, but s. 7 of the 1997 Act provides that
references to 'harassing' include alarming or causing distress to a person.

While the new offences under the 1997 Act are still in their infancy, it seems clear
that they could potentially be committed in the course of industrial action.

10.3.5.2   Harassment under the 1997 Act

10.3.5.2.1   Actus reus   The *actus reus* of the offence is committed where a person
pursues a course of conduct which amounts to harassment of another (see 10.3.5.1 above
with regard to harassment). A 'course of conduct' is defined in s. 7(2) as meaning
'conduct on at least two occasions', and 'conduct' is defined as including speech (s. 7(4)).

10.3.5.2.2   Mens rea   The *mens rea* of the offence is that the offender knows or
ought to know that the conduct amounts to harassment. As to when a person ought
to know, s. 1(2) provides that this element will be present where a reasonable person
in possession of the same information would think that the course of conduct
amounted to harassment. In other words, liability is objectively based.

10.3.5.2.3   Defences   Three specific defences are created under s. 1(3) of the 1997
Act: (i) where conduct is carried out in the investigation of a crime; (ii) where it takes
place so as to comply with any enactment or rule of law; or (iii) where the conduct
is reasonable. In *Huntingdon Life Sciences Limited* v *Curtin* (1997) *The Times*, 11
December, the High Court held that when an application for an injunction was made
in connection with alleged harassment under s. 1, harassment did not occur where
those allegedly harassing were exercising a right of free speech in a matter of public
interest or in a political demonstration.

10.3.5.2.4   Penalties   To the extent that a person is found guilty of an offence under
s. 1 of the Protection from Harassment Act 1997, under s. 2 the offender is liable to
a term of imprisonment not exceeding six months, or a fine not exceeding level 5 on
the standard scale or both.

10.3.5.3   Putting people in fear of violence under the 1997 Act

10.3.5.3.1   Actus reus   The *actus reus* of the offence is committed where a person,
on at least two occasions, causes another to fear that violence will be used against
him as a result of the actor's conduct (s. 4(1)). 'Conduct' includes speech for these
purposes (s. 7(4)).

It should be noted that if a defendant is found not guilty of this offence at a trial on indictment then under s. 4(5) a jury is still empowered to return a guilty verdict in relation to the s. 2 offence of harassment.

10.3.5.3.2   Mens rea   The *mens rea* is the same as for the offence of harassment (s. 4(2)) and regard should be had to 10.3.5.2.2 above.

10.3.5.3.3   Defences   The defences are the same as for harassment, save that the defence of reasonableness is qualified by the addition of a proviso that the conduct must be aimed at protecting the actor or another, or the actor's or another's property (s. 4(3)(c)). Regard should be had to 10.3.5.2.3 above.

10.3.5.3.4   Penalties   To the extent that an offender is found guilty of an offence then the penalty is either imprisonment for a term not exceeding five years, or a fine or both where the offence is tried on indictment; or, if the offence is tried summarily, the offender can be sentenced to a term of imprisonment not exceeding six months, a fine up to the statutory maximum, or both.

10.4   BAIL CONDITIONS

If a person is arrested and charged for the alleged commission of an offence during industrial action, the first stage in the criminal procedure that he will encounter after charge is a bail hearing. The right to bail is governed by the Bail Act 1976 (as amended by Pt II of the Criminal Justice and Public Order Act 1994), or, in the case of police bail, s. 47 of the Police and Criminal Evidence Act 1984 (as amended by s. 27 of the Criminal Justice and Public Order Act 1994). The main constraint that can be imposed in this area occurs in relation to conditions that can be attached to bail, in particular (in the context of industrial action) a prohibition on attending the site of an industrial dispute. The legality of this form of condition was challenged in *R* v *Mansfield Justices ex parte Sharkey* [1984] IRLR 496. In this case, the defendants were charged with offences committed during the course of picketing in the miners' strike 1984/5. They were remanded on bail by magistrates who attached a condition that they were: 'Not to visit any premises or place for the purpose of picketing or demonstrating in connection with the current trade dispute between the NUM and the NCB other than peacefully to picket or demonstrate at [their] usual place of employment.'

The defendants sought a judicial review and asked that the condition attached should be quashed and that the magistrates should be directed to admit the applicants to unconditional bail. The matter was heard by the Divisional Court which refused the application. Lord Lane, the Lord Chief Justice, held that s. 3(6) of the Bail Act 1976 conferred a wide discretion on magistrates as to the conditions that they could attach. The magistrates were required to address the question of whether the condition was necessary to prevent the commission of further offences while the defendant was on bail. If they thought that a real risk existed that could be met by the imposition of conditions, they would be justified in imposing a condition.

It does not follow from this that on every occasion where an offence has been committed in the course of industrial action bail conditions will be imposed. Nevertheless, what *ex parte Sharkey* does show is that such conditions can be imposed, and they are therefore another potential restriction that can arise in the context of industrial action.

Index